PALACES OF HOPE

This volume assembles in one place the work of scholars who are making key contributions to a new approach to the United Nations and to global organizations and international law more generally. Anthropology has in recent years taken on global organizations as a legitimate source of its subject matter. The research in this field gives a human face to these world-reforming institutions. *Palaces of Hope* demonstrates that these institutions are not monolithic or uniform, even though loosely connected by a common organizational network. They vary above all in their powers and forms of public engagement. Yet there are common threads that run through the studies included here: the actions of global institutions in practice, everyday forms of hope and their frustration, and the will to improve confronted with the realities of nationalism, neoliberalism, and the structures of international power.

Ronald Niezen holds the Katharine A. Pearson Chair in Civil Society and Public Policy in the Faculty of Law and the Department of Anthropology at McGill University. His work on public justice outreach includes the study of truth and reconciliation commissions, online lobbying, and human rights movements. These areas of study have involved research in a variety of forums, including the United Nations Working Group on Indigenous Populations, the Permanent Forum on Indigenous Issues, the World Health Organization, and the Arctic Council. His books include *The Origins of Indigenism: Human Rights and the Politics of Difference* (2003), *Public Justice and the Anthropology of Law* (2010), and *Truth and Indignation: Canada's Truth and Reconciliation Commission on Indian Residential Schools* (2013).

Maria Sapignoli is a Research Fellow in the Department of Law and Anthropology at the Max Planck Institute for Social Anthropology. She has done research on legal activism, indigenous rights, and social movements. These areas of study have involved work in a variety of global organizations, including the United Nations Secretariat Headquarters, the Permanent Forum on Indigenous Issues, and the International Fund for Agricultural Development. Some of her research involves San activism in southern Africa on issues related to indigenous peoples' rights and claims to land and resources in the context of resettlement. She is the author of several articles and book chapters on indigenous peoples in southern Africa, most recently in *Anthropological Forum* (2015) and the Political and Legal Anthropology Review (*PoLAR*) (forthcoming).

CAMBRIDGE STUDIES IN LAW AND SOCIETY

Cambridge Studies in Law and Society aims to publish the best scholarly work on legal discourse and practice in its social and institutional contexts, combining theoretical insights and empirical research.

The fields that it covers are: studies of law in action; the sociology of law; the anthropology of law; cultural studies of law, including the role of legal discourses in social formations; law and economics; law and politics; and studies of governance. The books consider all forms of legal discourse across societies, rather than being limited to lawyers' discourses alone.

The series editors come from a range of disciplines: academic law; socio-legal studies; sociology; and anthropology. All have been actively involved in teaching and writing about law in context.

Series Editors
Chris Arup, *Monash University, Victoria*
Sally Engle Merry, *New York University*
Susan Silbey, *Massachusetts Institute of Technology*

A list of books in the series can be found at the back of this book.

Palaces of Hope

THE ANTHROPOLOGY OF GLOBAL ORGANIZATIONS

Edited by

RONALD NIEZEN
McGill University

MARIA SAPIGNOLI
Max Planck Institute for Social Anthropology

CAMBRIDGE
UNIVERSITY PRESS

University Printing House, Cambridge CB2 8BS, United Kingdom

One Liberty Plaza, 20th Floor, New York, NY 10006, USA

477 Williamstown Road, Port Melbourne, VIC 3207, Australia

4843/24, 2nd Floor, Ansari Road, Daryaganj, Delhi - 110002, India

79 Anson Road, #06-04/06, Singapore 079906

Cambridge University Press is part of the University of Cambridge.

It furthers the University's mission by disseminating knowledge in the pursuit of education, learning and research at the highest international levels of excellence.

www.cambridge.org
Information on this title: www.cambridge.org/9781107566361
10.1017/9781316412190

© Cambridge University Press 2017

This publication is in copyright. Subject to statutory exception and to the provisions of relevant collective licensing agreements, no reproduction of any part may take place without the written permission of Cambridge University Press.

First published 2017
First paperback edition 2017

A catalogue record for this publication is available from the British Library

ISBN 978-1-107-12749-4 Hardback
ISBN 978-1-107-56636-1 Paperback

Cambridge University Press has no responsibility for the persistence or accuracy of URLs for external or third-party internet websites referred to in this publication, and does not guarantee that any content on such websites is, or will remain, accurate or appropriate.

Contents

List of Contributors		*page* vii
Acknowledgments		xi
List of Abbreviations		xii
1	Introduction Ronald Niezen and Maria Sapignoli	1
2	Heart of Darkness: An Exploration of the WTO Marc Abélès	31
3	Horseshoe and Catwalk: Power, Complexity and Consensus-Making in the United Nations Security Council Niels Nagelhus Schia	55
4	A Kaleidoscopic Institutional Form: Expertise and Transformation in the UN Permanent Forum on Indigenous Issues Maria Sapignoli	78
5	The 'Public' Character of the Universal Periodic Review: Contested Concept and Methodological Challenge Jane K. Cowan and Julie Billaud	106
6	Meeting "the World" at the Palais Wilson: Embodied Universalism at the UN Human Rights Committee Miia Halme-Tuomisaari	127
7	Expertise and Quantification in Global Institutions Sally Engle Merry	152
8	From Boardrooms to Field Programs: Humanitarianism and International Development in Southern Africa Robert K. Hitchcock	172

9	Global Village Courts: International Organizations and the Bureaucratization of Rural Justice Systems in the Global South Tobias Berger	198
10	Contrasting Values of Forests and Ice in the Making of a Global Climate Agreement Noor Johnson and David Rojas	219
11	The Best of the Best: Positing, Measuring and Sensing Value in the UNESCO World Heritage Arena Christoph Brumann	245
12	Propaganda on Trial: Structural Fragility and the Epistemology of International Legal Institutions Richard Ashby Wilson	266
13	The Anthropology *by* Organizations: Legal Knowledge and the UN's Ethnological Imagination Ronald Niezen	294

Index   318

Contributors

Marc Abélès (Directeur d'études à l'EHESS) is a leading figure in the development of institutional ethnography. In 1995, he established the Laboratoire d'anthropologie des insitutions et des organisations sociales (LAIOS) (Laboratory of the anthropology of institutions and of social organizations), which he directed until 2010. He has published several in-depth studies of legislatures, including *La vie quotidienne au Parlement européen* (Daily life in the European parliament, 1992) and *Un ethnologue à l'Assemblée* (An ethnologist in the Assembly, 2000). He has more recently built on these studies of power in institutional practice with a collaborative study of the World Trade Organization, resulting in an edited volume, *Des anthropologues à l'OMC* (Anthropologists at the WTO, 2011).

Tobias Berger is a postdoctoral research fellow at the Institute for Human Sciences in Vienna. Before moving to Vienna, he was a visiting research fellow at the Department of Law and Anthropology at the Max Planck Institute for Social Anthropology in Halle (Saale), Germany. He has studied at the School of Oriental and African Studies in London, the University of Oxford, and the Freie Universität Berlin, where he also obtained his PhD and served as Associate Professor in Politics and International Relations during the academic year 2014–2015.

Julie Billaud is Associate Researcher in Anthropology at Sussex Asia Center, University of Sussex. In May 2010, she completed a European DPhil in Social Anthropology and Law from the École des Hautes Études en Sciences Sociales and the University of Sussex. Her doctoral research has led to her recent book *Kabul Carnival: Gender Politics in Postwar Afghanistan* (2015). In 2010, she assisted Professor Jane Cowan in her ethnographic study of the Universal Periodic Review (UPR), a new mechanism of human rights monitoring within the reformed UN Human Rights Council in Geneva. She is now redirecting her research interests towards Islam in Europe, with an investigation of everyday uses and practices of Islamic law in Britain.

Christoph Brumann is Head of Research Group ("The Global Political Economy of Cultural Heritage" and "Buddhist Temple Economies in Urban Asia") at the Max Planck Institute for Social Anthropology in Halle, Germany, and Honorary Professor of Anthropology at Martin Luther University Halle-Wittenberg. He is the author of *Tradition, Democracy and the Townscape of Kyoto: Claiming a Right to the Past* (2012) and *Die Kunst des Teilens: Eine vergleichende Untersuchung zu den Überlebensbedingungen kommunitärer Gruppen* (The Art of Sharing: A Comparative Study of the Survival Conditions of Communitarian Groups) (1998) and the editor of *Making Japanese Heritage* (2010, with Rupert A. Cox), *Urban Spaces in Japan: Cultural and Social Perspectives* (2012, with Evelyn Schulz), and *World Heritage on the Ground: Ethnographic Perspectives* (2016, with David Berliner). He has also published numerous journal articles and book chapters on such topics as cultural heritage, UNESCO, urban anthropology, the concept of culture, utopian communes, and gift-giving in Japan. He is a member of the Academia Europaea.

Jane K. Cowan is Professor of Anthropology at the University of Sussex in Brighton, England. Her prize-winning first book, *Dance and the Body Politic in Northern Greece* (1990), explored the ways gender, power, and identity were performed and negotiated within social dancing. Doing fieldwork in the ethnically mixed region of Greek Macedonia – the target of rival nationalisms since the late nineteenth century – alerted her to the complex politics of rights claims based on culture and minority status, a theme investigated both in *Macedonia: The Politics of Identity and Difference* (2000) and in *Culture and Rights: Anthropological Perspectives* (co-edited with Marie-Benedicte Dembour and Richard Wilson; 2001). Her current research explores the social processes and contested meanings of the United Nations' new human rights monitoring mechanism, the Universal Periodic Review, situating this within a genealogy of the international oversight of rights.

Miia Halme-Tuomisaari is a research fellow at the venture Bodies of Evidence: Interplay of Documents, Narratives and Biotechnologies, funded by the Kone Foundation (2014–2016). She is an Affiliated Senior Research Fellow of the Program for the Study of Global Governance of the Geneva Graduate Institute, and an Affiliated Senior Research Fellow of the Erik Castrén Institute of International Law and Human Rights, University of Helsinki. She has recently co-edited the volume *Revisiting the History of Human Rights* (with Pamela Slotte, 2015).

Robert Hitchcock is currently Research Professor of Anthropology at the University of New Mexico. He is also a member of the board of the Kalahari Peoples Fund (KPF). Hitchcock has worked with indigenous peoples and refugees in more than a dozen African countries, as well as in North, Central, and South America. Part of his work has been with the United Nations family of agencies, including the United Nations High Commissioner for Refugees (UNHCR) and the World Bank, and with various non-government organizations, including the Ford Foundation, Hivos (the Netherlands), Open Society Initiative for Southern Africa (OSISA), and the International Work Group for Indigenous Affairs (IWGIA). He is the author/editor of 15 books and 250 journal articles and book chapters. His most recent books include

The San of Zimbabwe: Land, Livelihoods, and Human Rights (with Ben Begbie-Clench and Ashton Murwira, 2015); *The Ju/'hoan San of Nyae Nyae and Namibian Independence: Development, Democracy, and Indigenous Voices in Southern Africa* (with Megan Biesele, 2013); and *Vulnerable Children: Global Challenges in Education, Health, Well-Being, and Child Rights* (co-edited with Deborah Johnson and DeBrenna Agbenyiga, 2013).

Noor Johnson is a cultural anthropologist whose research focuses on knowledge politics and participatory processes in Arctic environmental governance. She has a PhD from McGill University (Anthropology), where she was a Vanier Canada Graduate Scholar. A Fulbright Arctic Initiative Scholar, her current work examines dynamics of community participation and knowledge practices in decision-making about Arctic offshore development. She is a Senior Advisor for policy and interdisciplinary initiatives with the Office of International Relations at the Smithsonian Institution in Washington, D.C., and an Adjunct Assistant Professor of Environment and Society at Brown University.

Sally Engle Merry is Silver Professor and Professor of Anthropology at New York University. She is also a Faculty Director of the Center for Human Rights and Global Justice at the New York University School of Law, and past president of the American Ethnological Society. Her books include *Colonizing Hawai'i* (2000), *Human Rights and Gender Violence* (2006), *Gender Violence: A Cultural Perspective* (2009), and *The Practice of Human Rights* (co-edited with Mark Goodale; 2007). Her recent book *The Seductions of Quantification: Measuring Human Rights, Violence against Women, and Sex Trafficking* (2016) examines indicators as a technology of knowledge used for human rights monitoring and global governance. She has co-edited two books on quantification: *The Quiet Power of Indicators* (with Kevin Davis and Benedict Kingsbury, 2015) and *A World of Indicators* (with Richard Rottenburg, Songi Park, and Joanna Mugler, 2015). She is the author/editor of 15 books and special journal issues and 125 articles and reviews. She received the Hurst Prize for *Colonizing Hawai'i* in 2002, the Kalven Prize for scholarly contributions to sociolegal scholarship in 2007, and the J. I. Staley Prize for *Human Rights and Gender Violence* in 2010. In 2013 she received an honorary degree from McGill University's Faculty of Law and was the focus of an Author Colloquium at the Center for Interdisciplinary Research (ZIF) at the University of Bielefeld, Germany. She is an adjunct professor at Australian National University.

Ronald Niezen is the Katharine A. Pearson Chair in Civil Society and Public Policy in the Faculty of Law and the Department of Anthropology at McGill University. He holds a PhD from Cambridge University (1987), with a thesis on Islamic reform in West Africa. He has also conducted research in Aboriginal communities in northern Canada and on the international movement of indigenous peoples. His work on international indigenism has involved research in a variety of UN forums, including the Working Group on Indigenous Populations, the World Health Organization, and the Permanent Forum on Indigenous Issues. His books include *The Origins of Indigenism: Human Rights and the Politics of Difference* (2003), *Public Justice and the Anthropology of Law* (2010), and *Truth and Indignation: Canada's Truth and Reconciliation Commission on Indian Residential Schools* (2013).

David Rojas is Assistant Professor at Bucknell University. He has a PhD in Anthropology from Cornell University and an MPhil in Social Anthropology from Cambridge University. Since 2009 he has pursued a multi-sited ethnography in Brazilian Amazonia and United Nations Environmental Forums that focuses on novel political responses to planetary-scale environmental crises.

Maria Sapignoli is a research fellow in the Department of Law and Anthropology at the Max Planck Institute for Social Anthropology. Since 2006 she has carried out ethnographic work in Botswana, most recently in Namibia, and in several international organizations, including the United Nations Permanent Forum on Indigenous Issues and the International Fund for Agricultural Development. Some of her recent work has focused on resettlement and rights related to conservation programs and extractive industries, as well as on international institutions and global governance. She is currently working on several book projects and is the author of numerous articles and book chapters on indigenous peoples in southern Africa, most recently in *Anthropological Forum* (2015) and *Political and Legal Anthropology Review (PoLAR)* (forthcoming).

Niels Nagelhus Schia is a senior research fellow at the Norwegian Institute of International Affairs. He is a former fellow of the New School for Social Research and holds a PhD degree in social anthropology from the University of Oslo. His research focuses on international organizations, diplomacy, global governance, and peace operations. In this work, he has been centrally concerned with the United Nations. Recent publications include "Being part of the parade – 'Going native' in the United Nations Security Council" *Political and Legal Anthropology Review* (2013). He is also head of the scientific committee for the annual Fulbright Norway award.

Richard Ashby Wilson is the Gladstein Distinguished Chair of Human Rights and Professor of Anthropology and Law at the University of Connecticut. He studies international human rights, and in particular post-conflict justice institutions such as truth and reconciliation commissions and international criminal tribunals. He is the author or editor of ten books and his most recent, *Writing History in International Criminal Trials*, was selected by *Choice* as an "Outstanding Academic Title." He is presently writing a book about the international law and social science of inciting speech and hate speech, titled *Propaganda on Trial*.

Acknowledgments

The chapters in this book were first presented at a workshop on the McGill campus in Montreal titled *Palaces of Hope: The Anthropology of Global Institutions*. This workshop was hosted by the Faculty of Law at McGill University and co-sponsored by the Pearson Chair in Civil Society and Public Policy and the Departments of Law and Anthropology, and Resilience and Transformation in Eurasia of the Max Planck Institute for Social Anthropology. The editors wish to thank the McConnell Foundation and the Max Planck Institute for Social Anthropology for the support that made this meeting possible, particularly given that it gathered together scholars from twelve institutions coming from eight countries (two via Skype). Our research assistants, Ian Kalman and Adam Fleischmann, were important not only for their part in the logistics of the meeting but also its content, to which they contributed through their careful note-taking and commentary. We are grateful to the contributors to this volume for their productive exchange during the workshop and the high quality of the work they produced subsequent to it, not to mention their patience with our suggestions along the way. We wish to thank the two anonymous reviewers of our proposal, who encouraged us all to be attentive to the many complexities and nuances of our subject matter. Finally, we are grateful to the many people we met during our fieldwork in and around the UN, who were essential both in the subject matter and the inspiration for this volume.

Abbreviations

AAA	American Anthropological Association
CBC	Canadian Broadcasting Corporation
CBD	Convention on Biological diversity
CBO	Community-Based Organization
CCA	Country Common Assessment
COICA	Coordinadora de las Organizaciones Indígenas de la Cuenca Amazónica
COP	Conference of Parties
CTBTO	Preparatory Commission for the Comprehensive Nuclear Test-Ban Treaty Organization
DG	Director General
DPI	Department of Public Information
DRIP	Declaration on the Rights of Indigenous Peoples
ECOSOC	Economic and Social Council of the United Nations
EIB	European Investment Bank
ELCIN	Evangelical Lutheran Church in Namibia
EU	European Union
FOTCD	Field Operations and Technical Cooperation Division
FPIC	Free, Prior, and Informed Consent
GATT	General Agreement on Tariffs and Trade
GDP	Gross Domestic Product
GNP	Gross National Product
HDI	Human Development Index
HDRO	Human Development Report Office
HRC-SPD	Human Rights Council and Special Procedures Division
HRTD	Human Rights Treaties Division
IAEA	International Atomic Energy Agency
IBRD	International Bank for Reconstruction and Development
ICC	Inuit Circumpolar Council
ICC	International Criminal Court
ICCPR	International Covenant on Civil and Political Rights
ICL	International Criminal Law

ICOMOS	International Council of Monuments and Sites
ICTR	International Criminal Tribunal for Rwanda
ICTY	International Criminal Tribunal for the Former Yugoslavia
IDA	International Development Association
IDPs	Internally Displaced Persons
IFAD	International Fund for Agricultural Development
IFC	International Finance Corporation
IFI	International Finance Institution
IFR	In-Stream Flow Requirements
IIFB	International Indigenous Forum on Biodiversity
ILO	International Labour Organization
IMF	International Monetary Fund
IPACC	Indigenous Peoples of Africa Coordinating Committee
IPCC	Intergovernmental Panel on Climate Change
IPO	Indigenous Peoples' Organization
IRN	International Rivers Network
ITC-ILO	International Training Centre of the International Labour Organization
IUCN	International Union for Conservation of Nature
IWGIA	International Work Group for Indigenous Affairs
LAC	Legal Assistance Center
LHDA	Lesotho Highlands Development Authority
LHWP	Lesotho Highlands Water Project
LLEs	Local Legal Entities
LRF	Legal Resources Foundation
MDGs	Millennium Development Goals
MFA	Ministry of Foreign Affairs
NAMA	National Asset Management Agency
NDF	Namibian Defense Force
NEPA	National Environmental Policy Act
NGO	Nongovernmental Organization
NRCS	Namibia Red Cross Society
OECD	Organisation for Economic Co-operation and Development
OD	Operational Directive
OHCHR	Office of the High Commissioner for Human Rights
OPCW	Organization for the Prohibition of Chemical Weapons
OTP	Office of the Prosecutor
OUV	Outstanding Universal Value
OXFAM	Oxford Committee for Famine Relief
PFII	Permanent Forum on Indigenous Issues
POE	Panel of Environmental Experts
PPP	Purchasing Power Parity
RAIPON	Russian Association of Indigenous Peoples of the North
REDD+	Reducing Emissions from Deforestation and Forest Degradation
RIS	Reservoir-Induced Seismicity

RMAs	Range Management Associations
RRDD	Research and Right to Development Division
SDGs	Sustainable Development Goals
SPFII	Secretariat of the Permanent Forum on Indigenous Issues
SRS	Serbian Radical Party
SSM	Special Safeguard Mechanism
SuR	State under Reveiw
TA	Traditional Authority
TK	Traditional knowledge
TRIPS	Agreement on Trade-Related Aspects of Intellectual Property Rights
UNAOC	United Nations Alliance of Civilizations
UNDESA	United Nations Department of Economic and Social Affairs
UNDG	United Nations Development Assistance Group
UNDP	United Nations Development Programme
UNEP	United Nations Environment Programme
UNESCO	United Nations Educational, Scientific and Cultural Organization
UNFCCC	United Nations Framework Convention on Climate Change
UNFPA	United Nations Fund for Population Activities
UNHCR	United Nations High Commissioner for Refugees
UNHQ	United Nations Headquarters
UNICEF	United Nations Children's Fund
UNICRI	United Nations Crime and Justice Research Institute
UNMOVIC	United Nations Monitoring, Verification and Inspection Commission
UNPFII	United Nations Permanent Forum on Indigenous Issues
UNSC	United Nations Security Council
UNSC	United Nations Statistical Commission
UNSD	United Nations Statistical Division
UNSO	United Nations Statistical Office
UPR	Universal Periodic Review
USAID	United States Agency for International Development
WBG	World Bank Group
WFP	World Food Program
WGIP	Working Group on Indigenous Populations
WIMSA	Working Group of Indigenous Minorities in Southern Africa
WIPO	World Intellectual Property Organization
WTO	World Trade Organization
WWF	World Wildlife Fund

1

Introduction

Ronald Niezen and Maria Sapignoli

CONFIGURATIONS OF AMBIGUITY

The near impossibility of identifying the common qualities of global organizations probably follows from the fact that their most publicly visible features seem to assemble into contradictions. They tend to be sources of popular prestige and gathering points of NGO activism, yet in the media every major calamity of international relations and global finance becomes a failure of global governance (the examples are too numerous to mention, though Kosovo, Rwanda, Iraq, and Syria come instantly to mind). Many of their goals involve correcting the wrongs of states, yet they are persistently, almost defiantly state-centric; and even with the creation of new norms and the dramatic rise of NGO participation in their initiatives, their decision-making remains dominated by states (Weiss and Daws 2007: 3). They trumpet their efforts to be transparent and accountable, yet regularly generate documents that heighten obscurity, while producing ideas and policies behind closed doors. They are commonly seen as epicenters of an oppressive neoliberal world order, associated with a dramatically widening global income gap between rich and poor, while being called upon to lead the way in ending hunger, reducing poverty, and promoting development. The list could go on.

The complexity of these organizations can also be seen in the challenge of naming them. Clearly they are international in the sense that states are always central to their structure and procedures; and they are multilateral in the sense that states coordinate their policies in groups or blocs and occasionally in consensus. Strictly speaking, the organizations that we consider in this volume are not all United Nations specialized agencies, even though they are all closely interconnected – the World Bank Group, for example, was created in the Bretton Woods conference in 1944 before the Charter of the United Nations was drafted a year later; and the World Trade Organization is one of four officially designated "Related Organizations" created between 1957 and 1997.[1] Our intention, therefore, is not just to offer a set of ethnographic studies of the

---

[1] The other related organizations are each concerned with weapons regulation: the International Atomic Energy Agency (IAEA), the Preparatory Commission for the Comprehensive Nuclear Test-Ban Treaty

UN, but to take a new approach to those entities often referred to as "global organizations."

The sense in which these organizations are global, however, is particularly complicated. In some respects, they are not global at all. State interests are often a deciding, and limiting, factor in what they are able to do. They struggle to transcend strictly national or even international frameworks, yet, as institutions of "global" governance, remain clearly dependent on them, and therefore take on qualities that are neither entirely global nor post-international (Fleischman and Kalman 2015). In these global spaces, particularities are asserted. The concept of indigenous peoples, for example, is very much based on the existence of distinct rights and identities. Forums of pastoralists and farmers in the International Fund for Agricultural Development (IFAD) similarly bring locality into universal space; and there are many more similar examples to be found. International law has universal aspirations, but often in support of locality, while the UN as a whole is now (together with the NGO boom of the past several decades) promoting a bottom-up approach in its advancement of human rights and development.

In other ways these institutions achieve their intended universality. Nothing they do can be in conflict with universal human rights, and an overarching sense of humanity is a more general reference point for their work. Certainly globality can be seen in the elaborate alchemy of actors that they bring together: bureaucrats with cosmopolitan backgrounds and identities, state-sponsored diplomats, and a bewildering array of NGOs, some with their own global mandates and others that are part of global networks and social movements. The common denominator of the contributions to this volume, then, is a distinct kind of institution, situated in intersections of the "local," the "national," and the "global," in which globality emerges as the central point of reference (although as much in the realm of ideals as in reality).

By setting ourselves the challenge of exploring these institutions using the methods of ethnography, the first obstacle we face is this seemingly deep-seated ambiguity. Or perhaps it is not an obstacle at all, but a place to begin, the kind of thing that characterizes the terrain that, as ethnographers, we want to explore.

Despite a growing awareness of their social and historical density, bureaucracies, (global organizations in particular) are still commonly reified, still seen as essentially rational, efficient, and dispassionate – or their opposite: dysfunctional and arbitrary. Only the people who work within structures of institutional incoherence can tell us how things actually work – or fail to work – as they act on multiple, sometimes conflicting interests. The ethnographic studies included in this book each question the monolithic representations of international

---

Organization (CTBTO), and the Organization for the Prohibition of Chemical Weapons (OPCW) (Alger 2006: 103–104). The common denominator in these agencies is that their mandate involves a topic of global concern, but in which the most powerful states do not want the scrutiny and regulatory mechanisms that tend to come with UN specialized agencies.

institutions produced by their mandates and by the outside perspectives that focus only on the content of their documents and public statements. Instead, ethnographers portray institutions by starting with the people who populate them, above all the ways that they maneuver through structural obstacles and opportunities, and in the process reveal the tensions and contests behind formal appearances. Reflecting on the contributions of the ethnography of institutions, Colin Hoag finds that, simply by shifting attention away from the products of bureaucratic process and toward the period of time before decisions are rendered, "bureaucratic practices appear not as the product of logics (a contextualized rational choice), orders of discourse, or superordinate powers, but as a tangle of desires, habits, hunches, and conditions of possibility" (2011: 86). The institutions of global governance as depicted by anthropologists are social worlds with distinct characters, influenced by their connections with civil society, states, transnational corporations, and publics. They are also influenced by the visions and personalities of the people who work in them, situated in an ebb and flow that includes diplomats, consultants, activists, lawyers, interns, translators, media representatives, office workers, archivists, housekeepers, and security personnel. They are worlds apart, united by cosmopolitan ideals in their inspiration and commitment to diplomacy in their methods.

As with any organized, goal-oriented setting of human interaction, much of what happens within global organizations is like a theater production. Everyone plays a role, some of course more important than others, but each indispensable. As with the unfolding of a good story, there are unexpected alignments of interests that complicate the usual division of roles. Diplomats, civil servants, and activists (NGOs, the private sector, etc.) do not always stay tidily in their places, but sometimes form alliances that cross boundaries, or come into conflict in efforts that are meant to be collaborative.

Finding themselves in the middle of this drama, ethnographers aim at unraveling and revealing the internal structures and unwritten rules and practices that are not always discernible to the outsider but that nevertheless establish the framework for the actions that follow. Following the interactions of experts through administrative or activist networks reveals the porous boundaries of institutions, their extensions of influence into other administrative and social realms. Listening to these experts talk about what they do and why they do it reveals the dominant attitudes that influence the priorities of policy – but that also dissent from them: the palace intrigues, resistance to dominant ideas, the contradictions internal to institutions, the thoughts that never find their way into the media or official publications. Whether their research involves tagging along with diplomats as they rush between office buildings in Manhattan, collating stacks of documents, listening for hours on end to NGO delegates delivering their prepared statements in UN meetings, or participating in any number of things that take place in global organizations, ethnographers at the same time develop a kind of "double vision" that picks up on informal exchanges, snippets of conversation, small, accidental insights that accumulate to reveal the complexity, diversity, and irrationality of organizational life.

Even in the process of rationalizing the world, of making (often excessive) use of numerical indicators, legal categories, and formal procedures, global organizations cannot help but take on some of the qualities of the people who create them and work in them. In essence, these institutions are expressions of human determination, ingenuity, error, and frailty in ambitious projects of human betterment. As subjects of anthropological inquiry, they appear quite different from the way they present themselves, in much the same way that individual persons, considered closely by a sympathetic observer, almost never appear quite like their self-representations.

CROSSING THE GATE

It is now taken for granted that ethnography takes for its subject matter a wide range of quintessentially "modern" settings, including courts, police forces, laboratories, and nongovernmental organizations, and, moreover, that this methodological approach is no longer the exclusive province of anthropology but is taken up by scholars in a wide range of disciplines. At the same time, it is a bit surprising how long it took for ethnography to make a transition in its subject matter, from people on the margins of states and empires to the "modern" institutions that sometimes exercised power in those settings. The anthropology of institutions – a term that includes both the sub-field and method at the foundation of this book – has been a legitimate part of the discipline for only a few decades. This development, Marc Abélès finds (Chapter 2 in this volume), is an outcome of globalization, of the rapid flow of information and images, which contributed to erasing the mythical and "exotic" qualities that once favored different societies as ethnological subjects. In these changed and rapidly changing circumstances, institutions have become the legitimate subject matter of anthropological inquiry.

An early example of institutional ethnography – one that is remarkable in its audacity, yet rarely acknowledged as part of the history of the discipline – comes from a series of "shop floor studies" by the Manchester School in the 1950s and 1960s, in which Max Gluckman's classic study of colonial ritual and relationships in Zululand became a source of inspiration for interpreting the dynamics between workers and managers in a British factory (Wright 1994: 10–14). This kind of extension of anthropological research methods to "modern" subjects did not occur with any regularity in the discipline until, in essence, it became impossible to ignore. In a globalized world, people could no longer be understood in isolation from transnational activist networks and powerful institutions. In the 1970s, the subject matter of anthropology, with its focus on former (or current) colonies and marginalized people, was being called into question, in a shift Laura Nader referred to as "studying up." "What if," Nader exhorted, "in reinventing anthropology, anthropologists were to study the colonizers rather than the colonized, the culture of power rather than the culture of the powerless, the culture of affluence rather than the culture of poverty?" (1972: 289). Corresponding with the tenor of this question, a new direction took place in anthropology, which eventually made it possible (and legitimate) to include such things as business, scientific enterprises, and government institutions among the "field sites" of anthropology (Gellner and Hirsch 2001). A literature (almost a sub-field in itself) emerged specifically dedicated to the "anthropology of the state" (Bierschenk and Olivier de Sardan 2014; Sharma and Gupta 2006; Trouillot 2001). The limits of the subject matter of anthropology, once defined largely by colonial projects, were transformed by applying the tools of ethnography to the loci that can be considered the essence of modernity: the sources of the power of states, courts, legislatures, financial institutions, the European Union, and, ultimately, institutions of global governance.[2]

A particularly important source for the ethnography of global institutions, and another kind of challenge to colonial projects, came from a direction that we might call "from below," with its origin in local settings – the people and communities on the margins of states that constitute the "classic" subject matter of anthropology. The invasion of global organizations into fields where anthropologists did research, usually among people on the margins of states, was suddenly evident in the form of projects, advisors, and funds (Müller 2013: 3–4).[3] In some cases, ethnographers also found catastrophic conditions of dispossession and displacement that accompanied this invasion, and that added powerful feelings of indignation to their research motivations. Anthropologists were able to see how local actors were both impacted by and able to navigate the agencies that appeared in their midst with the goal of their improvement. At this point it was almost to be expected that the anthropologists' curiosity would turn to these agencies themselves as part of the subject matter they were trying to understand, using the approach of "the ethnography of organizations." The participation of anthropologists in international development projects and the human rights movement especially favored this shift to the study of global bureaucracy. These researchers were ideally situated to investigate the movement from interventions and activism in the margins of states to meetings sponsored by major agencies based in Geneva and New York. This starting point tended to emphasize the networks that create links between local settings and global agencies (see Riles 2001). In these circumstances, the participation of anthropologists as observers in UN agencies was less a matter of finding the centers of power being exercised in local settings and more the challenge of following activists and experts as they moved through networks that converged into international meetings. That is to say, having discovered new forms of networking among the people with whom they worked, some anthropologists "followed" the people and their networks to the

---

[2] See, for example, Abélès (2001), Latour (2009), and Shore (2000).
[3] Examples of the ethnography of global institutions of development with a focus on local settings include Mosse (2005 and 2013) and Li (2007).

institutions of global governance, and, from there, developed research agendas that began from the institutional vantage point.[4]

Regardless of what combination of motivation, curiosity, and serendipity brought them to enter a multilateral agency as an observer, each of the contributors to this book at some point "crossed the gate" following a decision to better understand an organization with powerful impacts on peoples' lives. In some cases, the fundamental contradiction between power and participation (that key distinctive feature of the UN and its related bodies) stimulated their interest in institutional research, acting as both a basic finding and a source of impetus. As anthropologists, each found a way to stay or to keep coming back, to extend the time and depth of their observations. And to do their research, each developed a method or a regime of observation tailored to their unique circumstances as investigators. To put it simply, they not only had to cross the gate, they had to figure out what to do once they got to the other side.

CENTRAL THEMES

This leads to a question that now allows us to introduce the central themes of this book: what are the main qualities of global organizations, aside from their structures and mandates, that emerge from close attention to their human composition, to the shifts between formality and informality, the discreet sidebars and cafeteria conversations, and all the other accumulated experiences and observations that follow from long-term involvement in the daily life of the institution? Of course, the subheadings that we provide in answer to this question are not intended as a complete list of traits. Taken together, however, these different points of discussion help us to arrive at a complex picture of global institutions, in some ways an ethnographic account in itself, one that departs from the classic reifications of bureaucracy or knee-jerk reactions to their most visible powers and incapacities.

Method

One of the common themes of the papers assembled in this book centers on the distinct problems of entry and access to information associated with the ethnography of global institutions. Once they collect their badges and find their way beyond the gates, past security, and into the hallways, meeting rooms, offices, archives, and cafeterias of global institutions, what is it that makes an ethnographer different from other kinds of scholar, some of whom might be sharing the same space and working on the same topic? What is the *ethnography* of the United Nations and its related organizations?

[4] This grassroots-to-the-capital approach to the anthropology of international organizations is emphasized in Müller's historical overview of institutional ethnography (2013). Examples can be found in Niezen (2003) and Merry (2006).

Knowing the human qualities of institutions well enough to report on them in detail requires deep familiarity. An ethnographic approach therefore involves, above all, long-term research: time in the field is ideally measured not in weeks, but in months and years. This approach is also participatory. Even when the focus of inquiry is on one meeting, one brief event, the ethnographer engages in as much self-exposure to institutional work and collective activity as possible. Ethnographers set themselves the goal of practicing a kind of empathy, putting themselves "in the shoes" of others, understanding them as human, with their own motives, emotions, areas of competence, fields of action, and moral dilemmas. Their central task in institutional ethnography is to situate this personal empathy in its context, to "unpack" or "translate" the actions and attitudes of human actors within their professional setting. And, in so doing, they ideally approach their judgments at a remove, not content with basing them on public political contests or institutional policy statements. This empathy involves a process of critical immersion, learning the way things work from the inside, the terminology, procedures, values, and relationships. Such immersion is critical in the sense that, despite a shift in anthropology toward greater proximity of ethnographers to their objects of study, there is never fully a release from the perspective of the observer, the note-taker and would-be writer.[5] Admittedly, there are some who become completely immersed in the roles they take on as part of their entry to the field, in their professional lives as fieldworkers. But at some point there is a distance involved in observation, which means that one is never fully part of what one is observing, even as a participant. The inner voice of the writer intrudes, takes note, and situates the unfolding of social life in an exterior project.

There is wide variation in terms of the particular regimes of access within which the contributors to this volume did their work. Every organization, as a subject of inquiry, calls for boundaries and identities to be negotiated, and the duration of stay and focus of research to be formally approved, sometimes in ways that reflect the formalism of management consultants (Gellner and Hirsch 2001: 5). In meeting these requirements, the contributors to this volume differed in the periods of time in which they made use of their access and the roles they filled, whether as "researcher," "intern," "consultant," "delegate," etc. Several drew attention to the challenge of doing ethnography with interlocutors whose backgrounds were similar to their own, to the point of being able to collaborate with anthropologists in their observations and interpretations.[6] This experience is discussed by Holmes and Marcus (2005) and Deeb and Marcus (2011) in reference to what they call "para-ethnography" in "para-sites" in which there is a basic "epistemic partnership" with

---

[5] Annelise Riles (2006: 3), by contrast, emphasizes the recent emergence of multiple dimensions of ethnographic proximity.
[6] Abélès develops this point in his edited volume on the WTO, noting that, as a whole, the discipline Anthropology has changed, in part through the ethnography of institutions. Whereas for a long time it had for its object remote, alien, unfamiliar societies, "today," Abélès writes, "the Other is more and more taken up with the same problems we have: from one part or another of the same planet, one finds oneself subjected to transnational economic and political strategies" (Abélès 2011: 18).

subjects whose perspectives, curiosity, and intellectual ambitions closely resemble those of the ethnographer. This collaboration occurs in a sometimes difficult situation, a bit like attempting to be at the same time both a fish and an ichthyographer (Modzelewski 2001: 133).

This is not to say, however, that as sites of inquiry, global organizations are always readily familiar to the ethnographer, even when they share many things in terms of outlook and professional training with their interlocutors. Global institutions each possess their own culture, language, and daily practices, sometimes taking on deeply distinct, seemingly indecipherable forms. They are places where the ethnographer needs to actively cultivate understanding of the seemingly impenetrable. Familiarity is not a given that follows from the common qualities one might have with the people who occupy the agency's offices.

The ways to accomplish such familiarity constitute the foremost challenge of ethnography. The models offered by those contributors who discussed method as a central part of their work share a central concern with how to begin to investigate the wide-ranging, complex, rife-with-contradictions reality of global institutions. For Marc Abélès, this challenge was addressed through a team approach to the World Trade Organization, using a diverse, international team of ten researchers to cover a variety of institutional activities and to conduct interviews from various starting points or premises of interlocution. For Maria Sapignoli, the preferred approach was to diversify her roles and points of engagement with an institution (the Permanent Forum on Indigenous Issues). And for Jane Cowan, the solution involved entering the UPR (Universal Periodic Review) with a small team of researchers, which included Julie Billaud and another collaborator, taking on various statuses and roles while examining different aspects of the review process. These are only a few examples of the basic initial methodological challenge faced by every institutional ethnographer – establishing a regime of access in conditions of bureaucratic hierarchy, systemic secrecy, and control or "management" of knowledge.

These examples also reveal that methodological problems and their solutions are inseparable from the very nature of the organizations under investigation. The anthropologists' conditions of entry and engagement reflect significant qualities of bureaucratic hierarchy, cosmopolitan staffing, and rhizomatic extension of institutional activities and ideas through (and beyond) the institutional system. "Method" in this sense is more than a technology of research; it is also deeply informative, revealing in itself something essential about the institutional Other.

Officialdom, Expertise, and Experience

Mark Malloch-Brown, reflecting on his long career that culminated in the position of Deputy Secretary General of the United Nations, observed a Jeckyll and Hyde quality to the UN, manifested in a permanent tension among its different employees, whom he classifies as the "people who work there who just want to get by" and those "who have a personal sense of commitment to making a real difference" (Malloch-Brown 2015). The stereotype of "Gucci-shoed bureaucrats taking long lunches," he observes, is more than offset by the work of individuals acting on a sense of purpose, whose efforts, taken together, make the UN a "force for good." Hope for the betterment of the world, his reflections make clear, can be grounded in the visions and dedication of civil servants.

One of the things that sets apart global organizations from other kinds of institution is the tremendous variety of personal experience in officialdom. These agencies are made up of people with a starting point of cosmopolitan life experience and values, and who come together from many parts of the world, resulting in a kind of diverse, institutionally oriented statelessness, brought into being through a full range of human variety and life experience. To this diversity among officials we can add the variety of organizations in which they live and work, with their very different regimes or "cultures" of expertise, ranging from the econo-centrism of financial agencies such as the World Bank to the legal expertise favored in the Human Rights Council, along with the particular specialisms of smaller agencies such as the UN Interregional Crime and Justice Research Institute (UNICRI) or the United Nations Statistical Commission (UNSC).

At the same time, it is possible to arrive at the impression that there is something distinctive about their employees, that there are certain qualities they commonly share. The civil servants who populate UN agencies in particular often begin their careers motivated by personal idealism. Often they have chosen their careers not only because of the prestige and benefits that come with UN officialdom, but because they genuinely want to make the world a better place, starting with their small corner of responsibility. They might recognize from the outset that there will be obstacles to projects of human improvement, but in the midst of efforts being made to save lives and make them better they see themselves as agents of possibility.

Then the pressures of conformity to institutional agendas make themselves felt. They are sometimes called upon to apply policies with which they fundamentally disagree, or required to be diplomatic in circumstances in which they are personally outraged. The agency can act like a magnet applied to the wrong side of their moral compass. More often than not, they respond by subverting their personal convictions and passions and simply getting on with the job. After all, no UN employee wants to be responsible for a failure of diplomacy by straying from the limits of sanctioned policy discourse. So the language they use in public communication tends toward the cautious and conciliatory, replicating the patterns in place.

It is, of course, to be expected that there would be resistance to this repression of conscience. Officials might use different methods to express their frustration, such as subtly inserting their own opinions into documents, infiltrating the flow of information that appears in the form of such things as Internet postings, newspapers, reports, and policy recommendations. Or they might break the rules by arranging closed door meetings intended to facilitate dialogue between stalemated states and NGOs that were otherwise only supposed to communicate through formal mechanisms. These are the conditions in which the private experience of officials encounters the moral hegemony of the institution. Given such conditions, it is important to consider the possibilities for collaborative resistance on the part of officials, whether their private opinions might be at odds with the dominant goals and policies of the agency, and, if so, the extent to which they are able to collaborate with other officials in somehow acting contrary to the trajectory of the agency's official policy and practice.

There is a paradoxical ethic of statelessness among those who administer organizations that are centered upon the concerns of states. Ironically, states are sometimes the initial reference point for recruiting those who seek careers as UN civil servants, with preference given to hiring those from under-represented regions, and relatively fewer opportunities given to those from powerful and influential states, particularly in starting positions at the UN Headquarters.[7] But once a potential employee is vetted and approved, they go through a process of denationalization, swearing loyalty to the organization and its goals above any rival personal, organizational, or national interests or sources of membership.[8] The purpose is to eliminate, to the extent possible, the kind of state-oriented politicization that stands opposed to the principle of neutrality among international civil servants. An identity transformation ideally takes place, in which the employee's country of origin is made secondary to their institutional belonging. This is physically evident in the fact that some 30,000 UN employees carry light-blue United Nations laissez-passer identity cards, which accompany or supersede (depending on the policy of the state they are entering) state-issued passports at border crossings. Both the occupational and legal identities of the employee are ideally oriented toward statelessness.

One of the distinguishing things about global organizations is the extent to which labyrinthine bureaucracies are infused with experts, permanent or temporary appointees whose specialized knowledge goes beyond the requirements of bureaucratic administration, and is applied to the tasks of program design and implementation. To the extent that international institutions intervene *in* the world, they require expert knowledge *about* the world. Experts have distinct roles in the bureaucratic system, including permanent, hierarchically ranked, agency-specific staff and temporary consultants hired for specific, limited tasks. Special Rapporteurs are a distinct category of autonomous expert in the UN's human rights system, a cadre of highly qualified "volunteers," responsible for independent, victim-oriented, on-the-ground reporting of state compliance with human rights (see Piccone 2012: ch. 1). Experts

---

[7] This element of diversity as a recruitment priority is set out in Chapter XV, Article 101(3) of the UN Charter: "Due regard shall be paid to recruiting the staff on as wide a geographical basis as possible." While an ideal, it is not always met in practice, as is suggested by the finding in Kofi Annan's 2006 reform agenda that, "targets for increasing recruitment for unrepresented and underrepresented Member States have been met by one fifth of Secretariat departments" (United Nations 2006: 16).

[8] For a comparative view of the socialization of bureaucrats, in this case among those working for the state, see Zachary Oberfield's *Becoming Bureaucrats* (2014).

also have professional identities that influence one another, interpenetrate, and, at times, come into conflict and produce tensions. In David Mosse's (2005) terms, these are "transnational epistemic communities," networks of experts with common foundations in training and knowledge. These epistemic differences can have important consequences for the ways that policies are developed and programs implemented. Disciplinary norms can have profound influences on the inner workings of the institution and the wider impacts of its policies and projects (Sarfaty 2012: ch. 3).

At the same time, it is important to stress that, in the UN system at least, the boundaries between these epistemic communities and the various roles that fall into the categories of "official" and "activist" are porous. In practice, officials are sometimes able to push an agenda in their area of responsibility, becoming, in small ways, "activists" from within the UN civil service. Experts and expert knowledge are created by the institutions in ways that can be applied (in quintessentially diplomatic ways) to so-called activist causes; and activists in turn, as they learn to navigate the UN system and acquire the language and etiquette of diplomacy, sometimes, by incremental steps, take on careers as UN experts and officials (as in the case of the Permanent Forum on Indigenous issued discussed by Sapignoli).

The Fiction of the Non-Political

Global organizations have a remarkable capacity to conceal the uses (and abuses) of power that take place through the initiatives that they sponsor, downplaying their deeply rooted value judgments as they apply their policies and programs. They do this in part by employing the sanitized language common in the social science of development, which banishes explicit reference to politics through the use of such concepts as governance, best practice, and the language of managerialism (Mazower 2009: 11). Policy makers of all kinds often depend on making their unstable social products appear apolitical and self-evident, concealing from view both the origins of institutionalized actions and the contested, untidy ways in which they are received (Shore and Wright 2011). If anything, the distance between the managerial language and sources of policy and those whose lives are shaped by them are more significant in those institutions with field programs, such as the World Bank or the UN High Commissioner for Refugees (UNHCR), where "headquarters" can be especially remote and unreachable from "the field" (see Hitchcock, Chapter 8 in this volume).

Self-evidence and apolitical appearances also take the form of numbers, or "indicators." As Sally Engle Merry (Chapter 7) puts it, "numbers are political resources," meaning that those who decide what to count and what not to count are influential in ways that are disproportionate to the limited attention given to the emerging global architecture of statistics and its impacts on procedures of "evidence based decision-making," audit, and standards of accountability. Indicators constitute a form of knowledge with "quiet power" that in the process of categorizing, counting, and analyzing, is able to "not only make sense of the messy social world, but also help to manage and govern it" (Davis, Kingsbury, and Merry 2015: 2).

The fiction of the non-political also takes the form of participatory values and superficial structures of equality, including the techniques used to conduct business without reference to disparities of power among states, or to create spaces of inclusion and dialogue that turn into blind alleys, with the actual results of participation going nowhere. Global agencies commonly promote a formal display of equality among nations that are in reality profoundly unequal. The UPR of the Human Rights Council, for example, is structured according to principles of strict equality among states, yet states are informally grouped by diplomats into two categories: those from the Western European and Others Group (WEOG), which constitute the "confident," "criticizing" countries, and those that are constrained by a lack of resources and "capacity," as well as obligations to donors and lenders such as the IMF (Cowan 2014: 58). The arrangements by which states participate in agency initiatives and interact among themselves may indeed be equal, but at the same time misleadingly encourage the idea that states pursue their interests on a level playing field. Even the Security Council, with the explicit advantages it gives to its permanent members, masks the power disparities among states through formal structures of impartiality and egalitarianism (see Schia, Chapter 3 in this volume). The same can be said of NGO participation in UN initiatives, particularly those involving indigenous peoples. These are peoples and organizations whose aspirations toward self-determination and the remediation of state abuses of power are given expression in meetings that formally encourage equal participation with states, but in ways that do not reflect actual disparities in power, that ultimately distort the extent to which states participate from positions of control.

A basic tension can be felt in some degree in every global agency between the voluntary structure of many initiatives – which gives states the liberty to abandon or sabotage efforts with which they disagree – and the reforming mission of the organization, oriented toward changing the behavior of states when it departs significantly from the agency's (and the world community's) standards of state conduct. Global agencies regularly conceal their primary goal of influencing the behavior of those states that, sometimes on specific issues, are out of step with or even contemptuous toward international norms. They are rarely in a position to further their political goals directly, but are required to constantly engage in the more oblique politics of diplomacy and persuasion. Hence, one of the common agendas (sometimes built into the mandates) of the agencies of global governance is their avoidance, on the surface at least, of obstructing (or even offending with reference to) the political agendas of states. Their success depends heavily on collaboration with states, making use of those states that are constructive participants in particular global initiatives while avoiding the alienation and enmity of those that are not. If the central guiding moral imperative of bioethics is non-maleficence, expressed with the term "do no harm" (*primum non nocere*), that of the global organizations might well be expressed as "cause no offence" (*ne scandalum*), or, perhaps better, do not offend states (*non pecces civitates*). In keeping with this frame of reference, they aim to promote peace and the eradication of poverty through the particular means at their disposal: negotiation, mediation, transitional justice initiatives, humanitarian intervention, and the gathering and dissemination of information. Diplomacy from this starting point is an ethic that originates in the relational qualities of international law. If the behavior of non-compliant states cannot always be influenced by compulsion, and if directly invoking the wrongs of the state are likely to produce no other result than defensive denial and justification, then other means of persuasion must be found, means that do not cause offense but that at the same time communicate concerns and offer avenues to reform without losing face. Given this element of state voluntarism, the political nature of global initiatives is pushed into the background, with emphasis placed instead on the benefits of development and conformity with norms intended to apply universally.

Another way to consider the fiction of the non-political is provided by Máximo Badaró (2011) and Marc Abélès (in Chapter 2 of this volume), through their use of the concept of *regimes of visibility*. Badaró, a member of Marc Abélès's research team in the WTO, considers the ways that high-level experts engage in forms of diplomacy and publicity that reduce attention to the political nature of their work. They see themselves as having to act with "discretion" and "prudence" in their interactions with diplomats, NGO representatives, and journalists. "Even though the role that they play in the political dynamics of the WTO grants them a certain level of visibility, the need for neutrality prevents them from leaving explicit traces of their practices" (2011: 84). These experts, Badaró finds, all have very similar professional backgrounds, with previous experience in diplomatic corps, international organizations and/or NGOs, and/or universities. They are globally linked in their professional activities with other professionals like them who work on similar issues, a fact that connects them to powerful networks and that at the same time gives the organization a flexible boundary, projecting its internal political dynamics toward other institutional and political domains. They also share a similar tension in their work, between their high level of qualifications and experience in their chosen fields, reinforced by their connections to global networks of like-minded experts, which are suppressed by the vital need for professional "neutrality" and restraint in applying their powerful expertise or invoking their global access to knowledge and political influence. This tension leads them to create, and be subject to, a *regime of visibility* (or, depending on one's perspective, of invisibility), a manner of presenting and distributing their technical and political skills and the results of their efforts. "The intervention of these agents in social reality," Badaró writes, "is first founded on its transformation in a visible and intelligible field, with precise limits, and which demands the application of a specific technical expertise" (2011: 85–86). This is to say, there is no stark divide between the technical and the political. The interstices of international politics can be found in informal processes (in those less structured spaces to which ethnographers seem to gravitate), including the workshops, meetings, informal documents, and activities sometimes referred to as "technical assistance."

Audit and Accountability

The fiction of the non-political can also be seen in the rise of accountability as a basic criterion of institutional success. International organizations have a distinct capacity to divert highly political decisions into the supposedly neutral realms of measures and technical procedures. This diversion is especially significant when state practices come under direct scrutiny, as in the UPR of states' human rights records, with audit taking the form of a ritualistic, interrogative examination of state assertions (Authers 2015; and Cowan and Billaud, Chapter 5 in this volume). Marilyn Strathern (2000: 1) describes this phenomenon as "the twin passage points of economic efficiency and good practice" that make up the basic criterion of institutional success. "Audit culture" as an institutional phenomenon, she argues, "has broken loose from its moorings in finance and accounting; its own expanded presence gives it the power of a descriptor seemingly applicable to all kinds of reckonings, evaluations and measurements" (2000: 2–3). The calculative rationalities of modern financial accounting are proliferating, more commonly being applied to contexts far removed from the world of bookkeeping and corporate management (Shore and Wright 2015: 2–3). There is, therefore, a close affinity between audit culture and the growing use of indicators (as discussed by Merry in Chapter 7). "Contemporary forms of governance," Garsten and Jacobsson (2011: 384) observe, "build to a large extent on the assumption that what is critical and valued can also be measured and compared. By pushing for enhanced transparency, for openness and visibility, the valued objects may be rendered accessible to measurement and comparison." The impersonal, technocratic, and neutral representation of regulatory technologies reduces the complexity of social reality and translates ethical dilemmas into manageable formats (Garsten and Jacobsson 2011: 387–388). Perhaps most significant for our purposes is the observation that there is a socially constitutive element of audit that goes well beyond the concern with numbers, that brings particular things into focus and renders others invisible or unsayable. Audit culture recognizes (and thereby creates conditions for) certain social practices, those that will convince, that "will persuade those to whom accountability is to be rendered" (Strathern 2000: 1), whether they be the government or the taxpayer/public.

These insights into the political field of auditing mechanisms suggest that they can have a wider impact in international organizations than merely their influence on global policies and pressures on states; they can also influence the ideas at the foundation of global initiatives. This includes not only the way that auditing mechanisms seek precision in selecting what is to be measured and how; they also, as Halme-Tuomissari points out in Chapter 6, reinforce concepts such as "universality" through the tangible presence of participants in auditing processes. A recurring theme in the chapters assembled here concerns how the turn to accountability, together with the measures on which it is based, are "having subtle but powerful effects on the way the world is understood and governed" (Davis, Kingsbury, and Merry 2015: 21).

Fragility

It is only few short years ago, it seems, that Hardt and Negri (2000) published *Empire*, a hugely best-selling, post-Marxist study of what they saw as an emerging global order. To them, and to their numerous supporters and sympathizers, Empire was a "total" phenomenon that included the United Nations as a whole, along with a variety of international organizations such as the IMF, the World Bank, NATO, and even nongovernmental organizations. At the time that they wrote, it seemed conceivable to many that global organizations of the kind that are the subject of this book constituted a key element of a totalizing form of power. Hardt and Negri's work is perhaps the most extreme example of a common, persistent error that applies to global organizations, that exaggerates their control over political power. It is true that some agencies have mandates that supersede those of others. The Security Council, the IMF, the WTO, and the World Bank all do have far-reaching influence on world affairs. But it takes particular form, and the contributions to this volume offer another picture to that of centralized, unchecked, and unknowable forms of global power. Even the most powerful agencies as described here have their points of vulnerability. And few of the organizations in the UN system have direct influence on the actions of states and transnational corporations. Beyond this, most operate within the limits of structural fragilities, a sense of impermanence, and vulnerability to the collective politics of their constituent states.

"Fragility" is a term used by the World Bank (2014) to describe those unstable countries that are on the verge of both possibilities for growth or descents into violence and chaos. The fragility of states in the aftermath of social and political upheaval is a realm of possibility and peril, and, for some, ideal points of insertion for global governance initiatives. While fragility is a significant part of the discourse of state failure, it applies in analogous ways to global agencies themselves. The difficulties faced by prosecutors in constructing and communicating an evidence-based narrative of mass crime are discussed by Richard Wilson (in Chapter 12) as a clear illustration of the institutional fragility of international justice. Incompletion, fragility, and reversibility are universal features of global institutions as they come into being.[9] Well-established procedures can also be incapacitated. The moral persuasion behind torture monitoring processes, for example, is readily

---

[9] Much the same observation is made by Thomas Bierschenk and Jean-Pierre Olivier de Sardan about state-building processes (2014: 7).

diffused by arguments about procedure, much to the advantage of non-compliant states (Kelly 2013a: 24). Human rights and international development agencies in particular tend to be pulled in different directions by other transnational actors, sharing with them many of the same humanitarian goals, but finding themselves in struggles over the different means to be employed, in the context of an emerging transnational normative pluralism (Goodale 2007: 3). Each organization, according to its mandate, has some potential to make important differences to conditions of poverty, insecurity, and displacement, yet each, including the most powerful, faces perils that could plunge it – and, in some cases, the world – into chaos. Depending on their mandates, their room for maneuver in implementing programs, above all in terms of the cooperation they can rely on from states, is often narrowly circumscribed.

States are more direct sources of what is arguably the most significant peril faced by global organizations: funding. Global institutions and initiatives are financially supported by and dependent on states, notwithstanding the occasional, very public donations made by billionaire "philanthrocapitalists" such as Ted Turner and Warren Buffett. If states together decide that an agency, a forum, or a project is not in their interest, they can simply cut or dramatically reduce their support for it. Country offices can be closed, forums are no longer able to hold meetings, or if they do, only in diminished form, with limited civil society participation and minimal impact. This is a source of fragility that goes beyond budgetary considerations, that influences the scope and possibilities of organizational influence, the extent to which they are able to bring about change through meaningful sanctions, or even to present ideas and actions that are discomforting to the most powerful states.

The concealments of the agencies' political agendas include a rough covering-over of their own fragilities, contradictions, and incapacities. Consistent with their ambitions, they tend to exhibit an attitude of publicly soldiering on without revealing the weaknesses imposed on them. These are private failings, the kinds of thing that never make headlines, that are not part of the sterile discourse that questions the usefulness and capacities of international organizations in the twenty-first century.

NGOs, Activism, and Publics

Much of what takes place in global organizations cannot be properly understood without considering public opinion as a source of conscience or point of reference for those who wish to bring attention to abuses of power, and in equal measure for those who wish to achieve political goals by indirect means. Public outreach is therefore a prioritized practice of international institutions. Even when presenting seemingly banal information on such things as new initiatives and upcoming international meetings, international agencies have a certain flair for media. Like all political entities, they are concerned with image, or "optics," usually in the form of carefully crafted press releases, tweets with up-to-the-minute news on world affairs, and seemingly neutral Internet postings presented to a global audience. Exercises of knowledge control and "spin" shape the way that global agencies present themselves to the world.

NGOs tend to be less concerned about the politically impartial representation of information and more concerned with having a political effect. Rights claimants and protesters try to make simple, persuasive cases to mass audiences about the urgency and appeal of their causes. The politics of shame influences the work of global organizations through NGOs, with their heightened capacities for media outreach, and, by extension, their potential for influence on public audiences with messages of crisis, victimhood, and illegitimate uses of power (Niezen 2010: ch. 2). Shame, Tobias Kelly (2013b: 134) remarks, is for states and other institutions a deeply political process, the impact of which lies in the social implications of the exposure of wrongdoing. States tend to be sensitive to opinion, if for no other reason than that their power cannot survive long in naked form, with global visibility now being unavoidable whenever their police and military are used en masse against their own citizens.

The ability of NGOs to convey information and make claims through media is, sometimes against the limitations of state-sponsored censorship, creating unprecedented avenues of rights-consciousness. With this will to make injustice known, we have entered an age of "democratic" access to the tools of persuasion. NGOs are themselves primary, interested public consumers of injustice and arbiters of global policy, each with their own target audiences of sympathizers. The success of global initiatives, in turn, can be highly dependent on the willing participation of NGOs (as Johnson and Rojas illustrate in Chapter 10 with reference to the strategic choices made by NGOs in their participation in global climate change conferences). Through the ideas and technologies available to NGOs, the sense of indignation as a response to collective injustice is increasingly expressed in relation to a wider awareness of human rights, environmental justice, and an ideal of a global just society.

Global organizations and forums differ widely in terms of their regimes of NGO access, with some, such as the Security Council and the World Bank, almost hermetically sealed from NGO influence while others, such as the Permanent Forum on Indigenous Issues, the treaty body hearings, and the UPR of the Human Rights Committee, are reliant on NGOs, to the point that they would cease to function without them. Beyond the work of individuals, NGO participation in global initiatives is mainly contingent on the possibilities they have for furtherance of their specific goals. Non-participation suggests either closure or, where NGO participation is intended but not achieved, exhaustion of the venue.

Knowledge

Global organizations are not just sources of global policy, and are not merely concerned with the politics of mediation between states; they are also primary producers of knowledge. One of the basic findings shared by several of the studies in this book is that the experts who in almost every respect resemble the ethnographer are deeply engaged in (sometimes to the point of obsession) a knowledge system, one that in some respects seems familiar, but that in other ways, on closer examination, appears as alien to an uninitiated observer as the so-called savage or primitive thought systems described by the pioneers of French structuralism or British social anthropology. Exposing to view the knowledge foundations of institutions is one of the distinct contributions of anthropology, in part because ethnography makes it possible to clear aside the formal reports and public statements, to reveal the thinking and activity behind them, as (un)expressed by their authors.

The fragility of knowledge in global institutions (revealed particularly clearly in Wilson's discussion of international tribunals) cannot be generalized as a feature of "institutional thought," circumscribed as this knowledge is by standards of evidence and court procedure. Institutions are commonly secure in their understanding of the world. In fact, one of the most disconcerting aspects of the ethnographic encounter with global organizations derives from the fact that bureaucratic/legal thought, more than any other form of expert knowledge, has a remarkable power to produce certainty where it does not exist – or, better (as Brumann demonstrates), to attempt to arrive at it where it is inherently out of reach. What is more, the ideas that they produce are sometimes widely popularized, becoming part of our everyday speech through processes of entrenchment or naturalization.

The knowledge systems of global institutions have important and occasionally direct implications for the rights of those whose essential qualities are debated and defined. While the critical acumen of activism remains oriented toward the actions and policies of those states and corporate entities that have direct impacts on the lives of marginalized and victimized peoples, the management of diversity by global institutions articulates the basic ideas and creates the institutional arrangements for this activism.

As rights claimants become involved in picking up on the concepts and priorities of institutions and shaping their own legal and cultural identities, they incline toward self-knowledge and representation (as discussed by Niezen in Chapter 13). For this reason, controversies about group rights have centered on the validity and scope of such self-definition in the context of the centralizing projects of states. This would seem to imply a certain amount of claimant-based input into the way differences are expressed and represented in the defense of rights – human rights in particular. Recognizing the proclivity of global institutions to exercise conceptual authority also calls for considering the acts of making oneself heard by those who represent the conceptualized, the intended beneficiaries and claimants of rights and policies of development.

Hope and Disenchantment

Finally, we turn to a theme that in one way or another is included (even if latently) in each contribution, which makes it appropriate to refer to global organizations as "palaces of hope." These organizations tend to have a disproportionate sense of mission, to be infused with their own peculiar kind of utopianism, a kind of piecemeal ambition for the betterment of the world, with goals that are sometimes not only hopeful and ambitious, but willfully and blindly impossible. They are driven by the typically utopian intention to construct a better world using only human ingenuity and agency, without reference to any form of divine intervention (see Todorov 2001: 3–4). In one sense, the hope of global institutions is unlike other this-worldly ideals in the utopian tradition: it does not intend to bring about a *perfect* world – it is clear to all that this cannot ever exist – but finds a simulacrum of perfection in an ideal of constant perfectibility.[10] In another essential respect it arguably goes further than its utopian predecessors: it is firmly grounded in legalism, scientism, and technologism, in the expectation that crises have a rational solution based in the almost limitless possibilities of human genius. The underlying principle in this utopianism goes beyond the intervention in crises; it tries to cultivate and harness new forms of knowledge that have the potential to transform the world.

As our discussion of fragility has already suggested, a contradiction arises from the fact that the utopianism inherent in these agencies is structurally incapacitated. Extrapolating from Mark Mazower's (2009: 27) historical reappraisal, the UN is suspended between its twin functions as an instrument of the great powers and bastion of state sovereignty, while serving as a supporter of postcolonial liberation and human rights across the world, in accordance with the rousing moral language of the Charter. This incapacity manifests itself in, among other things, the UN's limited ability to intervene effectively in human rights violations. As Ted Piccone (2012: 4) observes, "Political resolutions that condemn violations may be massaged for months and ultimately watered down to have little effect or blocked entirely." What is more, international jurists are basically agreed that fundamental restructuring of the UN "will not materialize in the next decades or even within this century" and that all its relative merits and deficiencies are set and likely to remain in place for years to come (Cassese 2012b: 648). Of course, many (if not most) activists who regularly attend meetings sponsored by the UN are aware of the limitations of its agencies, knowing full well that its "soft" processes operate in the absence of meaningful compulsion. Certainly the civil servants who organize these meetings have insight into the structural incapacities of the bodies they work for. Yet, almost miraculously, there continue to be impressive numbers of NGOs that participate in UN programs, comprising a "veritable army of 'moral fieldworkers'" (Strathern 2000: 3). The annual UN General Assembly meeting in New York has increasingly become a destination for a particular kind of tourist, those who want to "connect themselves with the excitement" of an event referred to by one tourist/participant as

---

[10] For an overview of utopianism in international law, see Antonio Cassese's edited volume, *Realizing Utopia: The Future of International Law* (2012a). Martti Koskenniemi's (2012) contribution to Cassese's volume offers a useful discussion of the history of utopian ideals of world governance in international law.

"the Super Bowl of do-good space" (Krueger 2015). This kind of participation goes together with a profound disjuncture between, on the one hand, the groundswells of activism that emerge from a global (and seemingly growing) sense of humanity united by ideals of accountability, democracy, and justice, and, on the other hand, the limited capacities of those organizations tasked with formulating and acting on them.

Each global institution works at its own pace, with its own regime of possibility, in which the idea of the future and the way it can be shaped is expressed in different form. International agencies are known above all for their slow pace of work. Legislative projects sometimes take decades to accomplish. Consistent with the stereotypes of molasses-like progress or "mission creep," those engaged in such projects often express the idea that the outcome of institutional effort is something that arrives far in the future, that "we need to be patient," that change will eventually be accomplished through the everyday work of people, through persistent collaboration. Incremental slowness, distant vision, and calls for patience, however, are not to be found everywhere. There are also those who are driven by an urgent sense of sympathetic justice that goes no further than setting to right the greatest of wrongs, protecting the children, feeding the hungry, engaging in a kind of damage control wherever and whenever the world goes awry. The crisis units of peacekeeping missions, famine relief, and epidemic intervention easily lose sight of the future, engaged as they are in emergencies that take precedence over the *longue durée* of remaking the world. Then there is the fast pace of development agencies such as the United Nations Development Programme or financial institutions such as the World Bank that work with the artificial crises of contracted time, that need to spend money quickly, with the ideals behind the sponsored projects, along with their human costs, often pushed into the background.

Hope is most front-and-center in the publicity produced by global organizations, including their reports of the results of scholarly meetings. Like all visionaries, their intellectual leaders encourage belief in a kind of possibility-beyond-capacity as a source of motivation for the realization of grand designs. Jeffrey Sachs, in his capacity as the Secretary-General's Special Advisor on the UN's Millennium Development Goals, for example, expressed the utopian aspirations of the UN succinctly when he said, "this generation has the ability to eliminate poverty altogether by 2025, and to make the world safe and prosperous for all" (cited in Tharoor 2005: 12). It is in fact rare for UN leaders to put things quite so explicitly. The usual expression of grand aspirations involves a combination of great ambition in the face of equally great obstacles, in a form something like "together we can achieve X" (an unprecedented condition of human betterment), "if only we overcome A, B, C, etc." (a daunting list of impediments). The obstacles, in fact, go together with the utopian vision by providing an element of apparent realism and clarity about what must be overcome before "we" can usher in the new world order and propel humanity as a whole toward conditions of betterment. There is a way in which the grand vision and the struggle against obstacles go together in this vision, as in Shashi Tharoor's (2005:11) simple, succinct words, "ending poverty is no simple task." Hope in the face of seemingly insurmountable obstacles is the indispensable leitmotif of almost every undertaking, every expression of institutional accomplishment and aspiration.

At the same time, the publications and reports that express such grand visions of global betterment do not reveal the extent to which their authors actually believe them. The acuteness of the tension between agency directives and the individual consciences of their employees makes global organizations different from other kinds of institution. It is not difficult to find those who populate the so-called corridors of power who are not really motivated by hope at all, just by prestige and an interesting job, not to mention overcome by disillusionment. One of the consistent findings of ethnographers in global organizations is that the further one gets from the content of public relations, and the closer one approaches the opinions of those responsible for converting policies into practice, the more we find expressions of frustration, disaffection, and cynicism. They are sometimes witnesses to the human costs of failure in "the field," in the form of destruction, destitution, and death. For many UN employees at all levels, a structural condition of hypocrisy is manifested in the disconnection between grand aspirations and the day-to-day reality of intervention in the lives of people in conditions of poverty and crisis. The reality that they eventually encounter can be profoundly disenchanting.

If we look closely, however, we can see that hope – even in its extravagant forms – still often lies hidden behind the sordid reality of humans in conflict, in crisis, in poverty, in sickness, in conditions of injustice – behind all the ills of the world that together make up the agendas of global organizations. As we now see in the collection of papers that follows, hope even lies hidden behind institutional impediments, the slowly grinding wheels of law and diplomacy, which stand between imagination and intervention.

OVERVIEW OF THE CHAPTERS

During the workshop in which early versions of the chapters of this volume were first presented, we were struck by the discovery that each paper offered several kinds of insight and could be discussed under several subject headings. We have arranged the contributions in the absence of organizational categories, both to avoid restricting them to their labels and to encourage the sense that these very different bodies have essential qualities in common, that a collection of ethnographic essays of this kind can, taken together, form an overarching ethnographic description.

We begin with several chapters on the most powerful of these organizations. Marc Abélès's discussion of the WTO begins with a description of an unusual international collaboration and method of entry into the WTOs various spaces of diplomacy. He then emphasizes the interconnectedness of technical discussions, secret diplomatic meetings, and public spectacle that constitute nothing less than the "power relations that condition the economic future of the planet." His focus on the World Trade Organization's July 2008 Ministerial Conference, aimed a completing the Doha Round of negotiations after seven years of effort, reveals the multifaceted practices of negotiation, the uses of power and diplomacy, which constitute the most significant field of activity in the WTO. Throughout these negotiations, a new balance of power between "emerging" and "developed" countries appeared as the Director General, Pascal Lamy, led efforts to achieve consensus among states with divergent interests, all within the frenzied atmosphere of rumor, phone calls to capitals, private meetings, and press interviews. The WTO's negotiation process, as Abélès describes it, is both a private and public drama that provides a forum for the expression of divergent interests and tensions between developing, emerging, and developed countries – all of this occurring within a slow, cyclical temporality in which failure is an ever-present possibility, "consubstantial with the life of the organization."

The significance of expertise and experience as a source of global power is revealed particularly clearly in the case of the Security Council, as portrayed by Niels Schia. Here, as with the WTO, the exercise of power occurs within the complex interconnections between several kinds of interactive space, which interpenetrate and are not so easily defined as might appear from a simple look. The formal space is marked by strict rules of procedure and a complex diplomatic etiquette that can only be acquired by officials through years of experience. Less apparent to those who consider the Security Council only from the perspective of the interactions at the famous horseshoe-shaped table are the spaces that leave room for an "informal working culture." Schia focuses on these informal processes to reveal how experienced actors in the Security Council are able to switch between different levels of formality and effectively engage in interrupting the processes of conflict and their internal paradoxes. These experienced actors acquire dexterity and influence in the Security Council that give significant advantages to the permanent member states that they represent in international diplomacy. Schia's discussion of the relationships among diplomats reveals the significance of shared values and conformity in the work of powerful agencies such as the Security Council, even in a wider context of political differences among states. The "world community" is in this sense an elite group of diplomats who frequent the same bars and cafes in New York.

Another approach to gaining some measure of control over the priorities of the UN system from the inside has been through a kind of mass participation in the acquisition of expertise and experience. Maria Sapignoli, using an ethnographic method based on "multi-positioned" roles, starting with the United Nations Permanent Forum on Indigenous Issues (UNPFII), follows various avenues and kaleidoscopic patterns in which the indigenous agenda is pursued, from the training of experts in an International Labour Organization initiative to the development of new programs and forums in receptive UN agencies. United Nations' civil servants sometimes engage with the causes of indigenous peoples by abandoning their apparently apolitical and diplomatic attitude to become effectively part of the indigenous movement. Indigenous delegates readily take advantage of opportunities to be socialized and professionalized in the UN system as they bring their own experiences and objectives to a wide range of initiatives. The spaces in and around the Permanent Forum are not just loci of diplomacy and activism, not just gathering points of states, international civil servants, and civil society, but are places of education and training, an integral part of the way people learn to be experts on the UN and on indigenous peoples' rights. The people, documents, and Internet data that flow in and out of the meeting rooms of the Forum constitute a vast network of education, advocacy, knowledge, interests, and expertise, some kept purposefully in the background, others expressed though delegates vying for a chance at persuasion, influence, or at least a place in the report. Sapignoli's chapter thus looks into the role of international organizations in the production of knowledge, expertise, and justice-oriented social movements, illustrating the ways that issue-focused experts/activists quite possibly contribute to changes in the structures and priorities of the UN system, adding programs, protections, measures, guidelines, and forms of representation intended, despite seeming futility and persistent frustration, to break open the UN's closed doors of state centrism.

Jane Cowan and Julie Billaud explore the "audit culture" of human rights in the UPR (see also Charlesworth and Larking 2015). The Secretariat and states have primary influence over UPR, shaping how people can intervene in the process – enabling and disabling what can and cannot be asked or formulated as a recommendation. Nonetheless, civil society actors are present and active in the UPR. Starting out with the intuition that the UPR could productively be approached as a "public audit ritual," Cowan and Billaud in the course of their research gradually discovered the institutionally specific yet diverse meanings of "public" and of the related notion of "transparency," including how access to various sites was managed. This "management" was marked by constant struggles among actors involved in producing the UPR over what should be revealed and concealed, and to whom. Their work thus illustrates the ways that human rights norms are asserted, promoted, and resisted within the practices of diplomats, social activists, NGO lobbyists, and international civil servants, interacting – expressing their own motivations, values, and interests – within the framework of the UPR.

Miia Halme-Tuomisaari examines another aspect of human rights monitoring, with a focus on universality as a myth that is actively promoted and realized through the complicity of participants. Her ethnography builds on recent work on human rights monitoring as an example of contemporary "audit cultures," contextualized around ethnographic data on national and international NGOs at the sessions of the UN Human Rights Committee – the treaty body monitoring compliance with the International Covenant on Civil and Political Rights (ICCPR). What she finds there is not the abstract universalism that is often opposed to relativism or particularism, but one in which the range of human diversity is tangibly represented in the process of reviewing human rights compliance. As they sit in the public sessions of the main meeting room of the Palais Wilson, the NGO participants "embody" the world, thus bringing to life "the international" as something dependent on this monitoring mechanism. It is revealing to see how few people are actually involved in the participatory aspect of the hearings. In particular, she focuses on the actions of a Geneva-based umbrella NGO as it invites NGOs dispersed around the world to participate in UN monitoring proceedings, thus "embodying universalism" and bringing to life "an effect of the real." Such efforts are not always successful, and civil society presence can be desultory. The Finnish hearing, to which she pays particular attention, was minimally participatory only because of the fact that a state employee went to great lengths to solicit and support NGO participation. Paradoxically, the universal comes to life in human rights monitoring through the efforts of a few individuals.

Sally Merry takes this volume's observations and concerns about audit culture and accountability into the realm of the statistical data that is designed, generated, and circulated by institutions of global governance. A genealogical approach to such quantitative knowledge reveals the rise of what she calls "indicator culture": the progressively growing use of the technologies and rationalities of quantitative data as a foundation for decision-making (Merry 2011; 2013; Merry, Davis, and Kingsbury 2015). Her ethnographic approach to this phenomenon reveals some of its other, more often overlooked qualities, including its far-reaching political influence. Outside the UNSC, she finds, the politics of measuring is consistently disregarded, concealed by mistaken assumptions of technical neutrality and the objectivity of numbers. The UNSC lacks the burgeoning activity of NGO participation that we find in many other agencies and programs. In part this could be because it deals largely with technical issues relating to the quality of data, with its central concerns seemingly remote from the life-and-death circumstances of people in crisis, following rather from its narrow role of facilitating the work of national statistics offices and developing comparable statistics across nations. Her ethnography of the UNSC emphasizes how statistical knowledge is created and by whom. Measurement, she argues, is a deeply political process, centered most explicitly on the goal of protecting statistical knowledge from interference by states. Considering the influence of the UNSC further, the statistical competence of states is connected to their credibility and in some cases to their qualification for aid. Metrics and measurement also have political implications in and of themselves, in the sense that determining what and who gets counted has important consequences for recognition and resource allocation.

Tobias Berger introduces us to the structures of "legibility" that take form through documentary practices in his study of a project in which the United Nations Development Programme (UNDP), the European Union, and various local

NGOs try to "activate" the so-called Village Courts in Bangladesh. These courts are a colonial institution that never really materialized in the local practice of conflict resolution; the project "Activating the Village Courts in Bangladesh" tries to change this through systematic efforts toward justice reform. The thrust of this chapter is an ethnographic exploration of the ways in which the United Nations and the Village Courts in Bangladesh become interconnected within the project, with a particular focus on the circulation of written documents that move up and down hierarchical structures, between UN staff in Dhaka, EU bureaucrats in Brussels, NGO fieldworkers in rural communities, and local village court applicants. He shows how these documents, which were explicitly designed to neutrally record village court proceedings, also fulfill a less overt purpose: they render informal justice institutions legible to international donor agencies and thereby link global and local institutions.

Understanding the effects of managerial intervention in "the field" poses its own methodological challenges, which Robert Hitchcock meets with a long-term study of two large-scale UN-sponsored initiatives in southern Africa. Here the method has a long-term, multi-stranded, comparative dimension that considers the relationships between UN Headquarters and country teams, "the boardrooms and the field," between two loosely interconnected agencies, the UNHCR and the World Bank, and between these agencies and their sponsoring states, all of which he assembles to reveal the hidden pathways of power, misunderstandings, and sources of disillusion as global organizations undertake major initiatives of humanitarian intervention and development. Hitchcock finds that "where there is a convergence of local and global scales in institutions such as the UNHCR and the World Bank, the offices of the headquarters usually dominate" (p. 175). In both instances (though perhaps more overtly in the case of the Bank), those who reported their experiences of displacement confronted the façade of the non-political, the assertion, expressed one way or another, that "this is not an issue for us." The expertise that went into formulating refugee intervention in these two projects was startlingly ignorant of the local contexts in which the projects were being implemented, concerned as they were with the pre-eminent goal of reinforcing the powers of states and global organizations.

The relationship between the local and the global is also present in Noor Johnson and David Rojas's comparative study of the viability of NGO participation in the UN's global climate change standard-setting, focusing on the ways activists engage with the UN in international and regional climate change conferences. Their starting point is the observation that the environmental perspective on climate change is losing footing in the UN, and is being replaced by an economic approach more in line with neoliberal state and corporate interests. Here, a recently devised system that is best known by its abbreviation, REDD+ (Reducing Emissions From Deforestation and Degradation), places landholders at the center of a policy approach in which forests, as natural resources, are monetized. By contrast, policy makers have been unable to create an analogous system of value to protect the

Arctic. Quite simply, there is no way to economize ice and snow. The motifs of forests and ice are vastly different in the ways that they appeal to publics and influence global climate change policy. Under these circumstances, the obstacles to an Arctic-oriented climate change policy are a central problem, addressed here by considering the ways that the UN channels activist energy and creates (or fails to create) legal expressions of meaning and value that leave room for the aspirations of civil-society participants.

The struggle for certainty in the context of inherent ambiguity receives sustained attention in Christoph Brumann's account of UNESCO's efforts to arrive at official criteria for the designation of World Heritage sites (see also Brumann 2014a and 2014b). Central to the World Heritage project is the idea that some sites have "outstanding universal value" (OUV) and deserve a place on the illustrious World Heritage List, meaning that they rightfully belong to, but must also be taken care of by, humanity as a whole. An operational definition of OUV, Brumann points out, is nowhere to be found in the texts of the World Heritage Convention, the World Heritage List, or anywhere else in the agency's founding documents. There is no consistent logic that can be applied in practice in UNESCO meetings, and when political considerations do not provide guidance, the agency's expert bodies and delegates subscribe to a mystical ideology in which they follow nothing more than personal intuitions. Like the use of indicators discussed by Merry, the World Heritage endeavor seeks standards of authentication and certainty where they cannot necessarily be achieved. The heritage project is unique, however, in its recourse to human experience, the poetry of place, enchantment, and the promise of greatness, all subsumed within a pseudo-objective exercise of assessment and comparison.

A very different struggle for certain knowledge can be seen in the prosecutorial goals of the International Criminal Tribunal for the Former Yugoslavia (ICTY), as described by Richard Wilson. Epistemology, he argues, is not an epiphenomenon of geo-politics and structural factors. Legal fact-finding and the knowledge it produces have important influences on "the contingent and shifting assumptions, principles and strategies of the legal actors." It is revealing, for example, to see the difficulties faced by judges and prosecutors in the ICTY, particularly in their efforts to establish a causal link between speech and criminal acts (see also Wilson 2011). The court's difficulties are illustrated by the case against Vojislav Šešelj, accused of inciting paramilitary groups to commit atrocities (or violations of international humanitarian law) during the Balkan wars of 1991–1995. The causal connection between Šešelj's speeches and the violence that followed them was not approached through statistical correlation nor through expert witnesses, but through a tenuous use of chronology: again and again, the utterance of hate and threats was closely followed by acts of violence. The limitations of the court's use of legal rationality would not be so significant were it not compounded by a more obvious limit to the effectiveness of the tribunal: it relied on states to collaborate with the prosecution, often those very states with a vested interest in an acquittal. Under these circumstances, it was difficult to conduct an effective investigation, or even to protect witnesses. The fragility of the ICTY is therefore both epistemic – relating to the limits of law in achieving the standards of knowledge needed for successful prosecution – and political, relating to the ability of those states that are indirectly implicated in crimes against humanity to thwart the prosecution of the individuals standing trial for those crimes. For those of us who are used to thinking of courts as the epitome of power, it can be surprising to see the limits within which a court such as the ICTY does its work, with implications for institutional power and knowledge.

Finally, Ronald Niezen provides an overview of the UN's uses of anthropological knowledge, with his main examples coming from UNESCO, the (now defunct) Working Group on Indigenous Populations, and the Permanent Forum on Indigenous Issues. He draws attention to the categories and norms of human belonging that are produced in global institutions, arguing that the discipline of anthropology has, to a great extent, been superseded by these institutions as the primary source of popular knowledge of human life. His paper is party historical and partly ethnographic in its examination of how international experts approach their conceptions of human rights and, in turn, how they categorize the beneficiaries of these rights. The conceptualization of humanity and its communities is accomplished in more publicly persuasive ways by international agencies, in part through their use of new media, but above all by connecting categories of belonging with the rights and political recognition that apply to those categories. The anthropology of global governance is instrumental and strategic in its ideas about human belonging, involving identification of beneficiary peoples, groups, and communities, including conceptions about the nature of their oppression and their distinct human qualities that make them proper subjects of the rights and benefits of global governance initiatives. This is a mode of conceptual development in which connections are made between rights and identities, in which specific categorizations of people are given legal recognition and then naturalized through participatory, collaborative forms of justice lobbying.

REFERENCES

Abélès, Marc. 2001. *Un ethnologue à l'Assemblée*. Paris: Éditions Odile Jacob.
   2011. *Des anthropologues à l'OMC: Scènes de la gouvernance mondiale*. Paris: CNRS Éditions.
Alger, Chadwick. 2006. *The United Nations System: A Reference Handbook*. Santa Barbara: ABC-CLIO.
Authers, Benjamin. 2015. "Representation and Suspicion in Canada's Appearance under the Universal Periodic Review." In *Human Rights and the Universal Periodic Review: Rituals and Ritualism*, Hilary Charlesworth and Emma Larking, eds. Cambridge: Cambridge University Press, pp. 169–186.

Badaró, Máximo. 2011. "Le régime d'invisibilité des experts." In *Des anthropologues à l'OMC: Scènes de la gouvernance mondiale*, Marc Abélès, ed. Paris: CNRS Éditions, pp. 81–110.
Bierschenk, Thomas and Jean-Pierre Olivier de Sardan (eds.). 2014. *States at Work: Dynamics of African Bureaucracies*. Leiden and Boston: Brill.
Brumann, Christoph. 2014a. "Heritage Agnosticism: A Third Path for the Study of Cultural Heritage." *Social Anthropology*. 22(2): 173–188.
    2014b. "Shifting Tides of World-making in the UNESCO World Heritage Convention: Cosmopolitanisms Colliding." *Ethnic and Racial Studies*. 37(12): 2176–2192.
Cassese, Antonio (ed.). 2012a. *Realizing Utopia: The Future of International Law*. Oxford: Oxford University Press.
    2012b. "Gathering Up the Main Threads." In *Realizing Utopia: The Future of International Law*, Antonio Cassese, ed. Oxford: Oxford University Press, pp. 645–684.
Charlesworth Hilary, and Emma Larking. 2015. *Human Rights and the Universal Periodic Review: Rituals and Ritualism*. Cambridge: Cambridge University Press.
Cowan, Jane. 2014. "The Universal Periodic Review as a Public Audit Ritual: An Anthropological Perspective on Emerging Practices in the Global-governance of Human Rights." In *Human Rights and the Universal Periodic Review: Rituals and Ritualism*, Hilary Charlesworth and Emma Larking, eds. Cambridge: Cambridge University Press, pp. 42–62.
Davis, Kevin, Angelina Fisher, Benedict Kingsbury, and Sally Engle Merry (eds.). 2012. *Governance by Indicators: Global Power through Quantification and Rankings*. Oxford: Oxford University Press.
Davis, Kevin, Benedict Kingsbury, and Sally Engle Merry. 2015. "The Local-Global Life of Indicators: Law, Power, and Resistance." In *The Quiet Power of Indicators: Measuring Governance, Corruption, and Rule of Law*, Sally Engle Merry, Kevin Davis, and Benedict Kingsbury, eds. Cambridge: Cambridge University Press, pp. 1–24.
Deeb, Hadi Nicholas and George Marcus. 2011. "In the Green Room: An Experiment in Ethnographic Method at the WTO." *PoLAR: Political and Legal Anthropology Review*. 34(1): 51–76.
Fleischmann, Adam and Ian Kalman. 2015. "In Search of Hope." *Allegralab*. August 26, 2015. http://allegralaboratory.net/in-search-of-hope/. Accessed August 27, 2015.
Garsten, Christina and Kerstin Jacobsson. 2011. "Transparency and Legibility in International Institutions: The UN Global Compact and Post-political Global Ethics." *Social Anthropology*. 19(4): 378–393.
Gellner, David and Eric Hirsch (eds.). 2001. "Introduction." In *Inside Organizations: Anthropologists at Work*. Oxford, UK: Berg, pp. 1–18.
Goodale, Mark. 2007. "Introduction: Locating Rights, Envisioning Law between the Global and the Local." In *The Practice of Human Rights: Tracking Law between the Global and the Local*, Mark Goodale and Sally Engle Merry, eds. Cambridge: Cambridge University Press, pp. 1–38.
Hardt, Michael and Antonio Negri. 2000. *Empire*. Cambridge, MA: Harvard University Press.
Hoag, Colin. 2011. "Assembling Partial Perspectives: Thoughts on the Anthropology of Bureaucracy." *Political and Legal Anthropology Review (PoLAR)*. 34(1): 81–94.
Holmes, Douglas and George Marcus. 2005. "Cultures of Expertise and the Management of Globalization: Toward the Re-functioning of Ethnography". In *Global Assemblages: Technology, Politics, and Ethics as Anthropological Problems*, Aihwa Ong and Stephen J. Collier, eds. Oxford: Blackwell, pp. 235–252.
Kelly, Tobias. 2013a. *This Side of Silence: Human Rights, Torture, and the Recognition of Cruelty*. Philadelphia: University of Pennsylvania Press.

2013b. "The Politics of Shame: The Bureaucratisation of International Human Rights Monitoring." In *The Gloss of Harmony: The Politics of Policy-Making in Mutilateral Organisations*, Birgit Müller, ed. London: Pluto, pp. 134–153.
Koskenniemi, Martti. 2012. "Projects of World Community." In *Realizing Utopia: The Future of International Law*, Antonio Cassese, ed. Oxford: Oxford University Press, pp. 3–13.
Krueger, Alyson. 2015. "Forget Coachella and Bonnaroo: The U.N. Is the Place to Be." *New York Times*. October 4. www.nytimes.com/2015/10/05/nyregion/forget-coachella-and-bonnaroo-the-un-is-the-place-to-be.html?_r=0. Accessed October 6, 2015.
Latour, Bruno. 2009. *The Making of Law: An Ethnography of the Conseil d'Etat*. London: Polity.
Li, Tania. 2007. *The Will to Improve: Governmentality, Development, and the Practice of Politics*. Durham: Duke University Press.
Malloch-Brown. Mark. 2015. "The UN is an underfunded Bureaucratic labyrinth and a force for good in the world." *The Telegraph*. 26 July.
Mazower, Mark. 2009. *No Enchanted Palace: The End of Empire and the Ideological Origins of the United Nations*. Princeton: Princeton University Press.
Merry, Sally Engle. 2006. *Human Rights and Gender Violence. Translating International Law into Local Justice*. Chicago: University of Chicago Press.
  2011. "Measuring the World: Indicators, Human Rights, and Global Governance." *Current Anthropology*. 52 (3): 583–595.
  2013. "Human Rights Monitoring and the Question of Indicators." In *Human Rights at the Crossroads*, Mark Goodale, ed. Oxford: Oxford University Press, pp. 140–150.
Merry, Sally Engle, Kevin Davis, and Benedict Kingsbury (eds.). 2015. *The Quiet Power of Indicators: Measuring Governance, Corruption, and Rule of Law*. Cambridge: Cambridge University Press.
Modzelewski, Karol. 2001. "Lo studio del totalitarismo: comprendere or giudicare?" In *Storia, verità, giustizia: I crimini dello XX secolo*, Marcello Flores, ed. Milan: Bruno Mondadori, pp. 132–140.
Mosse, David. 2005. "Global Governance and the Ethnography of International Aid." In *The Aid Effect: Giving and Governing in International Development*, D. Mosse and D. Lewis, eds. London: Pluto, pp. 1–36.
  ed. 2013. *Adventures in Aidland: The Anthropology of Professionals in International Development*. Oxford and New York: Berghahn.
Müller, Birgit (ed.). 2013. "Lifting the Veil of Harmony: Anthropologists Approach International Organizations." In *The Gloss of Harmony: The Politics of Policy-Making in Mutilateral Organisations*. London: Pluto, pp. 1–22.
Nader, Laura. 1972. "Up the Anthropologist: Perspectives Gained From Studying Up." In *Reinventing Anthropology*, Dell Hymes. ed. New York: Pantheon, pp. 284–311.
Niezen, Ronald. 2003. *The Origins of Indigenism: Human Rights and the Politics of Identity*. Berkeley and Los Angeles: University of California Press.
  2010. *Public Justice and the Anthropology of Law*. Cambridge: Cambridge University Press.
  2014. "The Law's Legal Anthropology." In *Human Rights at the Crossroads*, Mark Goodale, ed. Oxford: Oxford University Press, pp. 185–197.
Oberfield, Zachary. 2014. *Becoming Bureaucrats: Socialization at the Front Lines of Government Service*. Philadelphia: University of Pennsylvania Press.
Piccone, Ted. 2012. *Catalysts for Change: How the UN's Independent Experts Promote Human Rights*. Washington: Brookings Institution Press.
Riles, Annelise. 2001. *The Network Inside Out*. Ann Arbor: University of Michigan Press.

2006. "Introduction: In Response." In *Documents: Artifacts of Modern Knowledge*, Annelise Riles, ed. Ann Arbor: University of Michigan Press, pp. 1–40.

Sarfaty, Galit. 2012. *Values in Translation: Human Rights and the Culture of the World Bank*. Stanford: Stanford University Press.

Sharma, Aradhana and Akhil Gupta, eds. 2006. *The Anthropology of the State: A Reader*. Hoboken: Wiley-Blackwell.

Shore, Chris. 2000. *Building Europe: The Cultural Politics of European Integration*. London: Routledge.

Shore, Chris and Susan Wright. 2011. "Introduction: Conceptualizing Policy: Technologies of Governance and the Politics of Visibility." In *Policy Worlds: Anthropology and Analysis of Contemporary Power*, Chris Shore, Susan Wright and Davide Però, eds. New York and Oxford: Berghahn, pp. 1–26.

2015. "Audit Culture Revisited: Rankings, Ratings, and the Reassembling of Society." *Current Anthropology*. 56(3): 421–431.

Strathern, Marilyn (ed.). 2000. *Audit Cultures: Anthropological Studies in Accountability, Ethics, and the Academy*. London: Routledge.

Tharoor, Shashi. 2005. "The Millennium Development Goals, WSIS and the United Nations." In *The World Summit on the Information Society: Moving from the Past into the Future*, Daniel Stauffacher and Wolfgang Kleinwächter, eds. New York: The United Nations Information and Communication Technologies Task Force, pp. 11–17.

Todorov, Tsvetan. 2001. "Il secolo delle tenebre." Maddalena Carli, trans. In *Storia, verità, giustizia: I crimini dello XX secolo*. Marcello Flores, ed. Milan: Bruno Mondadori, 1–8.

Trouillot, Michel-Rolph. 2001. "The Anthropology of the State in the Age of Globalization: Close Encounters of a Deceptive Kind." *Current Anthropology*. 42 (1): 125–138.

United Nations. 2006. Investing in the United Nations: for a stronger Organization worldwide: Report of the Secretary-General. General Assembly, March 6, UN Doc. No. A/60/692. www.globalpolicy.org/images/pdfs/0303sgreport.pdf. Accessed June 23, 2015.

Weiss, Thomas and Sam Daws. 2007. "World Politics: Continuity and Change Since 1945." In *The Oxford Handbook on the United Nations*, Thomas Weiss and Sam Daws, eds. Oxford: Oxford University Press, pp. 3–38.

Wilson, Richard. 2011. *Writing History in International Criminal Trials*. Cambridge: Cambridge University Press.

World Bank. 2014. Breaking the Cycle of Fragility: A High Level Panel Offers Suggestions. Washington, April 11. www.worldbank.org/en/news/feature/2014/04/11/breaking-the-cycle-of-fragility-a-high-level-panel-offers-suggestions. Accessed May 13, 2015.

Wright, Susan (ed.). 1994. "Culture in Anthropology and Organizational Studies." In *Anthropology of Organizations*. London: Routledge, pp. 1–31.

2

Heart of Darkness: An Exploration of the WTO

Marc Abélès

A MEMBER-DRIVEN ORGANISATION

Since its creation, the WTO (World Trade Organization) has generated a vast amount of literature, aimed mainly at two categories of specialists: those who work for and those who are interested in this organisation. In 2008, a team of ten researchers from different parts of the world (Africa, Asia, America, Europe) undertook an ethnographic research project inside the Centre William Rappard, Geneva, where the WTO is located; one of the results of this fieldwork, conducted over a period of two years, consists in offering an anthropological perspective on the representations and practices of the organisation. This is a truly original approach, in complete contrast with the studies usually devoted to institutions, which traditionally take a political, administrative, sociological and sometimes legal angle of approach. It contrasts also with the classical fields of anthropology, a discipline traditionally devoted to the study of alterity and difference. However, during the past ten years, more and more ethnographic work studying organisations and institutions has been published, looking at local or national structures as well as transnational ones such as the IMF (International Monetary Fund) (Harper 1998), the World Bank (Pincus and Winters 2002) or the UNHCR. In this paper I will present some of the relevant issues raised by our exploration of the WTO, especially those related to transparency as a focal component of the neoliberal governmentality. The WTO's overriding purpose is to help trade flow as freely as possible. As such, it is a place where international negotiation takes place, the objective of which is to counter any obstacle to free trade. It administers a whole system of rules and regulations that provides a framework for trade. Its main goal is thus to make sure that trade flows smoothly, predictably and freely. The WTO derives from the General Agreement on Tariffs and Trade (GATT), which was initiated after WWII. It was created in 1995 and is today at the very centre of a multilateral trade system that was implemented throughout the world more than half a century ago. Since then, several rounds of negotiation have contributed to the stabilisation of trade by implementing a whole system of rules and regulations, as well as a Dispute Settlement Body whose role is to solve trade disputes. The organisation now includes 160 countries, and China's new membership in 2001 marked an important step in its enlargement. Indeed, it acted on China's clear wish to be a part of the world's trade economy. The implementation of the Doha Round[1] took place throughout the first decade of the twenty-first century without ever reaching a conclusive agreement. Admittedly, the financial crisis of 2008, which shook the foundations of the world's economy, was not conducive to negotiation. Yet, in spite of the international conjuncture and of the threat of protectionist reflexes, the organisation held its ground. New countries now wish to apply for membership to the WTO; the Dispute Settlement Body has gradually prevailed and the institution tries to establish an efficient communication policy in order to shed its entrenched image as a capitalist-driven organisation, serving the interests of the rich and caring little for the increasing inequalities between its members. Both the rapid development of emerging countries and the importance of digital technology in developing countries within the organisation have deeply changed the balance of power in the WTO. Therefore, it should come as no surprise that the question of development was one of the key aspects of the Doha Round.

The WTO headquarters are located in Geneva, in the William Rappard Centre, which was for many years the International Labour Office building. The WTO is generally defined as a member-driven organisation, as the power of decision belongs to its various member states. Member states enjoy this prerogative in the frame of the Ministerial Conference, which gathers at least every other year. WTO members are represented in the General Council Meeting; they include ambassadors and heads of delegations in Geneva. Occasionally, civil servants are also sent by member state capitals. The council gathers several times a year in the organisation's headquarters in Geneva, also as the Trade Policy Review Body and as the Dispute Settlement Body. It is aided in its missions by the Council for Trade in Goods, by the Council for Trade and Service and by the Council for Trade-Related Aspects of Intellectual Property Rights, which each report regarding their relevant fields. Negotiation and decision-making in the WTO rely on two essential principles, namely single undertaking and consensus. Single undertaking means that a cycle of negotiation can only be concluded if all participants agree on all of the subjects treated. The point is to link together the various questions, which obviously results in a better balance between advantages and concessions. By contrast, the absence of a single undertaking would enable some members to successfully conclude negotiations on a given subject without having to return the favour. 'Nothing is agreed until everything is agreed' – a motto that stalled several Doha Round negotiations. Unique undertaking is considered as a means of reaching a consensus, thereby reinforcing the multilateral system at the heart of the WTO.

---

[1] A multilateral round of negotiation launched in Doha in November 2001, aiming at liberalising international trade and at sharing the benefits of globalisation with developing countries.

Consensus indeed lends legitimacy to the agreements that result from negotiations. At the WTO, each country is permitted one vote, regardless of its population or its role in world affairs. One single opposition can hinder the whole process, and obtaining the approval of 160 countries is no easy task. The system actually works by gathering groups of countries like so many concentric circles: at the centre lies a small group deemed to be representative of the interests of its members, and groups that share more specific common interests gravitate towards it. Before a consensus is reached, a whole set of consultations takes place under the aegis of the Director-General in the *Green Room* – a name that derives from Elizabethan theatre, the Green Room being the place where actors gather backstage before a performance. The name therefore has a mysterious connotation. Numerous specialised committees, work groups and expert committees operate in the various fields in which agreements are sought. These include the environment, development, WTO membership applications and regional trade agreements. The WTO Secretariat, also based in Geneva, is made up of 800 civil servants, 630 of whom are permanent, and it is headed by the Director-General. The Secretariat aims at offering technical help to the various councils and committees as well as to the Ministerial conferences. It also provides technical assistance to developing countries and constantly produces world trade analyses. Finally, the Secretariat deals with the WTO's communication with the media and with public opinions through parliaments and civil society organisations. The Secretariat can also provide judicial help within the frame of dispute settlement and has an advisory role for the governments of those countries that wish to become members. Its budget is relatively modest (€130 million). Compared to the World Bank and the IMF – the other two great international economic institutions, both located in Washington – its powers are clearly more limited, as is its staff (2,500 people work at the IMF and more than 10,000 work at the World Bank).

ANTHROPOLOGICAL PERSPECTIVE ON TRANSNATIONAL INSTITUTIONS

After this short presentation of the WTO, let us come back to anthropology. Here we have to deal with these two questions: Why are anthropologists now so interested in great institutions? What can be their specific contribution to the understanding of a globalised institution such as the WTO?

In order to answer the first question, one must go back to the recent history of the subject. Anthropology has dealt primarily with far-removed societies. It traditionally explored the lifestyles and traditions of remote populations considered by Westerners to be different or exotic. Now, in the context of globalisation, the object of anthropology has profoundly changed. Today, the gap has largely been bridged between the anthropologist and his or her object. The Other must increasingly deal with the problems faced by us all, subjected as we are to transnational economic and political decisions. The world has shrunk and the strangeness attributed to 'exotic' populations has truly disappeared. The rapid flow of information and images contributes to erasing the mythical aspect that different societies were once invested with and which turned them into favoured ethnological subjects. The point is no longer to study separate cultures, but to lead more investigations into the *relationships* between cultures – hence, the recent proliferation of research on migrations and the question of boundaries.

Transnational organisations are a pertinent object of study for intercultural relationships. Transnationalism is not just a characteristic of contemporary capitalism; it also conditions power relations and cultural referents. Works on the World Bank (Pincus and Winters 2002), on the European Union (Abélès 2000a; Zabusky 1995) and on other international institutions (Müller 2013) have highlighted the new supranational configurations of institutions. Representatives of different cultures and political traditions are gathered there and work together to harmonise legislation and build encompassing projects. For the anthropologist, this configuration raises several questions about the consequences of a permanent confrontation between different ideas, different languages and different administrative traditions within a common policy; questions about the invention of new forms of cooperation in an enlarged bureaucratic frame; and, finally, questions about the practical and symbolic consequences of the displacement of politics and of the change of scale in these new theatres of power.

Thus, a new field of research has developed that corresponds to the original vocation of anthropology whilst reviving the concept and offering an original perspective differing from that of political science and the sociology of organisations.

As to the second question – the specific contribution of anthropology regarding our knowledge of transnational organisations – let us first specify that anthropologists resort to a different method from that of other social sciences. Their involvement enables them to collect materials that will, in time, fuel their analyses. They have to fit into an organisation and stay there long enough to know it well. Time is an important parameter in such a project. Likewise, the fact that the observer is both an insider and an outsider, along with his or her detachment from the studied group, results in the unveiling of practices and relationships within the organisation that are usually glossed over (Abélès 2000b; Latour 2009). Anthropologists work according to an inductive logic and construct their objects through construed fieldwork. What matters most to the anthropologist are the representations of the various players as well as the logic behind their actions. Both the anthropologist and the objects of his or her investigation (i.e. the members of the organisation) enter a discursive relationship. It is this very relationship that gives insight into the workings of the organisation. As Holmes and Marcus have shown (2005), the people whom we deal with in our studies, by imparting their vision of the organisation and of its environment, develop a 'para-ethnographic' approach. And thus, just as the anthropologist progressively unveils the logic behind a society whose manners and customs are completely different from our own, when studying a great institution he or she underlines the coherence and the tensions at the heart of the structure.

This approach presupposes that the institution, rather than be thought of as a formal structure, be considered as a place of confrontation between various representations, a place where quests for power cross over. This multifaceted quest constitutes the very life of the institution, with the tensions and conflicts that heterogeneous representations of the institution can breed. One can now better appreciate the theoretical implications of a daily approach to organisations. Knowing what they do and what happens inside them is fast becoming more and more indispensable to a better understanding of the world we live in. And yet it looks as though the institution's entrenched reputation, borne from the very image it projects of itself, had tarnished most analyses. Words such as system, inertia or rigidity describe the reality of the institution. Yet, they only partially describe the processes that the anthropological approach tries to delve into. We apprehended the institution through its singularities and its subjectivities; we tried not to reduce it to a mere chart or to conform to the image that it constantly strives to project of itself through its communication department. This is why our analysis differs wholly from the literature aiming at presenting the WTO (Rainelli 2004) or at condemning it (Jawara and Kwa 2003). We did not enter the organisation with a view to chronicling its functioning (Blustein 2009). Nor did we intend to argue the evolution of capitalism today, or even to predict its future within the framework of international relations. Obviously, upon entering the WTO, one finds oneself embroiled in a debate on the future of multilateralism and on the issue of regulation in a globalised economic context, where the slightest imbalance is likely to weaken the whole system. Hence, the need for the anthropologist to step back and to consider the official line as yet another policy that needs interpreting. Failing this, the anthropologist is in danger of slavishly transcribing the official line and the dominant analytical frameworks that accompany it in the fields of economic and international relations. Admittedly, the fundamental question is whether, in the context of international trade, multilateralism – a defining part of the WTO – is not undermined by the rise of bilateral trade agreements (Bhagwati 2008) and whether this does not question the very vocation of the institution. Such issues are being raised even in the corridors and meeting rooms of the William Rappard Centre. However, our research tackles a different angle, and although it may help to better understand the way international issues are being debated, its goal is in no way to contribute to that debate.

In fact, what makes this ethnographic work within the WTO truly original is the device we used. Three elements played a key role here: first, the possibility to conduct research within the organisation; second, the participation of a diversified group of researchers; and finally, the duration of the research. Choosing a great international institution as investigative ground is courting difficulty. One cannot simply gain access to the building; a badge has to be worn, stipulating which of the two categories one belongs to, namely member or visitor. Now, strictly speaking, we belonged to neither category: we were neither visiting (which would have meant that our presence was only peripheral), nor were we involved directly in the activities of the institution. To carry out our research, it was important that we could spend time at the WTO.

DOING FIELDWORK AT THE WTO

As our research was mainly focused on the Secretariat of the WTO, we needed to get authorisation from the head of this organisation. When we undertook the project, Pascal Lamy was the Director-General of the WTO. I had known him about twenty years previously when I did fieldwork at the European Parliament. He was at the time the chief of staff of the President of the European Commission, Jacques Delors. Many people in the European Parliament had recommended that I meet Lamy in order to better understand relations between the Parliament and the European Commission. When I met him, he immediately spoke and explained to me that he considered that the anthropological approach was particularly relevant to study multicultural organisations. That is why he wanted to know if I would agree, once my work on the Parliament ended, to undertake an ethnography of the European Commission. It existed at that time as a Forward Studies Unit which sponsored research projects and seminars on very diverse subjects concerning Europe. It is this unit which sponsored the collective research which I conducted with two other anthropologists, Irène Bellier and Maryon McDonald. We had each chosen one of two DGs to lead our investigations. Besides the articles and books that it inspired, the report which we produced gave rise to discussions with the officials and persons in charge of the European Commission. Afterwards, we were invited to present our vision of the institution during internships in which the new state employees participated.

When, much later, I undertook a collective research project in the WTO, I thought that Pascal Lamy would support this initiative. We had often happened to discuss the issue of multiculturalism in the core international institutions. Lamy agreed enthusiastically to welcome the project to the WTO. It must be specified that our research was not funded by the WTO, which does not have the budget to promote such operations. This meant that we had to find another source of funding. The advantage of this situation was that it guaranteed our independence from the organisation. Furthermore, Lamy was worried that our presence should not appear as having been imposed in an authoritarian way by the Director. Thanks to the Director-General's agreement, we obtained the precious access in the form of a yearly pass; we were also granted an office that we shared with interns in the Economics and Statistics Department. Conversely, in view of the role of member states, it was clear from the beginning that the Director-General could not dictate our presence at meetings. Indeed, his only direct authority is over the staff of the Secretariat: anything to do with the activities of delegations is beyond his remit.

It soon became apparent that the presence of anthropologists at the WTO would be better accepted if they came from diverse continents, thereby reflecting the diversity at the heart of the organisation. This diversity, which we might have seen as an imposition, actually generated an unprecedented experiment in the field. Typically, anthropologists are rather isolated, and individualism is one of the defining traits of the subject. Collective work is rare and is generally carried out by researchers from the same country. Capitalising on the collaboration of ten researchers from such different countries as Argentina, Cameroon, China, Korea, Canada, the USA and France, our innovative approach moved away from the traditional approach at field level.

The team was numerically important. Generally, anthropologists are rather protective of their independence. Unlike other social scientists, who often work in a team, anthropologists are reluctant to engage in any hierarchical relation. The classical model of the boss surrounded by followers who share his theoretical framework and have to apply his conceptuality does not work among anthropologists. Here, we don't find the equivalent of Bourdieu's team, or of the way they worked out *The poverty of the world*. I did not think that this kind of functioning would make sense with our project. I remembered an important collective ethnography in a village of Burgundy, called Minot, undertaken by four researchers (Tina Jolas, Marie Claude Pingaud, Yvonne Verdier and François Zonabend 1990), who spent several years in the field. Lévi-Strauss, who had initiated this programme at the Laboratoire d'Anthropologie Sociale, never wanted to impose any frame of investigation on these ethnographers. At that time I was a PhD student of Lévi-Strauss and later on, for one decade, I was a member of the Laboratoire d'Anthropologie Sociale. I can testify that he never tried to favour his own conceptions or priorities and was eager to protect the autonomy of the researchers. He taught me that an ethnographer participating in a collective must keep a maximum degree of autonomy and initiative in the construction of their objects of research and the relations which he/she develops on the ground. Taking this principle into account, I thus encouraged each of us to choose the theme of their research and to develop his/her networks of informants according to what he/she observed, but also according to their own focus of interest. What interested me was not the homogeneity of our group, but its heterogeneousness, its internal diversity. We embraced diversity and rejected the idea of a homogenous vision or a shared doctrine. The fact of gathering people from different horizons, those not sharing the same theoretical background, but avid to work together, seemed to me more stimulating than to lock them into a pre-established frame. We not only exchanged information about our field's observations; it also gave us an opportunity to confront our different anthropological approaches toward politics and institutions.

What we wrote aimed at reflecting this diversity, and as such it differed from the kind of literature that the WTO has generated so far. It should be stressed that we were able to operate thanks to a tri-annual programme of the French National

Research Agency. We had enough time to truly immerse ourselves in this extremely bureaucratic world. Under these conditions, each member of the team was able to stay in Geneva for more or less extended periods of time and was able to further inquire and raise new questions. Various meetings between team members took place in the process, and the general consensus was that they played an important role in the global orientation of our work. Similarly, in the field, interactions between researchers were extremely stimulating.

Once the subvention of the ANR had been obtained, it was possible to start our collective project. In practice, the first two years of the project were dedicated to fieldwork. Some of the researchers made stays over a long period (up to one year and six months), others made regular comings-and-goings to Geneva. Sometimes there were two or three colleagues working at the same time at Center William Rappard; or one could go there and not meet anybody from the team – not because there were not any other anthropologists in residence, but because they were involved in meetings somewhere else in the city. If the WTO Secretariat was the focal place of our fieldwork, we were also interested in the functioning of the delegations, and we were extending our investigations to other part of the city where the embassies are located. We also studied the way the WTO is perceived by NGOs. I had a lot of contacts with Oxfam and other NGOs that had a critical approach to the liberalisation of exchange and promoted fair trade. With regards to the objects of investigation, Badaro was interested in the TRIPS, Jae Chung in the NAMA, Dematteo in communication and transparency, Cai Hua observed the Chinese delegation, Dima the Dispute Settlement Body. Pandolfi and Rousseau aimed to analyse the vision of the development inside the WTO. Marcus and Deeb conducted an ethnographic experiment in the Green Room with the Director-General. I was focused on the cotton issue, the accessions process and the process of Ministerial conferences.

At the beginning, Lamy and his staff gave us some introduction to the people who could answer our questions on these different subjects. These people then introduced us to others, and little by little each of us built his/her own network of informants. Having an office inside the Centre William Rappard gave us the opportunity to chat with the Secretariat staff, and we made contact with a lot of people. Part of our work consisted in interviews and observation of meetings. But the ethnography of institutions is grounded in so many informal exchanges, which take place in the lobby, at the cafeteria, etc. This kind of dialogue about everyday life sometimes affords more information than the formal interviews. It is a fabulous way of learning how people represent themselves, their own work and the institution.

What has come of this collective work? Has it opened the way for further analyses? What questions remain unanswered? In order to answer such questions, I would like to lay the emphasis on one of the most intellectually challenging aspects of the project, namely its experimental aspect. Indeed, when one reads extensive research describing organisations, one notices that they usually take for granted the boundaries of the object to be analysed and that they identify this empirical object with the research subject itself. In other words, these works do not aim at generating a series of questions or at outlining thematic priorities drawn from experiential data; on the contrary, they aim at describing at length the organisation as it is mapped out – from within and without – by a whole range of prevailing views.

Short of recording here the outcome of the research, one can stress the fact that the ethnographic work within the WTO has led to a larger questioning of the global politics that the institution incarnates so well. One could consider the WTO as a mere international organisation, as a place where diplomacy takes place at a global level but still in the traditional form of negotiation between governments. In this way, the WTO would only differ from the GATT in quantity (in the number of countries involved) and not in quality. Such is the implicit view of the older members of the organisation when they lament the expansion of structures and regret simpler times when the organisation was more of a club and less of a bureaucracy. It is to be noted, though, that their critical tone reflects their awareness of a profound change, one that we could better apprehend owing to our exteriority. Global politics (Abélès 2010) – as opposed to international policy – is a group of activities that includes diplomacy and decision-making on certain subjects (in this case, international trade), and also the production and circulation of norms and concepts applicable either locally or globally and the construction of a public space in a global sense. Global politics is where transnational organisations and civil counter-powers are constantly confronted and, therefore, one of the main results of our research is to have demonstrated that the WTO probably belongs more to the sphere of global politics than to that of international policy. This is probably the reason why the institution resists any kind of functional approach, one that would reduce it to a mere realisation of its explicit *telos*, namely the liberalisation of trade. In this framework, there is a mutually accepted system of rules, to which one might add the jurisdictional control of the Dispute Settlement Body. This is the heart of the matter. On the one hand, diplomats, jurists and economists clearly work at achieving what the organisation claims to be its main objective. They contribute, within their means, to the free flow of goods and services between member states. On the other hand, upon observation of the dynamic of the WTO, we notice the extent to which this 'functional' activity generates a clash between diverging interests, a clash which refers back to the rift between rich and poor countries and which the rapid development of 'emerging' countries has made all the more complex. This is not a mere process of further complexity – more countries, more diverse situations – but indeed a true transformation of the very nature of such an institution. In other words, we are dealing with a new political place, which does not mean that the WTO is a place of power. Behind extremely technical discussions, and with secret diplomatic meetings in the wings, there are quite clear power relations that condition the economic future of the planet. Let us be clear: international policy strategies already existed at the time of the GATT. The novelty of the situation is that while the latter, dominated as it was by the United States and its allies, only translated a stable hegemony into the field of trade negotiations, today the situation has thoroughly changed. The WTO has become the place where the imbalance of the world is most keenly felt and where the market economy is being questioned. This is probably why the well-oiled machinery that is the famous *Round* of negotiation seems to have seized up, incapable as it is, ten years on, of completing the Doha cycle. This is also the reason why the organisation is a place where debates take place not only concerning the future of multilateralism, but also about the necessity to link trade with what were so far seen as external concerns, i.e. social conditions of production (social dumping), the environment (with sensitive subjects such as the fishing trade), etc. If one considers the WTO as a political institution – though it in no way substitutes itself to existing governments – one better understands how it was forced to develop its own forum by reinforcing its communication strategy and by implementing an annual public Forum in which both negotiators and representatives of civil society (lobbyists, NGOs) participate.

Different themes emerge from our research, as so many unifying threads between our various contributions. We delved into the everyday life of the organisation by frequently attending the William Rappard Centre, a true microcosm of the WTO as it houses the civil servants of the Secretariat and holds the various committee meetings where delegation members are gathered.

At the WTO, we dealt not only with diplomats, but also with a whole set of jurists and economists who were either part of the Secretariat or who worked with the Secretariat as a delegation, a lobby or an NGO. One of our research efforts focused on the specificity of expertise, on the way knowledge is shared within the institution and on the use that is made of it. We focused attention on the activity of experts, on their relationship to diplomacy and politics, on the way that their roles vary from mere advisors – where utter discretion is necessary – to primary players in meetings on topical subjects or even to leaders of pedagogical sessions. The relationship between politics and expertise cannot be reduced to a simple opposition between light and shade or between the stage and the wings. It needs a deeper reflection on the *regimes of visibility*.

In order to question the notion of *visibility*, I will first focus on the cotton issue as an illustration of the overlapping of the technical and the political processes. Then I will consider the July 2008 Ministerial Conference, which was aimed at completing the Doha Round, the failure of which in fact mirrored the new balance of power between emerging and developed countries. As the WTO is one of the main places where what is called multilateral governance is being tested, and an arena within which the developing countries, the emerging countries and the developed countries are confronting their view on globalisation (Jawara and Kwa 2003; Kapoor 2004), the analysis of the negotiations round may offer an interesting perspective on the complexity of multilateral practices and the potential obstacles on their way.

CONTEXTUAL ELEMENTS

The Doha Development Agenda took a clear stand against the North–South imbalance issue, in the framework of international trade regulation:

> International trade can play a major role in the promotion of economic development and the alleviation of poverty. We recognize the need for all our peoples to benefit from the increased opportunities and welfare gains that the multilateral trading system generates. The majority of WTO members are developing countries. We seek to place their needs and interests at the heart of the Work Programme adopted in this Declaration. (Ministerial declaration, 14 November 2001)

Formerly concerned with business connections between developing countries dominated by the United States or the great European powers, the organisation was then theoretically at a turning point. In practice, things proved to be a lot more complex.

On one hand, the Ministerial declaration could be interpreted in various ways by the negotiators of big countries such as Brazil, Australia, the United States, South Korea and Japan. Concretely, there was no agreement regarding the issue of 'modalities':[2] how scaled-down would the custom tariff and the subsidies be – from 70 to 80 per cent, or from 20 to 30 per cent? Would these reductions be based on an average that would allow each country to determine for themselves the requested tariff and subsidies reductions? Or could there be a more gradual system that would ensure the highest rates to be the most reduced ones? Are there any exceptions? Which ones? The Doha Development Agenda was calling for negotiations on subjects such as anti-dumping, the fisheries subsidies, the services liberalisation and the elimination of the poor countries' export taxes. To put it plainly, the agenda stressed the need for substantial reductions and improvements in market access.

During the Cancun conference (September 2003), the organisation's main priority was to agree on the terms of agreement that would bring forth an important step in resolving other issues. At that time, the United States was not so keen on consensus politics. In March 2002, under the pressure of American iron and steel firms, the Bush administration forced a 30 per cent rate rise on imported steel, hence applying the safety rules that allow countries to raise the rates in case of a sudden importation inflow. In parallel, the *Farm Bill*, adopted in 2002, contradicted the WTO's proposal: to eliminate all rates in the field of industrial products and convenience goods in 2015. Criticised for this contradiction, American officials answered that the next *Farm Bill*, scheduled for 2007, would take into account the new rules adopted by the Doha Round. At Congress, Democrats had not stopped showing their hostility towards a politics of consensus, considered dangerous both for the economy and

---

[2] Way of processing. In the WTO's negotiations, the terms of agreement give the framework of the final commitments – like formulas or approaches for the tariffs reductions.

for employment. In early 2003, Stuart Harbinson, chairman of WTO's General Council at that time, encountered strong opposition when submitting his *Draft Text on Farm*, which was to be used as the framework for an agreement on the modalities.

In the meantime, in Europe, the EU had adopted the CAP reform, which modified the model by establishing the decoupling of the subsidies from production: the new rules were to take into account the cultivated areas. This was of course to do with the way subsidies were granted, and not with their value (€43 billion in 2003). The European Union was maintaining its high tariffs. On the United States' part, Washington was aspiring to a more progressive formula, where high tariffs would be cut more than low tariffs. The EU, supported by Japan, was going for a 36 per cent average cut of the tariffs. By setting an average, the progressive formula was not needed, meaning that some key products would remain untouched. The Commissioner for Trade at the European Commission, Pascal Lamy, suggested that Europe and the United States should jointly write the paper that would form the basis of the Cancun negotiation. After hours of negotiations in early August 2003, the EU and the United States' trade negotiators succeeded in producing a shared document. However, the problems were far from solved, since developing countries were asked to lower their tariff walls, whereas the EU and the United States were keeping their main agricultural subsidies. These conditions were widening the gap between Doha Development Agenda, planning sooner or later the total eliminations of subsidies, and from the EU's and the United States' standpoint, advocating the elimination of export subsidies on *products of particular interest for the developing countries*, but without naming them.

During the time preceding the Cancun conference, the Brazilian ambassador and his Indian colleague set up an alliance between developing countries against the United States' and the EU's approach towards agriculture. Two countries, whose interests and agrarian structure were often differing, were leading the coalition: on the one hand, India, the average production area of which did not reach 4.94 acres, on the other hand Brazil, with its huge and highly mechanised farm estates, the highest exporting country in the fields of sugar, coffee, orange juice and soy. This strategy proved to be a turning point as Argentina, South Africa, Thailand, China and around twelve other countries joined in. It is in this context that the G-20 was created, and that the cotton issue was brought out.

THE COTTON ISSUE

Since 2003, the cotton issue has been an ever-recurring one within the WTO. It is particularly emblematic of the direct opposition between rich and poor countries – on the one hand the two big players, the United States and the EU, and on the other hand Africa, whose interests are not easily reconcilable.

The cotton sector accounts for 8–12 per cent of the African countries' GDP, for 40 per cent of their total operating income, and for some of these countries, it reaches 70 per cent of their agricultural income. In the case of Burkina Faso, a country where agriculture employs 80 per cent of the working people, cotton is accountable for 60 per cent of the export revenues and feeds several millions of farmers. In Benin, it accounts for 50 per cent of its export revenues. The year 2003 saw the tension on the issue of cotton reach a new stage. In a general context marked by the fall in prices of raw materials, the competition between the southern and the northern producers intensified. It should be noted that, according to the IMF, the real costs (inflation deducted) of untreated cotton exports fell by nearly 45 per cent between 1980 and 2000. In the mid-nineties, the rate was at 42 cents per pound. The recurrence of the cotton price drop affected African countries as well as Brazil, especially as the United States and the European Union were giving priority to subsidies policy, allowing them to compete efficiently with the other producers. The 2002 Farm Bill had given preferential treatment to American farmers: compared to 2001, their production had increased by 40 per cent, thanks to economic aid. In 2003, Brazil was first to take a stand by bringing the United States before the Dispute Settlement Body. In 2009, the long procedure that followed delivered a judgement, on appeal, in favour of Brazil.

Once Brazil had filed its complaint, some African countries contemplated going into partnership with Brazil, but there were at least two reasons for not doing so. First of all, joining this country after the event would slow the procedure down. Moreover, procedures tend to be too expensive for these countries. They then considered a more spectacular process, which would stress the inequalities within the WTO. It was the NGO IDEAS Centre – created in 2002 by Arthur Dunckel, the former GATT Director-General, and Nicholas Imboden, a former Swiss representative for trade agreements and former ambassador in charge of the Swiss economic cooperation with developing countries – that was advising the African countries. The Swiss government had given them power of attorney to help the developing countries to fit into the trading system.

The collaboration between African and IDEAS leaders was born. According to Imboden (interview, 8 July 2008), the focus on cotton resulted in a simple alternative. Rather than enumerating a list of blatant inequalities, the choice of a precise point of impact would bring African trade problems into the limelight more effectively. This strategy had the advantage of informing public opinion in an efficient and spectacular way. Moreover, cotton represented the most important part of the agricultural resources in several countries, which were suffering due to unfair competition with the United States and the EU. From this context sprung the idea to submit a tender to the WTO. The countries that were more reliant on cotton – Burkina Faso, Mali, Chad, and Benin – went for this strategy. A fifth one, Togo, chose to stay out of it. In order to make their claim look impressive, Burkina Faso's president, Blaise Compaoré, came down to the WTO to hand their submission to the June General Council session, taking the opportunity to deliver a press conference. He said:

> Our countries are not asking for charity, nor are we requesting preferential treatment or additional aid. We solely demand that, in conformity with WTO basic principles, the free market rule be applied. Our producers are ready to face competition on the world cotton market – under the condition that it is not distorted by subsidies. (Compaoré 2003)

Concurrently, the English NGO Oxfam organised a demonstration. The event was created in order to gain large media coverage. At the time, the initiative achieved a good reception, including by the United States and the EU. But things went seriously downhill during the Ministerial Conference of Cancun.

On one hand, the African countries benefited from the support of the antiglobalists, within the framework of a vast communication campaign organised by Oxfam. On the other hand, Supachai, WTO's Director-General, broke his silence and described the cotton issue as a fundamental one, asserting that he would apply himself to set up an effective ruling system within WTO's framework. Yet, the Cancun conference ended in failure because of the absence of consensus regarding cotton. Considering that the subsidies granted to the producers of rich countries were bringing about an imbalance, African countries asked for the withdrawal of these subsidies. This initiative crystallised the opposition between the poor countries – led by India, Brazil, Kenya, and China – and the United States and Europe. In this trial of strength, the NGOs, Oxfam at the forefront, sided with the developing countries. Long before the Cancun conference began, Oxfam launched a petition called 'The Big Noise', which collected about 3 million signatures from across the world. The petition was presented (with great pomp and ceremony) to the Director-General of the WTO by Chris Martin, lead singer of the British rock band Coldplay, and by Adrian Lovett, Oxfam's director of campaigns and communication. The band, alongside a vast number of journalists, was back from visiting Mexican corn producers; this visit made them realise how difficult their living and working conditions were. In parallel, all kind of initiatives – events in the media (concerts, The Big Noise CD), a week-long course of actions to the European Parliament, echoed in press releases and analysis on the organisation's website – increased the pressure.

During the Cancun meeting, prompting demonstrations did not satisfy Oxfam spokespersons enough; they also played an important part in advising the poor countries, ensuring their overall presence in the media by increasing the amount of press conferences. According to a member of the EU delegation, the NGO had turned the conference into a 'morality play'. It is interesting to see that between the Commissioner for Foreign Trade at the European Commission and the NGO, a dialogue was established in the form of a contact group: the NGOs were being informed and asked for their opinion. Indeed, the knowledge of

Oxfam in the field of the food-processing industry meant they could not be overlooked: the organisation has its own experts – high-level economists – and the European Commission sought advice from it on tricky subjects such as the sugar issue, a field where pressure groups are very powerful. In Cancun, the European Union delegation included NGO representatives, but they kept their independence and fair-trade beliefs, and defended diametrically opposed ideas.

The 'sectoral initiative in favour of cotton' (Cotton Initiative), presented for the first time by the Cotton 4 in 2003, provoked strong reactions from the United States, firmly defending their cotton subsidies. And Supachai's intervention on the first day (10 September 2003) reinforced the US's position: 'the C4 does not need a special treatment, but a solution based on a fair multilateral trading system'. The next day, he announced that he had just agreed to lead the small working group dealing with the cotton issue. As Imboden was European, the United States suspected the Europeans of presenting them as the 'bad guy' in order to cover up their own subsidy policy. The United States rejected the elimination of subsidies and the financial compensation granted to Africans. They recommended diversification, suggesting that they could export something other than cotton, and that they needed the World Bank's financial help and loans to process cotton fibres and make clothes. Politics of diversion, from the Africans' point of view.

As Cancun was drawing to a close, tension was at its height between the United States and the Director-General Supachai, whom they blamed for failing to remain neutral. They made sure, though, that in the next draft, the WTO would commit itself to *'effectively direct existing programs and resources toward diversification of the economies where cotton accounts for a major share of their GDP'* (emphasis added). One of Africa's representatives summarised their feelings in one sentence: 'we are used to putting up with illnesses and starvation. Now, the WTO has also turned against us' (Blustein 2009, 152).

Supachai thought he was doing the right thing when he criticised the Swiss Minister for supporting the anti-globalist NGO, which initiated the scandal. The minister answered that the NGO in question was led by two irreproachable globalists, one of whom is the former GATT Director-General. Far from challenging the legitimacy of IDEAS Centre, other countries such as Germany, France, Great Britain, the Netherlands and Sweden joined forces with Switzerland, in effect supporting its project. Eventually, negotiations came up against another point, the Singapore issues (regarding investments, competition policy, transparency in government procurement and trade facilitation), which Europe wanted to bring up. The G20 representatives were wearing an 'Explicit Consensus' badge, referring to the promise made by India on the last day of the Doha meeting, to stand still on the Singapore issues until unanimity between the member states was reached. But Europe wanted these issues to be discussed. In the end, the European negotiator suggested the following compromise: keep only two questions. Zoellick wanted to make sure that one of the questions would deal with the competition policy, but he came up against Malaya's representative, Rafidah.

Derbez, the Mexican Foreign Affairs Minister who presided over the session, put an end to it at 1pm. During the adjournment, African countries agreed on refusing any kind of compromise. If someone was to suggest discussions about two questions from the Singapore issues, all of them were to refuse. Youssef Boutros Ghali (Egypt) tried to convince them that the Commissioner for Trade at the European Commission had made an important concession. When the session resumed, the African representative shared his colleagues' refusal to negotiate the aforementioned issues. The South Korean representative said the exact opposite, and the Singapore representative suggested that it was still possible to make progress on the agriculture matter. Suddenly, the Mexican representative, Derbez, threw out all opportunities of extending the negotiation and decided to close the session. On hearing that decision, African delegations jumped for joy. Some raised their fist in front of the cameras. Others sang 'Money can't buy the world', borrowing The Beatles' tune 'Can't buy me love'.

United under the C4 (Cotton 4) banner, the African countries deepened their actions by suggesting that the reduction of export subsidies and of the trade-distorting domestic support regarding cotton would bring stricter and quicker outcomes than the negotiations on the General Agreement on Agriculture. The United States was showing signs of hostility towards the Cotton Initiative and was even disclaiming the relation between American domestic support programmes and the prices slump, or denying the fact that the programme could have penalised any foreign competitor. A workshop was organised in Cotonou (Benin), including four sessions led by representatives of the World Bank and the African Development Bank.[3] The aim was to stress the role of the financial and technical assistance. From a development point of view, the trading issue was therefore coming second. The rich countries' response consisted in financing the assistance of the Least Developed Countries in return for their silence. Furthermore, Americans refused to dissociate the cotton issue from the rest of the agreements on agriculture, pretending that it was an agricultural commodity like any other. Within the C4, discussions occurred on the actions to be undertaken; their approach was to stand by their opinion on the trading matter. In December 2005, during Hong Kong's Ministerial Conference, despite American pressure on the C4 representatives to be more conciliatory, the representatives reinforced their requirements. The mandate adopted in Hong Kong came down to three points: the cotton issue was to be dealt in an *ambitious*, *quick* and *specific* way. The C4 suggested to the WTO Ministerials in Cancun (Mexico) and in Hong Kong that the reductions of export subsidies and of trade-distorting domestic support in the field of cotton would bring stricter and quicker outcomes than the negotiations on the

---

[3] Session I on Factors in African Cotton Production and Trade. Session II on Cotton-Specific Types of Financial and Technical Assistance. Session III and IV on the Roles and Contributions of Multilateral Institutions, and Bilateral Donors.

General Agreement on Agriculture. The C4 proposal (TN/AG.SCC.GEN/4: 1 March 2006) called for the elimination of all kind of payments included in the cotton's Aggregate Measurement of Support (AMS), but this was to be done within a third of the time limit, meaning 2010 rather than 2015. The C4 recommended the use of a mathematical formula, a 'correction coefficient', to be applied to the overall reduction of the already accepted MGS (TN/AG.SCC.GEN/4, paragraphs 5–7). The less ambitious is the overall reduction, the greater is the correction sought by the C4.[4]

The United States' 10 October 2005 proposal remains the US official position up to this date. Contrary to the C4's proposal, it suggests that the elimination of the cotton subsidies could only be possible if all other AMS were eliminated simultaneously before 2022, and under a number of prerequisites. Until then, there was no way of going below the line of €700 million of domestic support. On its behalf, the European Union announced that it could not go below a minimum threshold of €279 million.

The C4 members also wished for the cotton issue to be officially acknowledged. They were told that the Agriculture Committee was already in charge of this issue. Eventually, the *Cotton Sub-Committee* was created, hence taking into account the specific aspect of this issue. Today, there is no choice but to accept that nothing has really changed. The United States has never accepted the domestic support level going below €400 million, as asked for by the C4. In parallel, WTO's Dispute Settlement Body agreed that Brazil was right regarding their dispute with the United States. At the end of this procedure, the Dispute Settlement Body confirmed the judgement, while the United States persevered with their subsidy policy. In other words, if you look at things from the results' point of view, nothing much has changed.

The cotton issue remains unresolved. During the Ministerial Conference of July 2008, it was part of the twenty important points the Director-General wanted to bring up, but the negotiations ended before they even started, much to the C4 members' frustration. There are many ways of appreciating how the process has unfolded since Cancun. From a utilitarian point of view, it is a total failure: objectives have not been reached and issues have not been settled. Americans have not even dared to enter into the negotiations. They remained silent throughout the negotiations, keeping themselves from bringing up figures or even giving the outline of a proposition. The Sub Committee met, but they did not manage to get things moving again. And however relevant the means used and set up were, it did not come to an end.

Does this mean that the Cotton Initiative was a complete waste of time? In fact, the way the C4 came to life is in itself a significant event. It became the symbol of the

---

[4] AMS support for cotton shall be reduced according to the following formula: Rc = Rg + (100 − Rg) * 100 3 * Rg Rc = Specific reduction applicable to cotton as a percentage Rg = General reduction in AMS as a percentage.

construction of a political stage within the WTO. What is at stake is the 'distribution of the sensible', as the philosopher Rancière (1995) would put it. Until then, the WTO had set up an efficient ranking system that gave the big players the best deal, and that ensured their domination over the global economy. Europe and the United States have long had the upper hand; nowadays, China is gradually asserting itself, followed by the emerging countries. Even though the Doha Development Agenda mentions the development issue, it is clear that the solutions recommended by the rich countries turn a blind eye to the facts: considering the difficulties of the producers, what is put forward as a solution is not to make the cotton trade fairer, but to leave the field open to their competitors by switching to other kinds of production. This explains African countries' reluctance towards Western suggestions to stimulate diversification through financial aid.

By constituting the C4, African countries create a *dissensus*. They do not accept that their problems should be treated with respect to development, even if it is all about trading and if they refer to one of the WTO's undisputable principles: fair trade. Their attitude is reminiscent of the plebeian manners from the famous Menenius Agrippa fable: this tale sees the plebs meeting up on the Sacred Mount, and setting up their own assembly opposite that of the patricians, who have the monopoly of the trading system. When Rancière analysed the behaviour of the plebeians, he showed how they were actually challenging the configuration of the sensible, a cutting of the 'common' that allocates shares to one and another, a divisive sharing out in essence. 'They are setting up a new order, a new division of the sensible, not by forming into warriors equal to any other warrior, but into speaking beings sharing the same features as those who deny them' (1995, 53). The African countries followed suit when they created their own group and required the WTO to acknowledge the importance of the cotton issue, by constituting a specific negotiation authority within the organisation. This gesture can be considered as a political gesture, as defined by Rancière: 'a well-determined activity, antagonistic to the first one: one that upsets the sensible and fragile configuration, where parts and shares, or their absence, are defined by a presupposition that has, by definition, no room' (1995, 53). Beyond the cotton issue, what this example shows us is the way a political stage takes shape within an institution that manages nonetheless to carry on working according to its routine and its traditional diplomatic methods.

SCENOGRAPHY OF A NEGOTIATION : THE MINISTERIAL CONFERENCE OF JULY 2008

The definition of the WTO is that of an organisation aiming to liberalise trade. It is a forum for governments to negotiate trade agreements. It is a place for them to settle trade disputes. It operates a system of trade rules. Superficially, as a member-driven organisation, the WTO does not differ much from the other diplomatic traditional organisations. If we look at it more carefully, the WTO appears as one of the main places for experimenting with multilateral governance, an arena in which developing, emerging and developed countries are confronting their approaches of globalisation (Jawara and Kwa 2003; Kapoor 2004), I will now focus on this experiment, by looking at the most characteristic field of activity of the WTO, the practices of negotiation, and more specifically at the recent Ministerial conference of Geneva (21–30 July 2008).

This meeting was expected to complete the Doha Round after seven years of negotiations. However, this meeting did not reach these expectations: after nine days of intense negotiations, the talks collapsed over a disagreement concerning one of the twenty subjects that had been put on the table by the DG, Pascal Lamy. I will not describe the details of the negotiation. I treat this kind of event as a *'fait social total'*, whose analysis can shed some light upon the complexity of the so-called multilateralism and its limits (Bhagwati 2008) through the study of the WTO and the narratives of the actors. I try to shed light on the decision-making process, on the public dimension of the Ministerial conference and on the peculiar temporality of the negotiation cycle.

Pascal Lamy decided to call the Ministerial conference in order to complete the Doha Round by reaching agreement on a number of issues. The meeting was expected to adopt 'modalities' for agricultural and industrial goods, and to make progress in the services negotiations. In WTO jargon, 'modalities' mean the parameters on whose basis members would establish their new commitments, whether in terms of lower tariffs, subsidies or new disciplines. For the anthropologist, it is possible to describe the negotiation as a twofold process. On the one hand, there is the meeting itself: the ministers are working together and they don't have any contact with the outside. This process takes place behind closed doors in the Green Room, far from any external observer.

On the other hand, the Ministerial opens up a public space. By giving press conferences or talking informally with journalists, the main protagonists can deliver political messages and produce their own scenography of the negotiation. The journalists are located in a room at the ground floor. Spatially there is a separation, but the two worlds reconnect when the ministers leave the meeting room and go down or when some of their staff talk with the journalists.

Publicity is a key feature of the Ministerial. A lot of journalists from different countries follow the meeting. In Seattle and Cancun it gave an opportunity to the NGOs for transmitting their political messages. The Ministerial conference contrasts with the discretion that characterises the normal diplomatic process. In July, the Ministerial took place in the Secretariat building (William Rappard): it is the place where the members of the negotiation groups meet together every day. The arrival of the Trade Ministers radically transformed the atmosphere. They were surrounded by lots of advisors, senior officers, delegates and journalists. These people settled in the building for nine days.

In many respects, the Ministerial could be defined as a *public drama*. As the meeting progressed, the intensity of the commentary increased, changing focus from accounts of substantive issues to who-said-what-to-whom and the various tactics deployed to generate a consensus. Rumours, phone-calls to capitals, and frenzied work proliferated as the meeting neared an end.

When one tries to analyse what occurred during those nine days, one has to take into account not only the scenario of the negotiation but also the way the story was told to the media, and through them to the public. What I would like to point out is that the *performative* dimension of the event is in some way as important as the result of the negotiation. To complete the Doha Round means to find agreement on subjects as different and as technical as market access, internal agriculture subsidies, non-tariff barriers, trade facilitation, intellectual property, etc. The Secretariat must support the delegations in affording technical solutions, and in opening a path to a compromise between the different interests. At the same time, the intervention of the DG, as it is conceived by Lamy, consists in making sense of this process. I can briefly sum up the main events of the negotiation: one of the prerogatives of the DG was to determine the format of the meeting. He opted for calling a Green Room meeting including the thirty-five countries that were representative of the different categories (developing, emerging, developed): a sort of microcosmos of the economic and geopolitical diversity and of the complexity of the trade issues addressed. After a few days of discussions between these protagonists, it appeared that this format was not propitious to significant progress in the negotiation. Then Lamy decided to call the G7, a group formed by Australia, Brazil, China, Europe, India, Japan and the United States. On 25 July Pascal Lamy put a draft on the table, a proposition including twenty subjects. It seemed possible to reach an agreement, and a compromise was found on eighteen of the subjects. An atmosphere of optimism diffused inside the whole building, and was reflected in the media, which proclaimed: 'they are not far from an agreement', 'they will conclude'. However, one point appeared conflictual: the Special Safeguard Mechanisms. The issue was the right of India and other developing countries to protect agricultural products from competition in the event of a surge of imports. The issue neatly split the interests of import-sensitive developing countries and competitive farm exporters. The former wanted recourse to protection, the latter wanted predictable access to overseas markets. The SSM was intended to protect farmers against import surges and price declines by allowing them to raise tariffs beyond bound levels. Throughout the negotiation, the main point of contention had been whether, and by how much, countries should be allowed to use SSM to impose safeguard duties in excess of current (pre-Doha) tariff ceilings. Lamy made a compromise proposal: SSM remedies would be allowed to surpass pre-Doha tariff levels by up to 15 per cent when import volumes rose by 40 per cent. The US negotiator, Susan Schwab, agreed with this proposition: she said she would not accept a 'trigger' lower than 40 per cent because it could interrupt normal flows and would guarantee a new de facto tariff on US exports such as soy and cotton. However, India and China supported the G33's proposal. The trigger proposed by Lamy was too high to ensure that farmers would not be hurt by surges of 'subsidised' imports from developed countries. They wanted SSM remedies to be able to surpass pre-Doha levels by up to 30 per cent. The US did not accept this proposition, and after two days of discussions, the Seven did not reach an agreement. Efforts were made until the very last minute of the meeting to find a compromise over the SSM, especially by the EU, Australia, Brazil and Japan, but India and the US did not move from their respective positions, and China allied itself with India's negotiators in insisting on safeguard rules for agriculture. China and India insisted that developing countries be allowed to impose prohibitively high tariffs on food imports from affluent countries to halt imports that might put farmers in poor countries out of business. The mantra of multilateral negotiation reaching across several strands – manufacturing services, agriculture, legal trade rules, intellectual property rights – is that 'nothing is agreed until everything is agreed' (in the idiom of the WTO it is called the single undertaking principle). By consequence, the disagreement on one subject meant that all else that had been virtually accepted was now off the table. 'The Geneva headquarters of the WTO yesterday had an air of mourning after a party that started well but ended in tears' (Beattie 2008). The non-agreement on one subject meant the collapse of the Ministerial conference.

CONFLICT OF INTERPRETATIONS

I found it interesting to analyse the way people from the WTO talked about the negotiation and of its failure. I will first emphasise the use of *metaphors*: the terms used to qualify the negotiation refer to *gambling*. As a member of the Brazilian delegation said: 'It's a gamble: high risk, high return.' Another spoke of the 'tactical bet' to qualify the initiative of the DG when calling the conference. One can notice the repeated use of the expression 'to put on the table'; here, the idea is that the negotiators don't like to show their cards. What is extremely difficult for the chair of the negotiation is to make them admit to the concessions they could agree to.

When Lamy called the G7 into the Green Room, most of his time was dedicated to asking questions about what they could accept on such and such a subject. He himself put a draft compromise on the table in order to get their reactions. He asked the questions orally, but at certain moments distributed a written question. He then gave them time to respond, a little like a teacher questioning his students. Some participants compared him with a school principle. Another technique he used was the confessional: Lamy interrupted the meeting and invited one of the ministers to his office, situated down the hall. Sometimes he spoke with two ministers at a time in this fashion, and then the meeting continued. During this whole time, the others were waiting, continuing to discuss matters or meeting with their advisors. The ministers did not leave the negotiation room, and it could last from 9 o'clock in the morning to late at night.

The pressure mounted progressively; the protagonists felt as if they were locked in a bubble. Some became exhausted and asked whether there was a bed where they could sleep for an hour; others napped in a corner of the room, waiting for the confessional to end and the meeting to restart. Lamy was trying to find out the limits of each minister, their 'red lines'. The draft paper he had put on the table held at least one proposition that each person found unacceptable, but that, paradoxically, held the possibility for agreement, asking each person to move beyond, within certain limits, their red lines. When the draft paper was presented to the participants, here again the DG had to be in the role of initiator. He asked everyone's advice, skilfully beginning with those who, after admitting that the agreement would cause them to make considerable concessions, declared that they were nonetheless ready to make the effort to find a compromise. In a way, Lamy had to create a positive dynamic within a group of negotiators. In the negotiation itself, there was a very strong technical dimension. In order to try to find a compromise on the SSM, for example, they called not only on WTO bureaucrats but also on senior agricultural officers from the European Commission. Technically it was possible to propose a compromise between the Indian position and the American one. But what prevented agreement was foremost a political reason. The proximity of both Indian and American national elections led the two participants to harden their positions. The Indian minister wanted to appear as a protector of his country's agricultural interests. And there was no question that the American negotiator would accept the possibility of a limitation that only went one way.

An essential aspect of the negotiation was the staging of it, what each side performed. Let us now have a look at the public drama, the *story* that was told during these nine days. It is the story of a failure, but the importance lies in the *meaning* given to that failure. If we observe the attitude and commentaries of the Indian minister, we see how he gave a positive meaning to the failure, one that emphasised the resistance of the poor and the oppressed. He continually affirmed the fight for food security and his unwillingness to accept the commercial hegemony of the United States in the agricultural sector. For him, the failure of the conference marked the triumph of an alliance of emerging countries and developing countries against developed countries. Another message concerned the growing power of the emerging countries concretised by the presence of China and its alliance with India. The United States and the EU, previously the real powers behind world trade deals, would have to adapt to the rise of emerging economies such as China, Brazil and India. The Brazil Foreign Affairs Minister, Celso Amorim, proclaimed, 'In the past it was the EU-US business or at the most the Quad (Japan, Canada, EU, US); now it is a more complex trade system: you have to look at developing countries as a force.'

As usual, the US negotiator did not share these analyses: she denounced the stubbornness of the Indian trade minister, suggesting that he was mostly motivated by electoralist and demagogic reasons and that, due to this demagogic and populist attitude, he had forced the SSM to become a focal point for the developing countries (especially for African countries); hence, the cotton issue, about which the United States was ready to put a proposition on the table, was not addressed.

Last but not least, we have to consider the story as told by the DG in his press conference (Lamy 2008). He had to be neutral and not participate in the blame game. When he communicated about the failure in his speech to the G35, in his press conference, and later in two other circumstances (a speech to the parliamentaries, and a speech at the WTO Public Forum to an audience of NGOs and interest groups) he explained that the meeting collapsed to the detriment of the poor who would have benefited most from the lowering of prices that trade opening brings about, and to the detriment of the developing world that has fought to bring greater equity to international rules, in particular to the field of agriculture.

For Lamy, the Doha Round had 'a more fundamental *political* objective about renewing the "affectio societatis" – the vows of the original WTO contract. Its two fundamental principles being: one, that contributions to more open trade be made on the basis of a member's level of development and, two, that members be bound by a set of international obligations' (Personal communication 2008). This summed up Lamy's political conception of the WTO as an organ of regulation rather than a simple instrument for liberalising the world trade.

To conclude, I would like to address the issue of incompleteness as a constitutive element of the WTO culture. If we consider the temporality of this kind of negotiation, the Doha Round has to be seen as a very slow process, punctuated by accelerations. It took seven years from September 1986 to December 1993 to complete the Uruguay Round, and the Doha Round began in 2001. Slowness, the 'longue durée', characterises the temporality of the negotiation. Failure, as a major component of the cyclical temporality of the WTO, is consubstantial to the life of this organisation. The acknowledgement that meetings do collapse (six of these meetings have collapsed since 1982) is part of the normal rhythm of trade politics. First, we observe that each time a meeting has collapsed it has been followed by a period of reflection that in most cases enabled the agenda to be taken forward. Second, the negotiation as a public drama provides a forum for the different approaches of globalisation and for the tensions between developing, emerging and developed countries. For the anthropologist, looking at the structural incompleteness of WTO governance, reflecting on this culture of expectation, is a stimulating way of working on the multilateral process, its ambivalences and its contradictions.

REFERENCES

Abélès, M. 2000a. *Un ethnologue à l'assemblée*. Paris: Odile Jacob.
    2000b. 'Virtual Europe'. In *An Anthropology of the European Union. Building, Imagining and Experiencing the New Europe*. Eds. I. Bellier and T. M. Wilson. Oxford: Berg Publications, 31–52.

2010. *The Politics of Survival*, Public Planet Books. Durham: Duke University Press.

ed. 2011. *Des anthropologues à l'OMC. Scènes de la gouvernance mondiale*. Paris: Éditions du CNRS.

Beattie, Allan. 2008. 'Doha Collapse', *Financial Times*. 31/7.

Bhagwati, J. 2008. *Termites in the Trading System. How Preferential Agreements Undermine Free Trade*. London: Oxford University Press.

Badie, B., and Blustein, P. 2009. *Misadventures of the Most Favored Nation*. Philadelphia: Public Affairs.

Compaoré, Blaise. 2003. 'Allocution de son Excellence Monsieur Blaise Compaoré', Genève, le 10 juin 2003, Genève, Comité des négociations commerciales de l'OMC, www.wto.org/french/news_f/news03_f/tnc_10june03_f.htm.

Harper, R. H. R. 1998. *Inside the IMF. An Ethnography of Documents, Technology and Organizational Action*. Amsterdam Academic Press.

Holmes D., and Marcus, G. E. 2005. 'Cultures of Expertise and the Management of Globalization: Toward the Re-Functioning of Ethnography'. In *Global Assemblages. Technology, Politics, and Ethics as Anthropological Problems*. Eds. A. Ong and S. Colliers. Malden: Blackwell, pp. 235–252.

Jawara, F., and A. Kwa. 2003. *Power Politics in the WTO*. Bangkok: Focus on the Global South.

Jolas T., Pingaud M.C., Verdier Y., Zonabend, F. 1990. *Une campagne voisine: Minot, un village bourguignon*. Paris: Ed. de la Maison des sciences de l'homme.

Kapoor, Ilan. 2004. 'Deliberative Democracy and the WTO', *Review of International Political Economy*. 1(3): 522–541.

Latour B. 2009. *The Making of Law. An Ethnography of the Conseil d'Etat*. Cambridge: Polity Press.

Müller, Birgit (ed.). 2013. *The Gloss of Harmony: The Politics of Policy-Making in Mutilateral Organisations*. London: Pluto.

Pincus, J. R., and Winters J., (eds.). 2002. *Reinventing the World Bank*. Ithaca: Cornell University Press.

Rainelli, M. 2004. *L'organization mondiale du commerce*. Paris: La Découverte.

Rancière, Jacques, 1995, *La Mésentente, Galilée [Disagreement: Politics and Philosophy*, Minneapolis: University of Minnesota Press. 1998].

Zabusky S. E. 1995. *Launching Europe. An Ethnography of European Cooperation in Space Science*. Princeton: Princeton University Press.

3

Horseshoe and Catwalk: Power, Complexity, and Consensus-Making in the United Nations Security Council

Niels Nagelhus Schia

INTRODUCTION

The UN Security Council (UNSC) is the executive decision-making arena of the United Nations. What characterizes this arena is not only that the Council's decisions have effects across the world, from major capitals to small villages in isolated rural areas, but also that its decision-making is to a considerable extent affected by the micro-politics of the UNSC's informal processes. The Council produces far-reaching and extensive policy, but it has an inward focus.

In this chapter I argue that the significance of the informal processes and the micro-politics in the Security Council enforce inequality among the member states to a greater extent than is evident through the formalized veto right alone. I look at how an actor-oriented perspective on meetings between "countries" can result in a better understanding of how the Security Council works. I describe how informal processes overlap with formal structures in consensus-making and decision-making processes. I continue by examining how this overlap tendency favors "repeat players" (Galanter 1974: 3). When analyzing the American legal system, Marc Galanter distinguishes between those who have occasional recourse to the courts, and the "repeat players ... who are engaged in many similar litigations over time" (1974: 3). Rather than analyzing how a legal system such as that of the American courts influences the players, Galanter is interested in how the different parties impact on the way the system works. In his article the legal system is regarded as a society in which the actors, who are differently positioned and resourced, are in a relationship where they have opposing interests. The "repeat players" are typically larger and better-resourced units in terms of power, wealth and status (1974: 9). They are "the haves" and their stakes in any given individual case are smaller relative to the long run. The occasional players, or "the one-shotters" and "the have-nots," are smaller units with higher stakes in any given case when compared with the total worth. This difference gives the "repeat players" a whole series of informal advantages (ibid.: 3–6). My chapter is inspired by Galanter's argument about the advantages of the "repeat players." Whereas the permanent member states resemble the "repeat players," the elected member states play a similar role to the ones Galanter calls "the one-shotters."

Building on this, I combine aspects of expertise as sources of power and levels of formality as entry-points to my account of how the Security Council works. I continue by describing how the permanent members of the UN's Security Council know the rules of the game better than the elected member states, how they have shaped the rules and know how to phrase the questions and play the probabilities. Based on this, I argue that the five permanent members are able to effectively take control of conflict situations and dominate the Security Council without making use of their veto power.

ETHNOGRAPHY, THE UN AND THE SECURITY COUNCIL

The member states of the UN's Security Council spend considerable economic and political capital on influencing the Council's decision-making process in order to position themselves in world politics (Neumann and de Carvalho 2015; Schia and Sending 2015). Discussions around the Council's horseshoe-shaped table receive considerable international attention – they are, for international politics, not unlike the catwalk at fashion shows and beauty contests. Of course, there is more to the processes of the UNSC than mere outward appearance. Formal and public statements made by the countries represented in this arena were also relevant to my project – but a focus on the informal and internal dynamics within the Council may tell us even more.

Desktop studies may give the impression of the Security Council as a formalized and static organization. After all, it expresses itself through established channels such as resolutions, presidential statements and press statements, and conducts its meetings behind two security checkpoints in the formal Chamber with the horseshoe table. The Council may appear to be a highly formalized and static affair producing resolutions and statements that are merely results of the geopolitical interests of the member states. However, rushing between buildings, chambers and offices in midtown New York in order to meet and talk with diplomats, I increasingly came to believe that a focus on the internal dynamics between the delegates could reveal more about the rationality behind its decisions and autonomy. I had left Norway believing that the Security Council's decision-making process had a severely formalized character where everything passed along a chain of command and had to be cleared from the home capital – but as I began tracing processes and talking with stakeholders, this picture soon became blurred. Increasingly, I began to pay attention when delegates spoke about the "informal working culture" of the Security Council.

Turning back to my initial argument about repeat players and why it is necessary to include informal processes in order to better understand how the UNSC works, I found that, rather than becoming paralyzed when faced with inconsistent demands, the UNSC manages to deal with such challenges by means of informal processes.[1] These informal processes are dominated by the permanent member states or the "repeat players" of the Security Council. The delegates from the elected member states often enter these informal processes with a profound faith in the UN and its mandate, where being *part of the parade* becomes an important goal of its own for them (Schia 2013).

This chapter builds on six months of anthropological fieldwork (three months in Oslo and three months in New York) involving case studies and interviews conducted in 2002, and more recent follow-up interviews and shorter follow-up field-trips, as well as cross-checking of data and narratives with a wide range of informants. This entailed anthropological enquiries into what might appear as rather boring and uninteresting formal, static and transparent organizational structures. Nevertheless, I am interested in studying power and new forms of governance, and share Anette Nyqvist's enthusiasm for "the endless corridors of state authorities [as] real hot spots, the meeting rooms of public and private organizations are *the* place to be, official documents provide intriguing reading, and people in business suits are *the* people to hang around" (2013: 93). However, the distinction between work and leisure is blurred for delegates working with the Security Council. Informal negotiations and discussions also extend to the more informal spaces of the UN building and beyond, into the streets, bars and cafes of New York City.

Whereas Nyqvist highlights Sweden as the place to be for such studies, I would add the UN organization. There I was welcomed and generously granted access to people, places, documents, policies and strategies, as well as workshops, meetings and informal settings. However, it is important to consider *what* I have been granted access to and *where* I have been. I have not pursued an understanding of my informants as individuals; the focus has been on what these people do at work as officials, bureaucrats and diplomats. Nyqvist draws on Goffman's concept of front stage/back stage when describing and limiting her fieldwork and the private lives of her informants: "I am not interested in the private lives or personal backgrounds of these individuals; I am interested in who they are front stage and what they do there, not who they are back stage 'outside' and what they do there" (ibid.: 100). I am interested in the back stage/ front stage dynamics in the work relations of the delegates: this aspect is part of my focus on the interconnectedness between formal and informal processes.

Nyqvist further lists various ways of performing fieldwork in such locations (ibid.: 99): the first ones are to "follow suit" or "tag along" and "shadowing," which implies asking permission to follow people around during their working hours in order to observe what they are doing. Such activity was part of my more recent fieldwork (2009–2010), but I was generally more involved in the processes than merely a tag-along. Rather than

---

[1] Although some processes in the UNSC seems more deadlocked than others, such as, for instance, the current situation in Syria, and in Rwanda in 1993–1994 (see Barnett 2014).

doing *para-ethnography* as a collaborative ethnographic fieldwork with informants (Holmes and Marcus 2005), I engaged in the work of the UN officials in order to better understand their perspectives and their points of view. This was combined with something similar to what Hugh Gusterson (1977) has called *polymorphous engagement*. Such engagement is used in anthropological exploration where an ideal type of participant observation is difficult or even impossible. Gusterson coined the term *polymorphous engagement* as a way of:

> interacting with informants across a number of dispersed sites, not just in local communities, and sometimes in virtual form; and it means collecting data eclectically from a disparate array of sources in many different ways. Polymorphous engagement preserves the pragmatic amateurism that has characterized anthropological research, but displaces it away from a fetishistic obsession with participant observation. (1997: 116)

Such engagement, Gusterson continues, involves a combination of other methods, such as formal interviews and document study. In my fieldwork I was able to conduct participant observation, but where necessary I combined this with other methods. In order to fit in, I had to wear business suits and learn how to talk the "UN language," with all its abbreviations and organizational buzzwords. Because I was interested in my informants at work it was fairly easy to know where to draw the line, how to know where a connection could be traced and where it could not. Although it was relatively easy to understand when to stop tagging along, my polymorphous engagement took me to *off stage* places and happenings. Some of these were sorted out and rejected during the process of writing, while others contributed to illustrating demarcations, highlighting important aspects of my explorations. When meeting new people, I always made it clear that I was a researcher conducting anthropological fieldwork.

When I arrived in New York in 2002, the Norwegian Permanent Mission to the UN welcomed me and gave me an entry card and a place to work and invited me to join the morning meetings where the delegation discussed the UNSC agenda. This enabled me to follow the work of the Norwegian delegation as regards the UNSC. I could also see how the gatherings in the UNSC's formal meeting room were conducted and I observed Norwegian delegates in this room on several occasions. In addition to Norwegian delegates I also interviewed representatives from the US, Swedish, and Danish UN missions in New York (see Schia 2013). I started out with a series of interviews with staff in Oslo in the MFA's UN section and observed discussions at the meeting arenas established within the MFA in relation to Norway's seat on the Security Council. I was repeatedly told that everything Norway said or did in the UNSC was cleared with the home apparatus in Norway or was based on instructions from the ministry. I was also told that if I were to understand anything about Norway's role in the UNSC I would have to study the Council's working methods.

A challenge with any anthropological inquiry is that one's time in the field is spent with a limited set of people, and this may make it difficult to capture the larger picture. There are a great many people whose work is directly or indirectly related to the UNSC and the Norwegian MFA – but I could speak with only a fraction of the total. On the other hand, I was able to conduct good conversations and interviews, and I enjoyed the confidence of those who provided me with the data. I also benefitted from the fact that the UNSC has formalized its way of working through its Rules of Procedure,[2] an essential tool for social action between Council delegates from various countries. I could acquire information about cultural meaning and social relations through anthropological fieldwork while also gaining access to the larger picture through the UN Charter and the UNSC Rules of Procedure.

Several delegates used the word "skeleton" when they talked about the formal structures and the working methods of the Security Council, and emphasized that this formed the basis for how they organized their work there. Formal structure must be studied together with a perspective on human interaction, practice and relationships. In order to understand how formal structure has been shaped and developed through informal processes it is important to include a historically oriented perspective. The political and cultural context in which the Security Council was established, and in which it later evolved, is important to take into account when explaining its power relations, decision-making and internal dynamics today. Francis Fukuyama's assertion underlines the importance of this aspect: "we take institutions for granted but in fact have no idea where they come from" (2011: 3).

THE FORMAL STRUCTURE OF THE SECURITY COUNCIL

The UN was established on October 24, 1945, after the end of World War II. The structure of the organization drew on the international community's experiences with the not-so-successful League of Nations (1919–1946), which became irrelevant and failed in its primary purpose – to prevent a future world war. To avoid a repetition of the same fate as that of the League of Nations, the idea of a collective security pact backed by sanctions was introduced. The new UNSC was to have five permanent member states with veto power: the United States, the UK, France, China and the USSR – the victors of World War II. The mandate is formalized in the UN Charter, which defines the responsibilities of the Security Council in relation to the maintenance of international peace and security. The Security Council consists of fifteen member states: the five permanent members, and the ten remaining seats to be chosen by the UN General Assembly. These ten seats consist of two-year membership with a status as elected member states. Each member has one vote. Resolutions are binding under international law; adoption requires nine votes or more if they include the votes of the five permanent

---

[2] The Council's rules of procedure are in fact provisional and have never been made permanent.

members.³ The Council shall at the request of the Secretary-General determine whether there exists a threat to peace and security, and recommend solutions. Furthermore, the Security Council has the mandate to request member states of the UN to use military force or economic sanctions and other non-violent methods to stop an aggressor. It may also recommend new members and advise the General Assembly with regard to the election of a new Secretary-General.

CONSENSUS-MAKING, *PENHOLDERS* AND INFORMAL PROCESSES

At a meeting in one of the corner offices on the 40th floor of the Manhattan building that houses the Norwegian permanent delegation to the UN, I asked a Norwegian delegate about his views on Norway's role in the Council. He started to talk about informal processes and channels, outlining the kinds of informal options the Norwegian mission could use in its work with the Security Council. Simply phoning delegates from other Council delegations or the lead country about a certain process was pointed out as an effective way of influencing a process even before it had actually been started. Furthermore, delegates often talked with the President of the Security Council about the creation of the monthly program. This was, the delegate told me, "seen as an opportunity to inform and influence the agenda about topics that were important to Norway."⁴ Delegates could also tell the president that Norway would like to have a resolution on a certain topic, that it would like to see a text on a topic, or that the Council should arrange an "Arria meeting"⁵ (fieldnotes, Interviewee 1, October 10, 2002).⁶ According to a former Norwegian delegate to the UN, it is particularly those conversations taking place before and outside of the closed meetings in the Council that establish the basis for the outcomes around the horseshoe table in the Chamber. Those conversations are nurtured through frequent informal contact. Among the more influential ones are the conversations between three of the permanent five delegates – France, the UK, and the USA (together known as the "P3") – through phone calls, visits to their respective delegations or over a table at a cafeteria or a restaurant in Manhattan (conversation, August 19, 2015).

Another example of how informal practice may provide for an opportunity to set the case in the Council is the role of the *penholder*. Around 2008, the P3 began a new division of labor that evolved into a new informal system or practice. As a result of the increasing workload in the Council, the P3 – seen by many delegates and others as especially active among the P5 as regards legislation – began dividing situations that

---

[3] For more information on this, see the UN Charter, chapter 5.
[4] All translations from the original Norwegian are the author's.
[5] The term "Arria meeting" derives from the practice of Ambassador Diego Arria of Venezuela and refers to informal meetings that the UNSC can arrange, mainly to meet with other delegations, or NGOs or special representatives.
[6] Unless otherwise noted, all interviewees in this chapter were members of the Norwegian Permanent Mission to the UN, New York, at the time of my fieldwork.

emerged on the agenda among themselves and claiming the role of penholder, i.e., the de facto leader on an issue. This role includes taking the initiative on all aspects concerning the situation in question and the drafting of possible resolutions. The penholder produces a draft that the P3 usually agree on before they start what is often a meticulous process of negotiations with Russia and China. Thereafter, the text is circulated to the elected members, who are usually discouraged from making amendments after what may be a fragile consensus has been achieve among the P5.

Although these arrangements have been informal and unwritten, they seem to have become institutionalized to the extent that the practice will be difficult to change. In 2012, Portugal was an elected member of the Council and chaired the body dealing with Council working methods. When Portugal proposed changing this practice into a system where all members would get an opportunity to be penholders or co-penholders, the Council was unable to reach consensus and the idea was dropped. Thus, the gap between the permanent and the elected members seem to have increased substantially through informal processes and practices in the Council.[7] The penholder arrangement contributes to the marginalization of the elected members, preventing a more democratic distribution of burden, diversity and dynamics in important matters. This imbalance between the "P3" and "P2" (China and Russia) and the "P5" (the permanent five member states) and "E10" (the elected ten member states) seems to have become further segmented over the past decade. It can be argued that, in practice, the Council has become a battlefield of interests between the P5 where *the will* of the Council can be subsumed to what these five permanent members see as being in their own best interest. These five possess considerable institutional power vis-à-vis the ten elected members – often utilized in the internal and informal decision-making processes and preliminary negotiations of upcoming resolutions.

In addition, the UN building offers various informal meeting areas for Council members: the cantina, the lobby, the café and the delegates' lounge. There are two categories of spaces – formal and informal – with diametrically opposing functions. The main arena, the Chamber with the horseshoe table, is the formal meeting room. This is where the Council's official positions and statements are produced – the catwalk of the Security Council. Meetings here are usually open to other UN staff and UN missions outside the Council. Delegates read out their countries' statements and cast votes. Minutes are always written and distributed, and, as mentioned, these meetings are usually open to the public. In combination with the Chamber there is also a small meeting room with enough chairs only for the ambassadors and a few delegates. Meetings here are conducted under Chatham House Rules: no observers, and no minute-taking. Because it is not considered good form to quote

---

[7] See: www.securitycouncilreport.org/monthly-forecast/2013-09/in_hindsight_penholders.php. Accessed August 30, 2016.

from discussions that have taken place here, "this room allows for creativity and personality" (fieldnotes, Interviewee 3, November 6, 2002).[8]

Decisions pertaining to the Security Council are increasingly being made through informal processes, ahead of the formal meetings around the horseshoe table (See Schia 2015). The *street smarts* of the diplomats and their ability to navigate the internal culture of the Security Council, but also the informal space and the extension of these social relations beyond the meeting rooms and the UN building into the streets of New York (lunch-appointments, restaurants, bars and journeys), building networks with think tanks, NGOs, organizations and other UN delegates, have become increasingly important in order to influence the decision-making process. At the same time, the P3 are generally seen as dominating the *doxa* in the Council through cultural capital and, for instance, the power to define situations through the role as penholders.

I became curious about the internal dynamics, *the patterned ways of doing things*, of the Council and how informal processes may or may not "resist or oppose what is organizationally prescribed – at times even buttress official procedures – but it flows from a logic of institutionally segmented and stratified groups trying to accomplish what they regard as their real work" (Maanen 2001: 242). Turning back to the initial argument inspired by Galanter and the advantages of the "repeat players," I will now describe the relationship between the experts and the ambassador in the Norwegian UN mission during their previous membership in the Security Council in 2001–2002. This can help shed light on the internal dynamics and the production of official Security Council statements, mandates and resolutions.

EXPERTS AND AMBASSADORS

The delegations with the greatest impact on output (resolutions, presidential statements and press statements) were, according to my informants, those with skilled experts and an ambassador willing to stick with a case when it was being processed in the Security Council. This combination was the best, and there was no need for anyone in between these two. During Norway's time in the Security Council in 2001–2002, one of the Norwegian delegates told me:

> It's all about having as few intermediaries as possible, it is very much about two persons. One operating at the expert level, and one who speaks on behalf of the government. This is very English and French ... you have to synchronize the person who knows the case with the one who presents it in the UNSC. Between those two there should preferably be no one else. (Interviewee 2, Norwegian Permanent Mission to the UN, New York, November 2002)

---

[8] More about this meeting room is given later in the chapter.

According to this person, the Norwegian delegation had chosen the English and French way to organize their work. I asked why it was so important to have as few intermediaries as possible. The answer was: "you save time, you are on the ball immediately and thus can influence the process already at a very early stage" (Interviewee 2). The ambassador could present the case in the Council immediately after speaking with the expert. In that way, the delegation was able to stay on top of processes and at the forefront of cases being dealt with:

> France is incredibly good at this. They have a brilliant expert, Alexis. He is the conductor among the experts as he writes and moves and presents new stuff. Whenever he needs more ammunition to get his case through, he just goes to Lewitt [the French ambassador], who will run it in the Council. You see [laughter] they move terribly fast. Ok. While all the other countries have working groups and request instructions from the capitals and sit put wondering what will happen, France does this in ten minutes. (Interviewee 2)

Thus, the threshold for influence was in many ways defined by the French, especially for small states. The Norwegian delegation could not always wait for instructions from Oslo, which could involve a convoluted process with meetings in the ministry: "Norway's great advantage is that we have an informal system. This has to do with the character of the instructions: they cannot be too detail-oriented. Norway is at its best when we [the Norwegian delegates] have broad instructions, when we can clear things very quickly with the top" (Interviewee 3, Norwegian Permanent Mission to the UN, New York, November 2002). Although this is a self-serving statement from the Norwegian delegate, it resonated with how other informants described Norway and the internal dynamics in the Security Council. In short: if little Norway organized its work in a tight, bureaucratic way, it would probably lag behind. The pace in the Security Council, propelled by certain missions, triggered creative solutions among the delegates because there was no time to deal with the cases according to the formal Rules of Procedure. This point will be important for understanding how Norway came to support exclusive insight into Iraq's weapons declaration for the five permanent member states.

ORGANIZATIONAL PLASTICITY

In international politics there exists no legitimate overarching organ with the same functions as the state within its national borders. The Security Council may be the closest we can get on the international level. Its fifteen member states are tasked with maintaining international peace and security. Through its resolutions and by taking the initiative to establish UN organizations, the Security Council may deal with issues ranging from state sovereignty to individual rights. It is a unique organization, so it is important to understand how its actors relate to the structure and rules of procedure: "[T]he working method is set. Norway, a small country and member of the UNSC for two years only, cannot change the working method. For us it was a fait accompli" (Interviewee 3). To the Norwegian delegates, the working method was an "accomplished fact" (Constantinou 1996: 43). They had to adapt: "There is absolutely nothing you can do to change this, and this is the secret. You have to organize and adapt your instructions in order to exert influence on the internal working culture." According to this informant, the Norwegians had to accept this reality: "countries like the USA and China, together, can change this. For Norway that would have been a totally pointless activity" (Interviewee 3). But that also indicates that not all Council members saw the working method or patterns of action as a fait accompli. How fixed are these patterns of action, really?

The main function of the Security Council is to make decisions necessary for maintaining international peace and security, but there is an inherent dilemma about change and tradition. The Council's legitimacy depends on the maintenance of the original purpose as set out in the UN Charter and the Council's Rules of Procedure – but it also depends on continued relevance in an ever-changing world (Hurd 1999: 383). This dilemma propels an organizational plasticity, a flexibility defined by the interrelation between the formal structures and the informal processes.

Bounded by both tradition and change, Council actors require a certain degree of pliancy to manage this squeeze. This organizational flexibility in the Council can best be described as its "plasticity." Plasticity can lead to change of practice, even while the external body may appear quite stable. Take, for example, how the international atmosphere from the early 1990s to the present has made it unpopular and therefore difficult for the five permanent members to use their formal veto power.[9] That means it is not enough to look at structure alone: we need to explore whether these permanent members can exercise the same power through informal processes, without the veto action being externalized and made public.

IRAQ'S WEAPONS DECLARATION

It seems likely that informal practice will always be worth investigating because, on the one hand, the formal rules cannot specify every contingency, and on the other, human creativity seems to be naturally inclined to subvert formal procedure.

(Hurd 1997: 140)

If informal processes play a significant role in the Security Council, the human factor is relevant and plays an important role also in the most volatile issues: "the sense of freedom or confidence diplomats feel that they have in relation to the

---

[9] In the 1960s, a more introverted UNSC came to prefer closed consultations and informal arenas. This trend escalated after the end of the Cold War (Prantl 2005: 571). For an overview of the use of veto between 1946–2008, see www.globalpolicy.org/component/content/article/102/32810.html. Accessed August 30, 2016.

political leadership is crucial to how the human factor can come into play" (Interviewee 6, Norwegian Permanent Mission to the UN, New York, November 2002). Even though delegates told me that the cases referring to Iraq were treated at the most formal level (through formal channels, with formally clarified responsibilities), informal processes and internal dynamics also played a significant role (see Schia 2013). First, a quick reminder about what really was at stake when Iraq was on the agenda in late 2002. On November 8, 2002, resolution 1441 was unanimously adopted, requiring Iraq to divest itself of its weapons of mass destruction and to disclose all its nuclear, chemical, biological and missile programs, or face "serious consequences." One month later, Iraq submitted its 12,200-page weapons declaration to the Security Council. Immediately after having received the report, the Council agreed that the five permanent member states were to have exclusive insight into the document. Then, the weapons declaration was perceived to be incomplete, and pressure on Saddam Hussein increased. This eventually led to the Iraq War, which began with an invasion on March 20, 2003, and was not to end until 2011.

The Norwegian delegation's support for the decision to allow only the five permanent members to have insight into Iraq's weapons declaration illustrates the significant role of informal processes in cases dealt with also at the most formal level. In many ways, the Norwegian delegation had a dual role – on the one hand, national interests and politics; on the other, responsibility for the processes in the Council:

> One thing is our [the Norwegian] views, but because we have this role as a coordinator of the secretariat for the involved parties, the other neighboring countries, who are on the phone all the time, wondering what happens etc. and in relation to the other members of the Council, you accrue responsibility for the process that in a way is bigger than your national interests, and when your colleagues disagree you have to try to find solutions, bridge the conflicting parties or see to it so that we can find solutions. (Interviewee 7, Norwegian Permanent Mission to the UN, New York, November 2002)

On Sunday, December 8, 2002, Norway supported the proposal granting the five permanent members exclusive access to Iraq's weapons declaration. But the next morning, Norway publicly opposed the same decision. The matter had been settled through telephone meetings between the delegations over the weekend. On Sunday afternoon, the President of the Security Council (from Colombia) had received a visitor from the US delegation – UN ambassador John Negroponte. Negroponte came with instructions from the Bush administration, insisting that Washington should obtain Iraq's weapon declaration immediately, and before anyone else. From the residence of the Colombian ambassador/incumbent Security Council President, the two ambassadors made phone calls to the other delegations, one by one, seeking exclusive access to Iraq's weapons declaration for the five permanent members. Their justification was that these five countries had "special requirements for additional access through their status as nuclear powers" (Interviewee 8, Norwegian Ministry of Foreign Affairs, Oslo, May 2004). All Council member states except Syria supported the proposal. This put Colombia's diplomats in a squeeze: "The proper move was to call for council consultations that night to resolve the issue. But Colombia President Alvaro Uribe had no patience for the niceties of Council procedure. Cementing relations with Washington was his top priority. Give the Americans whatever they want, he instructed his UN team" (Bosco 2009: 228).

At 8.30pm the same night the case was settled, and Colombia handed over the declaration, still sealed, to UNMOVIC (the UN Monitoring Verification and Inspection Commission) to be passed on to Washington. All the Council member states, with the exception of Syria, had agreed to this through phone calls. No one called for consultations or proposed waiting until Monday to meet in the normal way in the UN building (Interviewee 8). According to the Security Council's Rules of Procedure, paragraph on agenda-setting, delegates shall receive the meeting agenda from the Secretary-General at least three days prior to a meeting, although in emergency situations the meeting agenda may be notified simultaneously with the meeting request. In this case, however, the meeting agenda was notified simultaneously with the actual "meeting," as the decision was made on the phone that very evening. This involved a shortcut between agenda-setting and meeting that prevented delegations from updating their capitals.

For Norway, this meant that their foreign minister was not updated on the situation and thus was unable to instruct the delegation. A Norwegian delegate explained to me that a precondition for the Norwegian delegation to accept the settlement through phone calls was that none of the fifteen member states had objections. The Norwegian delegation concluded thereafter, on the phone with the Security Council President, that Norway would support the proposal on the condition that none of the other Council members objected (Interviewee 8). In fact, however, according to UN diplomats, not all fifteen members were consulted before a US official obtained the massive report – 12,200 pages and hundreds of floppy disks. The sole public statement came from the UN ambassador of Syria, Mikhail Wehbe, who declared that it was contrary to all logic and unity among the Security Council's fifteen member states to hand over the copy to the USA. The Syrian deputy UN ambassador commented on the decision to the Associated Press on December 11: "a grave violation of the procedures of the Council, something which has never taken place ... This is a material breach of the resolution" (Lederer 2002).

A few weeks after the decision had been made, delegates confirmed to me that the case would probably have had a different outcome if it had been dealt with according to formal procedure. The Security Council President did not want to hold a separate meeting on the case because, I was told, the question came up during the weekend and it would represent unnecessary inconvenience to the delegates if they had to gather for a special meeting after working hours. Further, this was a matter of urgency and had to be dealt with immediately. According to members of the Norwegian delegation, the Council President wanted the case handled quickly because of the nature of the matter, but also to avoid massive media attention. According to David L. Bosco, the reason for this rush was that the US ambassador to the UN had put pressure on Colombia to get the declaration sent to Washington as soon as possible (2009: 228). Given the significant role of the informal processes indicated earlier in this chapter, the reason why the other member states accepted this procedure may have had just as much to do with the internal dynamics of the informal processes as with the weight of the US position. The Norwegian delegate "went native" in the Security Council's working culture, as consensus and the internal dynamics were the main priority when this decision was made. Later, several of the elected member states were unhappy with this resolution, including Mexico, Syria and Norway; and the Norwegian Minister of Foreign Affairs, Jan Petersen, publicly opposed the decision the day after it was passed.[10] Still, three days after the decision had been made, Secretary-General Kofi Annan insisted "the council is united and they are working together" (Lederer 2002).

Petersen and the Norwegian MFA in Oslo had not been updated on the situation. The Norwegian delegation could have opted to vote against the proposal through the phone calls, postponing the decision by one day. Instead, the internal dynamics and the way Norwegian actors adapted to this probably influenced how the delegation chose to act. Because of time pressures, organizational complexity and the rules of the game in the Security Council, Norway's delegates found themselves squeezed between responsibilities to their MFA on the one hand and to the Security Council on the other. If perceiving Norway as a "one-shotter" and the permanent member states as the "repeat players" in the way suggested by Galanter, this case could be explained through the architecture of the Security Council and how the micro-politics of its informal processes tends to fortify interlocking advantages of the permanent members.

THE CHAMBER AND THE SMALL MEETING ROOM

Procedures in the official meeting room, the Security Council Chamber, are strictly formalized. There are rules on everything – from where the delegates shall sit around the horseshoe table to when they may speak. Delegates normally read from prepared written statements. There is little room for improvisation. Individuality or personal roles are marginalized. Connected to the Chamber by a short, narrow corridor there is the second – and very different – meeting room for the delegates. In this small room where delegates meet for informal and confidential conversations, the activity was described as "real." Several interviewees spoke of how the human factor played a crucial role in these closed consultations. The importance of learning and playing

---

[10] Petersen said that the permanent five were treating Norway and the other 10 elected member-states as "B-nations" (Lederer 2002).

by the rules of this game was further pointed out: "the discussions around the table are real – knowing when and how to play your cards becomes important" (Interviewee 4, Norwegian Permanent Mission to the UN, New York, November 2002). The role of personality in the UNSC can be illustrated with Lord Caradon's proclamation of a poem at the end of one of his speeches in 1968:

> We know that we must send for him.
> When storms and tempests fill the sky
> "Bring on Kuznetsov!" is the cry.
> He comes like a dove from the communist ark
> And light appears where all was dark.
> His coming quickly turns the tide
> The propaganda floods subside
> And now that he has changed the weather
> Lion and lamb can vote together.
> God bless the Russian delegation.
> I waive consecutive translation.
> (Lord Caradon, Security Council, June 1968, Boyd 1971:37)

This proclamation exemplifies how the human factor can play a role in the decision-making process. The proclamation also illustrates Vasily Kuznetsov's important role in the Security Council during the middle of the Cold War. The incident happened only a week after the General Assembly had approved the NPT Treaty (Nuclear Non-Proliferation Treaty) in June 1968, and the poem was a greeting from Lord Caradon welcoming further Russian–US cooperation. The poem illustrates how different personalities and micro-politics impact decision-making processes in the Council. This point is also reinforced by the fact that Kuznetsov was replaced in September 1960 by Valerian Zorin in connection with a change in Russia's Congo policy.[11] By other member states, Zorin was considered an unpopular ambassador for Russia. There was a general perception in the Council that when Russia appointed Zorin as their ambassador, the efficiency of the decision-making process would decrease. Zorin held the position until October 1962 when Nikita Khrushchev withdrew Russian nuclear weapons from Cuba. Russian politics had changed course and, symptomatically, Kuznetsov replaced Zorin. Kuznetsov was a problem solver and a man who was good at concluding agreements; Zorin held the diametrically opposite characteristics (Boyd 1971: 36).

Normally, the first place to look if you want to learn more about decision-making procedures or working methods in an organization would be its Rules of Procedure. However, according to my informants, the Rules of Procedure for the UNSC were not particularly relevant in their daily work: "the UNSC decides by itself, a 100 percent, its own rules of procedure and how it chooses to work" (Interviewee

---

[11] Under Kuznetsov, Russia backed a UN resolution on Congo operations in July 1960. Two months later, Russia had changed their policy and replaced their ambassador to the Security Council.

4). How the delegates choose to work is most of the time based on established practices and custom. "It is incredibly informal. In 90 percent of the times the Security Council is gathered, it is gathered for closed consultations in a tiny room" (Interviewee 4). Several informants who had attended such meetings further pointed out how this was not an arena for reading out manuscripts, as elsewhere in the UN system. Because there are no records and because it is not considered good etiquette to quote from these meetings, they are the only place where people generally speak unscripted. This room is used to air opinions and thoughts, as well as for positioning in relation to the other Council member states. It is in this small meeting room that the important decisions are made.

Knowing how to play the game is important. Local knowledge in the Security Council means knowing how to master the relationship between "instructions," "influence," "work culture," and the dynamics in that small meeting room; further: "instructions have to be formulated as speaking points, you get cues and principles instead of whole sentences. This-and-that are important, we support this, we oppose that" (Interviewee 4). To what extent a country's interests have an impact is, in the end, up to the one delegate representing his country in this small meeting room. Naturally enough, most member states mobilize substantial resources at the top, so as to secure individual influence. Thus the institutional paradox: it all depends on the delegate with the microphone in his hand and the cases dealt with around that little table. (This point is further developed by Jane K. Cowan and Julie Billaud, Chapter 5, where they explore diplomats as individuals and spokespersons.)

The focus on informal processes illuminates how, by switching between different levels of formality, actors manage to resolve conflicting processes and internal paradoxes without fragmenting the external continuity and unity of the Council. Such organizational paradoxes are handled through delegates' manipulation of formal guidelines in the Charter and Rules of Procedures. With time and changes in the international atmosphere, this manipulation has propelled the importance and frequency of informal processes in the Council, and it has been able to adapt to shifts in international politics. But does this member-state effect lead the Council to work in line with the original intentions, as embodied in the UN Charter and its Rules of Procedure?

"REPEAT PLAYERS" AND *METIS*

Metis is an ancient Greek word used by de Certeau to describe "practical intelligence" (1984: 19) and by James C. Scott to describe the ability to know "when to apply the rules of thumb in a concrete situation" (1998: 317). This involves skills that cannot be learned from reading manuals or rules of procedures: they have to be acquired through local practice and experience. To return to the initial argument of this chapter, this aspect is particularly evident when exploring the differences between the "repeat players" and the "one-shotters," or between the permanent and elected member states of the Security Council. Even though Council delegates are normally skilled diplomats presumably familiar with the necessary *metis* in diplomacy, the formal structure of the UNSC has effects on the informal processes, making the internal dynamics in the Council quite distinctive in the world of diplomacy.

Learning to *play the game* in the Security Council can be done only through experience and practice as a member. Like most other elected member states, Norway began its membership without these skills, without local knowledge or knowing the *rules of the game* of the informal processes. Elected members, or the "one-shotters," have a mere two years to learn these skills: "Rapid turnovers admittedly mean that time, and opportunities, are lost while newcomers master the ropes; and that slowly nurtured personal relationships of mutual confidence are abruptly broken" (Boyd 1971: 36).

Delegates from permanent member states often serve longer, which gives them much better opportunities to learn, master and define the game and the skills needed in the informal processes. The permanent members are in a favorable position not only because of their status as veto powers: knowledge, cultural capital, networking and being permanent players of the game in the informal processes also matter. These members have an informal power base not reflected in any formal structures of the Council.[12] How the US ambassador pushed through the case of Iraq's weapons declaration in the Security Council in 2002 indicates how this works in practice (see Schia 2013). Another example is how the French delegation determined the pace of other processes in the Council. Norwegian delegates mentioned the effects of these internal dynamics:

> It is that simple, the Security Council is a very informal organ and in order to be taken seriously you must have something to contribute with in the debates. Make alliances and select a few priority issues that you will run with and work hard for. Still, influence is related to what kind of instructions you get, but also the working method and how the delegation and the delegates master this. The Security Council is in many ways a dream body for Norwegians, because of its informal character. It is informal yet structured. This suits us, when the structure and the traditions are strict, but the style is informal. (Interviewee 5, Norwegian Permanent Mission to the UN, New York, November 2002)

The informal character of the decision-making processes in the Council constituted what was described as a "dream body" by the Norwegian delegates – it enabled the Norwegian delegates to work efficiently, but simultaneously increased the potential for "going native" in the Security Council, one of the most powerful bodies in the world (Schia 2013). For the Norwegian delegates the working method was set, the human factor had to work accordingly and instructions had to be adapted to this:

---

[12] This view was confirmed by UN delegates in 2010.

How does this fit with Norwegian temperament and work style? We do not have a very authoritarian and hierarchical system, so the risk of making mistakes is greater. Everything moves very quickly. We are in New York, we have two levels, only two levels: expert – ambassador. No one in between. Is this irresponsible? What kind of restrictions are put, firstly on the expert, 28, 30, 32 years old, and secondly on an overworked ambassador with a thousand different things to remember, shared only between two men? (Interviewee 5, as above)

The internal dynamics of the Security Council's informal processes seem to favor the permanent members and countries familiar with the work style. The perspective offered by Galanter becomes useful in order to investigate power structures caused by factors other than the structural ones and how these favor the "repeat players." Knowing how to play the game, how to play the probabilities, how to raise the issues – or, in other words, being able to internalize good *metis* – are decisive skills for being able to influence the Council.

The internal dynamics have evolved through practice and custom over more than sixty years. The five permanent members have been working in the Council since it was established and have therefore played a more dominant role in defining good practice and style than the other UN member states. Practice and action generate social patterns that in the Security Council could result in an even more unequal distribution of power, making it even less representative than initially defined in the Charter. How does this affect small and medium-sized states?

DILUTION OF SMALL STATES' POLITICS?

Related to the main problem in focus here is the question of whether small states can have influence on international politics, where there exists no legitimate sovereign power. The Security Council is the arena that resembles such an actor the most, and through Norway's role in the Council in 2001–2002, I found a social field where it was possible to study small states and their role in shaping the internationally legitimate resolutions. As noted, the literature has focused largely on formal structure. Little has been written about Norway's Council membership 2001–2002,[13] and the ongoing debate on reform of the Security Council is generally centered on the formal structure (Schia 2013).

There are three main approaches to the study of order in International Relations. Two traditional perspectives oppose each other: the *Realpolitik* approaches (see, for instance, Vattel 1916 [1758]; Morgenthau 1973; Waltz 1979) and the liberalistic perspectives (see, for instance, Grotius 1853; Bull 1977; Keohane and Nye 1977; Wendt 1999). However, as both approaches use the state system as their entry point, they do have a common feature. The third tradition is more common in

---

[13] The most important contributions are parliamentary bill no. 22 (2002–2003) and Ambassador Ole Petter Kolby, Stein Tønnesson and Erik Sagflaat's discussion on Norway in the UNSC in *Internasjonal Politikk* no.2 (2003).

anthropology. It views order as a social phenomenon that exists prior to state sovereignty. This tradition is propelled by an understanding of order and social practices as regularity in interaction, and provides an opportunity to think about global politics without starting with the state. Consequently, a culture-analytical perspective should work well here, as long as social relations are taken as the basis for understanding.

In this chapter I have used the third tradition as the entry point, hoping that it can represent an original twist to literature on the Security Council and international organizations, which tends to take *formal structure* as its starting point (see, for instance, Ambrosetti 2012; Bailey and Daws 1969, 1998 [1975]; Bedjaoui 1994; Hurd 2007; Kirgis 1995; Malone 2004; Schweigman 2001). As these and others have argued before me, it is difficult to understand organizations solely through a focus on structure, pretending that these exist independently of the actors that constitute the various positions in the structures.[14] Actors bring flavor to the positions. Even Council delegates cannot divest themselves of their individual personalities, humor and roles. Furthermore, actors take shortcuts, find loopholes and interpret rules and norms differently. As we have seen, these variations may generate social patterns that are in conflict with the rules of the organization, and that perhaps ultimately lead to change. Drawing on Galanter, I was able to explore how informal processes in the Security Council enforce inequality between the permanent, "repeat players" and the elected, "one-shotter" member states in a larger degree than was defined by the formalized power structures.

Structures have influence on actors' values and, thus, their choices. Individual choices may generate patterns that have structural and social implications. Both structures and actors exist and are constructed in relation to each other.[15] Organizations, like societies, are not static: they are constantly *in the making*. Therefore, it is not enough to look at organizational structures in order to understand the roles of small states in international politics: we need to understand who does what, with whom, and why. An actor-oriented perspective with a focus on the interplay with structure is useful also in enabling conclusions on how the Security Council works.

When a democratic state produces policies and plans, it is, in principle, accountable to its parliament and its citizens; delegates to the Security Council are also, at

[14] Anthropology and other studies more informed by qualitative analyses have studied organizations through focusing on practice and social relations. Such studies on the UN organization are rare but they exist; examples include: Riles (2001); Merry (2006); Garsten and Jacobsson (2011); Müller's edited volume *The Gloss of Harmony* (2013); Schia (2015); Barnett (1999); Gosh (1994); Pouliot (2016); and Feldman (2010). Mahbubani (2004) and Schia (2013) are examples on anthropological studies of the UN's Security Council focusing on practice and social relations. The best ethnographic account of internal relations in the Security Council is probably Andrew Boyd's *Fifteen Men on a Powder Keg – A History of the UN Security Council*. It was published in 1971 and, although the Security Council is very different today, this book provides interesting and relevant observations regarding its internal dynamics.

[15] See Berger and Luckmann 1979; Giddens 1979, 1984.

least in theory, answerable to their home countries. The internal dynamics within the Council, however, are autonomous and accountable to no one. Once in the game, delegates from the elected countries (as opposed to the five permanent members) tend to abide by the informal rules, and responsibility toward their home countries becomes overshadowed by responsibility toward the Council.

In terms of Norway and its foreign policy, the Iraq case illustrated how the need to engage in real politics in the Security Council could mean a dilution of Norwegian foreign politics. For the Norwegian delegates, membership involved a responsibility for the Council's efficiency, in addition to their national responsibility. The significant role of the informal processes in the Council is a manifestation of this dilemma, which in turn put constraints on the Norwegian delegates – and most likely the delegates from the other elected member states as well. There was no sovereign entity that *did* this to "Norway" or to the Norwegian delegates. Through the Iraq case and the relation between experts and ambassadors, we have seen how this was a matter of ways of interacting – ways that appeared normal to the delegates, which in turn had effects on patterns of action. It was a shared mindset about the practices and activities that made the actions appear practical and appropriate for the actors involved. That was the effect of the Security Council. Whether Norway should be seen as a potent small state exercising *Realpolitik* or a mere follower depends on what is in focus: the Norwegian interests in upholding a well-functioning Security Council, or other Norwegian interests in international politics.

CONCLUSIONS

This chapter has investigated how the countries of the world manage to come together and make plans, programs and resolutions in the UNSC. Studying the various countries' positions in formal Council meetings reveals little about how this happens, so I chose to focus on actors representing member states and the rules of the game in the informal part of the decision-making process. This focus showed how the Security Council's introspective way of *seeing* comes from the organization's internal dynamics, internal working culture and interaction patterns, which have evolved through more than sixty years. Drawing on Galanter's analysis of the legal system, and in particular on his combination of "repeat players" and "one-shotters," it became possible to explore more than just how the five permanent members enjoy privileged status through their formalized veto power. We have seen how the internal dynamics put constraints on elected member states' delegations. The permanent member states draw several advantages from being continuously present in the Security Council. They have larger delegations, more experienced diplomats and more resources available over longer periods of time in New York than most of the elected member states are better able to mobilize. In this way, the delegates from the permanent member states have more opportunity to acquire *street smarts*, learn the rules of the game and the informal space than the "one-shotters" who only sit for two years. In this way, the permanent member states dominate the Council through the formal structure but also through cultural capital and informal knowledge. They enjoy an additional power component in that they simply master the Council, both the formal and the informal space, better than the others.

The asymmetrical distribution of power in the formal structure of the Security Council is being reinforced and strengthened by the dynamics between the formal structure and the particularities of the informal space. The distribution of power is thus more skewed than what is defined by the formal structure. Pessimists would argue that the informal consultations imply a loss of transparency and thus undermine the legitimacy of the Security Council. Optimists, on the other hand, would emphasize how informal consultations are "the oil in the machinery" that makes the Council able to function effectively and thereby invoke legitimacy. To be able to exert influence in the Council, Norway paradoxically had to adapt so much that its foreign policy at times became paralyzed (however, a well-functioning Security Council is also at the heart of Norwegian foreign policy). If Norway – admittedly a small nation, but also among the biggest financial contributors to the UN – had this experience, surely other small and medium-sized nations also encounter the same challenge in the Security Council.

We could see how permanent membership also usually places the veto powers in the center of the informal processes. By being able to establish accepted mindsets and patterns of interaction and defining the internal dynamics through good practices, the permanent five place constraints on the elected member states in the Council. The Iraq case demonstrated how this could be done. The French expert's way of setting the pace in decision-making processes illustrated how informal processes may *govern* the ten elected members. Through informal strategies and broad instructions, the Norwegian delegation was able to manage complexity in the Security Council on an everyday basis, without being subject to a stringent apparatus from the MFA in Oslo. And yet, the Iraq case, together with the focus on informal processes, revealed how Norway was rendered impotent in one of the main issues to be dealt with in its two years on the Council.

Norway, through its UN delegation, chose to vote for the "exclusive insight" proposal even though the Minister of Foreign Affairs, as well as traditions in Norwegian foreign policy in general, did not support it. The informal processes lubricated the organizational machinery, on the one hand, but also represented a potential for the permanent members to dominate the Council through the internal dynamics, on the other. This implies that the permanent members, or the "repeat players," have possibilities for acting as an authoritarian group within the UNSC to a greater extent than through their formal veto alone. In this way, political horse-trading and power struggles may easily come to dominate in the handling of cases. The micro-politics of the Council and the rules of the game further indicate that the focus on big politics and relations between the member states are more important in the Council's decision-making processes than the interests of those who are to be the actual recipients of its plans and resolutions. Supporting the consensus focus is at the heart of Security Council activities.

The Security Council has an introspective focus, but far-reaching policy. Thus, the risk of "going native" and ending up as a *believer* or a camp follower for the "one-shotters" or elected member states is high, as is the likelihood of gaps between plans and the challenges to be solved.

REFERENCES

Ambrosetti, David. 2012. "The Diplomatic Lead in the United Nations Security Council and Local Actors' Violence: The Changing Terms of a Social Position." *African Security* 5:2, 63–87.

Bailey, Sydney D. 1969. *Voting in the Security Council*. Bloomington: Indiana University Press.

Bailey, Sydney D. and Sam Daws. 1998 [1975]. *The Procedure of the Security Council*. Oxford: Clarendon Press.

Barnett, Michael N. 1999. "Peacekeeping, Indifference, and Genocide in Rwanda." In Jutta Weldes et al. (eds.), *Cultures of Insecurity. States, Communities, and the Production of Danger*. Minneapolis: University of Minnesota Press, pp. 173–202.

    2014. "The United Nations Security Council and Rwanda." Expert opinion paper for the "International Decision-Making in the Age of Genocide: Rwanda 1990–1994" project, co-sponsored by the Center for the Prevention of Genocide at the US Holocaust Memorial Museum, and the National Security Archive at the George Washington University.

Bedjaoui, Mohammed. 1994. *The New World Order and the Security Council: Testing the Legality of Its Acts*. Dordrecht: Martinus Nijhoff.

Berger, Peter L. and Thomas Luckmann. 1979. *The Social Construction of Reality: A Treatise in the Sociology of Knowledge*. London: Penguin.

Bosco, David L. 2009. *Five to Rule Them All – The Security Council and the Making of the Modern World*. Oxford: Oxford University Press.

Boyd, Andrew. 1971. *Fifteen Men on a Powder Keg – A History of the UN Security Council*. London: Methuen.

Bull, Hedley. 1977. *The Anarchical Society: A Study of Order in World Politics*. London: Macmillan.

Constantinou, Costas M. 1996. *On the Way to Diplomacy*. Minneapolis: University of Minnesota Press.

de Certeau, Michel. 1984. *The Practice of Everyday life*. Berkeley and Los Angeles: University of California Press.

Feldman, Ilana. 2010. "Ad Hoc Humanity: UN Peacekeeping and the Limits of International Community in Gaza." *American Anthropologist* 112(3): 116–129.

Fukuyama, Francis. 2011. *The Origin of Political Order: From Prehuman Times to the French Revolution*. New York: Farrar, Straus and Giroux.

Galanter, Marc. 1974. "Why the 'Haves' Come Out Ahead: Speculations on the Limits of Legal Change." *Law and Society Review* 9(1): 95–160.

Garsten, Christina and Kerstin Jacobsson. 2011. "Transparency and Legibility in International Institutions: The UN Global Compact and Post-Political Global Ethics." *Social Anthropology* 19: 378–393.

Giddens, Anthony. 1979. *Central Problems in Social Theory: Action, Structure and Contradiction in Social Analysis*. London: Macmillan.

———. 1984. *The Constitution of Society: Outline of the Theory of Structuration*. Cambridge: Polity Press.

Gosh, Amitav. 1994. "The Global Reservation: Notes toward an Ethnography of International Peacekeeping." *Cultural Anthropology* 9(3): 412–422.

Grotius, Hugo 1853. *De Jure Belli ac Pacis*. Cambridge: Cambridge University Press (orig. 1609/1625).

Gusterson, Hugh. 1997. "Studying Up Revisited." *Political and Legal Anthropology Review (PoLAR)* 20(1): 114–119.

Holmes, Douglas R. and George E. Marcus. 2005. "Cultures of Expertise and the Management of Globalization: Toward the Re-functioning of Ethnography." In A. Ong and S.J. Collier, (eds.), *Global Assemblages: Technology, Politics and Ethics as Anthropological Problems*. Oxford: Blackwell, pp. 235–252.

Hurd, Ian. 1997. "Security Council Reform: Informal Membership and Practice." In Bruce Russett (ed.), *The Once and Future Security Council 1997: Informal Membership and Practice*. New York: St. Martin's Press, pp. 135–152.

———. 1999. "Legitimacy and Authority in International Politics." *International Organization* 53(2): 379–408.

———. 2007. *After Anarchy: Legitimacy and Power at the United Nations Security Council*. Princeton: Princeton University Press.

Keohane, Robert O. and Joseph S. Nye. 1977. *Power and Interdependence*. New York: Little Brown.

Kirgis, Frederic L., Jr. 1995 "The Security Council's First Fifty Years." *American Journal of International Law* 89(3): 506–540.

Kolby, Ole Petter. 2003. "Norge i FNs Sikkerhetsråd 2001-2002 Erfaringer og Perspektiver" (Norway in the UN's Security Council 2001-2002 Experiences and Perspectivees). *Internasjonal Politikk* 61(2): 225–235.

Lederer, Edith. 2002. Facing UN Criticism, US Defends Deal to Take Possession of Iraq's Weapons Declaration, *Associated Press*, December 11, 2002. See: https://news.google.com/newspapers?nid=1891&dat=20021212&id=M_QwAAAAIBAJ&sjid=JtoFAAAAIBAJ&pg=1147,1182025, accessed August 31, 2016. The article can also be read here: http://usatoday30.usatoday.com/news/world/2002-12-11-us-iraq-report_x.htm, accessed August 31, 2016.

Maanen, John Van. 2001. "Afterword: Natives 'R' Us: Some Notes on the Ethnography of Organizations." In David N. Gellner and Eric Hirsch (eds.), *Inside Organizations: Anthropologists at Work*. New York: Berg, pp. 231–263.

Mahbubani, Kishore. 2004. "The Permanent and Elected Council Members." In David M. Malone (ed.), *The UN Security Council: From the Cold War to the 21st Century*. London: Lynne Rienner, pp. 253–267.

Malone, David M., ed. 2004. *The UN Security Council: From the Cold War to the 21st Century*. London: Lynne Rienner.

Merry, Sally Engle. 2006. *Human Rights and Gender Violence – Translating International Law into Local Justice*. Chicago: University of Chicago Press.

Morgenthau, Hans J. 1973 [1948]. *Politics Among Nations: The Struggle for Power and Peace*. New York: Knopf.

Müller, Birgit (ed.). 2013. *The Gloss of Harmony: The Politics of Policy-Making in Multilateral Organizations*. New York: Pluto Press.
Neumann, Iver B. and Benjamin de Carvalho. 2015. "Introduction: Small States and Status." In Benjamin de Carvalho and Iver B. Neumann (eds.), *Small State Status Seeking: Norway's Quest for International Standing*. London: Routledge, pp. 1–22.
Nyqvist, Anette. 2013. "Access to All Stages? Studying Through Policy in a Culture of Accessibility." In Christina Garsten and Anette Nyqvist (eds.), *Organisational Anthropology – Doing Ethnography in and among Complex Organisations*. London: Pluto Press, pp. 91–119.
Pouliot, Vincent. 2016. *International Pecking Orders – The Politics and Practice of Multilateral Diplomacy*. Cambridge: Cambridge University Press.
Prantl, Jochen. 2005. "Informal Groups of States and the UN Security Council." *International Organization* 59(3): 559–592.
Riles, Annelise. 2001. *The Network Inside Out*. Ann Arbor: University of Michigan Press.
Sagflaat, Erik. 2003. "Norge Meklet" (Norway Brokered). *Internasjonal Politikk* 61(2): 241–245.
Schia, Niels Nagelhus. 2013. "Being Part of the Parade – 'Going Native' in the United Nations Security Council." *Political and Legal Anthropology Review (PoLAR)* 36(1): 138–156.
   2015. *Peacebuidling, Ownership, and Sovereignty from New York to Monrovia: A Multisited Ethnographic Approach*. PhD Dissertation, Department of Social Anthropology, University of Oslo.
Schia, Niels Nagelhus and Ole Jacob Sending. 2015. "Status and Sovereign Equality: Small States in Multilateral Settings." In Benjamin de Carvalho and Iver B. Neumann (eds.), *Small State Status Seeking: Norway's Quest for International Standing*. London: Routledge, pp. 73–85.
Schweigman, David. 2001. *The Authority of the Security Council under Chapter VII of the UN Charter – Legal Limits and the Role of the International Court of Justice*. The Hague: Kluwer Law International.
Scott, James C. 1998. *Seeing Like a State. How Certain Schemes to Improve the Human Condition Have Failed*. New Haven: Yale University Press.
Tønnesson, Stein. 2003. "Hvorfor Mislyktes Norge Politisk i Sikkerhetsrådet?" (Why did Norway Fail Politically in the Security Council?) *Internasjonal Politikk* 61(2): 235–241.
Vattel, E. de, 1916 [1758]. *The Law of Nations or the Principles of Natural Law Applied to the Conduct and to the Affairs of Nations and of Sovereigns*. Philadelphia: T. and J. W. Johnson.
Waltz, Kenneth N. 1979. *Theory of International Politics*. New York: McGraw-Hill.
Wendt, Alexander. 1999. *Social Theory of International Politics*. Cambridge: Cambridge University Press.

4

A Kaleidoscopic Institutional Form: Expertise and Transformation in the UN Permanent Forum on Indigenous Issues

Maria Sapignoli

POSITIONING ETHNOGRAPHY

There is a tendency for people to think that United Nations (UN) agencies somehow correspond with their titles and acronyms, as discreet and bounded, with their own mandates, guiding principles, leaderships, hiring practices, and personnel. The proliferation of acronyms in the literature on the UN adds to the sense that there is shape and substance to those entities that are labeled organizations, institutions, agencies, forums, and working groups, with boundaries of inclusion and exclusion that go together with processes of accreditation, visitor and employee badges, and doors marked "closed meeting" and "staff only." This may be truer of some powerful organizations such as the Security Council than it is of the institutions that actively invite NGO participation. My experience in several of the organizations engaged in common efforts on behalf of indigenous peoples paints a very different picture from that of the agency-as-entity, reflecting more the change and permeability of the organization, the interpenetration of ideas and institutional efforts, with, through the years, changing patterns of collaboration and mutual influence among its participants.

The United Nations Permanent Forum on Indigenous Issues (UNPFII), which I discuss here, is one of those notoriously intricate global phenomena that defy categorization. Its annual session meets for ten days at the UN Headquarters in New York, accompanied by a pre-session meeting; an annual expert group meeting at the request of the Forum; and about seventy side events organized during the annual session by governments, UN agencies, NGOs, Indigenous Peoples'

I wish to thank the Department of Law and Anthropology of the Max Planck Institute for Social Anthropology for contributing to the funding of the research for this chapter. Other support was provided by the Katharine A. Pearson Chair in Civil Society and Public Policy at McGill University. I am deeply indebted to my former co-workers in the UN Secretariat, and to my many interlocutors in the Permanent Forum on Indigenous Issues, who over the years gave me the information and insights that are at the foundation of this chapter. Though inspired by the spirit of learning and collaboration at the UN, responsibility for the content of this chapter is solely my own.

Organizations (IPOs), and academic institutions. It usually includes dialogue with indigenous delegates, UN agencies, experts, and governments, and a special day of discussions on thematic issues and/or geographical areas. The session ends with an indigenous closing ceremony and the presentation of the session's draft report. These sessions are phantasmagorias of complex, sometimes shifting rules and alignments of power, navigated by actors with divergent interests, constituting a kaleidoscopic institutional form: complex, colorful, changeable, and illusory.

The annual session embodies in a heightened way all of the central qualities of civil society engagement in the UN's public space: there is not just an expectation of NGO input, but an often-voiced demand for full and equal participation with states. There is a tension between what Wilson describes, in the context of the growing legalization of rights claims, as the "false expectations" and "normalizing" effects of legal processes versus the "access to justice" and "accountability" that can follow from admittance to legal institutions (Wilson 2007: 352–353). To what extent does the participation by indigenous organizations in UN initiatives involve normalization of – or challenges to – the legal/bureaucratic system in which their delegates are making claims and attempting to influence human rights standards? How might increasingly structured human rights discourse and institutions shape the ways that rights claimants, state delegates, and UN officials apprehend and act upon the challenges facing the world? (Cowan 2006: 10). I address these questions ethnographically by situating indigenous delegates and UN officials in the ever-changing structures of the Permanent Forum, and offering an account of their efforts to operate – and to learn and institute reform – within it. I intend to show how the session is more than a place of activism, contest, and lobbying; it is also a site of encounter, knowledge production, and learning, a place for the acquisition and application of expertise, where people share experience and strive to influence international standard setting, institutional realignment, and reform.

In my first ventures to the UN, I was pursuing an interest that began elsewhere, in "the field," as part of a long-term research project that started in Botswana in 2006 on the state-sanctioned removal of indigenous peoples from the Central Kalahari Game Reserve (Sapignoli 2015). I was interested in following the activities of San activists and their supporters in any and all forums in which they found possibilities for expressing their grievances and seeking redress. Among these places, there were several UN offices in Geneva and New York, particularly the annual sessions of the UNPFII (Sapignoli 2012).

Once I entered the UN, my attention turned to more general features of the PFII and its space in the global institution itself. In preparing this chapter, I therefore decided to discuss the Forum as a "field-site," including its structure and activities throughout the year, in particular its annual session. To enter the field, I took on the positions of PFII observer (both NGO delegate and academic) and UN intern, positions characterized by distinct and overlapping status. Distinct because I had an official status in each; overlapping because my research project was a common denominator that crossed into each realm.

These various experiences I had in the UN between 2007 and 2015 gave me differing perspectives on its meetings, annual activities, and the ways that indigenous peoples circulate in the organization. I ended up doing not just a "multi-sited ethnography" (Marcus 1998), but what I call a "multi-positioned ethnography," in which the ethnographer takes on different formal roles within the same event and organization. Initially, my function as a registered "observer" in the Forum's annual session for the last nine years put me in the same situation as that of many other civil society delegates. It was important early on to familiarize myself with the context and the diplomatic roles. The fact that I was sharing the same processes of accreditation, meetings, and cafeteria breaks with indigenous activists and other NGO delegates involved me more as a collaborator in their lobbying and networking activities, and, in the process, learning about the UN from their perspective.

In order to overcome the limitations of being an outsider to the organization and to understand what happens out of the spotlight, I decided to enter the UN from another position. My goal was to pay close attention to the connections and relationships within and between UN agencies, through the people who work every day with the concept of "indigenous peoples." I therefore worked as intern for six months in 2009 in the Secretariat of the Permanent Forum on Indigenous Issues (SPFII) in the Department of Economic and Social Affairs (DESA) at the United Nations Headquarters (UNHQ) in New York; and for three months in 2010 in the Peoples and Tribal Issues Policy and Technical Advisory Division of the International Fund for Agricultural Development (IFAD) in Rome. In these capacities I had to learn not just the culture and dynamics of the social context I was in, but also the work itself: running errands such as photocopying, helping with the nuts and bolts of the accreditation process, assisting first-comers to familiarize themselves with the UN formalities, taking minutes, attending closed meetings, and helping disseminate the documents for the session according to the agenda. I was able to share with UN officers their daily feelings of frustration and anxiety when something went wrong, concern over the amount of work expected of them, and satisfaction when "things seem to work" at the end of the day or when they celebrated over drinks at the close of the Forum's annual session.

Adding further to my exposure to UN initiatives on behalf of indigenous peoples, I took part in training initiatives where indigenous, NGO, state, and UN delegates went to acquire official recognition and education as experts on indigenous peoples' issues. One such course I attended was entitled "Training for Trainers on Indigenous Peoples' Issues," hosted by the International Training Center ILO (ITC-ILO) in Turin in 2009.

In each of these roles, I was involved in promoting the very phenomena that became the subject of my work. I found myself in the predicament of contributing to the production of knowledge, notably the dissemination of indigenous rights talk, and the instauration of connections and networks that I intended to critically analyze, producing the knowledge that was the subject of my analysis (cf. Merry 2005: 243).

Consistent with this variety of experience, I will pay attention in this chapter to the spaces of interaction in and around the work of the Permanent Forum. I look at what the UN produces in terms of transformations in the areas of knowledge and learning, expertise, and identities. I highlight the way people – civil servants and delegates alike – struggle with structures that are largely controlled by states. This struggle goes beyond the usual dichotomy between co-optation and positive resistance. Bureaucrats and delegates participate in both the successes and limitations of the UN's efforts through their acquisition of expertise, above all through learning and the production of knowledge.

While the temptation to focus on the stories of injustice brought by indigenous delegates to the UN is always there, there is at the same time a great deal to be learned about the structures, events, and people away from the spotlight. As I try to show here, a shift in focus toward personal encounter, learning, and experience – including the disenchantment that can arise as experience is acquired – reveals that the organization is a place of production and transformation, in a permanent state of transition from one form to another. The changing convictions and capacities of the people who occupy the Forum are what give it creative power, and ultimately produce a global justice movement from within the UN, together with a range of institutional obstacles to its effective mobilization.

THE FORUM MEMBERS

The Permanent Forum cannot be understood separately from the rapid growth of civil society participation in the UN system. This is reflected in the number of NGOs having special consultative status with the Economic and Social Council (ECOSOC), which grew from 354 in 1991 (Osmańczyk 2003: 1624) to 2926 in 2014.[1] These figures tell only part of the story, since at the same time the participation of NGOs in the UN has significantly intensified, with new openings for the inclusion of NGOs that lack ECOSOC status. The Permanent Forum on Indigenous Issues is situated within this burgeoning growth of civil society participation in the UN, reflected in a wide array of forums and regular conferences, interconnected with overlapping participation, where each has its own mandate and form of sponsorship.[2]

---

[1] United Nations ECOSOC. 2014. "List of non-governmental organizations in consultative status with the Economic and Social Council as of 1 September 2014," UN doc no. E/2014/INF/5.

[2] The Permanent Forum is one of three UN bodies that is mandated to deal specifically with indigenous peoples' issues. The others are the Expert Mechanism on the Rights of Indigenous Peoples and the Special Rapporteur on the Rights of Indigenous Peoples.

Despite the dramatic conditions of oppression with which it is concerned, the Permanent Forum had a very prosaic beginning.[3] In 1993 the Vienna World Conference on Human Rights first recommended the establishment of a permanent forum for indigenous peoples. Two subsequent UN workshops on this idea were held: the first in the spring of 1995 in Copenhagen, Denmark, and the second in June–July 1997, in Santiago, Chile. Along the way, on the insistence of states, the term "peoples" in the title was replaced with "issues," much to the discontent of the indigenous delegates, who saw it as a way to limit their rights of self-determination (see Niezen 2003: 48). The Permanent Forum on Indigenous Issues convened its first session in 2002, as an "expert body composed of members serving in their personal capacity," a consultative body within ECOSOC. It has a mandate to discuss indigenous peoples' problems of economic and social development, education, wealth, environment, and human rights.[4]

Unlike its predecessor, the Working Group on Indigenous Populations (WGIP),[5] the Forum's mandate is not (as many delegates assume) to develop human rights norms, but to prepare and disseminate information, to raise awareness and develop cooperation (mainly within the UN system), and to submit recommendations and expert advice on indigenous issues to ECOSOC. The Forum members also have the authority to receive and investigate complaints or to address governments, UN agencies, and international institutions in the attempt to monitor the implementation of the UN Declaration on the Rights of Indigenous Peoples (UNDRIP).

Indigenous peoples' organizations, academic institutions, states, UN bodies, and governmental and non-governmental organizations may participate in the Forum's annual sessions as "observers." Although these observers have no formal voting rights, they can be invited to report on their activities regarding indigenous peoples and are entitled to present their point of view and make recommendations during the main session.

The Permanent Forum can thus be seen as two very different things: as a small group of sixteen experts that make up the Advisory Body to ECOSOC, and as a large annual gathering, known as a session. First, let me briefly describe the role of these members of the Advisory Body and other experts in the Forum, before turning to the annual meeting.

When the Permanent Forum was created it inherited many of those who had developed their expertise of the UN from previous initiatives such as the WGIP meetings, the twenty-year-long negotiations over the drafting of the UNDRIP, and

---

[3] The history of indigenous involvement in the UN has been discussed extensively by a variety of authors (Engle 2010; Peterson 2010; Xanthaki 2010; Minde 2008; Morgan 2007; Niezen 2003; Lâm 2000; Henderson 2008; Ewen 1994), as has indigenous peoples as a legal category and identity (Anaya 2004; Niezen this volume).

[4] United Nations. 2000. Economic and Social Council (ECOSOC) Resolution E/2000/22. Establishment of a Permanent Forum on Indigenous Issues www.un.org/esa/socdev/unpfii/documents/about-us/E-RES-2000-22.pdf. Accessed August 15, 2015.

[5] For a discussion on the WGIP, see Escarcega (2003), Muehlebach (2001), and Niezen (2003).

various workshops on the future of the indigenous agenda in the UN.[6] This group of experts is widely seen (by UN officials and other Forum participants alike) as an "international indigenous cohort," referred to by some as an "elite," comprising a network of individuals who year after year were invited by the UN to participate in meetings in a variety of functions as indigenous experts and representatives.

The Permanent Forum is formally composed of sixteen members: eight are nominated by governments and elected by ECOSOC, the other eight are appointed by ECOSOC's president following broad consultation with indigenous organizations (Thornberry 2002: 24). The members of the Forum participate as "independent experts," representing seven socio-cultural regions, and stay in office for three years, with the possibility of re-election or reappointment for one further period. These independent experts do not serve the indigenous peoples of their regions in any personal capacity, certainly not in the manner of elected representatives.[7]

The two kinds of Forum member differ greatly, following from the fact that one is nominated by the corresponding indigenous regional caucus and another by states. Representatives nominated by the indigenous caucus almost invariably come from well-established and respected NGOs in the UN and are popularly seen as advocating on behalf of indigenous interests, even though their mandate restricts their role to that of "advisor."

The experts nominated by states, in contrast, still sometimes have backgrounds in indigenous communities, but often as parliamentarians, civil servants, or persons in some other way connected to the state. Decisions among the sixteen experts are to be made by consensus. This means that any member can obstruct an initiative or recommendation, even though they are committed to be independent of states and their interests. This structural condition and the lack of transparency concerning the decision-making process are a point of concern among members of the Forum and its Secretariat; many indigenous activists have similarly expressed dissatisfaction with the Forum's structural limitations and sometimes weak commitment in representing their interests.

During the year (that is to say, between the annual sessions that punctuate their work), Forum members participate in a variety of activities oriented toward "saturating" the UN with the promotion of the rights of indigenous peoples: they attend regional and international meetings on women's rights, mining, climate change,

---

[6] For more on these earlier meetings, see Dahl (2012), Lindroth (2006), Escarcega (2003), Muehlebach (2001), Niezen (2003), Pritchard (1998), and Sanders (1989).

[7] The members nominated by the governments are elected based on the five regional groupings of states normally used at the United Nations (Africa; Asia; Eastern Europe; Latin America and the Caribbean; and Western Europe and Other States). The members nominated by indigenous organizations, on the other hand, represent seven socio-cultural regions (Africa; Asia; Central and South America and the Caribbean; the Arctic; Central and Eastern Europe, the Russian Federation, Central Asia and Transcaucasia; North America; and the Pacific), a geographical division intended to give broad representation to the world's indigenous peoples. The solution to this lack of fit between the seven regions and the need to nominate eight experts is that the additional seat rotates between the three regions with the highest number of indigenous populations, namely Africa, Asia, and Latin America.

and so on, participate in country visits, and write thematic studies. Most of the time, even when their mandate ends, they remain part of the "UN family" – for example, by becoming a Special Rapporteur or moving on to positions as experts in other agencies.

The personalities and drives of those who have achieved, in one form or another, the status of high-level experts in the UN are central to its processes of reform. The influence of the sixteen Permanent Forum experts, for example, varies greatly, depending on their ambition to effect change, the extent of their networks in the UN system, their experience, and, perhaps above all else, their personal charisma and commitment to the indigenous cause. As appointed members of the Forum, they are in a strong position to closely collaborate with UN personnel in drafting reports, to bring issues to the floor of the session (or silence them), to engage in dialogue with state representatives, and to train less experienced NGO delegates in ways to effectively make use of the Forum's session.

A particular amount of influence accrues to those who are appointed by the Forum to act as chairperson of the annual session. Chairpersons take differing perspectives on the mandate of the Forum, with some more accepting of its advisory role, while others press for and, to the extent possible, implement in practice, another agenda. For Dalee Sambo Dorough and Megan Davis, the 2014 and 2015 chairpersons respectively, this agenda was human rights, an unusual departure from the priorities of their predecessors, which Dorough expressed as "the most important aspect of the Forum" (author notes); both chairpersons have actively promoted this agenda through the Method of Work reforms (see below, p. 102). Davis also furthered this agenda in a subtle way, by congratulating indigenous speakers whenever they delivered a particularly moving or rousing statement relating to state violations of their human rights. If any of the state delegates objected to this practice, they did not do so publicly in the conference room.

BECOMING EXPERTS, BECOMING ACTIVISTS

It is important not to limit our discussion on expertise to the sixteen members of the Forum and what they do in their official capacities. As Summerson Carr (2010: 18) observes, "expertise is something people do rather than something people have or hold," and the categories of "doing" expertise have very different levels of prestige in the UN system. At a certain point, expertise ceases to be defined by formal education or official status and is considered a capacity for intervention. More significant, perhaps, is the *recognition* that accrues within the UN's network of indigenous delegates to those individuals who acquire this experience and capacity to act, especially the ability of people to navigate and maneuver the spaces left for individual actions in global institutions, and ultimately to effect reform.

During the years that I attended the session meetings it was possible to see how some inexperienced indigenous delegates acquired broader understanding of the

UN, sometimes becoming international civil servants and experts in their own right. In fact, as I hope to have illustrated by the end of this chapter, the UN produces another kind of expertise, where the indigenous activists who are periodically able to attend UN meetings learn about the organization's working procedures, etiquette, and language to the extent that they are able to take on a variety of roles, including that of Forum member. For some, in other words, the Forum becomes an entry point for a UN career.

For first-comers to a Permanent Forum annual session, knowledge of the UN had probably already started in their local communities though the work of NGOs, but it remains quite an abstract place for most of them. Most do not have any idea of what they will encounter in New York. Once they have arrived, their initiation to the UN system comes in the form of several indigenous caucuses where they are exposed to the experience of other long-term indigenous delegates, some PFII members, and the Secretariat of the Permanent Forum. Indigenous caucus meetings happen during the weekend prior to the main session and periodically throughout the meeting.[8]

The official purpose of the preparatory caucus meetings is to decide what agendas and strategies are to be followed, and to provide updates on what has happened in various international forums in relation to indigenous issues throughout the year. Here participants exchange information with others and become part of the indigenous movement. In order to decide on agendas and strategies, special guests are sometimes invited to address the main global caucus. Staff from the Secretariat and Forum members are invited to explain the activities that will take place during the session and to respond to questions from indigenous delegates regarding their participation.

Indigenous delegates often use this opportunity to establish a direct dialogue with members of the Permanent Forum and the Secretariat, relationships that they try to cultivate throughout their time in New York, something that is difficult to accomplish on the floor of the annual session. In the caucus they start to gain familiarity with the UN's limits and possibilities, their expected contributions to the session, how to write and deliver statements, and how to discuss their grievances. For instance, indigenous representatives are advised by their colleagues and members of the Secretariat to play a "diplomatic game," and to try their best to be strategic in their recommendations and behavior during the meeting. Staff members from the Secretariat usually remind those attending the caucus meeting that "individual statements" can be up to three minutes long, whereas "collective statements" can be up to five minutes, stressing the importance of situating recommendations in "joint statements." Furthermore, to make their involvement as effective as possible, indigenous delegates are encouraged to use legal and political frameworks that are comprehensible within the international community. The technicality of this advice emerged in the guidelines presented by the Secretariat:

---

[8] For a detailed discussion on the indigenous caucuses, see Dahl (2012), Sapignoli (2012), and Bellier (2013).

Please look at the documents for this session and prepare recommendations accordingly ... Each organization can only speak once under each agenda item/sub-item. Priority will be given to caucus and group statements and a time limit is set by the Forum at the beginning of the session. (author notes, 2009)

This preparatory meeting is possibly the first of many encounters that first-time participants will have with the UN's management of discourse. For those who come to the Forum meeting thinking of it as a place where they will vent their sense of injustice and be listened to, that their cause will be heard by an agency ready to intervene on their behalf, this can be a bitter disappointment. For others, however, it is above all a learning experience that marks the beginning of a new vocation.

Learning and advocacy in the Permanent Forum are not only practices of indigenous delegates. There are many other regular participants in the work of the Forum and in the sessions, such as state delegates and UN civil servants, who attend meetings where they acquire expertise about indigenous peoples' rights and issues, becoming the point of reference for their own state or agency (including, for example, the appointees of the Inter-Agency Support Group), sometimes then being responsible for the further circulation of the indigenous agenda in the UN. The important place of knowledge among civil servants as an instrument of sensibilization was evident in Secretary General Ban Ki Moon's recent effort to promote indigenous issues in the adoption of the 2030 Agenda (the UN's High-level Political Forum on Sustainable Development), with his comments oriented particularly toward the promotion of indigenous rights among those working in Country Teams, framing the furtherance of these rights as a moral responsibility, and posing the rhetorical question, "if the United Nations doesn't care, then who will care?"[9]

More than any other venue that invites civil society participation, the annual session makes a strong impression on the civil servants who work at the UN Headquarters in New York. The color of the event stands out from the norm, and employees can sometimes be seen in the hallways taking pictures of themselves with indigenous delegates dressed in traditional clothes. Members of the Secretariat or of agencies that regularly participate in the annual session are often strongly moved by the statements they hear. They are often personally attracted to the ways of life that indigenous peoples represent and committed to the justice causes that they bring to the UN.

Some civil servants go beyond their job descriptions and take on something resembling the role of activists, even though the requirements of diplomacy call for them to exercise tact and restraint.[10] As UN employees, however, the rules of bureaucratic practice, emphasizing the political neutrality of civil servants, prevent

---

[9] www.un.org/development/desa/indigenouspeoples/about-us/un-country-teams.html. Accessed February 5, 2016.

[10] Such activism among UN officials has long been true of the initiatives involving indigenous peoples in the UN, including initiatives that predate the establishment of the Working Group on Indigenous Populations in 1982 (See Minde 2008).

them from acting on their allegiances in the way they would prefer. Despite the constraints they face, officials are sometimes able to perform "indirect" or "soft" advocacy in their own personal capacity. In their free time, for example, they might use social media to post news and comments concerning government policies, legislation, or human rights abuses. Members of the Secretariat will occasionally facilitate private closed-door meetings between particular indigenous delegates and representatives of states when it is clear that they are at odds over a particular issue and could benefit from closer dialogue. It commonly happens that, upon their retirement, UN employees with experience working on indigenous issues take on even more activist roles. Freed from the constraints of their position as civil servants, they are able to more directly involve themselves in the global indigenous movement – for example, by teaching indigenous human rights, planning workshops, sponsoring museum displays, or collaborating with indigenous NGOs in the development of training programs and events.

TRAINING THE TRAINERS

The process of attending meetings is only one way that those who become experts on indigenous issues acquire their experience and legitimacy; there is also sometimes a process of formal learning that adds to an expert's knowledge of the UN system and the ways (or techniques) to impart that knowledge to others. Training in the UN's work on indigenous peoples' rights is offered mainly by the UN Institute for Training and Research (UNITAR) based in Geneva and the International Training Centre of the ILO in Turin (ITC-ILO), and is facilitated by fellowships from the International Labour Organization and the Human Rights Council. These training initiatives can be considered spaces in which "knowledge brokers" (Merry 2006) learn how to vernacularize and transmit international law and models of rights in their localities and retranslate ideas from their localities in institutional contexts.

In April 2009 I participated in a four-day course titled Training for Trainers on Indigenous Peoples' Issues, organized by the Secretariat of the PFII and implemented by the International Training Centre of the ILO. Among the other participants were indigenous representatives working in NGOs, employees of UN agencies working on indigenous issues (including UNICEF and UNDP), Permanent Forum members, indigenous parliamentarians, and members of the Secretariat. All the participants were staying in the ITC-ILO campus, spending most of their time together, socializing during meals, and participating in tours of the city organized by the training staff. With the cost of travel to Turin, in addition to a package that included tuition, lodging, meals, and tours, the course was expensive and could only be afforded by those with well-funded positions or grants in (or relating to) the global indigenous movement.

Here, people were trained to become experts in creating "capacity" for governments and UN personnel, NGOs, and institutions working on indigenous peoples, aimed at changing institutions, policies, and practices. The course had as its immediate aim the development of trainees' knowledge on five main topics: (1) to recognize who indigenous peoples are, starting with the guidelines offered in key UN reports; (2) the meaning (based on examples) of "indigenous issues"; (3) the main UN institutions working on indigenous peoples' rights; (4) the main international instruments that deal with indigenous peoples; and (5) how to present these issues in a manner likely to convince "our audience" of the need for a human-rights-based approach to indigenous peoples.

Several Permanent Forum members were there as experts on indigenous peoples' issues and brought their expertise to the training room, but there were also people who were there to be trained in how to train others. During the meeting, strategies were discussed for how to integrate an indigenous agenda in the Country Common Assessment (CCA) and in the UN Development Assistance Group (UNDG) framework that was adopted as a strategic and planning tool in the context of the Millennium Development Goals (MDGs) for the UN system. There were guidelines for UN Country Teams on how to relate to governments that do not recognize indigenous peoples and how to "sensibilize" people to indigenous issues. These points were reinforced by asking the participants to apply what they had learned in the training to scenarios based on "real world" situations. The training was thus centrally oriented toward promoting the concept and interests of indigenous peoples at key points in the UN system and beyond, to the most unaware, non-collaborative states, and "to get participants enthusiastic about making changes and achieving a shared vision of how things should be different" (UNSPFII 2009: 33).

At the end of the course, new trainers on indigenous issues were created, a group photo was taken, and a certificate of successful attendance was given to each of the participants (myself included).

ACCREDITATION

Let us now turn to the Permanent Forum's annual session, above all the behind the scenes activities that determine its participants and make it possible. The Secretariat is the engine of the Forum. All becomes quite crazy in the months before the annual session, when all the documentation has to be collected and uploaded online (until recently also printed and brought to the meeting rooms), the rooms for the side events have to be booked, people have to be registered, and so on. The Secretariat prepares questionnaires for governments (rarely completed and returned) in order to invite them to submit information on the ways they responded to the Forum's previous year's recommendations and to comment on the agenda of the current meeting. It also prepares reports based on contributions made by agencies, NGOs, and governments regarding the implementation of the Forum's recommendations.

The sessions are open to civil society organizations that do not have consultative status with ECOSOC. Located high in the UN hierarchy, and therefore subject to scrutiny from states that may not have an interest in seeing indigenous issues progress through the UN system, the PFII has adopted a set of formal procedures for the accreditation of indigenous representatives. In order to be accredited for the first time, the participants need to fill out an online application giving information about their organization. This is followed by a short email correspondence in which the Secretariat and the Civil Society and Outreach Unit of the Division of Social Policy and Development must decide whether to authorize or reject indigenous organizations that do not have consultative status with ECOSOC. In practice, the UN follows the principle of self-identification and does not inquire into the legitimacy or the specific mandates of indigenous NGOs seeking accreditation, although the criteria for the participation of indigenous delegates in the UN are currently under review.[11]

Many indigenous representatives have difficulties following the accreditation procedures since they do not know if they will be able to secure financial assistance until a few days before the meetings, or they do not have access to a fax machine or the Internet. Some organizations do not even know of the procedure. Others, simply "forget" to do it and say something like "it is not an indigenous way of working." The accreditation process selects those people who are literate in one of the UN languages, and who are affiliated with organizations that have recognized institutional elements, such as a formal commitment to indigenous issues and an office with an address. This is a problem for many indigenous representatives as some of them remarked during the 2015 PFII session: "indigenous peoples are not just NGOs but they have their own institutions and they are not recognized by the UN" (author notes). One result of the accreditation process is that the breadth of indigenous representation able to attend the PFII is limited to those who own the technical knowledge and resources to participate. This is a clear example of international institutions, through bureaucratic procedures, shaping the meaning and structures concerning what it is to be indigenous and thereby determining who is able to participate in institutional reform and influence international policy.

Once the organization or the representative gets accepted, an invitation letter is sent via email – the necessary first step to enter the gates in New York. Despite possible difficulties of accreditation and the high cost of travel, the number of indigenous and civil society organizations attending the Forum's annual meetings has remained constant and significant over time, with more than 2,200 people registered for the 2015 annual session.

After they are accredited and wearing the badges necessary to pass through the security gates, the delegates take their seats in the circular room where the meeting takes place. From this point, their experience of the session begins.

---

[11] Seventieth Session General Assembly, Agenda Item 69, July 25, 2016, www.un.org/ga/search/view_doc.asp?symbol=a/70/990. Accessed September 1, 2016.

WRITING A STATEMENT

The ultimate source of energy that powers the work of the Permanent Forum is the vast deposit of injustice resulting from imposed development projects, forced displacement, and assimilation policies aimed at the removal of difference, the elimination of distinct ways of life, and the potential of distinct peoples for claims to recognition and resources. The structure and procedures of the Permanent Forum session offer examples of the way that this sense of injustice can be responded to, particularly in ways that ensure (to the extent possible) that the chaos and potential violence that follow from collective suffering and claims-making are controlled: not so much silenced as given order, directed into bureaucratic pathways that convert emotional energy into "information" and "dialogue" (cf. Wilson 1997: 149).

Statement-making is the main activity by which official communication takes place on the floor, together with the presentation of special reports made by members of the Forum or UN agencies. The main session in which interventions are heard is a place of exchange, making knowledge public, and ideally educating or changing the minds of those who are uninformed about or obstructive toward the distinct identities, claims of dispossession and marginalization, and rights of indigenous peoples. Different kinds of intervention are made during the session from representatives of indigenous delegations, states, UN agencies, and experts. This "professionalization" has led many to specialize in particular kinds of struggles related to conservation, biodiversity, traditional knowledge, women's and youth's rights, development with identity, climate change, and so on, extending their expertise through many agencies and programs in the UN system.

For indigenous delegates, the passions of injustice are channeled into three- or five-minute interventions, limited by the requirements of diplomacy, and possibly, just possibly, taken up by the Forum in its report and passed on to other levels, and other audiences, in the UN. As a form of official discourse, the statement has structures to be followed by the compliant, and, on rare occasions, rejected by those for whom the rules of the Forum represent an unwanted constraint.

Over time, indigenous delegates have developed their own form of discourse in the statements they deliver, introducing a new language to the UN. This includes, for example, salutations in their own languages, prayers, songs, and the introduction of terms such as "sacred sites," "Mother Earth," and *"buen vivir"* (living well), which have eventually become part of the language of international governance.

On session days indigenous delegates and any others who wish to participate rush to the registration table, where the Secretariat includes their names and the name of the organization with which they registered at the meeting on the list of speakers for each agenda item. Indigenous participants submit four kinds of statements: (1) indigenous caucuses statements, (2) joint NGOs statements, (3) individual statements, and (4) "cooperative statements" made collaboratively among NGOs, UN agencies, and states. These statements are usually prepared a few days before or during the

PFII meetings, but not much in advance. One of the main reasons for this is that it is difficult for indigenous delegates who do not have extensive experience with the UN to obtain the background documents that will be used in the PFII meetings, even though they are published online weeks before the session.

An example of one of these drafting meetings took place in April 2008, when I met some representatives from southern Africa in the UN Headquarters cafeteria in New York. They, like me, were "observers," there to attend the 7th Session of the Permanent Forum. The cafeteria was just outside the meeting room in the basement of the UN Headquarters. The people at the table were San and Khoe from Botswana, South Africa, and Namibia, three men and three women who averaged around thirty to forty years old. They represented various Khoekhoe and San groups, such as the Nama, Griqua, Tse'xa, ǂKhomani, and Hai//om. One of them, a Hai//om man from Namibia, had extensive experience at the UN. He had attended the WGIP in Geneva during the 1990s, and the PFII for the past several years. He was offering advice and explaining the activities of the Forum and its dynamics, underling the importance of "being strategic," "building alliances" and acting as a collective voice in the delivery of interventions.

Gathered at the table with their laptops, they were also talking about the various problems their people were facing and, more generally, about the attitudes of their governments toward indigenous peoples. They had pages in their laptops linked to the ILO Convention 169, the United Nations Declaration on the Rights of Indigenous Peoples, a report on South Africa by the Special Rapporteur on the Rights of Indigenous Peoples, and a variety of other UN documents. Their goal was to use these reference points of international law and policy to make the recommendations in their statements impactful.

The group, aside from seeing me as a researcher interested in and supportive of indigenous peoples' rights, considered me an expert on the Central Kalahari Game Reserve (CKGR) situation in Botswana, a case that since the 1990s has had a strong international appeal and had been discussed in various forums (Sapignoli 2012, 2015). Because of this, I was part of the conversation. They were discussing whether to include this case in their collective intervention but none of them was from the area of the reserve, so they asked me for information (which I provided) on what was occurring there, particularly after the 2006 High Court verdict that ruled partially in favor of the CKGR inhabitants in their struggle against the government of Botswana. (There were also digressions, such as when they wanted to know ways to get around in New York other than by taxi – too expensive for those on a fixed budget.) After everybody expressed their concerns about speaking for others on things with which they had no direct experience, the more experienced representatives from Namibia and South Africa decided to include the case because they thought that it was important to speak about all the issues regarding San in a collective voice, due to the fact that they shared most of the same problems. Furthermore, "people are for sure interested in the CKGR" (author notes, 2008).

These issues of collaboration and finding a common voice are particularly striking in drafting collective caucus statements (i.e., Global, African, or Women's Caucuses). These statements have to unify the voices and concerns of many people. In the process of writing, differences emerge in relation to the wording to be used, the selection of issues, and the meanings of concepts. Delegates argue for inclusion of their own notion of indigeneity, the specific problems that their communities face, and their own views on issues in the studies and conclusions of the PFII (writing in such a way as to steer the Forum toward accepting their recommendations). Also in drafting these statements, people with more experience of the Forum stress the importance of speaking not locally but continentally, criticizing the cases where caucus statements are not really representative of regions' but, rather, delegates' local issues. A particular factor that makes it difficult to reflect all delegates' concerns in the global caucus is that statements are usually drafted in English, French, or Spanish, and are not always translated into the other official languages of the UN (excluding, particularly, Russian- and Arabic-speaking delegates).

This drafting process ends up with some groups prevailing over others in deciding the wording and the agenda, and tensions and questions regarding who represents whom sometimes arise. The people who are appointed as drafter are often left with the challenging task of incorporating and reconciling different voices and views and deciding what needs to be included and how. The statements that result from this drafting process are therefore the products of collaborations – or, better, "negotiations" – among delegates, some with much more experience in the UN system than others, who struggle to translate their different experiences of dispossession and marginalization into common grievances, expressed using the preferred concepts and categories of the UN.

The drafting of statements clearly illustrates how the UN has become the central place where networks are formed and expand. The representatives are not only brought together by their common interests; they are also compelled to collaborate by the rules and structure of the meeting itself, by the limits of time and the need to condense the world's crises and injustices into manageable forms. Through this process of statement-making, local claims are "translated back" in efforts to influence international standard setting and rights discourse.

TAKING THE FLOOR

The main conference room itself is unbounded, connected to the world through the flow of media during the session. This flow takes a variety of forms and addresses a variety of publics who are recipients of the knowledge produced. At the most formal level, UN-TV live-streams the main session on the web and organizes interviews with Permanent Forum members and other key participants at the meeting. A summary of the daily activities is posted on the SPFII webpage, and throughout the day the Secretariat tweets and posts on Facebook, sending out material that includes photos, summaries of interventions, and up-to-the-minute activities in the meeting room. At the less formal level, some participants request permission from the Secretariat to use video and recording devices, usually for purposes of journalism or for documenting the activities inside the Forum for the outside world. Finally, there is the ebb and flow of information from all the other participants, with their smart phones, small cameras, and laptops, whereby they tweet, post, and send emails to their families, friends, and communities. During the session, the exchanges through the web are not only between people inside and outside the UN room, but also among people within the room. Facebook and email correspondence are used to share ideas on how to organize statements, when and where to meet, how to lobby other participants for writing a statement together, who will be the drafter, and who will be the one willing to read. Often the draft statement is sent to people at home in order to gauge their reactions and include their suggestions in the final version.

During the session, when their name is called by the chair, it is important for delegates to hear what is happening on the floor and be prepared to present or defend certain positions. They have to be ready: sitting behind a mic, raising their hand, starting to talk when the light on the mic is green, and being prepared to conclude within their allotted time when it is flickering red. These strategies are crucial for developing the capacity to organize and improvise, just as other diplomats do.

Not all the statements that are prepared are delivered. Delegates may not have been in the room when the chair called their name, or they may not have arrived at the registration desk on time. Or the indigenous representatives may not have wanted to speak in front of their own country's diplomats. The potentially intimidating consequences of making a statement include the possibility that their government would question them upon their return to the country or not give them jobs because they were on a list of people who had raised objections to the country's policies. Others, on the contrary, hope that, with the presence of their government in the room, they will be better able to challenge and embarrass it in front of those present.

The agenda item on human rights has been by far the most popular, with indigenous delegates vying for the limited places on the speaker list. Human rights-oriented statements range from passionate indictments against acts of genocide, to measured, even technical, recommendations that make careful reference to international instruments. An example of the latter can be seen in the San intervention to the PFII in 2013:

We, the San recommend:

1) That the government of Botswana take into consideration and implement the recommendations of the Special Rapporteur on Indigenous Peoples Rights, document A/HRC/15/37/Add.2 and to ratify ILO Convention 169 and to implement the

UNDRIP in national and local legislation and policies. Botswana must ratify the UN Covenant on Social, Economic and Cultural Rights.[12]

Other statements are more direct and emotional, sometimes accompanied by tears and quavering voices, in their evocation of such things as forced removal, missing and murdered women, high rates of youth suicide, extra judicial killings, and loss of land and livelihood to extractive industries. Making human rights complaints was mentioned by several delegates as a means to increase the accountability of states vis-à-vis their indigenous inhabitants, which in some cases was seen as an impetus for change at a national level. First-time attendees of the Permanent Forum meeting, however, might well come away from their experience with the impression that the interests of states prevail when the Forum chair decides to interrupt their statement because they exceed the time limit, fail to conform to the agenda item, or make accusations against states without offering recommendations.

If they fail to get their name on the speakers list or are simply not called by the chair, indigenous delegates are often able to incorporate accusations of human rights violations through more indirect means. Sometimes they will leave papers outlining circumstances or rights abuse on a display table at the back of the room, or they will distribute papers or pamphlets directly to delegates at their desks, the key being to do so quietly, as in the manner of passing notes or information sharing on the floor, without attracting undue attention. Although these denunciations may not be taken up for consideration in the final report of the PFII, they do raise awareness among NGOs, governments, and UN experts of the situation of indigenous peoples in specific countries, and they may provoke responses from governments participating in the session. These dynamics make the PFII a unique open space where global politics are played out and international law on human rights can be challenged from below to incorporate the concerns and rights of indigenous peoples.

The statements and interventions made by states when they take the floor of the session commonly assert their rights to constitutional and territorial integrity, their duty to further the equal rights of all citizens, and their positive records of human rights compliance and development, which (so they claim) meet the broader aspirations of the international community. These positions often appear irreconcilable with those of indigenous delegates. However, looking more closely at the variety of relationships and dynamics among the people in the room reveals a more complex reality.

Rights claims are rejected, accepted, or translated in different ways by the various governments. There are states that more clearly project an oppositional image. For instance, Namibia and Botswana have talked about "marginalized communities," or

[12] May 22, 2013, Agenda Item 7 Human Rights. This statement did not appear on DoCIP's online database.

"remote area communities," instead of indigenous peoples, thus undermining the San claim to differential regimes of rights (author notes, 2015). It is also widely noted that the Declaration was not initially ratified by the United States, Canada, Australia, or New Zealand – these being the four classic "settler states" with large indigenous populations and with territorial and development interests most in opposition with those of indigenous peoples.

But these positions, as upheld by some states, should not be taken as representative of a common state position on indigenous rights in the UN. In fact, there are states such as Finland and Denmark that present joint statements with indigenous organizations, to emphasize their support of indigenous peoples' rights (even though Saami delegates on other occasions denounce these governments' lack of compliance with indigenous rights). At the furthest end of the spectrum, taking a distinct position as a state with an indigenous government, Bolivia has lobbied actively on behalf of the Forum's indigenous organizations, in particular those from Latin America. In the 7th annual meeting of the Forum in 2008, a head of state opened the session for the first time. Evo Morales, President of the Plurinational State of Bolivia, started his speech with a rousing condemnation of the destructive nature of capitalism and the hope to be found in the indigenous values of nurturance of Mother Earth: "We can continue on the route of capitalism and death or we can advance through the indigenous route of harmony with nature and life."[13] Whatever narrative they present (however distant from reality), public speeches in the Permanent Forum give states an opportunity for the promotion of their images and agendas, with little possibility of opposition.

The transformative nature of the Permanent Forum can be seen in the fact that state positions toward indigenous rights are not only variable but also undergo change – sometimes (albeit rarely) radical change, amounting to paradigm shifts. This corresponds with realignments in state governments, with new leadership sometimes having an almost immediate effect on the tone of state discourse in the UN, emanating from new directives given by foreign ministries to the states' Permanent Missions. The transition in the USA from the Bush presidency to that of Obama, for example, could be almost palpably felt in the style of diplomatic engagement, even if many of the US policies on indigenous rights remained unchanged. The same occurred more recently in Canada with the transition from the Conservative Harper government to the Liberal government under Justin Trudeau.

Change in government positions in the Forum is not merely a result of shifts in state politics or geopolitical realignments; it can also occur from within the Forum itself. States delegations are a steady target of information and education. Policies are challenged through efforts to persuade the individuals representing them that they

[13] Bolivia 2008, "Statement by H.E. Evo Morales Ayma President of the Republic of Bolivia." 7th Session, Permanent Forum on Indigenous Issues, New York, April 23, 2008: www.docip.org/Online-Documentation.32.0.html. Accessed March 5, 2015.

are harmful or out of step with widely accepted standards in international law. When the Central African Republic adopted the ILO's Indigenous and Tribal Peoples Convention 169 in 2010, for example, many were of the view that this was a result of efforts at persuasion that took place through the work of the Forum, of diplomats being "educated," "brought up to speed," and acting as agents of change (even if their actual compliance with the Convention remains to be seen).

A third source of intervention during the session comes from the UN itself, as agencies and related organizations participate in the Forum, offering statements that usually outline their activities oriented toward implementing the Forum's past recommendations. The 8th session in 2009 introduced a new way of proceeding in this regard; in fact, the Forum launched a new methodology by organizing an in-depth dialogue with six UN system entities. During the dialogue, when they were called upon to report on their activities, it was difficult for some agencies to justify the fact that they had done nothing to respond to the PFII recommendations. Often these agencies blamed the bureaucracy within the UN, which made them unable to respond. Just like states, the UN agencies are subject to the politics of shame – for example, during the 9th session in 2010, there was substantial critical discussion of indigenous peoples and forests and the potential impacts of the REDD+ program. In the discussion, questions were raised about the UN Environment Programme's (UNEP) activities in the Maa Forest of Kenya, where the Ogiek denounced plans to relocate them out of the forests without their consent. The Forum members accused the UNEP of acting against human rights standards for indigenous peoples while promoting the interests of industries and states. While the Permanent Forum would normally be reluctant to criticize a state for its rights abuses, it has fewer inhibitions when it comes to a UN agency or a related organization such as the World Bank. Just as efforts take place to change views and policies of states, the same occurs with UN agencies that are out of step with the Forum's promotion of indigenous rights. As an indigenous expert in a training side event for indigenous delegates put it, "the UN has to learn and is learning about indigenous peoples, and it is important to tell the UN what to do" (side event 14th Session 2015). This is the "hopeful" activist approach to the recalcitrance of some UN agencies that are unreceptive to the demands of indigenous NGOs, and that persistently maintain the gap between headquarters and Country Teams in implementing policy (see Hitchcock, Chapter 8 this volume).

A few agencies, such as IFAD, are generally considered good examples of how the UN should approach indigenous peoples' rights through collaboration with the Forum: financing indigenous projects, developing an internal policy that integrates key elements of the UNDRIP (such as the concept of "free prior and informed consent") in the operational guidelines and policy of the agency, and facilitating the participation of indigenous delegates through collaborative projects, participation in Country Teams, as well as international meetings of the agency. When I was an intern in its Rome Headquarters, IFAD was preparing the mandate for the creation of a new indigenous forum, internal to the agency (eventually established in 2011), an example that highlights the extension of the indigenous agenda, taking it beyond the Permanent Forum and into a range of agencies through much of the UN system.[14] This replication of the indigenous agenda in the "UN family" testifies to the potential reach of the Forum's recommendations (which are in turn a product of the statements and reports of the annual session) in influencing the institutions and policies of global governance, ultimately with consequences for peoples' lives.

From these dialogues, statements, and reports made in the session, the Forum drafts a final report and the chair reads it aloud during the last day of the two-week long session. Significant preparation goes into this pivotal event. Usually a Special Rapporteur is in charge of writing the final report, tasked with discussing each point in great detail. Behind closed doors, the Forum members, the Secretariat, and the session's Rapporteur meet to prepare and revise the draft report. Every single word and comma are discussed and possibly changed in order to reflect better the language of the UN and the emotionally neutral language of the law. The principle of consensus should govern the decisions regarding the drafting process, but it was clear to me that in the discussion not everyone participates in the same way; people who have a great deal of expertise at the UN and in international law and the best command of English take a central role in deciding which recommendations to adopt and how to formulate them. Even if translators are in the room it is difficult for everyone present to engage in the discussion, especially when the predominant language is English, or when not all the Forum members have legal training or are familiar with how to write a UN report, or simply when some are more interested in the debates than others. Sometimes the result falls below the expectations of indigenous delegates when the draft report is presented, and questions are raised about the influence of states in the drafting process and the issue of transparency in which recommendations are included.

In fact, the adoption of the session report by the PFII is not always accepted by the people present in the room. On the last day of the 7th Session in 2008, a group of indigenous delegates rose from their seats and started to clap their hands and shout *"queremos la palabra!"* (we want to speak!) and *"tenemos nostros derechos!"* (we have rights!). The chairperson conferred with the bureau and tried to continue the session as if nothing had happened, but was impeded by the noise from the delegates, which rose again. Finally, she suggested that the indigenous observers could speak after the adoption of the report, but they rejected the offer vehemently and insisted on speaking without further delay. UN security personnel entered the room. Someone exclaimed that if anybody had to leave, all the indigenous delegates would leave the room. The disturbance intensified, with people shouting insistently on their right to speak. Only after the chair asked the security staff to leave did the

---

[14] www.ifad.org/topic/ip_forum. Accessed September 5, 2016.

situation begin to calm down. In the end, the chairperson allowed the indigenous caucus to read out their statement.

Their statement expressed the view that their opinion and the recommendations concerning climate change and carbon markets made during the session had not been taken into account in the draft final report, and requested that they be allowed to change the relevant paragraphs. The final report brought to the attention of ECOSOC for its adoption and uploaded on the PFII website took into consideration the concern of the protesters, noting in paragraph 45 that "the current framework for REDD is not supported by most indigenous peoples."[15] This event, referred to on the web as the "May revolt,"[16] is one of the manifestations of indigenous discontent regarding the ways their rights and interests are unrepresented, and this experience was seen by many indigenous activists as a further demonstration of the fact that, even with gestures like the revision of a draft report, in the end, what matters in UN policies are the interests of the states and powerful international agencies, such as the World Bank. A UN civil servant, in solidarity with indigenous concerns, once remarked to me along similar lines, pointing to the structural connection between the UN and states interests: "The people that work in the UN are much too integrated into the system and they do not challenge state power – and sometimes they do not know that they are integrated into the system!" (author interview, 2009).

OUTSIDE THE MAIN ROOM: LOBBYING, EDUCATING, AND NETWORKING

The Permanent Forum meeting is much more than a conference-room gathering, more even than a focal point of global communication and mobility. It can be imagined as a central hub, with many venues, formal and informal spaces of interaction and knowledge production extending out from it.

The parallel activities that take place outside the main session, apart from the deliberations of the PFII and the meetings of the indigenous caucuses, are very important to understand how, in practice, the PFII annual meeting creates knowledge and how it interrelates with the other UN bodies, organizations, states, and indigenous peoples. These outside activities take three basic forms: (1) meetings approved and scheduled by the Secretariat referred to as "side events," including information, education, and training; (2) performative and representational activities, including film screenings, arts and crafts displays, exhibits of photographs and projects, receptions, and indigenous ceremonies and performances; and (3) informal activities in the form of meetings and lobbying that take place throughout the

---

[15] UN Permanent Forum on Indigenous Issues. Report on the 7th Session (21 April to 7 May 2008). ECOSOC Supplement n. 23. Doc. Number E/C.19/2008/13.

[16] The filmmaker Rebecca Summer shot a video on the May revolt which is possible to watch online on YouTube: www.youtube.com/watch?v=UtORVi7GybY. Accessed August 18, 2015.

Permanent Forum meeting in hallways, lobbies, and cafes in the UN building, states' embassies, and in bars and restaurants in New York City. Let me briefly elaborate on each of them in turn.

Some fifty or sixty official "side events" occur during the annual gathering, taking the form of book launches, film screenings, roundtables, training, information delivery, and so on, with their times usually scheduled during the two-hour lunch break, in the evening, or parallel to closed sessions of the Permanent Forum when the sixteen members meet among themselves. They are spaces of education and activism for civil society representatives, UN personnel, and state delegates.

They take place in the rooms used for the main sessions and in many other buildings of the UN on the other side of the street from the Headquarters Secretariat. These side events are proposed and organized by NGOs, UN agencies, financial institutions, universities, and indigenous organizations, with the help of the Secretariat. Organizers are in competition with one another to attract people to their event, especially considering that up to ten events take place at the same time. Serving food and drink is one way multilateral agencies and NGOs attract people to their side events, but they also sometimes distribute leaflets along the rows of desks during the main session (Dhal 2012). Participants must decide which event, if any, to attend; and often their selection is part of a broader strategy that takes into consideration not just the issues discussed in the event, but also the people who can be met and lobbied there. Most of the events organized by the agencies are intended for them to show off their recent work and there is not much space for indigenous representatives, who tend to be left with small, residual fragments of time for their interventions, as was the case in a UNESCO side event in 2011 reported by Dahl (2012: 56). During these informal meetings, discussions take place on several topics and people learn more about specific cases and the work of the UN, NGOs, academics, and states, including such things as intellectual property, traditional knowledge and language preservation, constitutional reforms, free, prior and informed consent (FPIC), development initiatives, policy reforms, and financial opportunities. Participants present their issues to, or ask information from, World Bank officers, agencies, governments, and corporations – entities that otherwise would be difficult (if not impossible) to access during the main Session. Much of the participation comes from the Forum members, who are often the key speakers in the events.

Then there are the "cultural events," craft markets, food stalls, and the daily photos taken of people dressed in colorful clothes, feathers, and beads as a statement of their rich diversity. Usually on the evening of the third day of the annual meeting this kind of event is organized by the Secretariat, to take place in the lobby of the UNHQ. Indigenous artists from different parts of the world perform dances and music, and the participants of the Forum and other peoples that have access to the UN lobby attend the event, drinking, eating, dancing, and watching the performances. Despite its image as an arid bureaucracy, the UN can be a place where a common indigenous peoples' identity is reinforced – and sometimes essentialized by the language of global unity-through-diversity, expressed in song, dance, traditional clothes, and a shared space.

This kind of event opens windows on indigenous identity politics and how culture is produced and used in the political struggles for rights: indigeneity is deployed, as illustrated by the importance of dressing in articles of clothing that characterize peoples' culture. Indigenous peoples share their ceremonies; each group attends and participates in the ceremony of the others. In fact, as indigenous representatives have stressed repeatedly, the "UN is an important space to share commonalities and not feeling so alone" (author notes, 2009). The sense of solidarity derived not only from shared forms of suffering, but from a sense of occupying a common space in the UN, being part of a social movement that brings together peoples under the banner of "proud to be indigenous."

During the PFII sessions, the areas outside the conference rooms, in the UN cafeterias and corridors, become even more important than the meeting room itself for indigenous organizations, but also for states and UN officers working on indigenous issues. This is very similar to what Richard Holbrooke, US Permanent Representative under the Clinton administration, describes when writing about the UN Headquarters in New York, referring to the UN as a village "with its own language and time zone… Food is probably the thing that holds the UN together … Boy, do those guys like to eat!" (cit. in Fasulo 2004: 91). In these spaces, indigenous representatives can organize themselves to create collective statements, share experiences, find funding opportunities, and exchange contacts and take pictures of each other "to show people at home how other indigenous peoples that have similar issues look." These are also spaces where indigenous delegates try to "saturate" the UN with their requests, terminologies, and priorities; and where, for instance, they approach states that are friendly to indigenous peoples' rights so that the latter, in turn, can raise questions concerning human rights compliance, directed toward the states slated to be under review in the next UN Universal Periodic Review cycle (see Cowan and Billaud, Chapter 5 in this volume). These are the spaces of advocacy, fundraising, and networking, and the spaces where the indigenous movements and their discourses are created and learned.

Besides all of this, they are spaces of diplomacy. Little of this work of diplomacy can happen on the floor. It calls for another kind of space, one that is less formal and more conducive to politics through social exchange. Nancy Soderberg, US ambassador in the UN (1997–2000), recalling her experience in the Security Council, describes a very similar situation to the Forum session. Formal meetings, she said, are "just a staged show … For the most part, you go in, there is a briefing that nobody pays attention to, and everyone reads prepared statements and nothing happens." She also stresses how often the informal still remains too formal for real negotiation and that "the actual decision may already have been made anyway. But where? In the back room" (cited in Fasulo 2004: 98).

Much the same point can be made about the Permanent Forum. That which is happening in the main session is the front-stage of relationships, networks, and decisions, all of which starts outside the main UNHQ, such as in the states Permanent Missions' offices in New York (for comparison, see Schia, Chapter 3 in this volume), as well as in government offices and NGO headquarters at the regional and local levels. The words expressed from the floor, conveyed by translators and formalized in documents, do not always say what people mean, and certainly do not express the sensitive issues at the heart of conflict situations, the goals that are at cross-purposes, above all the aspirations for indigenous recognition and autonomy that have the potential to challenge state and corporate interests – or are merely *perceived* by states to challenge these interests. Given the dominant position of Member States in the UN system, the so-called politics of shame are limited in their potential to change state policies; and some of the more diplomatically inclined indigenous delegates and UN personnel prefer to engage in dialogue with state representatives as a way to achieve subtle shifts of perspective that might eventually result in a change of position.

CONCLUSION: TURNING THE KALEIDOSCOPE

Much of what I have described concerning the organization of the sessions and the production and delivery of statements is provisional, undergoing a transition. The Permanent Forum is engaged in a process of self-examination and reform, discussed in the 2015 session with reference to a "Concept Note for Discussion,"[17] with changes being called for and planned that could well result in the Forum becoming a completely different organization from what it is today. These changes cover the entire spectrum of the Forum's structure and work, including addressing "conference room dynamics": problems of access to the speaker's list by developing a system of "equity" for indigenous representatives "to have the opportunity to speak." In response to repeated criticism, they also envisage improving the ways that the Permanent Forum report is adopted, to give delegates greater input into the drafting process. Beyond a concern with improving the annual Session, the reforms are oriented toward raising the Forum's political profile, both in the UN system and in its direct influence on states. Giving Forum members the authority to undertake consultations in the regions they represent, as is now being proposed, would make them, in effect, political representatives of the UN to their regional constituents (effectively overturning their current status as "experts" acting in an "independent" capacity). Limiting the number of the Forum's recommendations while implementing mechanisms to make them "actionable," along with the development of human rights indicators through a proposed "Indigenous Development Index," would make

---

[17] UN Permanent Forum on Indigenous Issues – 14th Session: Concept Note for Discussion: Method of Work of the Permanent Forum on Indigenous Issues. www.un.org/esa/socdev/unpfii/documents/2015/concept-notes/methods-of-work.pdf. Accessed July 17, 2015.

use of statistical data and "indicators" to raise the profile of the Forum's involvement with human rights issues and make violations more globally visible (cf. Merry, Chapter 7 this volume). Finally, there are reforms oriented toward more closely integrating the Forum within the UN system. This was expressed in the "Concept Note" as an effort to "strengthen its coordination with UN agencies" and to "improve dialogue with respective UN agency representatives."[18] In orally explaining this point in the main conference room of the Session, Dalee Sambo Dorough, former chairperson of the Forum, expressed it in terms of "saturation": "To saturate the UN system with the view, perspectives, and human rights of indigenous peoples."

At the time of writing, these reforms were articulated in preparation for the 15th annual Session in 2016, which envisions a "cultural change in the conduct of the session," introducing three closed meetings in which indigenous delegates, UN agencies, and states meet separately with Permanent Forum members.[19] The changes envisaged for the Forum also involve reform to the advance speakers' list during the open plenary, introducing new procedures whereby delegates will be able to pre-register for the speaker's list through the website of the Forum before the session, thereby eliminating the queues at the Secretariat's table during the session day, while placing greater reliance on computer literacy. Finally, a new, participatory structure for "interactive dialogue" will be introduced, in which speakers get the attention of the chair simply by pressing the microphone button on their desk and waiting to be acknowledged. Needless to say, these reforms face the imbalance of power and the overriding interests of states in the UN, which do not always have the interests of indigenous peoples at the forefront of their agendas, and which could very well end in treadmilling, making critics think they are moving forward while running in place. Such reforms to the structure of international institutions, with implications for how international law and policy are developed, are the focal point of the tension between false expectations and effective leveraging of rights, in which it remains to be seen whether the international organization is a site of autonomy or "part of a grand global scheme of subjection" (Wilson 2007: 352).

Organizational changes, whether illusory or real, constitute the main impetus behind what might be seen as the turning of the kaleidoscope, evident in the shifting alignments of global power, which find reflection in the priorities and diplomacies of states. There is a never-ending learning process that follows from the realignments of power and opportunity in the UN system. States do sometimes come to the Forum year after year with consistent positions on the major issues concerning the

---

[18] UN Permanent Forum on Indigenous Issues – 14th Session: Concept Note for Discussion: Method of Work of the Permanent Forum on Indigenous Issues. www.un.org/esa/socdev/unpfii/documents/2015/concept-notes/methods-of-work.pdf. Accessed July 17, 2015.

[19] Overview of the Changes to take place during the 15th Session of the UN Permanent Forum on Indigenous Issues. www.un.org/esa/socdev/unpfii/documents/2016/Docs-updates/Overview-of-the-Changes-PFII.pdf. Accessed May 4, 2015.

recognition and rights of indigenous peoples. But state delegations also occasionally come with major political changes, with implications for either greater receptiveness or rejection of the indigenous agenda, in the background of their participation in the Forum.

I have considered how the tension between activism and bureaucratic inertia is sometimes expressed in the way civil servants and activists take on aspects of one another's roles. The boundaries between their roles are permeable. Officials are sometimes powerfully influenced by their regular encounters with the experience and justice claims of indigenous delegates. And indigenous delegates, for their part, are often inspired by their experience in the UN to seek professional training, recognition as experts, and employment within it. The sum of these personal commitments helps to explain wider transformations in the UNs reception and institutionalization of the indigenous agenda.

The annual session is structured in a way that (both intentionally and unintentionally) promotes expertise and the bureaucratic legibility of indigenous rights claims, starting with the online process of accreditation and its inherent preference for delegates who are connected to organizations, and for organizations that are formally constituted and connected online. The acquisition of expertise is an essential part of the conditions of entry and effective participation in the UN. In preparation for their participation in the meeting room, delegates learn how to follow procedural rules in the structure and sequence of agenda items, the diplomatic language of an acceptable intervention, and the time allotted to speak (even though in practice these rules are often violated, and occasionally explicitly denounced and rejected).

In the absence of mechanisms of compliance, of the ability to make recommendations "actionable," the Forum's interventions and reports are oriented toward new structures of sensibilization, without, it is sometimes feared, having a "transformative impact on the underlying political-economic conditions" that perpetuate the vulnerability of indigenous peoples (Goodale 2015: 4). Many of the most experienced indigenous delegates, disillusioned by the Forum's limited influence on the behavior of states and corporations, have stopped attending international meetings and pursue their causes locally and nationally. Other delegates to the session see and understand the structural limits of the Forum, yet they still choose to attend, sometimes year after year. What do they see in the Forum that keeps these "regulars" coming back? The transformative potential of the organization is the focal point of hope for those who continue to participate, a quality that overrides all the deficiencies of the present. And the acquisition of expertise is the way toward enacting that potential, making of the expert a potential reformer, one whose knowledge of the UN system brings about the possibility of a world built upon the wisdom of its original inhabitants.

REFERENCES

Anaya, James. 2004. *Indigenous Peoples in International Law*. Oxford: Oxford University Press.

Bellier, Irene. 2013. "'We Indigenous Peoples…': Global Activism and the Emergence of a New Collective Subject in the United Nations." In Birgit Müller (ed.) *The Gloss of Harmony. The Politics of Policy-making in Multilateral Organizations*. London: Pluto Press, pp. 177–201.

Cowan, Jane. 2006. "Culture and Rights after *Culture and Rights*." *American Anthropologist* 108(1): 9–24.

Dahl, Jens. 2012. *The Indigenous Space and Marginalized Peoples in the United Nations*. New York: Palgrave Macmillan.

Engle, Karen. 2010. *The Elusive Promise of Indigenous Development: Rights, Culture, Strategy*. Durham: Duke University Press.

Escarcega, Sylvia. 2003. "Internationalization of the Politics of Indigenousness: A Case Study of Mexican Indigenous Intellectuals and Activists at the United Nations." PhD diss., University of Davis, California.

Ewen, Alexander. (ed.) 1994. *Voice of Indigenous Peoples. Native People Address the United Nations*. Santa Fe: Clear Light Publisher.

Fasulo, Linda M. 2004. *An Insider's Guide to the UN*. New Haven and London: Yale University Press.

Goodale, Mark. 2015. "Dark Matter: Toward a Political Economy of Indigenous Rights and Aspirational Politics." *Critique of Anthropology*, 0(0): 1–19.

Henderson, James (Sa'ke'j) Youngblood. 2008. *Indigenous Diplomacy and the Rights of Peoples: Achieving UN Recognition*. Saskatoon, SK: Purich.

Lâm, M. Clech. 2000. *At the Edge of the State: Indigenous Peoples and Self-determination*. Ardsley: Transnational.

Lindroth, M. 2006. "Indigenous-State Relations in the UN: Establishing the Indigenous Forum." *Political and Legal Anthropology Review (PoLAR)*, 42: 239–248.

Marcus, George. 1998. *Ethnography through Thick and Thin*. Princeton: Princeton University Press.

Merry, Sally. E. 2005. "Anthropology and Activism: Researching Human Rights across Porous Boundaries." *Political and Legal Anthropology Review (PoLAR)*, 28(2): 240–257.

—— 2006. *Human Rights and Gender Violence: Translating International Law into Local Justice*. Chicago: University of Chicago Press.

Minde, Henry. 2008. "The Destination and the Journey: Indigenous Peoples and the United Nations from the 1960s through 1985." In *Indigenous Peoples: Self-determination, Knowledge and Indigeneity*, Delft: Eburon, pp. 49–86.

Morgan, Rhiannon. 2007. "On Political Institutions and Social Movement Dynamics: The Case of the United Nations and the Global Indigenous Movement." *International Political Science Review*, 28(3): 273–292.

Muehlebach, Andrea. 2001. "Making Place at the United Nations: Indigenous Cultural Politics at the U.N. Working Group on Indigenous Populations." *Cultural Anthropology*, 16(3): 415–448.

Niezen, Ronald. 2003. *The Origins of Indigenism: Human Rights and the Politics of Identity*. Berkeley and London: University of California Press.

Osmańczyk, Edmund Jan. 2003. "Nongovernmental Organizations (NGOs)." In *Encyclopedia of the United Nations and International Agreements*. Edited and revised by Anthony Mango. New York: Routledge.

Peterson, M J. 2010. "How the Indigenous Got Seats at the UN Table." *Review International Organization*, 5:197–225.
Pritchard, Sarah. 1998. "Working Group on Indigenous Populations: Mandate, Standard-Setting Activities and Future Perspectives." In S. Pritchard (eds.) *Indigenous People: The United Nations and Human Rights*. London: Zed Books, pp. 40–65.
Sanders, Douglas. 1989. "The UN Working Group on Indigenous Populations." *Human Rights Quarterly*, 11(3): 406–433.
Sapignoli, Maria. 2012. "Local Power Through Globalized Indigenous Identities: The San, the State, and the International Community." PhD diss., Essex University, Colchester, United Kingdom.
  2015. "Dispossession in the Age of Humanity: Human Rights, Citizenship, and Indigeneity in the Central Kalahari." *Anthropological Forum: A Journal of Social Anthropology and Comparative Sociology*, 25(3): 285–305.
Summerson Carr, E. 2010. "Enactments of Expertise." *Annual Review of Anthropology*, 39: 17–32.
Thornberry, Patrick. 2002. *Indigenous Peoples and Human Rights*. Manchester: Juris Publishing, Manchester University Press.
United Nations Secretariat of the Permanent Forum on Indigenous Issues (UNSPFII). 2009. *Training Module on Indigenous Peoples' Issues. Facilitator Handbook*. April 2009, prepared by the UNSPFII.
Wilson, Richard. A. 1997. "Representing Human Rights Violations: Social Contexts and Subjectivities." In Richard Wilson (ed.) *Human Rights, Culture & Context: Anthropological Perspectives*. London: Pluto, pp. 134–160.
  2007. "Tyrannosaurus Lex: The Anthropology of Human Rights and Transnational Law." In Mark Goodale and Sally Merry (eds.) *The Practice of Human Rights: Tracking Law Between the Global and the Local*, Mark Goodale and Sally Merry, eds. Cambridge: Cambridge University Press, pp. 342–369.
Xanthaki, Alexandra. 2010. *Indigenous Rights and the United Nations Standards: Self-determination, Culture and Land*. Cambridge: Cambridge University Press.

5

The 'Public' Character of the Universal Periodic Review: Contested Concept and Methodological Challenge

Jane K. Cowan and Julie Billaud

In this chapter, we examine the 'public' character of a new mechanism within the Geneva-based United Nations human rights system, the Universal Periodic Review (UPR), based on an ethnographic and historical research project we initiated in the final year of its first cycle, which ended in October 2011.[1] The adjective 'public' is a central but ambiguous notion within the UPR, as well as within the wider United Nations context (see Niezen 2010), and we explore it both as a contested concept and as a methodological challenge. Starting out with the intuition that the UPR could productively be approached as a 'public audit ritual', through fieldwork we gradually discovered the institutionally specific yet diverse meanings of 'public' and of the related notion of 'transparency'; how access to various sites was managed; and the constant struggles among actors involved in producing the UPR over what should be revealed and concealed, and to whom. The contested 'public' character of the UPR within our primary fieldsites in Geneva was an object of our research, yet as a social fact, it also posed distinct methodological challenges: it was a phenomenon in the face of which we had to adapt our methods. As the fieldwork unfolded, moreover, another sense of 'public' emerged: we came to realise the degree to which the three-hour reviews are the 'tip of the iceberg' to a plethora of activities stretching across time and space, well beyond the meeting rooms of the Palais des Nations. Indeed, the UPR has produced a new 'political field' of transnational dimensions; we use this analytical concept to think about the networks which connected (more or less well) the Geneva ritual with national and transnational 'publics'. We end with a reflection on the benefits and limits of an anthropological approach for illuminating questions about the public character of an international institutional process.

---

[1] We gratefully acknowledge the support of the British Academy which funded the research project 'International Human Rights Monitoring at the Reformed Human Rights Council: An Ethnographic and Historical Study' (BR100028), October 2010 to September 2011. Field research was carried out intensively during that period and has continued intermittently until the present.

WHAT IS THE UPR?

The UPR is a periodically held, peer-based supervisory review of a state's human rights situation, in which participants are encouraged to be constructively critical and to share best practice. Introduced as part of an extensive reform of the United Nations human rights system in 2005–2006, and launched in 2008, its architects drew ideas from peer reviews in other public international institutions (including the Organisation for Economic Cooperation and Development [OECD] and the African Peer Review Mechanism). Responding to widespread accusations that the UN's long-standing Human Rights Commission had been guilty of 'politicisation' and of applying 'double standards', scrutinising some states for human rights violations while allowing other states to escape scrutiny (Alston 2006; Gaer 2007), the UPR is organised on the principle that all states will be reviewed according to rigorously equal and comparable parameters. Moreover, the UPR discourages 'naming and shaming', aiming instead to cultivate a monitoring practice that is 'objective, transparent, non-selective, constructive, non-confrontational and non-politicised' (HRC Res 5/1 on Institution-Building, Annex, para. 3(g)).

The review is based on three reports: a National Report written by the State under Review, a Compilation of extracts from reports of UN agencies, treaty bodies and special procedures and a Stakeholders Summary, based on submissions from civil society. According to the modalities of the first cycle (2008–2011) in place during our fieldwork,[2] the review took place in the magnificent Salle XX, *La Salle des Droits de L'Homme et de l'Alliance des Civilisations*, whose dramatic multicolour stalactite ceiling, created by the abstract artist Miquel Barcelo and offered to the United Nations as a gift from the Spanish Government, has since its installation in 2008 become the icon for the Palais des Nations. As each review unfolded, its proceedings were webcast in real time via the UN website. The government delegation of the State under Review, chaired by the Human Rights Council President and assisted by a senior Secretariat staff member, would present its National Report describing the country's 'human rights situation' to the community of UN member states, known in this context as Participating Governments, as well as observers (UN agencies, multilateral organisations, NGOs, academics and the press). After a roughly 30-minute presentation, the Interactive Dialogue was opened: following the order of the designated Speaker's List displayed on a large video screen, with a digital clock counting down, each Participating Government would read out a short prepared statement,[3] which would contain, in some combination, greetings, comments, questions and recommendations. Periodically, the one-after-the-other flow of statements was paused – so that the State under Review could answer questions or present

---

[2] Some changes in the modalities have been introduced for the second cycle (2011–2015), as discussed later in the chapter.
[3] Members of the Human Rights Council had three minutes, Observer States had two minutes, but if the number of states wishing to speak was high – as frequently happened – the President would declare a two-minute limit for all states.

further information, sometimes calling on representatives of various government ministries who were part of the delegation – and then resumed. When the time allocated to Participating Governments (two hours) was used up, the State under Review was given the final minutes to wrap up.

Forty-eight hours later, the collectivity would gather again for the Adoption of the Report. In this shorter session (10–30 minutes), the Troika (three states charged to assist the State under Review during the few days of the Working Group review) would present the Draft Report, indicating the decisions of the State under Review regarding the recommendations it had received, and deal with technical issues and queries. The State under Review was free to accept or reject[4] recommendations, bearing in mind both its own priorities within the vast field of human rights, the legal human rights obligations it had assumed and the nature of its bilateral relations. In a final one-hour slot at the plenary of the subsequent Human Rights Council session several months later, the Draft Report of the Working Group would be formally adopted under Agenda Item 6. This launched the implementation phase for those recommendations that the State under Review had accepted.

The UPR has been widely lauded as the 'success story' of the new Human Rights Council. The stated intention to create a 'level playing field' has been key to its appeal to states and to the high degree of 'buy in' it has achieved. Formal equality among states, a matter of fundamental symbolic importance, is enacted mathematically: the fixed amounts of time and space allocated to the UPR process are divided absolutely equally among the states to be reviewed. Even the time *between* a state's performances, such as between the Review of the Working Group and the Adoption of the Draft Report – normally 48 hours – has been a focus of delegates' concerns, the principle being that no state should enjoy an unfair advantage by receiving more preparation time than its peers.[5] Maximum times for specific speakers to speak and maximum page lengths for documents on which the review is based are scrupulously policed. Similarly, ordering (which by definition requires that some party goes first) is left to 'fair play', such as being determined by one's time of arrival in the queue. Avoidance of unfair advantage is assured by utilising chance, as when the State under Review selects its Troika by picking out slips of paper from a bowl.

THE UPR AS A 'PUBLIC AUDIT RITUAL'

Although the UPR is variously described as a 'peer review', a 'periodic review' and, more informally, as an 'exam' (see Cowan and Billaud 2015), we see the practices

---

[4] During the second cycle, certain actors encouraged a shift in terminology: recommendations that were not accepted should, they insist, be referred to as 'noted' and not as 'rejected'. Claiming this to be closer to the 'original' intention of UPR architects, this approach also keeps the non-accepted recommendation 'on the table'.

[5] We observed the expression of these concerns during the 2011 discussions reviewing UPR's modalities and suggesting changes for its second cycle.

surrounding the UPR to exemplify what Marilyn Strathern (2000b) has dubbed 'audit culture', in which actors are enrolled, through myriad micro-practices, in providing an account of themselves and of others. Specifically, we believe that it is useful to view the three public moments of UPR (the 3-hour review of the Working Group, the Adoption of the Draft Report and the final Adoption of the Report at the Human Rights Council plenary) as elements of a 'public audit ritual'.[6] Why have we chosen this phrase, and what does it allow us to see?

Let us consider each term, starting with 'audit'. Whereas most analysts assessing the UPR are concerned to determine *how well* the UPR 'works' as an accountability mechanism, we take a few steps back from these practical concerns in order to reflect on *how* it works, in a broader sense. We examine the UPR through the lenses both of critical anthropologies of human rights and of recent interdisciplinary work on 'audit culture', an arena of discussion within the wider literature inspired by Foucault's work on governmentality, which aims to understand the new ways that power operates within contemporary practices of 'good governance' (Shore and Wright 1999; 2000a; Strathern 2000b; Rose 1999). Adopting these lenses enables us to interrogate critically the UPR's own self-description and to reframe it theoretically. Whereas the peer review model emphasises the structural equality among 'peers', ignoring or downplaying the asymmetries existing 'outside' of the review, we ask: what are the implications of those asymmetries among 'peers'? Whereas that model takes as axiomatic that peers 'share' values and commitments, we ask: to what extent are these actually shared? We also ask: what is kept off the agenda – and, by extension, what cannot be said – through the very form and modalities of the peer review? Contextualising the UPR within wider practices of neoliberal governance, we suggest that UPR exemplifies the trend of increased auditing of public institutions, up to and including the state, and that it should be thought about in relation to other mechanisms of so-called soft power at the international level.

In sum, by using the language of 'audit', we hope to highlight power relations obscured in the UPR's disconcertingly friendly phrases. Whereas the term 'review' conveys the idea of repeated surveillance – literally: re-viewing, looking again – the term 'audit' can be defined as 'an account of compliance with a set of expectations or standards' (Beitz 2011: 34). We believe that this better captures the nature of UPR as a form of 'soft power', involving a combination of coercion and voluntary engagement, and of external (collective peer) oversight plus self-revelation and anticipatory self-regulation.

Why ritual? Our starting focus has been with the audit and the way that this audit is publicly enacted through a ritual. Indeed, the UPR contains many elements which Moore and Myerhoff (1977) identified within 'secular rituals': it is highly ordered in time and space, involving formalised modes of speech (e.g. a rigidly ordered 'interactive dialogue', the reading out of timed written statements, use of diplomatic

---

[6] This section draws heavily on Cowan (2014:49–53).

codes) which require particular presentations of the body, voice and demeanour. Although the UPR is a ritual of audit, it simultaneously expresses commitment to other core propositions and values, including universality, equality and cooperation. Not least, through its state-focused review, the UPR invokes and ritually performs national sovereignty. Its smaller rituals – of greeting, solidarity and confrontation – enable States to express the tone of their bilateral relations, even as they are compelled to act as a collective body (e.g. in the adoption of country reports).

Acknowledging the positive aspects of its ritual dimensions, the international legal scholar Hilary Charlesworth has pointed to the danger that the UPR may also encourage 'ritualism', which she defines as a 'technique of embracing the language of human rights precisely to deflect human rights scrutiny' (Charlesworth 2010: 12–13; see also Charlesworth and Larking 2014). We agree that actors representing a state may use human rights language with varying degrees of commitment, and even insincerely, as well as with divergent understandings of what human rights mean and entail. But we think that the conceptual opposition of ritual vs. ritualism may be unhelpful, in as much as it diverts our attention from the wider effects for states, both as auditor and auditee, of participating in a universal and public ritual. Staying inside a problematic of compliance, it under-theorises the effects of 'just' going through the motions, and, especially, of the cumulative effects of 193 UN Member States, one after the other, going through the same motions within a ritual that is highly orchestrated and relatively unvarying. Following Butler (1990), we see the repetitiveness of the UPR as productive, as well as key to its power and persuasiveness. Repeated embodied participation in the ritual of the UPR serves to make habitual, customary and normal a specific discourse regarding the nature of state sovereignty in relation to human rights. The focus on issues of sincere vs. insincere commitment can be a distraction when 'going through the motions' itself has such powerful effects.

THE CONTESTED MEANING OF THE 'PUBLIC' AND THE ISSUE OF 'TRANSPARENCY'

Why, finally, do we describe the UPR as 'public'? Since its establishment, advocates of the UPR have stressed its 'public' character. As a review that was designed to be both holistic, encompassing the entire range of a state's human rights commitments, and relatively non-technical, many hoped that it would appeal to a wide public – particularly to a 'national' public keen to see how its own government performed. Some NGO activists, for instance, saw it as a way for that public to become aware of human rights issues on their doorsteps and perhaps to become drawn into more active participation in civil society initiatives addressing them. From the first cycle in 2008, the OHCHR (Office of the High Commissioner for Human Rights) supported this accessibility by making available on its UPR website the three key documents on which the review is based. In light of its anticipated appeal, it was also decided to webcast all public UPR sessions: anyone with access to the internet and the right computer equipment could watch the proceedings of the UPR Working Group as they were webcast in real time or, in theory, view them later through archived webcasts. UPR participants – especially the State under Review and States participating in the Interactive Dialogue – immediately had to get used to the idea that they were being watched and evaluated not only by their colleagues in Salle XX, but often by critical domestic audiences back home.

Yet the meaning of 'public' in the United Nations context is not straightforward. As one enters Door 40 of the UN Palais des Nation complex into the spacious reception hall, one sees a large board announcing the day's meetings, indicating each as 'Public' or 'Private'. The UPR is marked as 'Public'. A member of the public coming in from 'off the street' could, with valid identification documents, get this far with a visitor's badge, but she would not be able to enter Salle XX, located just beyond the top of the escalator. Even to sit in the Public Gallery, a glassed-in unit three floors above the meeting room floor from which one can observe proceedings, she would have had to stumble across information on the OHCHR website directed to civil society organisations, indicating an email address to which she should submit a request at least 24 hours in advance. Although the OHCHR (2014: 7) advises that a 'limited number of seats' are available 'for persons wishing to observe the proceedings of the Working Group without being accredited as participants (e.g. students and academics)', the general public is not invited to be physically present. Only in their 'organised' form as members of civil society organisations may ordinary people enter Salle XX, but here, too, only if their organisation has ECOSOC-recognition, or, alternatively, if they can persuade an ECOSOC-recognised NGO to provide them with a badge under their auspices.

It did not take us long to discover that virtual access to Salle XX was almost as contentious as physical entry for a community of diplomats who in no way agreed on what degree of 'publicness' was appropriate or desirable for the UPR. Posted on the OHCHR's UPR Extranet (a virtual institutional space which members of the public may, ironically, enter by electronically requesting, then using, a password) is a document witnessing an early gesture of resistance. In April 2008, a few months before UPR was launched, the Africa Group, the Arab Group and the Organisation of Islamic Countries produced a 'non-paper' setting out their views on 'the remaining UPR modalities'. There, the authors point out that the 'IB [Institution Building] text ... does not provide for webcasting of the WG [Working Group] proceedings' and that doing so would go, unacceptably, beyond existing UN practice (Shoukry, Abu Koash and Khan 2008). This coalition of regional groups was not successful in resisting the innovation of webcasting, an institutional practice that is now presented as evidence of UPR's 'transparency'.

The importance that both advocates and opponents of webcasting placed on the UPR performance, and on determining who would be able to see and hear it, is itself notable, indicating that much is thought to be at stake. Yet we can ask: what is actually captured in the webcast? Moving back and forth between the government delegation seated on the dais at the front and centre and the succession of speakers at diplomatic desks around the room, the camera shields from view the constant movement and background buzz that rises and falls as individuals enter and leave, greeting and chatting or consulting with colleagues on the way in or out. The webcast records the flow of formal statements, but with its static and inevitably limited camera angles, it offers only a very partial perspective on what happens on the floor. Needless to say, those numerous discussions that occur outside the room which precede, inform and give sense to the UPR performance are not observable either.

Significantly, since 2008 the virtual visibility of the UPR has been buried and, literally, lost in the proliferating abundance of UN webcasts. After several redesigns of the UN website, 'UN Web TV: The United Nations Live & On-demand' now delivers thousands of webcasts, many of them in tiny parcels: a single speech, one country delegation's statement or other minute excerpts from meetings that last many hours. It has become almost impossible for the general public to find the archived webcasts of previous UPRs, especially those that occurred in the first cycle. A keyword search in February 2016 of the phrase 'UPR' brought up 1,306 results in no particular order, but attempts to narrow down to a particular review – 'Universal Periodic Review Greece 2011', 'UPR Greece', 'Greece Universal Periodic Review', 'Greece UPR' – all came up with '0 entries'. The somewhat counter-intuitive phrase 'Belgium Review' finally hit the jackpot for Belgium, but 'Greece Review' brought up nothing. (Belgium was reviewed for a second time in January 2016, while at the time of the search, Greece had been reviewed only once, in May 2011; that webcast was presumably archived elsewhere.) If a diligent web searcher does manage to find the desired webcast, she may still be unable to open or 'play' it, given technical difficulties with 'RealPlayer' and 'Quicktime' interfaces. Viewers 'in the know' – those already familiar with the UPR – will be aware that all documents relating to previous UPRs, including webcasts, are now available from the easy-to-use and comprehensive upr-info.org website, but even here, viewing relies on the smooth workings of technological interfaces, which frequently fail. In these various ways, therefore, 'public' access to the UPR space is either highly controlled or rendered difficult due to technological complexity or incompatibility.

These impediments notwithstanding, what is the rationale for making the UPR 'public' in the first place? It is that citizens should be able to – indeed, 'have the right to' – see how their governments talk about human rights and how they propose to respect, protect and promote them. Like other human rights monitoring mechanisms, the UPR requires the State under Review to give an account of itself, and to show itself accountable, with respect to human rights, in a manner that acknowledges both achievements and challenges. What is being demanded of the state is an attitude of openness to scrutiny and a willingness to give public reasons for its actions. What is being demanded of other actors is a willingness to ask pertinent and probing yet respectful questions. This orientation is often glossed as 'transparency'.

The involvement of Non-Governmental and Civil Society Organizations (NGOs and CSOs, glossed officially as 'Stakeholders' but more informally as 'NGOs') in the UPR process is seen by some as a means to improve the UPR's 'transparency'. The contribution of such organisations is substantial, even in this primarily state-based peer review mechanism. Given that 'the state can say whatever it wants', as activists often remarked, many UPR participants look to NGOs to act as 'watchdogs' and 'whistleblowers'. In these roles, they compose 'submissions' to the OHCHR in advance of the review which provide information on the country's human rights situation, in ways that may supplement, challenge or provide an alternative interpretation to the state's account. In the months and weeks before a state is reviewed, NGO staff often approach diplomats with requests that they make particular recommendations during the Review on issues that their organisation deems important. In these ways, NGOs make visible issues that the State under Review might hide or neglect. At the same time, not all critical human rights issues in a country will have an NGO champion: NGOs generate visibility, but selectively and in a way that is reflective of their own priorities. With the emphasis in the UPR on cooperation and non-confrontation, moreover, notions of the NGO role are also shifting. In UPR contexts, NGOs are being encouraged to act both as critical watchdogs and as 'partners' in the state's implementation of its recommendations. Indeed, we have observed NGOs being praised when they voluntarily took on responsibilities that actually belong to the state, such as birth registration.

The hegemonic quality of transparency as a self-evident good within the UPR could be observed in a key debate during the review of UPR modalities towards the end of the first cycle, as part of a larger Review of the Human Rights Council. A proposal supported by certain states and NGOs called for making it mandatory – rather than optional – for states to submit mid-term reports on their progress in implementing accepted UPR recommendations. When other states – including many Developing and Least Developed Countries – objected to the proposal, their diplomats did not question the value of transparency as such; rather, they argued that mandatory reports were, for certain Developing Countries in particular with already overstretched state bureaucracies, overly burdensome (Cowan and Billaud 2015). The value of transparency went unchallenged, even as the proposal for mandatory mid-term reports was defeated.

Making documents 'transparent' was equally central to the Secretariat's mission. In this specific bureaucratic context, it involved a myriad of 'rituals of verification' (Power 1999) which aimed at ensuring the validity of the information shared in reports. The drafting of the Stakeholders' Summary, for instance, necessitated classifying stakeholders according to their status (ECOSOC or non-ECOSOC), identifying the 'best and most effective quote' in a report consistent with the word limit and organising footnotes so that the author of each quote could be easily identified. With the inflation in the number of stakeholder submissions as the first cycle of the UPR progressed, compiling the Summary could easily turn into a brain-twister, requiring an extra labour force usually drawn from the large and constantly renewed pool of interns. Some states did not hesitate to interfere in the process, accusing the UPR Secretariat of accepting contributions from Civil Society Organizations that were 'illegitimate' in one way or another. In order to protect the 'voices from the field' while maintaining diplomatic relations with states, drafters had to devise intricate narrative strategies. During their weekly coordination meetings, drafters engaged in animated conversations on how to justify the inclusion or exclusion of particular Stakeholders in the Summary. Although the Secretariat had devised internal guidelines for compiling the Summary, those were constantly negotiated on a case-by-case basis.

Our ethnographic research enabled us to understand both the high stakes surrounding the public moments of the UPR, and the fact that these were the 'tip of the iceberg' – or, in Erving Goffman's (1969) metaphor, the 'frontstage' – of a much more extended process, both temporally and spatially. We quickly realised that the public audit ritual could not be understood in isolation, and might not even be the most interesting site from which to observe the UPR drama. Many of the most intense moments of the drama took place off-stage: in the offices where OHCHR drafters crafted Summary texts that manifested 'the voices of civil society' and in meeting rooms where they defended their texts or negotiated compromises, in the Palais des Nations corridors where diplomats bargained over the wording of recommendations and in the ministries of governments where bureaucrats wrangled over what should be put in and what kept out of the National Report.

METHODOLOGICAL CHALLENGES

Like other anthropologists studying international institutions, we found the sheer extent and complexity of the 'political field' that constitutes the UPR extremely daunting. We wrestled with the methodological challenges it posed. How, we asked, does one conduct participant observation when 'the field' is so dispersed across time and space? How does one investigate the different moments in the UPR process and the distinctive ways that the UPR is seen and experienced by the various UPR participants, depending on their role? How does one understand the identities and motivations of UPR participants when those individuals – diplomats, NGO staff, visiting activists, UN civil servants, interns and trainees of various stripes – are leading such transient lives, constantly moving from one job to the next and one organisation to the next, often literally moving across the boundaries that are supposed to exist between 'the state', 'the international' and 'civil society'? And, finally: how does one access spaces where the 'public' is not allowed or where 'publicness' becomes an issue? As our fieldwork progressed, we had to develop strategies to deal with these issues.

Participant Observation at the Secretariat

From her long-term archival research on the handling of minority petitions by the League of Nations Minorities Section during the interwar period, Jane had learned just how crucial the work of an international organisation's Secretariat was in managing the implementation of international agreements (Cowan 2003; 2007b; 2007a; 2010; 2013). In this UPR project, too, we were interested in the contribution of the OHCHR Secretariat to the UPR process. As we anticipated, Secretariat staff played a key part in the production, as well as the social life, of UPR documents. We were particularly interested in the document-making process: how information was selected, reformulated and organised in the final UPR documents. For instance, we wanted to know in detail how the stakeholders quoted in the Stakeholders Summary, one of the three reports which serve as a basis for the review, were selected, which of their issues were represented and how and what kinds of concerns informed such decisions. Yet in the initial months of our research on the UPR, even as we attended UPR sessions and side events and developed relationships with diplomatic delegations, NGOs and some OHCHR Secretariat staff, we had no real access to the everyday work of the Secretariat in preparing for and supporting the UPR process, and thus little insight into how these decisions were made.

During a conversation with the OHCHR Secretariat staff member in charge of coordinating the preparation of Stakeholders Summaries, Julie saw up close the limitations of interviews for grasping the nature and materiality of the myriad bureaucratic procedures in which drafters were routinely involved. It was clear that the only way to get a sense of these was to observe the working practices of the Secretariat from within, ideally by undertaking them as a participant. Because the Secretariat's UPR unit – like the OHCHR Secretariat and the UN system generally – was chronically understaffed, it regularly used the support of interns to produce the documents for which it was responsible. Julie's offer to work in the UPR unit as an intern was therefore enthusiastically received, although it took several months of administrative procedures before she was able to start her work within the Field Operation and Technical Cooperation Division. From April to June 2011, she became an apprentice UN civil servant, attending weekly team meetings, learning how to draft UPR documents and following the everyday bureaucratic work of the division.[7]

The team of UPR drafters was spread across the four divisions of the OHCHR – namely, the Research and Right to Development Division (RRDD), the Human Rights Treaties Division (HRTD), the Field Operations and Technical Cooperation Division (FOTCD) and the Human Rights Council and Special Procedures Division (HRC-SPD). Drafters worked collaboratively, using their respective knowledge and expertise to select and compile the information relevant for each report.

---

[7] For a more detailed account of preparation of UPR documents in the OHCHR Secretariat, see Billaud (2014).

Julie was able to follow closely the document drafting processes for the twelfth and final session of the UPR's first cycle. She was herself tasked with drafting the key UPR documents, including the Stakeholders Summary and FOTCD's input to the Compilation, for several countries, and it was through the process of actually doing the Secretariat's work that she was able to witness the complex negotiations taking place which aimed to construct the texts required while upholding the fragile and always contested legitimacy of the institution. By spending time with drafters and attending the various meetings that took place during the drafting process, she gradually gained a greater understanding of the nature of the interactions between the OHCHR, NGOs and states in general, and of the complex arts of diplomacy in particular. Although the internship provided Julie with an ideal position from which to observe other 'backstage' scenes, such as the Troika meetings which followed states' reviews, civil servants' bureaucratic work during UPR sessions and the adoptions of states' final Working Group reports in the Human Rights Council plenary, it was the UPR report drafting processes that she got to know most intimately.

Perhaps because the UPR was a new mechanism and all the actors were trying to figure out how to use it most efficiently, Julie's temporary colleagues were surprisingly reflexive and strategic regarding their work. Although work guidelines existed, each of her colleagues had developed quite personal and creative techniques for drafting documents; they also formulated arguments for defending their texts which drew, idiosyncratically, on knowledge of human rights conventions, the socio-political context of the country and their own moral commitments. At the same time, they attempted collectively to develop procedures that increased the reliability and validity of the information provided in UPR documents. Because they envisioned their role as 'keepers of the truth' (Billaud 2014), they spent considerable time strategizing how best to preserve 'the voice from the field' despite the myriad bureaucratic constraints imposed. For instance, OHCHR policy prevented drafters themselves from summarising key issues in their own words, since that was thought to give too much authorship to OHCHR staff. Thus, the Summary of Stakeholders' Contributions (also known as the Stakeholders' Summary, or simply the Summary) was approached as a 'collection of best quotes' which drafters carefully selected from the reports they had received.

Despite the drafters' concern to ensure inclusion of what they saw as a country's key human rights issues, producing the Summary was an exercise in translation according to the negotiated and agreed political requirements of this bureaucratic genre within the UN system: a set of requirements which, paradoxically, could often make the documents very difficult for the ordinary lay public to decipher. For instance, in neither of the two reports produced by the Secretariat is there much space to explain the history (for instance, of colonial domination) of the State under Review, nor its current political and economic context, such as its position within regional systems of conflict, trade or migration, the existence of wars and civil strife or its condition of indebtedness, which might be relevant for understanding its human rights situation, although such information might be included in the Compilation (if already mentioned in existing UN reports) under a section entitled 'Achievements, best practices, challenges and constraints'. The State under Review has more leeway to include this information in its National Report, as Uganda did in its Introduction and as Timor-Leste did in its General Description, but in many National Reports in the first cycle, this information was brief or entirely absent. The general lack of emphasis on history or context perpetuates an impression that discussion of what may be the root causes of a country's limited achievements in the field of human rights is somehow off-topic (Marks 2011; see also Cowan 2014: 60–62).

How is such decontextualisation justified? Within the international human rights system, the state – a form of political organisation that encompasses a very large spectrum of realities – is the primary duty-bearer, with overall responsibility for protecting and promoting human rights. Apart from vague references to the 'progressive realization' of rights, therefore, the documents do not address the material constraints faced by particular states. They remain silent on the broader economic and political context in which, for instance, developing states have to operate, including the pressures of donors, multinational corporations and international financial institutions such as the International Monetary Fund and the World Bank.

In *This Side of Silence: Human Rights, Torture and the Recognition of Cruelty*, Tobias Kelly (2011) underlines similar dynamics when it comes to evaluating, measuring and calculating acts of torture. Even though international, regional and national bodies are in place to protect individuals against torture, rarely are the personal details of torture recognised in legal proceedings. The UN Committee Against Torture, which monitors compliance with the UN Convention Against Torture and Other Cruel, Inhuman, Degrading Treatment or Punishment (CAT), moreover, tends to work with and reproduce a depoliticised definition of torture. As Kelly rightly argues: 'Human rights indicators, in the shape of statistics, legislation, and codes of practice are much easier for the Committee to deal with than the often messy day- to-day reality of prison guarding or interrogation techniques' (Kelly 2009: 778; see also Merry 2011; Merry et al. 2015). The UPR process has normalised a similar mode of engagement with 'measurable facts' at the expense of contextual analyses.

Caught between inside pressures from their management to produce more reports with fewer resources, on the one hand, and, on the other hand, outside pressures from certain states that questioned the impartiality of the information they included in their reports, drafters had to develop intricate narrative strategies for presenting human rights claims, criticisms or patterns of violation that preserved both the legitimacy of their institution and their own sense of justice and moral integrity. Moreover, they had to do this while remaining alert to state sensitivities and respecting diplomatic etiquette. During the thrice-yearly, two-week UPR sessions, the intensity of work increased dramatically; with only 48 hours between the public review and the Adoption of the Draft Report, and normally with two states being reviewed each day, OHCHR staff often worked well into the early morning hours, night after night, in order to finish the draft reports on time. As if this weren't difficult enough, OHCHR staff depended on – and were sometimes let down by – diplomatic colleagues who shared responsibility for finalising the Draft Report. Members of the Troika were supposed to assist by approaching states that had made recommendations or statements that the State under Review 'did not understand' and asking for clarification. But the efficacy of this assistance varied greatly from one review to the next – each review having a different Troika – and not infrequently some questions remained unanswered until the very last minute, adding extra stress for already exhausted OHCHR staff. For those staff, the constantly changing configuration of diplomatic actors who varied in their skills and their modes and levels of cooperation was a crucial human dimension of the context in which they attempted to fulfil their duties supporting this state-centred mechanism of human rights monitoring. It was only through Julie's participant observation at the Secretariat that such hidden struggles were revealed.

Pre-review Fieldwork in Two National Spaces: Greece and Belgium

Although our research was Geneva-based, we realised from the start that it would be essential to try to get a sense, even if a very modest one, of how the UPR was perceived and being engaged with in the national context. We thus arranged to undertake a brief period of fieldwork in two countries that were preparing for their first UPR reviews, with Jane travelling to Greece and Julie to Belgium. Jane had spent many years living and researching in Greece since 1975, and speaks Greek fluently. In addition to a broad knowledge of Greek society and history, she had also become familiar through her own research and reading over the years, and through research by a number of her doctoral students, with issues surrounding the Macedonian and Turkish/Muslim minorities. Greece interested us, moreover, as a county positioned at the margins of Europe that was facing intense popular unrest since the financial crisis, ballooning debt and Eurogroup policies forced the government to slash public spending. Belgium, by contrast, represented the administrative heart of the European Union that intriguingly, despite its apparent tranquillity, had been unable to form a government since June 2010. As in other European countries, migrants and asylum seekers, as well as linguistic minorities, were controversial issues. These two countries presented significant and intrinsically interesting human rights issues; equally important, they were 'known' to us and affordable to visit within our research budget. We hoped that by soliciting accounts of the preparations 'in country' of two reviews, we would get a 'glimpse' or a 'taste', at least, of the national process, leading to a more rounded picture and greater insight into the mechanism.

Jane drew on her forty years' worth of contacts, including many academic friends and colleagues in Thessaloniki and Athens, to gain access to some of the people and institutions that were involved in preparing for Greece's first UPR review in May 2011. She spent two weeks in these two cities in November 2010, six months before Greece's UPR review, meeting Ministry of Foreign Affairs civil servants, staff at the Greek National Commission for Human Rights, NGO representatives, human rights activists and lawyers. As for Julie, she had a large network of friends working in the human rights sector and in the European institutions in Brussels. It was relatively easy for her to get the contact details of the civil servants and NGO representatives who had taken part in the process, either through consultations with public authorities during the drafting of the Belgium National Report or through the writing of contributions to the OHCHR. Like Jane, she also spent two weeks in Belgium, 'touring' the NGOs and the federal administration, in order to get a sense of how Belgium was preparing for its UPR. These short periods of fieldwork gave us a more concrete picture of the ways in which states and civil society actors engaged – or not – with the UPR. It also gave us a greater insight into the on-the-ground meaning of terms such as 'participation', 'consultation' and 'transparency' – terms that were widely mobilised in the context of the UPR.

From these fieldtrips, we saw important variations in governments' understanding of principles of participation, consultation and transparency, and in their approaches for putting them in practice. These variations were not necessarily reducible to a government's political will to enable civil society participation, as NGO rhetoric tended to imply; they could also be linked to resources and even to the complexity of governmental structures. Whereas only a few NGOs in Greece were aware of the existence of the UPR in November 2010 and the Greek government's consultation with them did not happen until early December, by the same time in its planning process the Belgium federal government had already organised several consultations with civil society organisations. The Belgian consultations, however, remained largely symbolic and pro forma since internal consultations within the administration itself were already cumbersome. Indeed, given the federal structure of the Belgium administration, the writing of the National Report took an entire year. To complete this task, civil servants at the federal, community and regional levels were mobilised, and a coordination body called 'coor multi' was set, which met six times altogether. About fifty civil servants participated in these meetings, and ten were directly in charge of writing the report.

If the differences between these two European countries alerted us to the broader lesson that our first year of fieldwork confirmed – that governments consulted with NGOs in different ways and to widely varying degrees – we saw that NGO engagement was affected by other factors, too. NGOs might be hampered by their own lack of familiarity with this still relatively new mechanism and sometimes also by technical problems in communications with the OHCHR. Two Belgian NGOs that Julie had visited during her fieldtrip had submitted contributions for the Summary which, as Julie later learned only by virtue of her internship, OHCHR staff in charge of drafting the Summary never received. It turned out that although submitted electronically, stakeholder contributions to the OHCHR were received and registered manually, without any possibility for NGOs to verify whether their contributions had reached the right person. The Secretariat, in effect, functioned as a 'black box', a centre of circulation where documents were gathered but whose transformation processes remained hidden. As Latour convincingly argued in *Essays on Science Studies* (Latour 1999: 304), the working methods of scientists are generally made invisible by their very success. Once scientific discoveries become 'matters of fact', their internal complexity tends to be ignored and attention is redirected towards 'inputs' and 'outputs'. The opacity of the document-creating and document-negotiating processes underpinned the Secretariat's appearance as neutral and objective, qualities upon which its authority depended. Nonetheless, many NGOs complained about their contributions being watered down and decontextualised in the Summary.

In crisis-stricken Greece, where the government had to make important cuts in administrative spending, the National Report and the UPR-coordination was led by a small team of legal advisors and civil servants in the Ministry of Foreign Affairs. When, Jane visited and interviewed two of them, both of whom had extensive experience with UN and European human rights mechanisms, in November 2010, they admitted to being both daunted and excited by the holistic character of the National Report they were tasked to write, which left rather open the selection of issues to highlight. They had an established, though not tension-free, working relationship with the Greek National Commission on Human Rights, but the expectation of 'consultation' with civil society organisations was novel and intriguing for them; at that point, they had not decided how this would be handled, who they would invite and on what basis. Clearly, they were finding their way with a process which bore a family resemblance to other human rights report-writing obligations, yet was distinctive. One NGO representative who attended the early December 2010 consultation found the Ministry staff receptive to NGO representatives' suggestions on which human rights issues to cover, but she criticised the Minister who met them as surprisingly ill-informed and, in her view, insincere; she judged the consultation to be 'something they had to do', rather than demonstrating an authentic openness towards Greek civil society. The director of a Turkish minority organisation based in northeast Greece complained vociferously of being excluded altogether from any communications regarding the consultation. Staff at the Greek National Commission for Human Rights described the challenges of carrying out their work in a society where human rights were not an everyday issue: the 'defensiveness' of successive Greek governments, the 'suspicion' towards civil society activists not only on the part of governments but also of society generally, and the long road ahead before human rights activism became established as legitimate and accepted.

Fieldwork in Informal Sites and the Creation of Collaborations

Even with our focus on the UPR as a public audit ritual, our research required a lot of time spent with participants in other spaces. Alongside the formal events of the

Working Group, Adoption and UPR-related agenda items in the Human Rights Council plenary, we attended numerous 'side events'. (The two-week UPR sessions normally had a full schedule of side events thematically related to the specific reviews, most of them timetabled during the lunch break between the morning and afternoon reviews, in the meetings rooms one floor below Salle XX; many included a trolley or table of sandwiches, coffee and cakes for the quickest to arrive, and a chance to meet and chat with other participants.) We also attended occasional meetings, trainings, receptions and parties.

Most important, however, was the fieldwork we conducted in the informal spaces of the Palais des Nations where participants gathered before, after or in between reviews, when taking a break and in the weeks between the thrice-yearly UPR sessions. The Serpentine Bar, with its magnificent view on Lac Léman, was a major meeting point for diplomats to exchange information, for NGOs to lobby states' representatives and for international civil servants to exchange information. As we became more familiar with the space, we were sometimes able to join conversations around a cup of coffee and discuss the UPR informally. It was often easier to approach diplomats directly in the bar than through more formal channels such as emails or phone calls. These ad hoc discussions allowed us to get a glimpse of the 'person' behind the position and to gain a deeper understanding of the motives guiding formal statements made public during a state review. This is also how we became acquainted with the intricate rules of diplomatic etiquette and modes of sociability in an inherently transient space, where faces and positions constantly shifted.

The Palais des Nations ground floor cafeteria was another space conducive to informal exchanges with diplomats, Secretariat staff, Geneva-based NGO staff, in-country NGO representatives visiting for a few days or weeks and the interns attached to any of these kinds of organisations. Sharing a lunch with them was often the most appropriate way to follow our informants' own work pace, some of whom stayed only for short periods of time in Geneva before returning to their home country or moving on to the next internship or job. Like many academics studying and/or directly involved in the work of international organisations, the people we met led transnational lives. Moreover, for many, the UPR was just one of a myriad of activities with which they were involved. For instance, like many ambassadors of small missions to Geneva, the Ambassador of Nepal, whom Jane got to know well, juggled a diversified brief: he was responsible not only for the UPR but also for Nepal's engagement in the Human Rights Council as a whole, plus development negotiations with UNCTAD and trade negotiations with the WTO, as well as being diplomat to three countries. Children's rights charities' staff routinely dealt with UNICEF and the treaty-body system, particularly the Committee on the Rights of the Child, as well as the UPR. Many of Julie's colleagues in the OHCHR Secretariat contributed not only to the UPR but also to treaty-body reporting, to field operations and often to other parts of the human rights system. These individuals' understandings of and hopes for the UPR were informed by various factors: their experience with other human rights monitoring mechanisms, their familiarity with other international organisations and their academic and practical knowledge of international law and various national contexts. Our conversations together, therefore, were, for us, very often conversations with 'people like us' rather than with people with a radically different cultural background or worldview. Our fieldwork thus involved collaboration with people who had considerable expertise and who were themselves reflecting on and analysing, as well as producing, the human rights culture in which they were embedded; it would have been not only wrong but also counterproductive to approach them as simply sources of raw data. Although distinct from academic critical theorising, their interpretations of the UPR came to inform our own conceptualisation of the mechanism, even when we disagreed with them.

Significant epistemological and ethical questions about the practice and, indeed, the purpose of ethnography are raised when anthropologists attempt to create ethnographic descriptions of the knowledge and worldview of expert subjects whose parallel theorising already incorporates sociological analysis. Miyazaki and Riles (2007) regard the ethnographic failure that is associated with attempts at research on or with expert subjects as an 'end point' of anthropological knowledge. For an anthropological project premised upon difference, the 'epistemological sameness' between the ethnographer and her subject results in a 'failure to know the ethnographic subject' – or, rather, a failure of ethnographic knowledge to be accepted as such (Miyazaki and Riles 2007: 327). This descriptive failure arises due to the inability to 'objectify' or to 'localise' expert subjects and thus to maintain a defining distance between ethnographer and subject.

Holmes and Marcus suggest that rather than accepting this end point, ethnography can be 'refunctioned' by recourse to experts' own sceptical or self-critical moves. Writing of financial professionals doing their work, they observe a 'self-conscious critical faculty that operates ... as a way of dealing with contradictions, exception, facts that are fugitive, and that suggest a social realm not in alignment with the representations generated by the application of the reigning statistical mode of analysis' (Holmes and Marcus 2007: 237). Making use of this 'para-ethnographic' dimension of expert domains, Holmes and Marcus invite anthropologists to find a 'collaborative' mode of research among those expert subjects who are neither natives nor colleagues but, rather, counterparts (2007: 248). Anthropologists may then draw on the 'kind of illicit, marginal social thought' (2007: 237), anecdotal or intuitive, that exists among managers, international experts and field staff, scientists or consultants, whose practices are dominated by official technical discourse, yet which is deployed 'counter-culturally and critically' (2007: 241) by both privileged and subordinate actors within development systems. Anthropologists can make this a bridge 'to further the production of fundamentally anthropological knowledge' (2007: 246).

Similar forms of collaboration arose in our fieldwork, where many encounters were marked by a common desire to analyse and evaluate the potentialities and constraints of this new mechanism. We gathered from a wide range of participants, occupying a variety of roles, descriptions of their practices and experiences of the UPR. Over time, with some of them with whom we had built relationships, we shared intuitions and used them as sounding boards for our analyses. If our interlocutors did not always share our views and were often more prescriptive than we were – in the sense that they were primarily interested in assessing how well particular states complied with UPR procedures and whether they did so in good faith – they nonetheless claimed to find our approach 'really interesting', not least because we often focused on things that 'everybody knew' but 'nobody talked about'. Some of them read drafts of articles or chapters we were writing, and responded with elaborate comments. It is through these conversations and through our awareness of the very particular relationships we developed with our 'counterparts' that we have managed to fine-tune our analysis.

CONCLUSION

Anthropology is the science of bringing the tacit or implicit into consciousness – of making the invisible visible. Human rights monitoring in the UPR similarly aims to bring 'human rights situations' to light, exposing the actions of governments to 'constructive criticism' by peers in order to facilitate human rights improvement. For anthropologists such as ourselves, who also teach in European universities, the ostensibly benign practices of peer scrutiny elicit feelings of ambivalence. Being acquainted with the constant evaluation of our research, writing and teaching by our peers, we sympathise with the values audits are supposed to preserve (accountability, good governance) yet we feel uncomfortable with the real-world side-effects such auditing practices can have. In an influential article entitled 'The Tyranny of Transparency', Marilyn Strathern (2000a) reminded us that 'making society visible' involves much more than simply new technologies of visibility. She pointed out that academics trained to give an account of themselves in the context of periodic Research Assessment Exercises – these have now transmogrified into the Research Excellence Framework – in British institutions of higher education tend to anticipate what auditors will consider 'valid scientific knowledge' to the extent that a consensus is gradually built around performance criteria. Instead of being collegially discussed and decided, these criteria are simply imposed and even become naturalised for those (especially among young academics) who have never experienced a different order of things. Audits have contributed to a standardisation of research formats, as well as a new hierarchy among the previously diverse genres of academic writing, with the twenty-plus page article in an international peer-reviewed journal prioritised over all other forms of dissemination of knowledge, including edited volumes such as this one. Audits have contributed to the defining and fixing of what can and cannot be considered as scientific knowledge.

A human rights monitoring mechanism such as the UPR presents similar ambiguities: if, on the one hand, the relatively public character of the exercise has rendered human rights issues visible at the global level, it has at the same time compelled states to comply with the injunction to monitor themselves, putting in place internal procedures of action and measurement (action plans, targets, indicators) which may have unintended and sometimes even insidious consequences (see Merry 2011; Merry et al. 2015). Through peer pressure to participate and through the sharing of best practice, states are guided towards and encouraged to internalise certain norms and standards and particular approaches to talking about, defining, addressing, counting, protecting, respecting and fulfilling human rights. We have discussed these issues elsewhere (Cowan and Billaud 2015), but for the purposes of this chapter it is perhaps sufficient to say that our anthropological work on human rights monitoring aims to discern, and then to unpack, the array of micro-practices that constitute such a complex mode of governance.

By observing the people, relationships and power struggles behind the official documents, webcasts and reports – those materials that are usually used as primary sources by most researchers studying international organisations – the anthropologist can reveal, at least partially, the inner workings of the system. We believe that without first posing a more open question about the UPR, as we have done (Cowan 2014: 42–43), asking *how* it works and what it *does* – what are its effects? – it is not possible to assess *how well* it works to 'improve human rights on the ground'. This is because the UPR outcome is much more than a simple list of recommendations offered by some states to another. In fact, the key outcome is the UPR process itself, including what it sets in motion and the new phenomena that it generates. In the specific context of the UPR, these include the setting up of new institutions in charge of monitoring states at the national level (national human rights institutions), the production by states of more reports (mid-term reports on the progress of implementation of accepted recommendations), the encouragement of an arguably conflicting role of NGOs to act as 'watchdogs' prior to the review but as 'partners' (in effect, as providers of what are normally state services) in the implementation phase and, finally, a focus on quantity in human rights monitoring, rather than quality or substance, through the increasing emphasis on counting and ranking of 'recommendations'.

Anthropological research on a 'universal' human rights mechanism nonetheless remains challenging since our field is dispersed in time and space. As the second cycle of the UPR is coming to an end and the third cycle is about to start, it is difficult to predict what will become of a mechanism that is constantly reshaped as new actors enter the field and as new practices emerge. As researchers faced with time and budget constraints ourselves, we recognise that fieldwork cannot go on forever or be carried out in every corner of the planet where the UPR has generated a distinctive political field. Our aim here has been to identify certain trends in this evolving field of political action on the basis of what we can grasp 'just now'.

REFERENCES

Alston, Phillip. 2006. 'Reconceiving the UN Human Rights Regime: Challenges Confronting the New Human Rights Council'. *Melbourne Journal of International Law* 7: 185–201.
Beitz, Charles R. 2011. *The Idea of Human Rights*. Oxford: Oxford University Press.
Billaud, Julie. 2014. 'Keepers of the Truth: Producing "Transparent" Documents for the Universal Periodic Review'. In *Human Rights and the Universal Periodic Review: Rituals and Ritualism*. Hilary Charlesworth and Emma Larking, eds. Cambridge: Cambridge University Press, pp. 63–83.
Butler, Judith. 1990. *Gender Trouble*. New York and London: Routledge.
Charlesworth, Hilary. 2010. 'Swimming to Cambodia: Justice and Ritual in Human Rights after Conflict'. *Australian Year Book of International Law* 29: 1–16.
Charlesworth, Hilary and Emma Larking. 2014. 'Introduction'. *Human Rights and the Universal Periodic Review: Rituals and Ritualism*. Hilary Charlesworth and Emma Larking, eds. Cambridge: Cambridge University Press, pp. 1–21.
Cowan, Jane K. 2003. 'Who's Afraid of Violent Language? Honour, Sovereignty and Claims-making in the League of Nations'. *Anthropological Theory* 3(3): 271–291.
  2007a. 'The Success of Failure? Minority Supervision at the League of Nations'. In *Paths to International Justice: Social and Legal Perspectives*. Marie-Bénédicte Dembour and Tobias Kelly, eds. Cambridge: Cambridge University Press.
  2007b. 'The Supervised State'. *Identities: Global Studies in Culture and Power* 14(5): 545–578.
  2010. 'Coincidences as Connections: "Reading across" Disciplines while "Reading from" Anthropology'. *Focaal* 56: 99–105.
  2013. 'Before Audit Culture: A Genealogy of International Oversight of Rights'. In *The Gloss of Harmony: The Politics of Policy-making in Multilateral Organisations*. Birgit Müller, ed. London: Pluto, pp. 103–133.
  2014. 'The Universal Periodic Review as a Public Audit Ritual: An Anthropological Perspective on Emerging Practices in the Global Governance of Human Rights'. In *Human Rights and the Universal Periodic Review: Rituals and Ritualism*. Hilary Charlesworth and Emma Larking, eds. Cambridge: Cambridge University Press, pp. 42–62.
Cowan, Jane K. and Julie Billaud. 2015. 'Between Learning and Schooling: The Politics of Human Rights Monitoring at the Universal Periodic Review'. *Third World Quarterly* 36 (3): 1175–1190.
Gaer, Felice. 2007. 'A Voice, Not an Echo: Universal Periodic Review and the UN Treaty Body System'. *Human Rights Law Review* 7 (1): 109–139.
Goffman, Erving. 1969. *The Presentation of Self in Everyday Life*. London: Allen Lane.
Holmes, Douglas R. and George E. Marcus. 2007. 'Cultures of Expertise and the Management of Globalization: Toward the Re-functioning of Ethnography'. In *Global Assemblages: Technology, Politics and Ethics as Anthropological Problems*. Aihwa Ong and Stephen J. Collier, eds. Oxford: Blackwell, pp. 235–252.
Kelly, Tobias. 2009. 'The UN Committee Against Torture: Human Rights Monitoring and the Legal Recognition of Cruelty'. *Human Rights Quarterly* 31(3): 777–800.
  2011. *This Side of Silence: Human Rights, Torture and the Recognition of Cruelty*. Philadelphia: University of Pennsylvania Press.
Latour, Bruno. 1999. *Pandora's Hope: Essays on the Reality of Science Studies*. Cambridge, MA: Harvard University Press.
Marks, Susan. 2011. 'Human Rights and Root Causes'. *Modern Law Review* 74(1): 57–78.

Merry, Sally Engle. 2011. 'Measuring the World: Indicators, Human Rights and Global Governance'. *Current Anthropology* 52 (S3): S83–95.
Merry, Sally Engle, Kevin Davis, Benedict Kingsbury and Angelina Fisher. 2015. *The Quiet Power of Indicators: Measuring Governance, Corruption, and Rule of Law*. Cambridge: Cambridge University Press.
Miyazaki, Hirokazu and Annelise Riles. 2007. 'Failure as an Endpoint'. In *Global Assemblages: Technology, Politics and Ethics as Anthropological Problems*. Aihwa Ong and Stephen J. Collier, eds. Oxford: Blackwell, pp. 320–331.
Moore, Sally Falk and Barbara G. Myerhoff. 1977. *Secular Ritual*. Uitgeverij: Van Gorcum.
Niezen, Ronald. 2010. *Public Justice and the Anthropology of Law*. Cambridge: Cambridge University Press.
OHCHR, Office of the High Commissioner for Human Rights. 2014. *The Universal Periodic Review: A Practical Guide for Civil Society*. Geneva.
Power, Michael. 1999. *The Audit Society: Rituals of Verification*. Oxford: Oxford University Press.
Rose, Nikolas. 1999. *Powers of Freedom: Reframing Political Thought*. Cambridge: Cambridge University Press.
Shore, Cris and Susan Wright. 1999. 'Audit Culture and Anthropology: Neoliberalism in British Higher Education'. *Journal of the Royal Anthropological Institute* 5(4): 557–575.
Shoukry, Sameh, Mohammed Abu Koash and Masood Khan. 2008. 'Non-paper on Remaining UPR Modalities', submitted by the African, Arab and OIC groups'. Available from the Universal Periodic Review Extranet.
Strathern, Marilyn. 2000a. 'The Tyranny of Transparency'. *British Educational Research Journal* 26(3): 309–321.
  2000b. *Audit Cultures: Anthropological Studies in Accountability, Ethics and the Academy*. London: Routledge.

6

Meeting "the World" at the Palais Wilson: Embodied Universalism at the UN Human Rights Committee

Miia Halme-Tuomisaari

Finally the doors of the main conference room at the Palais Wilson swing open. The crowd rushes forward in uncharacteristic haste; the group is larger than usual, and slow movers will likely be left without seats. Consisting of people with differing shades of complexion and textures of hair who have traveled to this occasion from all around the world, the group embodies "the universal" that is the bedrock of human rights ideology and UN operations. The group has been waiting in the corridors patiently, yet in palpable anxiety. Participants were supposed to be allowed in an hour ago, but the Committee's previous hearing had run exceptionally late. It is the first day of yet another session of the UN Human Rights Committee, which is the expert body responsible for monitoring compliance with the International Covenant on Civil and Political Rights (ICCPR). The stage is once again set for the subsequent weeks of "ritual and ritualism" (Charlesworth and Larking 2014), also known as UN treaty body proceedings.

Inside the conference venue the air is dense; if only someone had opened the windows for a few minutes in between sessions. The conference room located on the first floor of the Palais Wilson – former headquarters of the International League of Nations and today the headquarters of the UN Office for the High Commissioner for Human Rights in Geneva – is spacious and usually more than adequate to accommodate the audience that follows the Committee's proceedings. The painstakingly detailed sessions of UN treaty bodies are not the biggest tourist attraction of this grand global organization, to put things mildly. Yet today things are different, as the room is packed to the very last seat. Eyes are fixed to the front, expressions somber; a few beads of sweat already run down nervous foreheads. The shared importance of the moment is tangible.

This chapter has benefitted from generous funding by the Academy of Finland project "Human Rights: Law, Religion, Subjectivity" in 2009–2012, the Department of Law and Anthropology, Max Planck Institute for Social Anthropology, in 2013, the venture Bodies of Evidence: Biotechnologies, narratives and documents (2014–2016, Kone Foundation), and the Law Faculty of the University of Turku, Finland. Warm thanks to comments on an earlier draft to this volume's editors, Ronald Niezen and Maria Sapignoli, as well as all the participants of the authors' meeting at McGill in April–May 2015.

Then, the session opens with a sharp bang of the chair's gavel. Seated far at the front, and barely audible without earphones, he declares this hearing of NGOs open, informing those present of the two-minute time limit for their statements. All those with previous experience know that this limit is to be respected; those attempting to exceed it will be cut off. The session to follow will prove once again that, whereas most NGO delegates have done their homework well and prepared statements tailored to this short duration, a few will find themselves silenced in the middle of articulating urgent concerns. Some experienced delegates clearly take advantage of the mildly confrontational occurrence of being stopped by the chair after their time is up, skillfully employing it as an opportunity to add urgency to the issues that they represent as being just *slightly* more compelling than those presented by others. Many read their statements with confidence and skill; a few voices of first-timers tremble. NGO interventions soon form a steady stream of statements interspersed with customary UN jargon, with each one attempting to grasp the attention of the UN experts seated at the front to highlight the wrongs of which governments around the world are guilty.

This scene embodies one of the most cherished elements of UN treaty body hearings. More concretely, the above sketch describes a specific session of the "most prestigious" of all UN treaty bodies – the Human Rights Committee – which is closed to state representatives and features NGO delegates from around the world. The session in question is the shared NGO hearing on the reports on Russia, Cambodia, the Ivory Coast and Cypress – a two-hour event made up of two-minute speeches by NGO representatives prepared in advance. Simultaneously, the above description builds on material acquired via participant observation from similar sessions from the 108th and 109th session of the Human Rights Committee from 2013. This shared hearing of NGOs is one of the two types of events in which NGOs can formally participate in the sessions of the Human Rights Committee. The other category is the smaller, one-hour lunch-time briefings arranged for NGOs and Committee members – events that are likewise closed off from state representatives, on which I elaborate later.

The explicit purpose of the above session is to allow direct interactions between treaty body members and NGO delegates – or interactions that are as direct as the contours of these elaborate international meetings permit. Once a rarity, now these NGO sessions form a staple in UN treaty body sessions, or at least the program of the Human Rights Committee. States may be the only formal parties to UN human rights treaties, yet, as these sessions testify, they certainly hold no monopoly in the dialogue they have with the UN Committees.

What, fundamentally, is going on in these sessions? Why do these exchanges between this high-profile UN body and NGOs exist? What about UN treaty body sessions in general? What kind of roles might they have beyond the most evident ones? I have also addressed these questions earlier (Halme-Tuomisaari 2012; 2013a; 2013b), and my arguments thus far could be summarized as follows: although formally the most important element – the raison d'etre – of UN treaty body proceedings is the exchange of information on how state parties to UN human rights covenants realize their obligations as parties to UN human rights treaties, these sessions hold also numerous "informal" reasons for existing.

I have in previous instances examined these reasons from the perspective of knowledge: how moments that appear as empty from the perspective of information exchange in fact embody sharp tensions over which type of data – and presented by whom – is accepted as reliable information by UN treaty bodies, and, in contrast, what kind of data – and from whom – is dismissed as propaganda (Halme-Tuomisaari 2013a). I am continuing this analysis by linking these moments to their intrinsic role in initiating "dialogue," and thus sustaining perpetual movement as one of the most fundamental purposes of the UN treaty body system (Halme-Tuomisaari 2013b).

In this chapter I develop yet another approach as I link these moments that transpire between NGO delegates and UN experts into one of the most crucial concepts of the entire contemporary human rights phenomenon: universalism (Alfredsson 1999; Morsink 2000; Lauren 2011). Rather than seeing it as a condition grounded in ideology or culture, or even the consequence of geographic spread, I discuss universalism as a dynamic entity, the outcome of specific types of action engaged in by key human rights actors at the global centers of human rights. I link the notion of universalism to NGO interventions as tangible evidence of the "curious grapevine" that Eleanor Roosevelt felt would be needed for bringing the abstract provisions of the Universal Declaration of Human Rights (UDHR) to life, as has been recounted by William Korey. In his treatises, Korey has shown how today this position is commonly seen as having being filled by NGOs (Korey 2001).

My discussion of universalism finds wider context in my recent work on the history of human rights. The first angle relates to the role that "the myth of universalism" holds in descriptions over the history of human rights (Halme-Tuomisaari and Slotte 2015). The second angle relates to the drafting history of the UDHR, and how in reality its "universalism" is likewise an attractive myth, not an empirical fact (Halme-Tuomisaari 2015). The latter angle also has distinct consequences for analysis of human rights action today: it appears as being equipped with a distinctly expansionistic dynamic (Halme-Tuomisaari 2010a; 2010b). Simultaneously, "universality" is cast as a delicate entity that requires constant maintenance and cultivation.

In this chapter I discuss this process by focusing on the concrete, physical bodies of NGO representatives gathered at UN sessions. I examine in particular the role that they hold in sustaining and reproducing the ideal of human rights as "universal," simultaneously preserving this ideal's continued legitimacy. I discuss examples from treaty body sessions that emphasize the importance of this embodied "universal representation." Further, I glance at moments in which this representation is actively supported – cultivated, even – by key actors "at the center," that is to say, the insiders of Geneva-based UN human rights bureaucracies as well as – surprisingly – state actors who act as activist "intermediaries"(Merry 2006).

In many ways it appears odd, in this scholarly moment in time, to dedicate such excessive attention to a concept that feels outdated, trite, even irrelevant. Yet, I argue, universality has both continuous, multi-faceted importance as well as significant unexplored dimensions, which could be summarized as follows: today it is evident that – in terms of geographic spread – human rights form "universal" notions that are a staple of political rhetoric, even in most national legislation throughout the world. Ratification of UN human rights treaties enjoys virtual universality, in that some of them have been ratified by all, or close to all, states of the world. Simultaneously, human rights NGOs exist today in most parts of the world.

These observations can be recognized as key ingredients in impatient statements that wish to silence, once and for all, the nagging voices of "relativism" that attempt to continually challenge the genuine "universal essence" of human rights ideology (Alfredsson 1999). Universalism and relativism, of course, form the most persistent adversarial pair within the contemporary phenomenon that has formed around human rights since the post–World War II era. To elaborate this train of thought, the objective "universal" spread of human rights legislation, covenant ratifications and advocacy organizations thus becomes evidence of the intrinsic "universality" of human rights ideals as something that is common to humankind the world over. Simultaneously, such an approach leaves many things unexplored. Just how and by what processes – both on the micro and macro levels – have human rights ideas spread globally, first in terms of state ratifications of human rights treaties, then in incorporation of human rights notions in national legislations? How have human rights NGOs been created around the world – by whom, via what kind of international processes, and with what kind of financial support? How is the continued relevance of UN human rights monitoring as truly universal ascertained in action?

All of these questions have been discussed by recent anthropological work on human rights (see, among others, Merry 2006; Rottenburg 2009; Englund 2006; Allen 2013; Dembour and Kelly 2007; Kelly 2011; Curtis 2014; Cowan 2013). I contribute to this work by arguing that these questions have more than historical implications, and instead hold continued relevance for a deeper understanding of the contemporary human rights phenomenon today – and in the future. This chapter analyzes these questions via the minute details of action in what I argue continually forms one of the global "centers" of human rights work. The concepts of center and periphery are familiar from the world systems analysis of Immanuel Wallerstein, who has utilized them to describe structural positions in a world economy (Wallerstein 2004). Ulf Hannerz has expanded the significance of these concepts to the flow of meanings, which is also the principal sense in which they are utilized in this chapter, similarly to my earlier work (Hannerz 1993; Halme-Tuomisaari 2010c: 34).

The center–periphery dynamic borrows also from Sally Merry's influential analysis of the human rights regime. Merry characterizes transnational consensus building characteristic to the international human rights regime as something that occurs in a social space – a center – where actors from all parts of the world come together. This space has its own norms, values and cultural practices; it is an English-speaking, largely secular, universalistic, law-governed culture organized around the formal equality of nations as well as their economic and political inequality (Merry 2006).

In many ways the center(s) of the human rights phenomenon can be construed as being "de-territorialized," and thus temporary centers may emerge in any place that becomes the site of transnational human rights activity, such as a large international, high-profile meeting of human rights experts and policy makers. Yet a few more permanent centers can also be identified, the most important ones in the UN context being the organization's headquarters in New York and Geneva, the geographic focus of this chapter's analysis.

My analysis focuses on the proceedings of the "most prestigious" of all UN treaty bodies – namely, the Human Rights Committee monitoring compliance with the ICCPR – located at the headquarters of the UN High Commissioner for Human Rights at the Palais Wilson in Geneva, former headquarters of the League of Nations. Further, this chapter examines how the processes to produce universalism at this center disseminate into different parts of the world, and thus how *universalism of human rights in action* is also an empirical consequence of active cultivation by key actors at the "center." Thus, the notion of universalism discussed in this chapter also connects to the impact that UN treaty body work has around the world.

Ultimately, the focus of this chapter has been an outcome of the data that emerged as relevant in my fieldwork. Contrary to increasingly dominant trends in academia in general and anthropology specifically, my fieldwork has not been conducted with a definite "action plan" in mind, namely a list of just what and whom I would be observing in my field, via exactly what method and theory. Rather, my research over the past decade has been and remains loosely directed by the same over-arching questions: How should we understand the vast global phenomenon that has formed around the discourse and ideology of human rights after World War II? What kind of visions of a new world order are presented by the institutional frameworks created around this discourse and ideology? What kind of fantasies, utopias and fears do key actors in these frameworks seek to both realize and suppress?[1]

[1] It is with this set of questions that I have observed human rights expertise, knowledge and learning in a Nordic context (Halme-Tuomisaari 2010c). In 2010 I moved onto studying documentary practices around human rights reports produced at the Finnish Foreign Ministry and processed by UN Human Rights Treaty Bodies (Halme-Tuomisaari 2012), and in 2013 I commenced an ethnography of the UN Human Rights Committee. This same set of questions has guided me to the past, specifically to the archives of the International League for the Rights of Man, the first human rights NGO in the 1940s, and lobbying efforts for a document then known as the International Bill for the Rights of Man, which in 1948 became the Universal Declaration of Human Rights.

In other words, my fieldwork at the Human Rights Committee redirected my attention to the notion of "universality." This fieldwork brought to life this slogan that felt familiar yet empty from much of the "mainstream" human rights scholarship that I first encountered a decade and a half ago. Via my ethnographic data, this concept acquired a dynamic quality as a fascinating, often unarticulated category, an ideal held by the actors at my multi-sited field, further finding a distinct presence in the continually negotiated relationship of the "center" and "peripheries" of the contemporary human rights phenomenon. As my fieldwork progressed, universality became cast as a delicate entity that has a complex plural existence, accompanied by a fragility that needs special cultivation and protection.

INTRODUCTION TO THE HUMAN RIGHTS COMMITTEE AND THE UN TREATY BODY SYSTEM

Despite its decades of existence, the UN treaty body system remains little-known outside the UN framework. Very briefly, in the absence of an international court of human rights with universal jurisdiction – a UN-operated equivalent of the European Court of Human Rights, for example – human rights treaty bodies are the highest authoritative bodies of the UN to address human rights violations – or, rather, state compliance with treaty-based obligations. Ten treaty bodies exist today, of which the best-known are the Committees on ICERD (the International Convention on the Elimination of All Forms of Racial Discrimination) and ICEDAW (the International Convention on Ending All Forms of Discrimination Against Women), as well as ICESCR (the International Covenant on Economic, Social and Cultural Rights) and the Human Rights Committee monitoring compliance with the ICCPR (the International Covenant on Civil and Political Rights).

In recent years, the treaty body system has been significantly overshadowed in visibility by the newcomer of UN monitoring practices, the Universal Periodic Review by the Human Rights Council (Cowan 2014; Billaud 2014; Charlesworth and Larking 2014). The fundamental difference between these two monitoring systems is that treaty bodies are based on contractual obligations and are thus "legal" – even if the relationship of treaty body work and "the law" is a significantly complex matter. The UPR, by contrast, is thoroughly "political," even if human rights treaty obligations and the work of treaty bodies are frequently highlighted in them. The treaty body system as a whole is currently under review (Pillay 2012; UN Office for the High Commissioner for Human Rights n.d.), with influential voices supporting its unification – a plan starkly opposed by others as it is seen to diminish the bite of this monitoring mechanism. A large internal review of the matter is scheduled for 2020, and with the remodeling of the UN Human Rights *Commission* into the *Council* it would not be surprising to see dramatic changes in the composition of treaty bodies as well – even if a significant modification would be more complicated to execute due to the covenant-bound nature of treaty body mandates.

The Human Rights Committee was founded in 1976 in accordance with treaty provisions when the ICCPR entered into force. The Committee's mandate is based on covenant provisions, as is the case with most other treaty bodies. The Committee's operations as a part of public international law are best contextualized by recent contributions to international law, many of which summarize the general "forward looking progressive ethos" of much human rights scholarship (Bayefsky 2000; Kamminga and Scheinin 2009; Crawford 2010; Cassese 2012; Bassiouni and Schabas 2011; Simmons 2009). That the Human Rights Committee is regarded as the most authoritative of all the UN treaty bodies finds succinct echo in the Committee's title: where the names of all the other treaty bodies are more restricted and linked to the substance of the covenants that they monitor – the Committee on the Elimination of All Forms of Discrimination Against Women (CEDAW), as one example –the very name of the Human Rights Committee indicates a certain generality: it addresses "human rights" in their full scope.

The Human Rights Committee has 18 members, nominated for candidacy by their governments and selected as members by elections via processes that remain a combination of state politics and respect for their personal, independent human rights expertise. Echoing the overall porous nature of the treaty body system as well as its somewhat obscure impact is the fact that, whereas the actual work of the Human Rights Committee, like other UN treaty bodies, occurs today predominantly in Geneva, elections for membership occur at the UN headquarters in New York and are conducted solely by states. This practice produces a curious disconnect between the work of the Committee and the procedures through which its composition is determined. Thus, exactly who gets nominated to treaty bodies and why remains obscure, even to members of the treaty bodies themselves as well as the personnel at the UN secretariat who handle the practical work around their operations. This reality also contributes to the importance of the Secretariat in creating a sense of continuity in Committee proceedings on a practical level.

Like other UN treaty bodies, the Human Rights Committee convenes annually in three sessions of four to five weeks, three weeks of which are open to the public. The primary and most visible part of treaty body work is the processing of periodic reports submitted by state parties in public sessions, which are also open to NGOs and other observers, such as scholars. These sessions are concerned with how states comply with the provisions of the human rights treaty in question. The intervals for periodic reports are today defined by the Committee. In practice, the Human Rights Committee invites states to submit periodic reviews at intervals of between five to ten years, and on this basis examines how the state has met the obligations that it has undertaken as a party to the ICCPR. It also assesses how state compliance has changed from the previous evaluation. In reality, many states fall behind in these obligations, and some have never participated in treaty body proceedings, all problems which – together with the low visibility and compliance with the Committee's work – pose serious problems, giving rise to the aforementioned pressures to reform their work fundamentally (Krommendijk 2014).

In each session, the Committee processes between five and eight periodic reports submitted by states. In addition, it issues documents known as Concluding Observations, in which the Committee compliments and reproaches states for their conduct, forwarding suggestions for improvement. The other principal element of Committee work is to process individual petitions, which occurs in closed sessions and is both referred to and considered as the most "court-like" of the Committee's operations. In addition, the Human Rights Committee produces General Comments, which are elaborate statements intended to clarify the meanings of specific treaty provisions due to legislative and other changes, including the work done by the Committee itself, which have occurred in the four decades since the covenant entered into force.

Participants of treaty body sessions fall into five main categories: (1) expert members of the Committees, who in the case of the Human Rights Committee are commonly (male) law professors; (2) members of state delegations, who, with few exceptions, only participate in the "constructive dialogue" of their states; (3) members of the UN Secretariat, including the secretary of the Committee and her staff; (4) members of UN Conference Services, including press secretaries and interpreters who jointly oversee that the sessions run fluently; and (5) outside audience. Of these categories – and with the exception of introductory speeches and short occasional informational announcements made by the UN Secretariat – only members of the Committee and State delegations have the possibility to make oral interventions (with the evident exception of interpreters). Thus NGOs – which fall into the fifth category – are without formal possibilities for public interventions. Yet, in other significant ways they are included in the program – including the two hearing categories already outlined – and thus hold important possibilities for making interventions of diverse kinds.

NGOs AS "PHYSICAL CHECK-UP LISTS"

It's two pm and the doors of the meeting room close. The NGO lunch briefing – open only to members of the Human Rights Committee, their assistants, representatives of NGOs from the state whose periodic report is to be processed next, and staff of the UN secretariat – is about to start. It is *hot* in the room. Someone opens the window. In the background, distant sounds of protests unfold in a language impossible to identify. This is unusual, as protests usually stay further up the hill, in front of the Palais des Nations, the Geneva headquarters of the UN. No demonstrators are visible, and it is impossible to make out what their complaints are about. Soon the traffic of the lakeside road muffles the sound of the protesters. Someone closes the window, and silence sets in.

The mid-sized meeting room has ornate ceilings and is divided by a large, oval-shaped table. One can easily imagine that, for decades, meetings of high-caliber international diplomacy have been held in the room. On the side of the doorway sit eight members of the Human Rights Committee; the scorching afternoon sun entering through the large windows facing the lake must feel uncomfortable in their eyes. The remainder of the room is filled to the brim with representatives of NGOs from the country in question, as well as a few representatives of international NGOs from their headquarters, often from London or Geneva. This is the most intimate encounter that takes place between NGO representatives and Committee members, and is usually the only moment in which they see each other face-to-face – excluding the fact that they often have lunch at adjoining tables in the cafeteria located down the hallway, oblivious to each other's presence.

A middle-aged delegate, evidently a seasoned conference participant, opens the session, briefly introducing herself and the NGOs present. After that, there are short statements by other NGO delegates, many presented in fluent English and professionally organized in such as way as to indicate strong familiarity with the forms containing practical information for Committee members. Other statements are forwarded with heavy accents and flawed grammar, in prose that makes identifying relevant pieces of factual information a strenuous task for Committee members. Committee members listen attentively; a few look visibly exhausted. These four weeks of sessions, from 10am to 6pm, often extended with breakfast meetings and dinners, as well as reading and drafting work in the evenings, take their toll. Yet, all signs of fatigue vanish as the Committee members begin their round of questions after preliminary statements have been forwarded by NGO delegates.

These hearings are closed off from state representatives – allegedly, there have been instances in which NGO representatives faced reprisal from states as a consequence of having presented unfavorable information on the state to UN treaty bodies. Thus, I will offer no further detail here on which state this particular hearing regards. Simultaneously, such detail is not relevant for the current debate: rather than highlighting distinctiveness, this ethnographic glimpse holds importance in illustrating commonalities in the current analysis of "universalism" of human rights action. In this instance, the actual presence of NGO participants and their capability to embody "the international" becomes relevant. What is going on in these proceedings? Why are they so important? I have previously addressed similar questions in a desire to gain a more profound understanding of the numerous layers attached to treaty body proceedings – how, instead of merely functioning as sites of information exchange, treaty body proceedings entail, among other things, intense contestations over who has the capacity to make legitimate representations in front of UN bodies on behalf of distinct populations. Using the example of China, I have argued that its single-party regime, seen widely by the international community as being constitutionally illegitimate (Simpson 2004), also reduces China's capacity to offer information that is seen as reliable in UN treaty body proceedings (Halme-Tuomisaari 2013a).

Whereas the official purpose of treaty body proceedings is to transfer knowledge on how states comply with covenant obligations, in reality this function is more complicated – a finding that certainly applies to these NGO hearings that take place only moments before the public "constructive dialogue," as it is known in Committee parlance. This "constructive dialogue" is exchanged between Committee members and state representatives in the public session held at the main conference room of the Palais Wilson. Given the extensive preparation that takes place in anticipation of this dialogue, the timing of these closed NGO meeting raises important questions on the nature of these exchanges – what happens in these meetings from the perspective of information transfer?

In principle, in treaty body proceedings Committee members and NGOs are "on the same side": the mandate of both is broadly to safeguard the well-being of humanity whereas, unfailingly, in these proceedings the state is cast as "the bad guy." Information presented by NGOs is predominantly treated with great respect and it holds a high status as a source of reliable information, echoing the general position of NGOs in the contemporary human rights phenomenon. Thus, the dynamic of the NGO briefings is in general strongly set toward a positive exchange. However, this underlying dynamic by no means suggests that NGO representatives are "in for a picnic" in these lunch-time hearings –Committee members frequently come across as rather strict. Their questions are sharp, and target surprisingly minute details of national legislation as well as recent local events; often, Committee members request exact statistics or figures, such as the number of inmates of a given prison. Evidently, this exchange is not suited for dilettantes, and offering satisfactory answers is challenging even for the most well-versed of NGO delegates. In discussions after these hearings, many NGO delegates confess to feeling surprised, even overwhelmed, by the level precision sought by Committee members.

Wide differences in their professional profiles might contribute to the evident nervousness accompanying these hearings: whereas members of the Human Rights Committee are leading international experts in their fields, many NGO representatives are very young, often taking their first aspiring professional steps as NGO workers or interns. Occasionally the hearings resemble oral university exams, as NGO delegates sometimes remark afterward – an understandable comparison as most Committee members serve as university professors outside Committee sessions. Yet it is not solely because of these background profiles or the pleasure of exam giving and taking that results in this dynamic. It is more likely linked to the function that these proceedings hold as "personified check-up lists."

This point becomes understandable from a continued overview of the "formal" description of treaty body work that I began earlier. Officially, the most important role of NGOs in the proceedings is to submit ancillary or "shadow" reports to complement periodic reports submitted by states. Ideally, NGO reports are submitted simultaneously or close to state reports; both genres of documents are deposited publicly at the UN website and disseminated to Committee members prior to the constructive dialogue taking place between state parties and the Committee. Overall, the weight given to NGO reports is significant, and they hold the important capacity not only to contest the veracity of information offered by states in their reports, but, as was already mentioned, also gain importance also for their ability to challenge the state's capacity to make legitimate representations over the population that the state reports target. Thus, Committee members often rely on them extensively as they prepare for the constructive dialogue with state representatives.

Yet the influence that NGOs hold in treaty body proceedings does not end with these written documents. Some additional detail illustrates this point: state reports are submitted around 18 months before being processed by the Committee in the "constructive dialogue" described earlier. For example, the periodic report of Finland, processed by the Human Rights Committee in the July session of 2013, which was the 108th session of the Committee, was submitted by Finland in late Autumn 2011. The deadlines for NGO submissions are slightly later, but they should ideally arrive a full year before the oral exchange takes place in Geneva. The interim period between submission of documents and their processing in the "constructive dialogue" now includes one additional round of documentary exchanges, as the Committee sends state parties clarifying questions, to which states commonly send complementary information. These clarifying questions are linked to the "List of Issues" adopted by the Committee two sessions prior to the actual constructive dialogue with the state party – with regard to the report of Finland, the List of Issues was adopted in the October session of 2012, in the 106th Session of the Committee.

Adopting the List of Issues is the one moment in which the impact of NGOs may be the greatest. Today at the Human Rights Committee this phase includes direct consultations with NGOs, and often the concerns elevated by NGOs in these consultations will be strongly reflected in the issues that are eventually addressed by the Committee in its constructive dialogue with the state. Participating in these preliminary hearings for the adoption of the List of Issues is tricky, however, mainly because receiving funding for this purpose is difficult. Most commonly, funds are available primarily for NGOs to attend the actual sessions. Thus, for example, with regard to the report of Finland, I found that no Finnish NGO representatives were present physically in the 106th Session when the List of Issues was adopted.

Simultaneously, the weight of *any* individual moment in these proceedings is restricted, as these steps are by their nature cyclical and all individual steps conjoin with the preceding and subsequent ones. This not only illustrates the intrinsic difference between treaty body proceedings and court proceedings, it also concretizes an important overall purpose: to create a movement of forward-looking progressiveness in which individual moments receive their importance in their capacity to connect seemingly isolated events into a continuum of "dialogue" (Halme-Tuomisaari 2013a; Riles 1998).

In this ongoing dialogue, the role of the UN Secretariat is crucial, and is perhaps the most under-represented element in all the scholarship on treaty bodies and UN human rights monitoring more generally (for an important exception, see Billaud 2014). In reality, preparing the background material needed in treaty body sessions, including the preparation of "Lists of Issues," is done by individual members of the Secretariat. One central technique for carrying out this task is to go over previous reports on the given state by other UN treaty bodies, and incorporate relevant issues and recommendations that these reports have raised with appropriate modifications and elaborations. This task is complemented by updated information on developments that have occurred since, and often involves straightforward copy-and-pasting. In updating previous documents, the information provided by NGO ancillary reports holds significant importance, in addition to data gathered by UN regional offices, for example.

The crucial role of the Secretariat in this background work contributes to the "dialogical" or chain-like nature of treaty body proceedings. Individual members of the Secretariat are well positioned for this task as they are likely responsible for preparing background material for two or even three treaty bodies at any one time – thus, one member of the Secretariat may be in charge of preparing the background material on, say, Belize, as well for the Committee on CERD and for the Human Rights Committee. Consequently, there is a likelihood that they have personally prepared the material on a given state's report for another treaty body previously, and it is on the basis of their own work that they then draft new background material for Committee work.

All these findings bring us back to the NGO lunch-time briefing that opened this section, allowing us to re-examine what transpires in it, particularly its qualities of oral exams and functioning as a "personal check-up list." What does this latter characterization mean in light of these proceedings? How do these NGO briefings appear in light of information exchange? In essence, it casts their nature differently: instead of moments where fundamentally new information is introduced by NGOs to Committee members, they are moments in which Committee members test and confirm whether the information they have received from various NGO reports on specific detailed events, statistics or legislative reforms is accurate.

These face-to-face interactions, in other words, offer moments for the Committee members to test whether the understanding that they have acquired of, say, the number of inmates at a given prison, or the percentage of children from a specific ethnic background that continue into higher education, from the massive background information for each state report is accurate. This also explains the occasional severity that characterizes the tenor of the Committee members: examined from this perspective, NGO representatives are the last "test ground" for Committee members before they engage state representatives in the oral exchange, using knowledge as the weapon with which to address the state and its potentially fraudulent portrayal of reality: they are the last moment to stock up on the arsenal with which, moments later, they go into the main conference room and the public session of *constructive dialogue* to engage with state representatives.

In this capacity, they bring to mind Marilyn Strathern's analysis of university mission statements: she finds that one approach for making sense of why institutions of higher education produce documents which, from the viewpoint of information, are nonsense, is to regard them as "bullet-proofing," in an echo of the analysis of John and Jane Comaroff (Strathern 2006; Comaroff and Comaroff 1992). In a similar vein, these NGO hearings come across as physical check-up lists with which Committee members fortify their armor for the constructive dialogue in between state parties and itself. Simultaneously, these hearings also hold another kind of importance, connecting this discussion to the notion of embodied universality, as I discuss next.

FINLAND'S REPORT AND "CENTRALLY" SPONSORED "PERIPHERAL" PARTICIPATION

Is there anyone here who knows of the situation of the Roma people in Finland? What about claims that the Finnish government was aware of Guantanamo Bay prisoner transfer flights by the US military through Finnish air space? The treatment of under-aged asylum seekers? LGTBI-issues, gender-corrective surgery and forced sterilization?

(Fieldnotes, UN Human Rights Committee)

Committee members look inquisitively at the NGO representatives seated on the opposite side of the oval table. The representatives squirm slightly; these issues do not fall under their competence and thus they have no information to share. It is yet another hot afternoon during the 107th Session of the Committee in July 2013. The week has been an intense one, with reports from numerous high-profile states with conflicting human rights records. The seats of the main conference room have been consistently packed, as have the NGO hearings taking place in this smaller meeting room. The contrast between the charged atmosphere of the NGO hearings and this one could not be more pointed, even if the NGO delegates present are no less committed to forwarding their causes. With slight reluctance, so it seems, Committee members abandon their questions, and the meeting is declared to be over.

This hearing on Finland has not been the greatest triumph among NGO briefings. In the end, there were only three people in the room representing Finnish NGOs – and of those, only one was from Finland himself: the representative of the Sami people. The other two NGO delegates were a representative of the Sami people from Sweden – the Sami people inhabit a unified geographic territory, which extends to the regions of Finland, Norway and Sweden – and a representative of a Geneva-based single-issue NGO focusing on conscientious objectors. A representative of another Geneva-based NGO focusing on LGTBI issues and collaborating with a Finnish-based NGO was due to appear, but she never showed up. In discussion afterward, NGO participants wonder whether the tepid quality of this hearing will resonate with the forthcoming constructive dialogue between the state delegation of Finland and the Committee. Were this to be the case, the Committee could easily be excused: how could it possibly spend an equivalent time discussing the human rights situation in Finland as the situation of Indonesia or Ukraine, both of which were discussed during the same week, a seasoned member of the Human Rights Committee remarks humorously.

These predictions, however, prove to be grossly misguided as the exchange between Finland and the Committee in no way lags in intensity when compared to the constructive dialogue on states with far more evident human rights violations to account for. In fact, the hearing is almost exceptionally precise – it feels as if the legal predictability, high degree of available quantified data and the overall bureaucratization of the Finnish state machinery form an ideal match for the monitoring instrument that the Committee embodies. Ultimately, the "constructive dialogue" ironically exceeds the time reserved for it – even if, admittedly, only because of the verbose final statement of the Finnish delegation head.

As the intense one-day hearing concludes with yet another bang of the chair's gavel, all parties exit from the conference room with smiles of satisfaction. Members of the Finnish state delegation – both directly afterward as well as in discussion a year and more after the fact – compliment the Committee on the fact that it had, as a whole, been very well informed. Save for a few questions that – the Finnish state delegates note with dismay – "circulate from one UN report on Finland to the next," and with the exception of one particularly lengthy question focusing on gender inequality that most labeled as totally incomprehensible, the questions raised by the Committee were seen as being on-point and relevant. Also, most of the recommendations in the Concluding Observations issued by the Committee were approved of, even if some more experienced state representatives again raised charges of the "same old," which they say applies to most UN treaty body documents on Finland. Committee members, in turn, praised the state delegates for their careful advance preparation and diligence – although the high number of internal committees that the Finnish civil servants have the habit of highlighting as solutions to problems of various kinds was not left unnoticed.

In all, the parties agreed that this constructive dialogue was a success – save for one element: that there were practically no NGOs from Finland physically present to participate in the NGO briefing or listen in on the constructive dialogue. This fact came up in numerous discussions with members of the Committee and the UN Secretariat in retrospect, and it was singled out as the sole disappointment of these proceedings on Finland. The absence of NGOs also manifested itself in the public session of constructive dialogue with the Finnish state delegation. Throughout the day, the mood of the audience was, to put things mildly, calm: only a handful of people were seated at the audience section, and there were virtually no genuine "outsiders" – that is, no people who were present solely because of professional tasks linked directly to the Committee's session.

More specifically, during the constructive dialogue on Finland, there were only the customary representatives of UN conference and press services seated at the back, as well as a few interns of Committee members. The Geneva-based umbrella NGO targeting the work of the Human Rights Committee in general was stationed at the seats reserved for it; the "Committee anthropologist" was present, diligently taking notes of the goings-on – but again because of scholarly interest, not because of embodying a member of the genuine "outside world." In addition, only the same three NGO delegates who participated in the NGO briefing were present, valiantly representing "the world" and "embodying the universal" in the midst of a sea of empty seats.

Why were there no other NGOs present, and why was the contrast so notable with the proceedings on numerous other states? Certainly, with Finland being relatively close to Switzerland, Finnish NGOs could find the means for this journey, which, on a global scale, is of modest expense. Or so one might assume. Yet discussions with Finnish human rights NGOs "back home" consistently highlighted the difficulties in summoning resources for attending. The airfare from Helsinki to Geneva may be a modest expenditure, but Geneva is one of the world's most expensive cities, and thus carving out money to attend is no simple matter for NGOs, even for a relatively prosperous state such as Finland.

Ironically, this material reality also manifested itself in the only Finnish NGO representative who *was* present: the aforementioned representative of the Sami Council. Her presence was paid for by the Finnish Foreign Affairs Ministry. This finding might come as unexpected, even troubling. As has been highlighted, the presence of NGOs serves a vital purpose in these proceedings precisely *because* of their independence from states – it is only because of this independence that NGOs are invested with their legitimate position as challengers of the veracity of information offered by states and are widely seen as representatives of humanity. As this chapter has shown, protecting this independence is engraved in the work of the Committee and the Secretariat through sessions closed to state representatives – the exclusive purpose of which is to ensure the integrity and even concrete physical safety of NGO representatives who appear before the UN Committee with possible sensitive information on the state's conduct. Are these functions and the entire division of labor that gives this monitoring mechanism its legitimacy compromised if the participation of NGOs is paid for by states? And why would a state organ pay for the presence of an NGO at a UN treaty body in the first place?

Answers to these questions are in part linked to the status of the state of Finland as a "model student" of the UN human rights framework (Halme-Tuomisaari 2010a) – a status cherished by Finnish civil servants and also frequently commented on by members of the Committee and UN Secretariat with regard to Finland's report. Because of this status, Finland's collaboration with NGOs is viewed not as something compromising the integrity of NGO representation, but, rather, as strengthening the adherence of the state of Finland to international human rights commitments. As I have discussed elsewhere, a similar reaction from a state with a constitutionally "illegitimate" single-party regime such as China would be utterly impossible (Halme-Tuomisaari 2013a).

Yet there are also crucial, more intimate layers at stake here, connected to distinct inside contours of international UN human rights bureaucracies, which simultaneously reconnect this discussion to the notion of universality as well as to the concepts of center and periphery. With regard to the report of Finland, all these elements are personified in a civil servant whom I will call "Mark." In addition to being one of the key figures in human rights policy at the Foreign Affairs Ministry of Finland, Mark is a prominent figure in Finnish human rights activist circles more broadly – the country and circles both being very small. Importantly, despite being a career civil servant at the Finnish Foreign Ministry, Mark is in many ways also an insider of the UN human rights framework, having worked at the UN Secretariat in Geneva as well as collaborated with various Geneva-based human rights NGOs before that. In his professional capacity he, like many civil servants at foreign affairs ministries around the world, participates frequently in UN human rights meetings. He knows many key people of UN human rights bureaucracies in person – or, at a minimum, is aware of their "inside" reputation through his extensive personal contacts.

In light of most scholarship on UN treaty bodies authored primarily by activist international lawyers, Mark's profile appears unexpected – most of this scholarship reifies the above-described stark division of participants into the categories of "state," "NGO" and "UN treaty body." Yet, as one of my most consistent ethnographic findings has become, in reality these categories are much more fluid precisely because of the professional profiles of human rights bureaucrats in which these categories merge. Thus, my findings suggest that instead of representing genuine "outsiders" – the "bad state" whose actions these UN monitoring mechanisms are geared to address – many civil servants handling human rights issues in foreign ministries around the world embody both knowledge and association with the "inside" and the "outside," making the borders between these abstract categories much softer and more malleable in the reality of UN human rights monitoring than the existing scholarship suggests.

My lengthy interaction with the Finnish civil servants has suggested that, in fact, they are likely among the most pro-human rights bureaucrats in existence. My data also suggests that, like Mark, this shared professional space in between UN offices and state positions is intensified by concrete professional profiles: experience in any UN-related position – whether as an intern or an UN-related NGO worker – is highly prestigious, and thus I suggest that a broader overview of state bureaucrats working with UN human rights reporting would show many of them to have similar professional portfolios. To date, however, such extensive comparative work has not been done, and thus elaborating this point will have to wait.

Yet, even with the absence of sufficient ethnographic data to generalize extensively – studying state representatives remains the single most difficult group of actors at the Human Rights Committee – I will argue that this finding has explanatory weight that extends beyond civil servants at the Finnish Foreign Affairs Ministry. Thus, the real opposition of "bad" state officials who belittle international human rights obligations and "good" human rights defenders cannot be neatly connected on the borders drawn on the divisions of "state," "NGO" and "INGO." Rather, the empirical professional and social space is much more nuanced and shared.

These findings have concrete importance for the discussion on "cultivated universality." It is evident that Mark's actions vis-à-vis the Sami representative far exceed what one would expect from a mere civil servant solely carrying out professional duties according to his station. A continued overview of Mark's actions strengthens this finding: in addition to overseeing the preparation of Finland's official state report, Mark worked actively to inspire Finnish NGOs to attend and submit ancillary reports. In spring 2013, leading up to the "constructive dialogue" on Finland's report by the Human Rights Committee in July 2013, Mark informed Finnish NGOs of the relevant deadlines for submitting parallel reports. He attended NGO meetings in person, where he instructed NGOs on what UN treaty body proceedings are, and how and why NGOs could and should participate. As the spring progressed, he distributed guidelines for NGO participation generated by an umbrella NGO operating in Geneva, with hopes of encouraging them to participate in the ongoing "documentary cycle," and even sent out last-minute reminders as the deadline for submitting shadow reports approached.

Yet he did not stop there, as was already mentioned with regard to the travel expenses of the Sami representative. What had happened, more concretely, was that the Sami Council had received funds from the Finnish Ministry of Foreign Affairs to attend another UN Expert meeting ongoing simultaneously at the UN Palais des Nations, the meeting of the Permanent Forum on Indigenous Issues. While the representative of the Council was already in Geneva, Mark had encouraged her to also participate in the hearing of the Human Rights Committee at the nearby Palais Wilson. Thus, were it not for Mark's insistent urging, there would, in fact, have been *no* Finns to represent NGOs or the Finnish civil society in Geneva at the Human Rights Committee's hearing – something that would have been quite embarrassing, in context.

Mark's actions initially appear difficult to comprehend: after all, he *is* a civil servant of an individual state – why would he engage in all of the above? Strictly speaking, not only does he evidently extend what the mere call of duty dictates, but his actions could also be seen as almost intrusive due to their impact on the rudimentary division of labor that forms the bedrock of UN human rights monitoring. I argue that in order for these actions to become sensible, one needs to view Mark in a different light: yes, as a civil servant, but also something more – a devoted human rights believer who in the course of his duties does not see himself as representing merely his own government, but also as someone whose devotion extends to the safeguarding of human rights and their realization via the UN regulatory framework.

Further, in this capacity Mark illustrates a crucial feature of human rights experts: on the one hand they may be, as is also the case for Mark, detached professionals and lawyers working with diverse, clearly outlined professional mandates; on the other, they may be keenly engaged "human rights believers" who also act as activists for human rights. In this duality, Mark embodies the two sides of human rights expertise, combining – to borrow Bruno Latour's classic comparison between natural scientists and lawyers – elements from both sides (Latour 2004; Halme-Tuomisaari 2010c).

In this sense, Mark in important ways resembles what Sally Merry has influentially denoted as "intermediaries": people who operate on the in-between terrain of global human rights centers and peripheries, translating diverse local concerns into the vernacular of human rights, thus both informing diverse people around the world that their issues are, indeed, "human rights concerns," and simultaneously engaging them more closely with the discourse and action on human rights (Merry 2006). Yet, so I argue, to fully comprehend the scope of Mark's actions one needs to add a crucial dimension to it. It is not a neutral navigation between these global centers and peripheries that Mark's actions entail, but, rather, an activity that is also importantly linked to the interests of the center, which in the present case is embodied by the UN Human Rights Committee. Although Mark's actions are undoubtedly intended to safeguard the interests of the Sami people and their plight, they also serve another vital purpose: to support the continued legitimacy of the UN monitoring mechanism, represented here by the UN Human Rights Committee via the concrete, physical participation of the Sami people as representatives of "embodied universalism," which serves to verify, time and time again, the ideology of human rights as shared by all mankind.

As my fieldwork progressed, I was impressed to discover that, in fact, Mark was far from unique in his actions as there was an important "central actor" who occupied a largely similar role to him, the difference being that this role was far more systematic and broader in scope. Here I refer to the already mentioned Geneva-based umbrella NGO which I will call Co-Ordinate. Co-Ordinate has numerous parallel organizations which all focus either on a distinct UN monitoring mechanism – for example the UPR – or on a distinct issue, such as conscientious objection or LGTBI-rights. Similar to many umbrella organizations, Co-Ordinate is a small centralized lobbying body, which has its offices in one concrete locality in Geneva, yet the scope of its operations is thoroughly global. What Co-Ordinate does is quite impressive, and echoes the actions of Mark: it selects a few states that are up for review from each session of the Committee, and approaches NGOs from this target country to inform them of the upcoming hearing of the Committee, with the purpose of inspiring them to submit ancillary reports. In this communication it provides NGOs with a set of guidelines on how to draft a report suitable for the purpose – no simple endeavor, given the distinct nature of Committee work embedded in UN jargon, linked to distinct covenant provisions as well as a distinct legalistic aesthetic via which information is favored by the Committee.

Yet, like Mark, Co-Ordinate does not stop there. Instead, it welcomes draft reports by its target NGOs, and, resources permitting, it revises these drafts and assists NGOs in their report submissions, work commonly carried out in its headquarters only a stone's throw away from the Palais Wilson. Further, it works with a range of funding agencies to attempt to secure funding that allows NGOs, particularly those from the Global South, to participate in Committee hearings, assisting them with travel arrangements and visas; it even arranges many of the NGO hearings described in this paper. This funding, in turn, is commonly provided by funding agencies that echo the geographic focus of Co-Ordinate's operations – in other words, Swiss – or the most decisive funding patterns of the UN treaty body system in general – to generalize broadly, emphasis on Scandinavian and Dutch funders. In short, in the sessions of the Committee, Co-Ordinate acts as the "inside guide" to the "outsiders" flown in from around the world as they frequent these Geneva-based meetings for a few short days. Co-Ordinate also contributes to the general visibility of these sessions via webcam and social media during public hearings; it issues press releases of Concluding Observations and follows-up on certain states in collaboration with the Committee.

Thus Co-Ordinate – like other international umbrella organizations – performs a crucial role in extending information of the Committee's sessions "around the world." Here it is important to recall that although the UN is a thoroughly global organization, due primarily to budget cuts most human rights treaty bodies now only meet in Geneva, instead of the previously regular sessions also held at the UN headquarters in New York. The sessions of treaty bodies are themselves quite localized, and the circles relatively small. In the end, only a minimal number of people stay put – the secretary of the Committee and other key staff of the UN Secretariat, the UN Conference Services, the fantastic lady at the cafeteria of the Palais Wilson, and Co-Ordinate.

EMBODIED UNIVERSALISM AND THE CONTINUED QUEST FOR LEGITIMACY

How can we understand the work of Co-Ordinate in light of this chapter's discussion on "universality"? What about the actions of Mark? Why did Mark invest so much weight in securing Finnish NGO participation in these hearings and go out of his professional way to keep NGOs informed of relevant deadlines, not to mention finding the means for the representative of the Sami people to attend? Why did it matter so much to Committee members and personnel at the UN Secretariat that there were next to no NGO representatives present in the hearing on Finland's report? After all, the above description suggests that from the perspective of information this would hardly have a crippling effect on the "constructive dialogue," the primary content of which was based on research commenced months earlier.

To begin, consider the issue of resources and whether Finnish NGOs really have them or not, and whether this was the reason for their absence from these proceedings. Realistically, even in situations of restricted resources, funds can often be found for purposes that are seen as imperative – does this apply here? Why did Co-Ordinate help Finnish NGOs secure funding? The answer is predictable: with Finland being a Western European democracy with a well-established human rights record – a party to the "model students" of the international human rights regime – it is very difficult for such international actors as Co-Ordinate to persuade local funders to support NGO participation. Rather, funders easily see that these resources are needed for NGOs from the geographic "other" – aka the Global South and the developing world.

What about the resources of Finnish NGOs themselves? Certainly they have some, as otherwise their operations would be hard-pressed, and realistically the more prosperous among them also have some leeway toward international collaboration. Why did they not tap into those resources to attend the Committee's constructive dialogue? In discussions with Finnish NGOs – the Finnish League for Human Rights; the Finnish chapter of Amnesty; as well as the Finnish umbrella organization for sexual minorities, SETA – nobody elevated participation in UN treaty body proceedings as a top priority. Or, more directly still: the Finnish chapter of Amnesty International was aware of the forthcoming constructive dialogue on Finland at the Human Rights Committee and was sending the Committee its own ancillary report – on the basis of the report that they had drafted for the Universal Periodic Review that the Human Rights Council had carried out the year before. Yet they had no plans to send a representative there in person – which would have been difficult anyway, according to Amnesty's guidelines that local chapters are not supposed to target local contexts but, rather, human rights violations occurring elsewhere (Hopgood 2006).

For the Finnish League for Human Rights, one of the oldest human rights NGOs in the country and commonly seen as an "umbrella association" of sorts to safeguard human rights issues in general, the director of the League (who had just assumed her position) was not aware of the forthcoming hearing by the Human Rights Committee *at all*, and thus, not surprisingly, the League was not planning to submit a report of any kind or send a representative in person. The NGO on sexual minorities, SETA, had, by contrast, heard of the hearing, yet due to a shortage of personnel resources, submitting the report had been left on the back burner. Ironically, after my visit to the organization, the organization's head was reminded of the deadline; simultaneously, she remembered the recent reminder of this deadline sent in by Mark; and eventually the NGO did submit a report, which was thus deposited on the UN website and discussed in the Committee's hearing.

In other words, none of these NGOs had any plans to attend the hearing of the Human Rights Committee in Geneva – not so much because of restricted resources but, rather, because attendance was not seen as a priority on any level in their operations, irrespective of the monetary costs involved. All the NGO workers that I interviewed described the UN system as distant, unfamiliar and with uncertain usefulness in its low impact and visibility. Curiously, despite its almost four decades of existence, all of the NGO workers also described the treaty body system as a "new" system which, because of its "recent nature," was still unfamiliar to them. The latter characterization was particularly puzzling in the case of the Finnish League for Human Rights, as I later learned that more than a decade ago, in the late 1990s, the organization *had*, in fact, been active in submitting shadow reports and even attending. Clearly, the sentiment of "newness" was in this instance not an accurate description of things, but a subjective sentiment held by the new head of the organization and created *after* previous participation by the League on the Committee's monitoring cycles.

Recent research suggests that rather than being isolated instances, these sentiments capture a relatively prevalent view of UN treaty bodies. In his comparative study based on extensive interview data as well as documentary analysis in Finland, the Netherlands, and Australia, Jasper Krommendijk found largely similar patterns – except, if possible, more prominent still: the hearings of treaty bodies implied very few consequences of any kind, whether measured in newspaper articles, civil society action, parliamentary debates or legislative changes (Krommendijk 2014).

These findings are deeply troubling for the continued legitimacy of UN human rights treaty bodies in particular, and for the global monitoring framework around human rights in general: in order for it to remain credible, relevant and *alive* it needs to be – or least give the impression of being – genuinely relevant to people, as something that is needed and adhered to by people *all around the world*, as something that is *universal* in its embrace and existence. Against this background, the message emanating from Finnish NGOs is deeply worrying, and sufficient in itself to contribute to the declining importance of this discourse and ideology that has formed the most visible "last global utopia" of recent decades (Moyn 2012). This lack of interest, or sense of irrelevance, poses a tremendous threat to this utopia. More potently than any ill-intended governments or malignant sovereigns, it is these sentiments that have the potential to reduce it from an ideology of "universal" scope into one of restrictive, "particular" relevance.

CONCLUSION: EMBODIED RELEVANCE

It is with these words that we arrive at the last ironic turn of this chapter: for almost seven decades – with greater or lesser intensity – scholars have been engaged in a regularly revived debate on whether human rights notions and language form universal phenomena or are merely "particular" in their scope and origin.

Simultaneously, we have collectively ignored what is really at stake in this debate, particularly after human rights have undoubtedly and genuinely become thoroughly global, or "universal." Especially in the first decade of the new millennium, scholars, particularly those in international law but also in the anthropology of human rights, have discussed these concepts as if they were connected in meaningful ways to "cultural difference."

My suggestion is not that this debate is entirely insignificant – it is not this debate that I am engaging with here, nor is this the argument that I wish to forward with these ethnographic glimpses from UN treaty body proceedings. Rather, I wish to highlight how "universalism" is an entity that is actively cultivated by actors at the "centers" of the contemporary human rights phenomenon so as to make human rights notions and the work of regulatory frameworks around human rights relevant for actors in the "peripheries" – or at least to create an impression to that effect. It is in both of these capacities that the concrete, physical bodies of the representatives of humanity "from the peripheries" – such as NGOs from Finland – gain their importance for participating at the "center" – such as the sessions of the UN Human Rights Committees at the Palais Wilson in Geneva.

First, when NGOs around the world participate in the monitoring cycles of UN human rights treaties, they are informed not only of the possibilities of participation within these monitoring mechanisms, but also of their very existence – not to mention the scope of specific human rights covenants. When they articulate their diverse concerns via the language of human rights, they simultaneously contribute to the salience of that language and the framework for processing complaints through that language. When they travel physically to Geneva, they, through their bodies, become complicit in the realization of the ideal of universalism into a living reality. When they engage in the NGO hearings in the meeting room of the Palais Wilson with members of UN Committees, they, through their physically present bodies, testify to the importance of these hearings, simultaneously reifying the importance of the work of the Committee. As they sit in the public sessions of the main meeting room of the Palais Wilson, they embody "the world," thus bringing "the international" alive as something that *needs* this monitoring mechanism.

So far, the over-arching assumption of UN human rights treaty body work has been that it exists for "something" or "someone" – both of which are in existence in the world, but often removed from view. By definition, they are "peripheral" to this action occurring at this "center." While sitting in the Palais Wilson, one never encounters this "something" or "someone." Yet the belief in the existence of both, as well as the relevance of the action at the center, forms a crucial accelerating factor for the continued action at the center. Further, without belief in this "outside," UN monitoring mechanisms would be reduced to a mere self-sustaining cycle of perpetual motion which operates and exists in an autonomous realm cut off from reality, engaging in action that is meaningful only to itself.

The assumption remains that the constructive dialogue taking place between the state and the UN Committee travels back – ideally assisted by local NGOs – and that the views presented by the Concluding Observations by the Committee similarly find tangible existence in reality. Yet, so recent scholarship contends, in reality all this is doubtful: very few people take notice of what goes on in Geneva during the events themselves, and even fewer notice after the fact. More often than not, no attention is paid to the Concluding Observations of Committees, save by the civil servants whose professional duty it is to read them and consider them for the next report due to a UN human rights body.

This chapter suggests that instead of the dynamic emanating merely from the "center" to the "periphery," we need to, if not replace it, at a minimum accompany it with the reverse dynamic and ask: what kind of energy does the sustained movement of actors from the "peripheries" offer to the "center"? What does this movement do to contribute to the continued vibrancy and legitimacy of action occurring at the "center"? My argument is that instead of ultimately contributing to the transfer of information or the outcomes of these proceedings back to the peripheries, the ultimate importance of their participation is a contribution to strengthen the impression of human rights work as being truly universal, important to people around the world – and it is this work that the physical bodies that subject themselves to this ritual of audit effectively support.

REFERENCES

Alfredsson, Gudmundur 1999 *The Universal Declaration of Human Rights: A Common Standard of Achievement*. 1st edition. Cham: Springer.

Allen, Lori 2013 *The Rise and Fall of Human Rights Cynicism and Politics in Occupied Palestine*. Stanford: Stanford University Press.

Bassiouni, M. Cherif, and William A. Schabas, eds. 2011 *New Challenges for the UN Human Rights Machinery: What Future for the UN Treaty Body System and the Human Rights Council Procedures?* Cambridge: Intersentia.

Bayefsky, Anne F. 2000 *The UN Human Rights Treaty System in the 21st Century*. The Hague: Kluwer Law International.

Billaud, Julie 2014 "Keepers of the Truth: Producing 'Transparent' Documents for the Universal Periodic Review." In *Human rights and the Universal Periodic Review: Rituals and Ritualism*. Hilary Charlesworth and Emma Larking, eds. Cambridge: Cambridge University Press, pp. 63–84.

Cassese, Antonio 2012 *Realizing Utopia: The Future of International Law*. Oxford: Oxford University Press.

Charlesworth, Hilary, and Emma Larking 2014 *Human Rights and the Universal Periodic Review: Rituals and Ritualism*. Cambridge: Cambridge University Press.

Comaroff, Jean, and John L. Comaroff 1992 *Ethnography and the Historical Imagination*. Boulder: Westview Press.

Cowan, Jane 2013 "Before Audit Culture: Towards a Genealogy of International Oversight of Rights." In *The Gloss of Harmony: The Politics of Policy Making in Multilateral Organisations*. Birgit Müller, ed. London: Pluto Press, pp. 103–133.

Cowan, Jane K. 2014 "The Universal Periodic Review as Public Audit Ritual: An Anthropological Perspective on Emerging Practices in the Global Governance of Human Rights." In *Human Rights and the Universal Periodic Review: Rituals and Ritualism*. Hilary Charlesworth and Emma Larking, eds. Cambridge: Cambridge University Press, pp. 42–62.

Crawford, James 2010 *The Future of UN Human Rights Treaty Monitoring*. Cambridge: Cambridge University Press.

Curtis, Jennifer 2014 *Human Rights as War by Other Means: Peace Politics in Northern Ireland*. Philadelphia: University of Pennsylvania Press.

Dembour, Marie-Bénédicte, and Tobias Kelly, eds. 2007 *Paths to International Justice: Social and Legal Perspectives*. 1st edition. Cambridge: Cambridge University Press.

Englund, Harri 2006 *Prisoners of Freedom: Human Rights and the African Poor*. Berkeley: University of California Press.

Halme-Tuomisaari, Miia 2010a "From the Periphery to the Centre: Emergence of the Human Rights Phenomenon in Finland." In *Finnish Yearbook of International Law*. Leiden: Brill Academic Publishers, pp. 257–281.

— 2010b "Absolute and Undefined: Exploring the Popularity of Human Rights in Finland." *Redescriptions: Yearbook of Political Thought, Conceptual History and Feminist Theory* 15: 46–71.

— 2010c *Human Rights in Action: Learning Expert Knowledge*. Leiden: Brill Academic Publishers.

— 2012 "The State Is One: Examining What 'Fact' Means in the Compilation of a Human Rights Report." *Suomen Antropologi: Journal of the Finnish Anthropological Society* (1): 22–30.

— 2013a Contested Representation: Exploring China's State Report. *Journal of Legal Anthropology* (1): 333–359.

— 2013b "Mobile yet Stagnant: Examining Human Rights Monitoring." Unpublished paper presented to the EASA Anthropology and Mobility Network's Workshop *Fielding challenges, challenging the field: The methodologies of mobility*, Oxford, UK, September 27–28.

— 2015 "Lobbying for Relevance: American Internationalists French Civil Libertarians and the UDHR." In *Revisiting the Origins of Human Rights*. Pamela Slotte and Miia Halme-Tuomisaari, eds. Cambridge: Cambridge University Press, pp. 330–361.

Halme-Tuomisaari, Miia, and Pamela Slotte 2015 "Introduction." In *Revisiting the Origins of Human Rights*. Cambridge: Cambridge University Press, pp. 1–36.

Hannerz, Ulf 1993 *Cultural Complexity: Studies in the Social Organization of Meaning*. New York: Columbia University Press.

Hopgood, Stephen 2006 *Keepers of the Flame: Understanding Amnesty International*. annotated edition. Ithaca: Cornell University Press.

Kamminga, Menno T., and Martin Scheinin, eds. 2009 *The Impact of Human Rights Law on General International Law*. Oxford: Oxford University Press.

Kelly, Tobias 2011 *This Side of Silence: Human Rights, Torture, and the Recognition of Cruelty*. Philadephia: University of Pennsylvania Press.

Korey, William 2001 *NGO's and the Universal Declaration of Human Rights: "A Curious Grapevine."* New York: Palgrave Macmillan.

Krommendijk, Jasper. 2014 *The Domestic Impact and Effectiveness of the Process of State Reporting Under UN Human Rights Treaties in the Netherlands, New Zealand and Finland: Paper-pushing or Policy Prompting?* Cambridge: Intersentia.

Latour, Bruno 2004 *La Fabrique Du Droit: Une Ethnographie Du Conseil d'Etat*. Paris: Editions La Découverte.

Lauren, Paul Gordon 2011 *The Evolution of International Human Rights: Visions Seen.* Third Edition. Philadephia: University of Pennsylvania Press.

Merry, Sally Engle 2006 *Human Rights and Gender Violence: Translating International Law into Local Justice.* Chicago: University of Chicago Press.

Morsink, Johannes 2000 *The Universal Declaration of Human Rights: Origins, Drafting, and Intent.* Philadephia: University of Pennsylvania Press.

Moyn, Samuel 2012 *The Last Utopia: Human Rights in History.* Reprint. Cambridge: Belknap Press.

Pillay, Navanethem 2012 Strengthening the United Nations Human Rights Treaty Body System: A Report by the United Nations High Commissioner for Human Rights.

Riles, Annelise 1998 "Infinity Within the Brackets." *American Ethnologist* 25(3): 378–398.

Rottenburg, Richard 2009 *Far-fetched Facts: A Parable of Development Aid.* Cambridge: MIT Press.

Simmons, Beth A. 2009 "Mobilizing for Human Rights: International Law." In *Domestic Politics.* 1st edition. Cambridge: Cambridge University Press.

Simpson, Gerry 2004 *Great Powers and Outlaw States: Unequal Sovereigns in the International Legal Order.* Cambridge, UK; New York: Cambridge University Press.

Strathern, Marilyn 2006 "Bullet-Proofing: A Tale from the United Kingdom." In *Documents: Artefacts of Modern Knowledge.* Annelise Riles, ed. Michigan: University of Michigan Press, pp. 181–205.

UN Office for the High Commissioner for Human Rights N.d. Treaty Body Strengthening. www.ohchr.org/EN/HRBodies/HRTD/Pages/TBStrengthening.aspx. Accessed August 15, 2015.

Wallerstein, Immanuel 2004 *World-Systems Analysis: An Introduction.* Durham: Duke University Press.

7

Expertise and Quantification in Global Institutions

Sally Engle Merry

Every year at the end of February, about four or five hundred statisticians from countries around the world convene in the United Nations building in New York for a four-day conference on global statistical issues. The conference, the annual meeting of the United Nations Statistical Commission (UNSC), oversees global agricultural, industrial, developmental, and other economic and social statistics. The attendees represent the twenty-four member countries, elected for four-year terms by the UN Economic and Social Council and allocated evenly among the UN's world regions. Representatives from other countries are free to attend the annual meeting as well. The participants discuss issues such as revisions to the system of national statistical accounts, updating the purchasing power parity measure, measuring new concepts such as violence against women, and the importance of upgrading gender statistics. The responsibilities of the UNSC have gradually expanded from its core concern with economic and demographic statistics into many new areas, including development, gender, crime, the environment, and other social phenomena.

Many of the country representatives are chief statisticians or work for their national statistical offices. They speak for the interests of official statisticians. They share concerns about the autonomous status of official statistics, the authority of the UNSC, and the importance of good statistical practices. They recognize the challenges of working within an economically and statistically unequal world with ongoing political pressures on their work. This chapter is an ethnographic foray into this social world. I attended the annual meetings for six years (from 2009 to 2014), went to other events happening alongside the conference, and spoke to many statisticians about their work in the context of my research on measuring human rights, violence against women, and sex trafficking (Merry 2016). My ethnography offers insights into the central concerns of the global statistical community as well as the tensions inherent in global collaboration among vastly unequal countries. After analyzing the UNSC as an international organization, I describe an intense debate in a commission meeting that exposed fault lines between rich, statistically sophisticated countries and poor ones that produce limited and even questionable data.

The UNSC meetings are largely professional gatherings, united by expertise and commitment to the profession of statistics. Unlike other commission meetings, such as those of the Commission on the Status of Women or the Human Rights Council (formerly the Commission on Human Rights), they are not the site of a major gathering of civil society activists eager to influence the commission and engaged in producing a large number of panels and discussions called side events. These meetings consist of an intellectually homogeneous population of statisticians: those representing countries, usually from their national statistical offices, as well as those that work for other UN agencies such as the UN Development Programme (UNDP) or the World Bank, or that are employed by the secretariat of the UNSC, the United Nations Statistical Division (UNSD). Despite the wide national differences among them, there seems to be consensus about the importance of official statistics, the need to resist political pressure from states on official statistics, and the challenge of producing adequate official statistics given sharp inequalities in wealth among countries. The attendees participate in other international statistical conferences and share concerns about how to measure old and new phenomena and how to manage government expectations. They are part of a global cultural world of statistical expertise.

The UNSC sees itself as responsible for the statistical knowledge produced by the UN. It claims oversight of the UNDP's Human Development Index and the new indicators of global development, the Sustainable Development Goals (SDGs), which were considered at the 2015 UNSC meeting. The UNSC plays a supportive and technical role, assessing data availability and advising in the formulation of indicators. For example, the UNSC supported the creation of SDGs by suggesting new technology for data collection, assisting in setting numerical targets, and preparing potential indicators, but did not develop the indicators themselves (UN Statistical Commission E/CN.3/2015/36, para. 10).

The Statistical Commission is also concerned with protecting statistical knowledge from political interference. During the meetings I attended, there were long discussions on the need to revise the preamble to the Fundamental Principles of Official Statistics. The Statistical Commission is guided by its statement of Fundamental Principles of Official Statistics.[1] These principles were adopted in 1994 to establish the independence of statistical offices from government influence at the time of the transition in Central Europe from planned to market-based economies (unstats.un.org/unsd/dnss/gp/fundprinciples.aspx, visited March 2, 2012). In 2011, UN Statistical Commission members sought to update the Fundamental Principles of Official Statistics and strengthen their implementation. At this meeting there were discussions of country situations in which governments had interfered in the statistical offices' production of data and analysis, such as in the provision of financial data from Argentina. In the 2012 meeting, country

---

[1] Official Records of the Economic and Social Council, 1994, Supplement No. 9 (E/1994/29).

representatives discussed the need for governments to respect these statistical principles and the threats to credibility if they do not.

A UNSC committee charged with implementing the fundamental principles developed a new preamble to this document and a practical guide to be used by countries and international organizations which was presented at the 2012 meeting.[2] The new draft of the preamble stated that "statistical principles in order to be effective have to be enshrined in the institutional frameworks that govern official statistical systems and be respected at all political levels and by all stakeholders in national statistical systems".[3] Delegates at the 2012 meeting expressed concern about government interference with statistical offices in Argentina, Greece, Ghana, and several other countries and emphasized the importance of the independence of statistical offices. Paradoxically, it is up to governments to maintain this independence.

The revised version of the Fundamental Principles was approved with much celebration at the 2014 UNSC. This included passing around individual small plastic bottles of champagne to all of those present in the large conference room and an enthusiastic toast to the acceptance of the revised principles by all present. A draft resolution of the Fundamental Principles was endorsed by the General Assembly of the UN in 2014. At the 2015 meeting, the UNSC considered a report from the Friends of the Chair committee, made up of twelve member nations (the term refers to a committee created by the UNSC), on implementation of the Fundamental Principles of Official Statistics that reports on an implementation survey and the development of guidelines for strengthening implementation. The final implementation guidelines were to be available on the UNSD website by March 2015 (UNSC E/CN.3/2015/18: paras. 1, 6, 10). Thus, the UNSC and its secretariat constitute a relatively coherent, if deterritorialized, social world committed to the ideal of reliable official statistics and to establishing the standards of professionalism that encourage populations to have faith in their country's official statistics.

However, the work of the UNSC does not always run smoothly. It sometimes erupts into intense debates. These conflicts reveal the fundamental tension of the global international system: the importance of maintaining the appearance of equality and sovereignty even though nations differ deeply in economic and political power and technical expertise. All countries are considered equal members of the United Nations, with the same rights to speak and participate, despite their size. Both Tuvalu (population 10,000) and India (population 1.3 billion) exercise one vote. As an Indian friend pointed out to a colleague from Peru, his state of Gujarat in India is larger than all of Peru. Sovereignty is

---

[2] UN Statistical Commission 2011: "Implementation of the Fundamental Principles of Official Statistics," December 20, 2011, E/CN.3/2012/14.

[3] Statistical Commission, Forty-third session, February 28 to March 2, 2012, Item 3 (k) of the provisional agenda, Implementation of the Fundamental Principles of Official Statistics, Background Document.

a fundamental principle of the international order, and is jealously guarded. It is protected by relying on multi-lateral treaties for global governance, in which countries choose to submit themselves to various mechanisms of control such as human rights treaties.

Despite the public emphasis on equality and sovereignty, a small fraction of the 193 member nations of the UN bear most of the costs and hold the vast majority of global power. Many of the rich countries are former colonial powers and the poorer countries former colonies. Meetings at the UN manage these disparities by using polite and indirect diplomatic language, producing shared documents which paper over deep differences through ambiguous wording, and adhering to the formalities of voting. Inequalities of power are rarely mentioned or acknowledged. All countries emphasize their national reputation and virtue, and representatives seek to present their countries in the best possible light. In some ways, these global institutions are fragile, and holding them together requires delicate management of such vast differences.

From time to time these differences produce conflict, even in the staid space of the Statistical Commission. Sometimes what is at stake is the reputation of a country's statistical system, at other times it is projects to measure practices such as female genital cutting that are prevalent in some countries but globally condemned. There are ongoing tensions over demands for poor countries to produce better statistics and allegations about inadequate or even corrupt statistics. Poorer countries typically respond to these demands by asking for more resources from the global community. There are also conflicts over expertise, particularly over the use of Global North experts to shape global statistical systems that apply to all countries. This chapter analyzes the role of the UNSC in the global statistical system, and then describes one meeting that exposed these underlying tensions. In the face of a contentious debate, the leaders of the UNSC sought to contain it in a way that allowed the international system to survive, despite its fragility.

THE DEVELOPMENT OF THE INTERNATIONAL STATISTICAL SYSTEM

Quantification systems are fundamental to the project of global governance, but typically receive little analytical attention from theorists seeking to understand how global governance works. They are generally seen as technical mechanisms, requiring refinement and attention to problems of validity and reliability as well as protection from cheating and political meddling, but not as fundamental mechanisms for creating the knowledge base for governance decisions or for shaping public attitudes toward these decisions. Yet, a historical view of the creation of statistics for governance shows that they were essential to the creation of the modern nation-state and the contemporary global system of governance (see Hacking 1990; Merry 2011). The statistical knowledge available at the global level for systems of governance is to some extent dependent on national-level statistical enterprises. Indeed, the tensions between national sovereignty and global control exist in the world of statistics as well as in many other domains of international governance.

The United Nations statistical system has been fundamental to the creation of a global political order. The UNSC was created in 1946 and was a core part of the United Nations system. It expanded from an initial focus on economic statistics to a broader range of social and environmental foci. Its central mission is to systematize global statistical systems and to support national statistical offices. It also seeks to protect national statistical offices from political pressure by developing and asserting fundamental principles of official statistics. Yet, recent conflicts within the UNSC reveal ongoing tensions between national sovereignty and global governance. These conflicts replicate those found in other areas of global governance even though statistics is not usually seen as a domain of contestation.

Historically, the creation of the modern nation-state and the project of governing colonial possessions were the two key forces driving the use of statistical data for governance. Under these pressures, the use of quantitative knowledge for policy and decision-making expanded throughout the nineteenth and twentieth centuries. More recently, these technologies of knowledge and governance have been adopted by international organizations. The shift has been particularly dramatic since the mid-1990s. Great increases in the availability and transfer of data via the Internet, improvements in census and data-collection efforts in countries around the world, and the expansion of measurement into new and previously uncountable spheres of social life have all produced a massive growth in the reliance on quantitative knowledge for international as well as national governance. At the same time, national and international organizations have developed new and successful indicators.

In the early nineteenth century, nation-states began to focus on managing populations rather than securing territory. It became important for states to count their population and to assess their state of health, ethnicity, gender, and capacities. The wealth of a country depended on its workforce and population, requiring knowledge of this population in order to govern it. Knowledge of populations became ever more important with the consolidation of the modern industrial state. As European countries expanded into new colonial domains, counting and classifying these populations was also critically important. Projects of surveying lands, measuring population sizes and capacities, and counting ethnic groups, castes, and races were fundamental to establishing colonial control (see Mitchell 2002; Cohn 1996). Thus, the notion of governing a population by quantifying its characteristics grew from these nineteenth-century projects of state-building and colonial expansion. Early empires used tax rolls and trade numbers as a mode of governance as well, but they did not assess the condition of the population by age, disability, race, gender, and nationality as nation-states did.

During the nineteenth century, an increasingly broad range of phenomena were subject to counting, with some states, such as Prussia, collecting data for its own sake while others, such as France, endeavored to turn this data into social laws about phenomena such as suicide (Hacking 1990). Numbers helped policy-makers make decisions between alternatives such as building railroads or canals, for which cost-benefit measures were valuable (Porter 1995). Reformers also relied on data on mortality and public health to press for improved health care and urban design (Schweber 2006). The use of numerical measures of population by age, birth and death rates, health, poverty, and other criteria constituted the population as a measurable entity that could be known in new ways (Poovey 1998; Porter 1995; Schweber 2006). Increasingly, statistics became the basis on which governments assessed their resources, human and natural, and developed policies for promoting public health, diminishing population decline and "degeneracy," and alleviating poverty.

It was not until the twentieth century that there were substantial efforts to generate comparative global statistics and composite indicators, those made up of multiple sources of information and multiple variables, combined to produce a single rank or score. The United Nations played a critical role in building technical capacity and developing international systems of measurement that facilitated cross-national comparison (Ward 2004). The first efforts focused on counting populations and measuring economic behavior shifted during the second half of the twentieth century to social phenomena such as well-being and quality of life (Ward 2004: 154). The social survey became increasingly well-known and used during the twentieth century in the United States, beginning with political opinions and expanding into new terrains such as sexual behavior in the Kinsey Reports of the 1940s and 1950s (Igo 2007). Starting in the 1930s, economists developed basic economic indicators such as gross domestic product and gross national product, while the international system of national accounts was established in 1952 (Ward 2004: 45) and widely accepted by statisticians during the 1950s. With the increasing focus on measurement and governance at the global level in the late twentieth century, particularly in the sphere of economic development, scholars recognized that counting things makes them visible and that what is not or cannot be counted is made to disappear (see Davis et al. 2012).

WHAT CAN BE COUNTED? WHAT IS COUNTED?

The use of quantitative knowledge for governance depends on processes of data collection and analysis. Numbers are political resources, valuable to whoever is able to harness them. To use the power of numbers, social life must be converted into measurements. Some things are more easily measured than others, however. Infant mortality is easier to count than the rule of law, for example. However, even phenomena that seem quite countable, such as infant mortality, depend on practices of birth and death registration and reporting mechanisms (see Merry and Wood 2015). Many indicators assess phenomena that are very difficult to quantify, such as justice or the protection of human rights. One solution is to create quantifiable proxies for the phenomenon. For example, if the goal is increasing the consciousness of human rights, this could be assessed by an attitude survey or by a count of the number of training sessions that an organization has carried out. The latter is clearly less expensive.

Contemporary global statistics are dependent on local data-collection processes in the places that are being governed, even when they are created and managed at the international level. These local actors may understand the process differently from global institutions. They may use different categories for classifying information, count different things, or resist cooperating with national and international expectations. Categories that miss important forms of behavior produced skewed results, often with serious policy flaws. For example, the failure to incorporate phenomena such as women's unpaid labor or environmental factors into economic measures such as the system of national accounts undervalues women's work and environmental degradation and therefore distorts economic decision-making (Waring 1990; 1999). It clearly matters who is deciding what to count and how to categorize it (see also Ward 2004: 186–187). Many statistical systems have been developed by the Global North, so that relatively affluent countries set the agenda, name the measurements and indicators, and assemble the criteria for measurement. Many global data systems, such as the Demographic and Health Surveys which are funded by USAID, are produced by wealthy countries to assess poorer ones.

Historically, both economic and social phenomena have been subject to measurement, although the relative enthusiasm for social and economic indicators has changed over time (Cobb and Rixford 1998; Dickinson 2011; Duncan 1984; Innes 1989; Sheldon and Freeman 1970). In the early part of the nineteenth century, social reformers in the United States, Britain, and France began using statistics to reveal public health problems and to advocate for improvements such as sanitation, factory conditions, prison reform, and temperance. The British General Register Office was created in 1836 and the US Bureau of Statistics in 1869. During the early twentieth century in the United States, there was interest in social indicators on topics such as population, communication agencies, education, metropolitan and rural communities, health and environment, and the social and economic activities of women. During the Depression of the 1930s, however, interest shifted to economic indicators. In 1937, the economist Simon Kuznets at the US National Bureau of Economic Research introduced the concept of the GDP as a key measure of national progress. It was adopted as a standard measurement of national progress by the Bretton Woods conference of 1944 as GDP.

During the 1960s in the United States, given the interest in the Great Society and the War on Poverty, social indicators again became important, particularly as a way to document racial disparities in health, education, and poverty. In 1967, Raymond Bauer, a researcher associated with NASA and the Harvard Business School, published a book called *Social Indicators*, which is credited with the re-birth of the social indicators movement in the United States. In the same year, Walter Mondale called for the creation of an annual government report on social indicators, which was published by the Office of Management and Budget and the US Census Bureau periodically until 1981. Under the Nixon administration, US government interest in social indicators waned, although academics continued to work on them. European countries including the UK, France, the Netherlands, and Germany established systems for collecting and reporting social indicators data during this time.

Although US government interest in social indicators evaporated in the 1980s, there was a new movement to create human rights indicators at the same time (Tomaševski 1984). An important conference in 1984 discussed right to food indicators (Alston and Tomaševski 1984). In 1990, the UNDP introduced the Human Development Index (HDI), created by economist Mahbub ul Haq, who said the purpose of the HDI was "to shift the focus of development economics from national income accounting to people centered policies" (UN Development Programme 2010a).

Thus, there have been significant changes in what is counted. There are also changes in how counting is done. Those who design statistical systems must decide which data-collection methods they can use depending in part on how much they can spend in collecting information. Collecting data is very expensive. The cost of data collection by states is an ongoing issue in the UN Statistical Commission meetings that I observed. For example, in 2012 Ghana said that there was a question raised during their census about the wisdom of spending $50 million on the census rather than investing it in development. Cameroon commented that generating statistics is a high-cost activity for them, and that the international community needs to rise to the challenge to provide funding and to have the flexibility to take into account the special situations of each country. Bangladesh made the same request. This plea from poorer countries to wealthier ones to fund activities that the wealthier ones advocate was expressed by several other countries as well, along with the stipulation that the poorer country should nevertheless retain control.

THE EMERGENCE OF GLOBAL STATISTICS

Since its formation, the United Nations has worked to develop the statistical capacity of its member nations. Initially, the UN focused on creating "a universally acknowledged statistical system and ... a general framework guiding the collection and compilation of data" (Ward 2004: 2). An early mission was to foster national censuses. Between 1955 and 1961, 195 national censuses were conducted on population, agriculture and industry, housing situations, earnings, age groups and available skills, and population density of different areas (United Nations 1961: 290–291). The UN has long played an important international role in fostering data collection, including the publication of surveys such as one it does on the state of the world's women, and teaching and supporting the development of statistical capacity. The UN works through its member nation commission, the UNSC, and its permanent secretariat, the UNSD, formerly the UN Statistical Office (UNSO).

The UN Statistical Office initially focused on developing economic statistics. The goal was to provide governments with tools for their economic decision-makers as they developed macroeconomic policies. Michael Ward observes that this system "set out a comprehensive framework that established the appropriate standard format for collecting and compiling all economic statistics. It created an interrelated network of concepts and definitions that remain more or less unchanged to the present day" (2004: 45). Thus, the categories and framework developed in one site in Europe shape the way economic relationships are now analyzed throughout the world. Although there are frequent debates about the details of these economic indicator systems at UNSC meetings, the basic framework remains unchallenged.

Economic measurement continued to be the central concern of the UN statistical system until the 1970s, when social indicators took on new importance as the movement developed outside of governments (Ward 2004: 161). During the 1980s, interest grew in gender, health, and nutrition statistics; composite social indicators; and labor participation measures, although by the end of the 1980s social indicator work was being sidelined (Ward 2004: 163). The 1990s and 2000s added concerns about the environment; governance issues such as freedom, corruption, and human rights; and poverty and global inequality. In 2000, the UNDP promoted the Millennium Development Goals (MDGs) and their targets and indicators (see Rittich 2014). Thus, the UN system has expanded from its initial focus on economic measurements to a wide range of social measures that include questions of inequality, development, and the effects of globalization (Ward 2004: 15–17).

The mission of the UNSD is primarily to advise government statistical offices rather than to develop its own indicators (Ward 2004: 159). It focuses on creating statistical concepts and appropriate classifications for processing the new social data that is of use to national statistical offices. In 1960, the UNSO, precursor to the UNSD, published *A Short Manual on Sampling*, including both theoretical discussions and examples. This was an important and widely used manual on statistical theory and sampling techniques (Ward 2004: 166–167). In the 1970s, the UNSO launched the National Household Survey Capability Program to help all national statistical offices develop an in-house survey capability and, ideally, to put them in a routine integrated survey program (Ward 2004: 170). The UNSD continues to produce and refine statistical systems, providing guidelines for their use and offering training sessions to national statistical offices that request them. For example, recently tasked with producing measures of violence against women, the UNSC produced a set of guidelines to be used by national statistical offices (UN Statistics Division 2013; Merry and Coutin 2014; Merry 2016).

The Population Division was formed in the 1940s to estimate global population and its changing demographic composition. Although its tasks were statistically straightforward, national cultures, local laws and customs, religion, and language all affected the technical measurement of population. As Ward notes, "Demographic statistics, however neutral they may be in any auditing or accounting sense, are invariably political in the wider meaning of the term" (2004: 192). Questions of citizenship and residence are clearly political, as are what constitutes a birth or death record in different countries (Ward 2004: 191–192). As with the rest of the UN statistical system, the Population Division has published recommendations and ideas about estimation procedures, the conduct of population and housing censuses, the construction of life tables, and other issues. It relies on the views of experts in demographic statistics and disseminates advice and guidelines through UN manuals and journal articles (Ward 2004: 192). The Population Division set up the UN Fund for Population Activities (UNFPA) and the USAID support for the Demographic and Health Surveys under the Johnson administration. The UNFPA now focuses on women and has sought to promote women's reproductive health. The Population Division has tried to remain outside political debates on morality and human rights, such as the right to life (Ward 2004: 193). In general, the UN stance toward producing statistical knowledge is to define it as a technical problem and not a political one, to which it brings expertise and advice that will support national initiatives.

However, as interest in measuring social development and the conditions leading to well-being and the quality of life increased, it became clear that it was much easier to measure economic phenomena, translated into real output and prices, than social ones (Ward 2004: 158). This statistical uneasiness has only grown. On February 27, 2012, just before the 2012 UNSC meeting in New York, I watched a panel of high-level statistical officers and academics from the EU, USA, Finland, India, Japan, and Qatar debating the issue of "Measuring the Unmeasurable: Challenging the Limits of Official Statistics." This panel considered the problem of being asked by governments to measure the unmeasurable. Of particular concern was the difficulty of measuring non-objective phenomena such as happiness or well-being, even though there are efforts to do so. One speaker pointed to the need for new methods and techniques to measure things like feelings as well as facts. Speakers debated questions such as, if a statistician measures feelings, can there be a loss of credibility? How far should we go?

One speaker pointed out that there are things that might be unmeasurable, such as opinions, prices when there are no markets, the future, clandestine activity such as human trafficking, or fictions. The head of the Finnish statistical service asked if measuring such things "is our business," but lamented that if something is not measured by official statistics, it will be measured by someone else. "Are there limits? Are there things that our governments are asking us to do that we should not do?" she asked. Forecasting the future, measuring non-material things, non-observable things, subjective things, and transnational and global phenomena are all difficult. New technologies might make things measurable in the future that are currently not measurable, but where is the boundary? She argued that it was appropriate to produce statistics needed for national and international decision-making and for monitoring national and international policies, such as MDGs, but that other needs are not the responsibility of national statistical offices. She pointed to the need to maintain credibility and the fundamental principles of statistics, such as impartiality, professionalism, scientific principles and standards, statistical relevance, reliability, quality, and transparency.

Another speaker at the conference, the head of the statistical office of India, pointed out that measurements that are useful for policy differ from those useful for description, and that what is unmeasurable depends on the purpose. He gave an example of measuring poverty in India based on population samples taken over time. This produced a series of snapshots of the proportion of people who are poor over time, but the particular people who were poor differed. Thus, this system provided a good description of the proportion of people who are poor but did not indicate which people required additional support. The head of statistics from Qatar noted that traditional socioeconomic and environmental indicators do not adequately measure what a country wants, since it may be different from what the indicators measure. For example, Qatar focuses on public engagement, so that measures such as GDP and MDGs are inadequate. The country values engagement, belonging, and trust, so measuring the impact of health and sports, such as the impact of sponsoring world soccer competitions, is important. A speaker from Japan noted that there is a long history of developing the ability to measure the unmeasurable, such as the system of national accounts and the international comparison program that computes purchasing power parity. In the discussion that followed this panel, some pointed to the fact that in the past, economists such as Keynes did not think that GDP was measurable but we now think both GDP and national accounts can be measured. The chair of the UNSD observed that statistics as a field is like an elephant: it is very big and moves very slowly, but it moves. He also noted that it is this community, attending the UNSC from statistical bureaus around the world, who will decide how to move forward with these questions.

CONTESTATION WITHIN THE UNSC: THE HUMAN DEVELOPMENT INDEX

In order to get an idea of how the UNSC operates, I describe a fight over the HDI in the Statistical Commission. The HDI is a prominent, widely used measure of economic and social development, yet it has generated considerable controversy (Ward 2004: 200–203). The HDI is based on a theory of development that sees education and health as critical dimensions of development, along with income levels. The fight over the HDI in the UNSC in 2011 (discussed below) indicates both ongoing sovereignty battles as well as how important their HDI rank is to countries around the world.

Developed in 1990 to replace GNP per capita as the measure of development, the HDI expresses the theory that social and economic development are inextricably related and need to be considered together. Instead of focusing only on growth in gross national product, this indicator combines economic and social factors in what is called a "capabilities" approach that emphasizes ends, such as a decent standard of living, over means, such as income per capita. The index measures access to health, education, and goods that give individuals the capacity to achieve their desired state of being (Stanton 2007: 3; Sen 2003). This approach constituted a new understanding of development itself. As a recent study observes, "In 1990, the United Nations Development Program (UNDP) transformed the landscape of development theory, measurement, and policy with the publication of its first annual Human Development Report (HDR) and the introduction of the Human Development Index" (Stanton 2007: 3). Advocates find it effective for advocacy and policy analysis. For example, sub-national HDI figures can reveal sharp inequalities in human development within one country, such as between urban and rural areas or between racial or gender groups (Fukuda-Parr and Kumar 2003: xxvi).

The HDI combines proxies for three human capabilities: longevity, knowledge, and a decent standard of living. Longevity is represented by life expectancy at birth; knowledge by adult literacy and mean years of schooling, weighted 2/3 to literacy and 1/3 to schooling; and a decent standard of living by GDP per capita based on US dollars purchasing power parity (PPP) adjusted to eliminate differences in national price levels (Haq 2003: 129). It is measured by a cut-off point defined as an income level regarded as adequate for a reasonable standard of living and reasonable fulfillment of human capabilities. The cut-off point comes from the current global average real GDP per capita in PPP dollars. These three measures are given equal weight and averaged together.

The HDI, and the Human Development Reports which include it, were developed by the major UN development agency, the UNDP, and its Human Development Report Office (HDRO). It grew out of almost thirty years of work and thinking in the field of development economics and represented a significant shift from a focus on utility to welfare. Efforts to produce such welfare-focused indicators began in the 1960s along with a critique of the dominant focus on growth in GNP since this measure neglected issues of employment, income distribution, jobs, and justice (Streeten 2003: 94). By the 1970s, there was increasing interest in a "basic needs" approach. By the 1980s, however, the basic needs approach seemed too narrow as new concerns arose about women and children, the physical environment, human rights, political freedom and governance, and the role of culture. New theories of economic growth focused not on technological progress alone, but also on the behavior of people, highlighting the importance of education and knowledge for productivity. Amartya Sen proposed an approach that expanded the basic needs idea by emphasizing the importance of freedom to choose as the basis for well-being (Sen 1999). He argued that a standard of living should be judged by a person's "capability" to lead the life that he or she values, including being well-fed and healthy, achieving self-respect, and participating in the life of the community (Streeten 2003: 94–100).

The HDI was created by a small group of elite development economists who served as advisors to the UNDP. The principle architect of the concept, Mahbub ul Haq, had experience in the World Bank, while his advisors held academic positions at Oxford, Cambridge, London School of Economics, Yale, and Boston University (Fukuda-Parr and Kumer 2003: 85–91 and 393–395). Mahbub ul Haq himself was an economist trained at Government College, Lahore (1948–1953), King's College, Cambridge (1953–1955), and Yale University (1955–1957). From 1989 to 1995 he served as Special Advisor to the Administrator of the UNDP and chief architect of the HDRs. A second major contributor was Amartya Sen, a professor of economics at Harvard. Sen himself was Master of Trinity College Cambridge, taught at Oxford, London School of Economics, and Delhi University, and was awarded the Nobel Prize in Economics in 1998 (Fukuda-Parr and Kumar 2003: 394). The creators and consultants behind the HDI came largely from the UK, India, Pakistan, Europe, and the USA. They belonged to prominent academic institutions as well as the World Bank and the UN, and were linked by long-term personal ties.

Despite widespread acceptance of the HDI in theory, there have been periodic struggles over its content and source of data. These fights underscore how important this indicator is to individual countries. Countries care a great deal about their HDI ranking because if it is too low they will not win foreign investment and if it is too high they will not receive foreign aid. Critiques of the HDI have surfaced in the UN Statistical Commission several times, both about its methodology and its use of data. In 2000, in response to a complaint from Australia about the choice of indicators and the statistical content of the Human Development Report 1997, an expert group met and agreed that there was a lack of transparency in the sources of data in that year's report. A similar issue emerged again in 2010 when some delegates expressed concern about the fact that the UNSC did not have oversight over the HDI, among other problems. The UNSC appointed a "Friends of the Chair" committee as an expert group to investigate the problem. In March 2010, the UNSC expert committee met with a team from the HDRO of the UNDP. The committee stressed the importance of using official statistics rather than unofficial ones, including academic ones (UN Statistical Commission 2011a). The HDRO office replied that it had held an extensive series of consultations with a wide range of experts, and that the HDRO "did not have a mandate within the United Nations to collect primary data from countries, and therefore relied extensively on the data series produced by international and regional organizations with the relevant expertise and mandates in the given subject-matter areas" (UN Statistical Commission 2011a: 4). The HDRO did not respond to the UNSC expert group's offer for further technical reviews or consultations.

In December 2010, Brazil, Morocco, and South Africa presented a joint report on their concerns about the choice of indicators and their methodology, focusing in particular on a lack of consultation with the UNSC and the methodology and data sources used in a new "Multi-dimensional Poverty Index" developed at Oxford University (UN Statistical Commission 2011b: 2). The report noted that criticisms of the HDI had been circulated since 2000 and generated two expert group committees to discuss it, and that similar issues had been debated concerning discrepancies between national data and the data used by international agencies for the MDGs (UN Statistical Commission 2011b: 2–4). The report was concerned about a lack of transparency in how data was collected and used, the use of imputations and estimations for countries when no data is available, and the failure to use official country data or the misuse of this data (UN Statistical Commission 2011b: 6).

At the 2011 UNSC meeting, this report generated a protracted debate. For three hours, country after country complained about the latest HDI report, a substantial investment of time in a very short four-day meeting. A total of forty-one delegations spoke. Complaints focused primarily on the use of non-official statistics in the report, as well as the failure of the HDRO to consult with national statistical offices about discrepancies between national and international data. There were complaints that six countries in the Caribbean and about twelve in the Pacific had not been ranked at all because their statistics were deemed inadequate. These countries said that the failure to include them because their statistics were too poor undermined faith in their statistics both domestically and internationally. Some other countries complained that the report discussed the inadequacy of their statistical data, again giving them trouble with their citizens, who were critical of their statistical office.

Another set of complaints concerned the use of dummy data or other extrapolated information when data was not available. Some countries said that if there was not adequate data available on their countries, then they needed technical assistance and support from other countries in order to collect it. The request for added resources from richer countries to improve the statistics of poorer countries was a frequent theme.

Many countries complained that the indicators had been changed. While education, one of the three criteria, had been measured in the past largely by literacy rates, a UNDP staff member who worked on the report told me that they had decided it was a bad indicator, since it is only a yes/no variable and 100 countries claim 100% literacy, so there is not much variation. Instead, they introduced expected mean years of schooling. But UNESCO did not carry out an educational survey, so the relevant data came from a study by a Harvard University professor and his student, now at the University of Korea. Several countries were angry that the HDI relied on this non-official data – i.e., data not collected by a UN agency. The HDI also introduced a multi-dimensional poverty index that included an assessment of assets. According to a UNDP staff member at the meeting, this index asks whether a person has a roof over his head, a toilet, and so on. One indicator is whether the family has a bicycle. Some countries complained that they have camels, not bicycles. But the HDRO official I talked to said that it does not work to substitute a camel for a bicycle since this means the measures are not comparable.

Moreover, he added that the UNDP mandate is to use international statistics, not to consult national statistical data. If countries want their statistics included, they can send them to the World Bank, which will harmonize them and they can then be considered. He also noted that not all countries have strong statistical capacity. He added that the non-official report on education that countries were complaining about was widely respected in the academic community, and that if UNESCO had produced this data it would have been used.

Another major complaint was that there was no consultation with the UNSC. For example, the issue of this new index was raised by South Africa at the UNSC meetings in 2010. At the time, South Africa complained that the UNDP was developing a new indicator without consulting the UNSC. At the time, the chair of the UNSC said that there really was not anything he could do about this, and that the authority of the UNSC over all statistical efforts was not clear. The report lodged by South Africa, Brazil, and Morocco before the 2011 meeting complained about the use of the international statistics and the failure to resolve discrepancies with national ones. An expert group met and advocated consultation, but countries complained that this did not happen. The UNDP staffer I talked to pointed out that there had been some consultation, but that the report is produced by an office of only 20 people, working 12–15 hours a day to put this index together. They are very dedicated and want to do good work. He found all this complaining very discouraging. On the other hand, a staff member of the UNSD said that the HDRO is seen as too independent, too arrogant, and too close to the academic community by country representatives.

Thus, the major issues in the debate were the failure of the HDRO to consult with the UNSC during the preparation of the report and index, the failure to even rank some countries on the basis of their poor data, and the use of non-official statistics that were produced by US academics rather than a UN agency to measure education. Underlying these complaints was a concern on the part of many countries about their HDI rank, which affects their ability to attract foreign investment or their eligibility for foreign aid. Many more countries were angry that the HDRO refused to use their national statistics, claiming that they were inadequate and relying on international data instead. This widespread concern showed that countries value having the international community recognize them as having good statistical systems. Countries also complained about the failure of consultation and the use of non-official data. The latter points both speak to the status of the UNSC. They represented slights to the authority of the UNSC within the UN system and showed overreliance on private expertise rather than official statistics.

The course of this debate, and the broad participation of many countries, suggests a surprising level of unanimity on these points despite disagreement about the HDI itself. While some countries supported the HDI, most complained. In UNSC discussions, country representatives speak for their countries rather than themselves, so I describe the debate in terms of country opinions rather than individual ones. Cape Verde noted that discrepancies in data, especially about health and education, make national data look less credible and create problems since aid is attached to rankings. Samoa complained that seven countries in the Pacific were excluded for lack of data, which is unfortunate since it provides misleading information to states and development partners. Caricom, representing the Caribbean countries, noted that six countries in its region were not included in the report because of data inadequacy. Several countries referred to the importance of following the fundamental principles of official statistics and placing greater reliance on national statistical offices. Developed countries such as France, Germany, the UK, the USA, and Australia expressed concerns about a lack of consultation and the use of non-official data. Canada said it recognized legitimate concerns about the availability of data and its quality, but noted that the selection of indicators is part of policy decisions that are beyond the concerns of statisticians. Germany noted the need to proceed with "utmost caution" on the use of composite indicators. Some countries suggested that the 2010 HDRO report and index should be withdrawn, while others suggested that they should issue a statement of deep regret about the situation and ask for a response from the HDRO.

While many countries asked for more consultation, some wanted to pass a resolution criticizing the report, and a few, including the Netherlands, wanted to pass a resolution rejecting the report. Although this plan was suggested by a few other countries, it did not generate sufficient support. At the end of the long discussion in the commission, the countries asked the UNSD (the UNSC secretariat) to negotiate with the UNDP, to ask the HDI to change, and to work with them. The chair and head of the UNSD commented that new things were being asked of the UNSD all the time and yet they had no increase in staff. He seemed unenthusiastic about the project, and a UNSD staffer told me he thought it was not likely to happen. By the end of the meeting, the HDI was not condemned, but the desire for greater consultation before the HDI was finished was firmly established.

The head of the UNSD who was chairing the UNSC meeting summarized the debate by saying that the UNSD would mediate between agencies, that it expresses deep regret that the UNDP (the parent organization for the HDRO) did not consult with the statistical community before issuing the HDI with new indicators and non-official data, and that it emphasizes the importance of the fundamental principles of statistics. He also stated that the UNSC regrets that some countries were not covered because of lack of data. It is, he concluded, the prerogative of the UNDP to pick indicators, but the quality of the data is a matter for the UNSC.

The HDRO responded that on some issues, only non-official compilations existed: for example, UNESCO did not produce data on adult mean years of schooling, a component of the revised HDI, but used estimates from a UNESCO database developed by a university research team whose work was first published in 1993 and "has been validated by extensive academic discussion" (UN Development Programme 2010b: 6). Moreover, the HDRO pointed out that it is not mandated to consult national data. It did, however, offer to improve consultation procedures.

The various challenges to the 2010 HDI and other HDRO indicators were considered by the UNDP Executive Board in 2011. It welcomed the HDRO's further efforts "to engage with the international statistical community on statistical matters" and its consultations with governments. It supported efforts to improve the quality and accuracy of the HDRs, but "while also preserving the Report's credibility and impartiality, and without compromising its editorial independence" (UN Development Program Executive Board 2011). The HDRO was thus left to take what guidance it wished from expert statisticians. As this example indicates, the HDRO has considerable autonomy despite these political wrangles. It is striking that actors on all sides of the debate invoked professionalism, impartiality, scientific standards, transparent methods, and the Fundamental Principles of Official Statistics themselves.

At the next UNSC meeting in 2012, several delegations commented that consultation had improved, although they still had complaints. Fourteen countries talked about the HDI. Most thanked the HDRO for better consultation procedures. Some still complained about a lack of transparency and the use of incorrect information. Iran objected to the practice of equally weighting all three factors when not all countries view them as equally important. Angola suggested that, given the high visibility of the report, it would be good to have training programs to deal with the tensions around discrepancies between HDRO and national statistical data. Turkey reiterated the importance of using official national data. Oman complained that the 2011 report used old data, which affected its ranking.

This debate underscored the importance of the index itself. In general, the complaints focused on the data, not the conception of the index. Despite considerable national complaining, the HDI survived essentially unchanged. Many of the complaints concerned the procedures of the HDRO office and its failure to consult countries, particularly over the use of national and international data. Inequalities in statistical capacity and the quality and reliability of data parallel the divisions between powerful and powerless countries. Many poorer countries argued that if they were given more resources, they could produce better data. There is also a clear worry about countries' statistical reputations, at home and abroad.

CONCLUSIONS

The UN Statistical Commission represents a shared field of expertise and social networks, situated between national political offices and international statistical experts, such as the staff of the HDRO. While they share the principles of autonomy and non-interference, the members of the UNSC also represent their governments, who face the loss of aid and the loss of face and credibility if their statistics are deemed inaccurate for international assessments. In these discussions, there is a clear distinction between advanced industrial countries that have highly developed statistical systems and poorer developing ones for whom gathering statistical data remains an expensive and perhaps less essential government function. The latter constantly say that if the former wish to have certain forms of statistical data available, they will have to provide them with the resources to collect it. As Morton Jerven notes, the statistical offices of many poor countries in Africa are greatly understaffed and may be closed down between census rounds (2013). In this setting, it appears that statistical competence becomes a marker of modernity. It is also clearly a dimension of sovereignty, since those with the resources to do so can measure themselves, while poorer countries are measured by international agencies.

This is a field of expertise with unequal participants, whose relative capacities serve to underscore and reinforce their inequality. The UNSC represents a formal scene of national equality and sovereignty, yet the debate reveals the vulnerability of poor countries that lack sophisticated statistical systems and are subject to the decisions of global experts who design measurement systems and collect the statistics that determine their position in the world, at least as measured by the HDI and other global indicators.

REFERENCES

Alston, Philip and Katarina Tomaševski. 1984. *The Right to Food: Towards a System for Supervising States' Compliance with the Right to Food*. Leiden and Boston: Martinus Nijhoff Publishers.
Cobb, Clifford and Craig Rixford. 1998. *Lessons Learned from the History of Social Indicators*. San Francisco: Redefining Progress Foundation. Retrieved from www.humanrightsimpact.org/ru/resource-database/publications/resources/view/32/user_hria_publications/. Accessed November 2, 2011.
Cohn, Bernard S. 1996. *Colonialism and Its Forms of Knowledge: The British in India*. Princeton: Princeton University Press.
Davis, Kevin E., Angelina Fisher, Benedict Kingsbury, and Sally Engle Merry, eds. 2012. *Governance by Indicators: Global Power Through Quantification and Rankings*. Oxford: Oxford University Press.
Dickinson, Elizabeth. 2011. "Anthropology of an Idea: GDP: One Stat to Rule Them All." *Foreign Policy* Jan/Feb 2011: 37.
Duncan, Otis Dudley. 1984. *Notes on Social Measurement: Historical and Critical*. New York: Russell Sage Foundation.
Foucault, Michel. 1991. "Governmentality." In *The Foucault Effect: Studies in Governmentality*. Graham Burchell, Colin Gordon, and Peter Miller, eds. Chicago: University of Chicago Press, pp. 87–105.
Fukuda-Parr, Sakiko and A.K. Shiva Kumar, eds. 2003 (2nd edn: 2005). *Readings in Human Development: Concepts, Measures and Policies for a Development Paradigm*. Second

Edition. New York: Human Development Report Office, United Nations Development Program; New Delhi: Oxford University Press.

2003. "Introduction." In Sakiko Fukuda-Parr and A.K. Shiva Kumar, eds. 2005 (2003). *Readings in Human Development: Concepts, Measures and Policies for a Development Paradigm*. New York: Human Development Report Office, United Nations Development Program and Oxford University Press, New Delhi, pp. xxi–xxxi.

Hacking, Ian. 1990. *The Taming of Chance*. Cambridge: Cambridge University Press.

Haq, Mahbub ul. 2003. "The Birth of the Human Development Index." In Sakiko Fukuda-Parr and A.K. Shiva Kumar, eds. 2003. *Readings in Human Development: Concepts, Measures and Policies for a Development Paradigm*. New York: Human Development Report Office, United Nations Development Program and Oxford University Press, New Delhi, pp. 127–138.

Igo, Sarah E. 2007. *The Averaged American: Surveys, Citizens, and the Making of a Mass Public*. Cambridge, MA: Harvard University Press.

Innes, Judith. 1989. "Disappointments and Legacies of the Social Indicators." *Journal of Public Policy* 9(4): 429–432.

Jerven, Morten. 2011. "Users and Producers of African Income: Measuring the Progress of African Economies." *African Affairs*. 110/439, 169–190.

2013. *Poor Numbers: How We Are Misled by African Development Statistics and What to do About It*. Ithaca: Cornell University Press.

Merry, Sally Engle. 2011. "Measuring the World: Indicators, Human Rights, and Global Governance." In *Corporate Lives: New Perspectives on the Social Life of the Corporate Form*. Damani Partridge, Marina Welker, and Rebecca Hardin, eds. Wenner-Gren Symposium Series. *Current Anthropology*, Vol. 52, Supplementary Issue 3: S83–S95.

2016. *The Seductions of Quantification: Measuring Human Rights, Violence against Women, and Sex Trafficking*. Chicago: University of Chicago Press.

Merry, Sally Engle and Susan Coutin. 2014. "Technologies of Truth in the Anthropology of Conflict." *American Ethnologist*. 41(1): 1–16.

Merry, Sally Engle and Summer J. Wood. 2015. "The Paradox of Measurement: Child Rights in Tanzania." *Current Anthropology*. 2015. Vol 56 (2): 205–229.

Mitchell, Timothy. 2002. *Rule of Experts: Egypt, Techno-politics, Modernity*. Berkeley and Los Angeles: University of California Press.

Poovey, Mary. 1998. *A History of the Modern Fact: Problems of Knowledge in the Sciences of Wealth and Society*. Chicago: University of Chicago Press.

Porter, Theodore M. 1995. *Trust in Numbers: The Pursuit of Objectivity in Science and Public Life*. Princeton: Princeton University Press.

Rittich, Kerry. 2014. "Governing by Measuring: The Millennium Development Goals in Global Governance." In *Law in Transition: Human Rights, Development and Transitional Justice*. Ruth Buchanan and Peer Zumbansen, eds. Oxford: Hart Publishing Ltd, pp. 165–185.

Schweber, Libby. 2006. *Disciplining Statistics: Demography and Vital Statistics in France and England, 1830–1885*. Durham: Duke University Press.

Sen, Amartya K. 1999. *Development as Freedom*. New York: Anchor Books.

2003. "Foreword." In Sakiko Fukuda-Parr and A.K. Shiva Kumar, eds. 2005 (2003). *Readings in Human Development: Concepts, Measures and Policies for a Development Paradigm*. New York: Human Development Report Office, United Nations Development Program and Oxford University Press, New Delhi, pp. vii–xiii.

Sheldon, Eleanor Bernert and Howard Freeman. 1970. "Notes on Social Indicators: Promises and Potential." *Policy Sciences* 1: 97–111.

Stanton, Elizabeth A. 2007. "The Human Development Index: A History." Political Economy Research Institute, UMass Amherst, Working paper series no. 127.
Streeten, Paul. 2003. "Shifting Fashions in Development Dialogue." In Sakiko Fukuda-Parr and A.K. Shiva Kumar, eds. *Readings in Human Development: Concepts, Measures and Policies for a Development Paradigm.* New York: Human Development Report Office, United Nations Development Program and Oxford University Press, New Delhi, pp. 92–105.
Tomaševski, Katarina. 1984. "Human Rights Indicators: The Right to Food as a Test Case." In P. Alston and K. Tomaševski, eds. *The Right to Food.* Leiden: Martinus Nijhoff Publishers, pp. 135–167.
United Nations. 1961. "Statistical Questions." In *Yearbook of the United Nations*, 1961, pp. 290–291. New York: Department of Public Information.
UN Development Programme. 2010a. History of the Human Development Report. http://hdr.undp.org/en/humandev/reports/. Accessed October 2, 2011.
   2010b. *Report on Statistics of Human Development.* UN doc. /CN.3/2011/15.
UN Development Programme Executive Board. 2011. *Executive Board Resolution* 2011/11, 16 June 2011. UN doc. DP/2011/32.
UN Statistical Commission. 2011a. *Report of the Bureau of the Statistical Commission on Statistics of Human Development.* 7 December 2010. E/CN.3/2011/14.
   2011b. *Report of Brazil, Morocco and South Africa on Member States' Concerns with Indicators Released by the United Nations agencies.* 7 December 2010. E/CN.3/2011/16.
UN Statistics Division. 2013. Guidelines for Producing Statistics on Violence against Women: Statistical Surveys. 9 September 2013. http://unstats.un.org/unsd/gender/docs/guidelines_VAW.pdf. Accessed August 1, 2014.
Ward, Michael. 2004. *Quantifying the World: UN Ideas and Statistics.* United Nations Intellectual History Project Series. Bloomington: Indiana University Press.
Waring, Marilyn. 1999. *Counting for Nothing: What Men Value and What Women Are Worth.* Toronto: University of Toronto Press.
   1990. *If Women Counted: A New Feminist Economics.* New York: HarperCollins.

8

From Boardrooms to Field Programs: Humanitarianism and International Development in Southern Africa

Robert K. Hitchcock

EXPLORING THE UNHCR AND WORLD BANK COUNTRY TEAMS

As an anthropologist interested in human rights issues and working as an expert with indigenous peoples and minorities in southern Africa for more than forty years, I have more than once found myself involved in the work of government, global institutions, and international and local NGOs in matters related to resettlements, land policy and development, displacement, and refugees. In this context, and over this lengthy period, I was what might be called a "casual" expert: an anthropologist with field-based experience who was occasionally called upon to put my expertise to use in the service of marginalized peoples directly affected by large-scale projects of humanitarian intervention and development. The method that I employed in this work was long-term or "longitudinal," which gave me some advantages in being able to report on the work of the agencies in the field at various points in time, including being able to track the transformations that occur at the local level as a result of changing United Nations High Commissioner for Refugees (UNHCR) and World Bank and state policies.

The UNHCR and World Bank were established at the close of the Second World War, a time in which the world community was dealing with large numbers of refugees, and issues of human rights and social justice were high on the global agenda; these issues helped shape the global institutions that were created (Betts, Loescher, and Milner 2012; Rich 2013). Today, there is a new era of global crisis. The 1980s and 1990s and the post-9/11 periods have seen significant sociopolitical changes, including widespread concern with security and transformations in the global economy, which have led to changes in the policies and practices of global protection and financial institutions. At the same time, out of keeping with the widely declared urgency of their missions, many local offices of the UNHCR and the World Bank have seen budget cuts and personnel reductions, reflected above all in the decline of socially oriented assistance programs.

The UNHCR has a humanitarian mandate, in contrast with the World Bank, which is a financial institution that has a development mandate. Both the UNHCR and the World Bank have to deal with issues of involuntary displacement and resettlement of people. In the case of the UNHCR, humanitarian assistance is provided to those people who are forced out of their homes and who cross borders. The World Bank, for its part, finances development projects that may lead to physical dislocation of people as well as the loss of assets, land, income, resources, and livelihoods. In many cases, the two organizations operate in the same states, as was the case in two of the contexts that I consider here: Windhoek (Namibia) and Maseru (Lesotho). Currently, much more of the work than in the past is being handled by outside consultants, some of whom see themselves as obliged to follow the dictates of the global multilateral institutions. Wanting to avoid giving "bad news" to the home office or risk the slowing down of funds disbursements for projects, they sometimes tend to downplay the negative social, environmental, economic, and political impacts of the programs they are working on.

Both the UNHCR and the World Bank have to deal with issues of involuntary displacement and resettlement of people. For this reason, both agencies are discussed in the context of an "anthropology of humanitarianism" that addresses the alleviation of suffering and how and why this has become a moral imperative (McNeill and Stclair 2009; Wilson and Brown 2009; Bornstein and Redfield 2010; Feldman and Ticktin 2010; Redfield 2013).[1] In the case of the UNHCR, humanitarian assistance is provided to those people who are forced out of their homes and who cross borders. An important objective of the UNHCR is to see that people are repatriated voluntarily to their home countries. Where this is not possible, alternative strategies are sought, including integration of the refugees into the populations of host countries (if states allow this to take place) or, alternatively, resettlement in third countries such as the United States or the United Kingdom. In line with the humanitarian principles pursued by the UNHCR, protection of refugees is paramount. Where refugees wish to stay in the countries where they have sought refuge, the goal of the UNHCR is to support governments in these efforts. According to UNHCR policy, the objective of the organization is not just to restore living standards, but to *improve* the lives and livelihoods of the resettled population and their hosts (Weiss and Minear 1993; Gilbert 1998; Crisp 2001; Loescher 2001b; Betts, Loescher, and Milner 2012; UNHCR 2012). The problem has been that refugee resettlement programs have often failed to achieve this goal.

The same is true of the World Bank projects, though the goals of the World Bank are simply to *restore*, rather than improve the living standards of project-affected people, which have been the cause of impoverishment of a substantial number of households in Lesotho. This policy is something that the World Bank supervisory teams were deeply concerned about and that put them at odds with policy makers in the Washington D.C. headquarters. The World Bank itself is occasionally itself

[1] For literature on the internal policy-setting and decision-making processes of humanitarian and development agencies see, for example, Hyndman (2000); Loescher (2001a); Lewis and Mosse (2006); Mosse (2011a, 2011b); Sarfaty (2012); Fresia (2013).

responsible for refugee crises, in that it finances development projects that may lead to physical dislocation of people as well as the loss of assets, land, income, resources, and livelihoods.

In this chapter I focus in particular on the way that the two agencies intervene in this process of human displacement. In Namibia my ethnographic work related to the refugees-resettled issues – the work started in 1987 and lasted until 2015; while in Lesotho I followed the development-resettlement work of the World Bank and of the Panel of Environmental Experts since 1990, which was ongoing to 2012, followed by work for the Millennium Challenge Corporation on Lesotho wetlands in the highlands (Hitchcock 2015).

Let me briefly offer some background to my research as a consultant for these agencies. First, I conducted interviews and observations in the UNHCR Liaison Office in Namibia and in its headquarters in Geneva. The focus of these interviews was on the professional staff of the office, from the UNHCR Namibia director and assistant director to the human resource officers and other staff, including social workers, accountants, logistical personnel who would handle travel, security officers, secretaries, domestic staff workers, and cleaners. I also made observations in meetings of interventions attended by UNHCR staff and consultants.[2] I carried out ethnographic work on the UNHCR, the refugees in the UNHCR–Government of Namibia refugee camp Osire, and the people and organizations in the area where the refugee camp was supposed to be resettled, in M'Kata, Tsumkwe District, and Otjozondjupa Region, who consisted mainly of !Kung, Khwe, Vasekele, and Ju/'hoansi San (Hitchcock 2001, 2012a). Activities that I participated in ranged from group meetings about the potential resettlement to agricultural and plant-gathering work by local people in the area where the refugee camp was going to be moved.

I used similar methods in the World Bank study in Lesotho. In this case I visited the World Bank Headquarter in Washington D.C., and at the local level I was a member of a Panel of Environmental Experts (POE) that monitored and evaluated the Lesotho Highlands Water Project, a large-scale water transfer project involving two countries, Lesotho and South Africa. The years that I worked in Lesotho were 1990–2013, usually two times a year with the POE and the Lesotho Highlands Development Authority. I worked directly with the World Bank supervisory mission teams that visited Lesotho, and I interviewed all of the members of these teams, from the two-team leaders to hydrologists, economists, engineers, biologists, and anthropologists. I also worked in the offices of the Maseru World Bank, where I conducted interviews of the staff, many of whom were similar to the staff of the UNHCR liaison

---

[2] I used a questionnaire in the interviews of the UNHCR staff and held group discussions in which I asked personnel about their jobs, their opinions of the management, their sentiments about UNHCR and Namibia policy, and their concerns about the ways that matters were being handled at the Windhoek headquarters level, at the Osire refugee camp, at the transit camps, and with the staff who had been posted to Otjozondjupa Region in anticipation of the resettlement. The years that I worked in Namibia were 1987, 1992 (twice), 1994, 1995, 2001, 2005, 2011, 2012, 2014, and 2015.

office in Windhoek. Building on work monitoring and evaluating a World Bank-funded water transfer project in Lesotho (the Lesotho Highlands Water Project Phase 1) (1990–2013), I examined the degree to which the Bank's expert and civil servants followed its own operational guidelines on indigenous peoples and resettlement as the two governments involved in the project observed treaty obligations. I paid particular attention to the degree to which the World Bank personnel at the field level observed safeguard protections in its programs involving economic development at the local level, and whether they attempted to argue for social and environmental safeguards protections at the headquarters of the Bank in Washington, D.C.

Drawing on field-based experience with the UNHCR and humanitarian nongovernment organizations in Namibia and work with experts from the World Bank in Lesotho, I examine the activities of these two global institutions in the field and in the relationships between field offices and headquarters in Geneva and Washington D.C., particularly those involved in refugee intervention. Through these two examples, I show that where there is a convergence of local and global scales in institutions such as the UNHCR and the World Bank, the offices of the headquarters usually dominate, often by refusing responsibility for the political, social, or environmental consequences of projects that they present to the world as strictly economic, developmental, or humanitarian.

UNHCR IN NAMIBIA

Founded in 1950 in response to the global concern for refugees and displaced persons, and based in Geneva, the UNHCR is a United Nations specialized agency that operates in most countries. International diplomacy is a key part of the work of the UNHCR, which has to negotiate with nation-states in order to operate within their borders. While the UNHCR at the outset was seen as a temporary institution, the refugee crises that have persisted over the past six and a half decades have resulted in its becoming a permanent institution with highly trained and committed staff and a well-worked-out mandate and set of goals and objectives. What started out as an organization with 34 staff based mainly in Geneva is now a global institution operating in some 120 countries with a staff of over 7,500, not including local field staff. The inability of the international community to deal with conflicts and protracted refugee situations has resulted in severe pressures on the UNHCR, the global community, states, and local NGOs. The local field staffs of the UNHCR are often overstretched, but they continue to do as much as they can to resolve the complex problems facing refugees and other displaced persons.

The UNHCR Liaison Office in Namibia consisted of twenty persons, including a director, deputy director, humanitarian affairs officer, public relations personnel, and secretarial staff. The UNHCR also had a presence at Osire, the refugee camp in Otjozondjupa Region.

The Republic of Namibia, like some other countries in Africa, has had to cope with sizable numbers of refugees coming into the country. Refugee flows into Namibia intensified in the late 1990s, particularly in 1999–2001, with several thousand people coming to Namibia from Angola after the resumption of hostilities between government forces and some of the opposition groups. Others came from southern, central, and eastern Africa in response to conflict and other kinds of pressures. Once they entered Namibia and encountered Namibian authorities, people seeking protection as refugees were supposed to contact either the Namibian government or United Nations High Commissioner authorities. The potential refugees were interviewed and, if they were found to be people legitimately seeking protection because of fear of persecution in their home countries, they were transferred to a refugee camp at Osire in central Namibia, located on a former white-owned farm in the commercial ranching part of the country.[3]

The Osire refugee camp was opened in 1992. By the latter part of 2001, there were more than 21,000 refugees in Osire, some of them relatively recent arrivals. The refugees housed at the Osire camp were provided with technical assistance, training and advice, and they were supplied with food, medicines, and other goods by the government of the Republic of Namibia, the UNHCR, the World Food Program, and various NGOs, including the Namibia Red Cross Society (NRCS). There were sometimes tensions between the UNHCR and Namibian government refugee camp staff members and the refugees, some of which resulted in demonstrations and, occasionally, riots. Dissatisfaction with food, blankets, and other goods and with camp sanitation conditions were some of the reasons for the hard feelings on the part of the refugees. While there were medical personnel assigned to Osire who saw patients and dispensed medicines, a complaint of some of the refugees was that there were too few trained medical personnel to handle their health-related problems.

Commercial farmers in the region surrounding Osire, most of whom were Germans or Afrikaaners, lobbied long and hard for the removal of the refugee camp away from their freehold farming area to another part of the country. Eventually they achieved some initial success in October 2000 when the government of Namibia announced a plan to resettle these refugees at M'Kata, in Tsumkwe District West in the Kalahari Desert region of northeastern Namibia. M'Kata, however, was already home to some 4,200 mainly !Kung

---

[3] To put this figure in a more contemporary context, in 2014, there were 136,000 official refugees in southern Africa, 1,519 of whom were in Namibia. There were even larger numbers of asylum-seekers: 278,000 in southern Africa, 1,158 of whom were in Namibia (UNHCR and government of Namibia data). Namibia does not recognize internally displaced persons (IDPs) within its borders, although there are some people who see themselves as being internally displaced as a result of development projects or the establishment of conservation areas, as occurred in Otjozondjupa Region (N≠a Jaqna, Hitchcock 2012a; Welch 2013) and in West Caprivi, now Zambezi Region (Taylor 2012). It should be noted that the UNHCR does not recognize what some analysts have termed "development refugees" or environmental refugees (for discussions of these terms, see Kane 1995; Oliver-Smith 2009a, 2009b).

and Khwe San, whose development hopes were riding on a very different agenda: approval of their Community Based Natural Resource Management (CBNRM) project, which was to become in 2003 the N≠a Jaqna Conservancy sponsored by the !Kung Traditional Authority. Several reasons were given for the proposed resettlement, including overcrowding of the Osire refugee camp, the lack of sufficient land and natural resources in the present location to sustain the population, the desire to establish a refugee resettlement area that had sufficient land to allow agricultural activities to take place, and the need for greater security.

The plans for the Osire refugee camp relocation became a very public battle, fought out in meetings at the UNHCR; the Ministry of Home Affairs and Immigration; the Ministry of Agriculture, Water, and Forestry; the Ministry of Lands and Resettlement; the Office of the Deputy Prime Minister; and in public meetings in M'Kata, Tsumkwe, Otjiwarango, and Windhoek. The Namibian media paid close attention to the issues of the relocation, and people writing op-ed pieces generally opposed the refugee camp relocation.

Interviews related to the resettlement planning assessments for a possible move from Osire to M'Kata were done under the auspices of the UNHCR by a sociologist, some field enumerators who were graduate-level sociology students, and myself, an anthropologist. We also worked with translators who spoke various Angolan languages (e.g. Oshiwambo) as well as !Kung, Khwe, Vaseleke, and Ju/'hoan. The interviews of refugees, UNHCR and GRN personnel, and members of the potential host community consisted of questions about people's backgrounds, livelihoods, current circumstances, and desires. There were also a number of questions that focused on people's sentiments about resettlement and what impacts they thought the resettlement might have. Careful attention was paid to questions of confidentiality since many of the people that were interviewed were concerned about their opinions being revealed either to the government or to UNHCR and refugee camp authorities. The majority of refugees to whom I spoke were opposed to the relocation of the Osire refugee camp. Some people in Osire saw it as potentially problematic because the area to which they would be moved was remote and had fewer natural resources than did Osire.

Local people from the potential host community in M'Kata felt that the area is known for its unique habitats, heritage, and people, and that the presence of refugees potentially could adversely affect the natural and social environments of the area. There were also those – admittedly a minority – who believed that the presence of a refugee camp would have positive spin-off effects, such as increased employment opportunities, expanded infrastructure, and larger markets for goods and services. A more commonly expressed opinion about the potential movement of refugees into the area was that it would place much greater pressure on natural resources, such as water, firewood, and wild plant foods, and could exacerbate inter-group conflicts. These opinions, however, were rare. Most people were unwilling to express their views for fear of being targeted by the government for not going along with national-level policy decisions.

There was also widespread concern over the issue of the proposed resettlement of refugees from Osire to the Tsumkwe District West area on the part of NGOs and conservancies in Windhoek and in the M'Kata area (Hitchcock 2001; Pakleppa 2001). I conducted a number of interviews of personnel in Namibian non-government organizations, including the Working Group of Indigenous Minorities in Southern Africa (WIMSA), and had meetings with the organization along with the lawyer working with them. WIMSA was working closely with people in Tsumkwe District West to form what came to be known as the N≠a Jaqna Conservancy in 2003 (Hitchcock 2012a). There was already a communal conservancy in Tsumkwe District East known as the Nyae Nyae Conservancy, which had been established in 1998 (Biesele and Hitchcock 2013). The majority of people in the M'Kata area had expressed deep opposition to the relocation of the Osire refugee camp to their area, saying that it would disrupt their plans to form a conservancy, the N≠a Jaqna Conservancy (NNC), and would also prevent them from establishing a community forest at M'Kata in Tsumkwe District West. Similar views were expressed by people in the Nyae Nyae Conservancy to the east.

Together, the !Kung Traditional Authority, the Ju/'hoan Traditional Authority, Tsamkxao ≠Oma in Nyae Nyae, the Nyae Nyae Conservancy, the Working Group of Indigenous Minorities in Southern Africa (WIMSA), and other local indigenous and environmental NGOs sought to get the government and the UNHCR to change their minds about the resettlement. The traditional authorities also tried to meet with UN officials who they hoped would take a stance against the positions of their agencies, but found that nobody in the headquarters of the UN agencies would lobby on their behalf. Several of the M'Kata people also met with World Bank officers to seek support, but these individuals were reluctant to take sides in issues that the World Bank defined as political and therefore outside of their mandate.

They further realized that they could not sue the UNHCR because of its standing as an international organization. What is more, a current of public opinion was against them since many of the people of Namibia were supportive of the efforts of UNHCR to assist refugees and asylum seekers who had come into the country.

At UNHCR headquarters in Geneva, there were intense debates over whether the relocation of the main refugee camp in Namibia should take place. These debates took place in the UNHCR headquarters office in Windhoek, in the offices of the Namibian Ministry of Home Affairs and Immigration, in Otjiwarongo, and at M'Kata.[4] Several of the people who I interviewed in the course of this study indicated that they thought that a reason for the resettlement of the refugees was to establish greater administrative control and protection, something that might be

[4] Minutes of these meetings were kept by UNHCR and government personnel, and these minutes were assessed as part of the research. Analysis was done of media coverage of some of these meetings, some of which were called by the Namibian government.

done more effectively in a remote area instead of one close to population centers in Namibia.

Others in the UNHCR in Geneva and Windhoek said that the relocation was a bad idea because it was too expensive. They also said there was chance that the conflict in Angola would be resolved relatively soon and then Angolans in the camp, who formed the majority, could return home. Several UNHCR staff members at headquarters in Geneva said that the UNHCR was "not in the policy-making business" and that the decision about refugee camp relocation should be left to the government of the Republic of Namibia. There was also headquarters staff who argued that the results of the social and environmental impact assessments of the proposed relocation should be evaluated before any decisions were made. There was clearly a diversity of opinion about the relocation of Osire, but the stated official position in Geneva was that the UNHCR was following the lead of the government of Namibia.

At the liaison office representing the headquarters of UNHCR in Windhoek there were similar debates during Country Team meetings and in meetings with both government and non-government organizations. Most of the personnel in the UNHCR liaison office were either management staff, consisting primarily of people who had extensive experience in humanitarian assistance in various parts of the world, or were locally hired people who were low-level administrators, secretaries, or service personnel. Much of the time of the professional staff was spent writing reports. Relatively few of them went to the field, and most of the people in the office had not been to Osire, nor had they been to the transit camps or to the Angola–Namibia or Zambia–Namibia border. The only exceptions to this condition of distance were two professional social workers in the UNHCR liaison office who tended to be most supportive of the refugees and of the civil society organizations working with them (e.g. the Evangelical Lutheran Church in Namibia [ELCIN] and the Namibia Red Cross Society [NRCS]).

Some UNHCR staff members said in interviews that they felt that they should go along with the Ministry of Home Affairs and Immigration and make plans to relocate Osire to Tsumkwe District West. Others argued off the record that the relocation should not take place because it would cause disruptions at the camp level and in the area where the new refugee camp was to be established. The latter, however, were almost always careful not to voice these opinions in public meetings or in discussions in the local headquarters, as they felt that their chances for advancement in UNHCR would be harmed if they did not go along with the decisions of UNHCR headquarters and UNHCR management in Windhoek. This was true also of virtually all of the staff members in the UNHCR liaison office, who were careful not to express any opposition whatsoever to the ideas and objectives director or the UNHCR headquarters personnel from Geneva who visited Windhoek. (The UNHCR consultants, as external experts, were much more willing to express their views about the drawbacks of the proposed refugee camp resettlement.)

In discussions with personnel from UNHCR headquarters and field staff in the period from 2001 to the present, I learned that many of the UNHCR staff believed that they would risk foregoing advancement in the organization if they opted to speak out in support of local organizations and individuals seeking to oppose government decisions. While some of the agency staff said in private interviews that humanitarianism was a major part of the mission of UNHCR, they also said that decision-making was more often made "in the interests of saving money rather than lives." They applauded the role of the UNHCR in protecting persons who feared persecution, but they were concerned about the costs of protection, and especially the care and feeding of the refugees. A number of UNHCR staff members noted some of the shortcomings in the organization, which included "letting states call the shots" and were "trying to remain neutral in highly charged political situations." The result was that there was no substantive opposition to the ways that the government of Namibia wanted to handle the refugee relocation situation. They were also concerned that they would be seen as "too friendly to local non-government organizations" who were vehemently opposed to the relocation of Osire.

Given their reticence to speak out, it should come as no surprise that the views of UNHCR staff did not find their way into policy. The UNHCR Liaison Office in Namibia examined some of the reports on consultations undertaken in Tsumkwe District West and came to the conclusion that the relocation of the refugee camp posed serious social, economic, and environmental risks. Nevertheless, the UNHCR office in Geneva did not come out against the relocation in spite of the concerns that a number of staff in the UNHCR's Geneva headquarters and Windhoek office had about the relocation strategy. The Director and management staff in the UNHCR liaison office were making the decisions along with Namibian government personnel such as those in the Ministry of Home Affairs and Immigration and the Prime Minister's office. The UNHCR Liaison Office in Namibia similarly went along with the government's decisions to relocate a refugee camp in spite of the fact that the relocation would cause serious difficulties not only for the refugees and host populations, but to the UNHCR itself.

As it happened, international politics overtook the decision-making process. After the Peace Accords were signed between the Angolan government and its opponents in April 2002, 170,000 Angolan refugees from throughout southern Africa were resettled in the first phase of repatriation (between July 2002 and May 2003), and another 70,000 were resettled in the second phase in 2004. A significant number (several thousand) of the Angolan refugees in Osire elected to go back to Angola. In 2006, however, the repatriation process of Angolans was suspended by the Angolan government. In June 2010, a tripartite commission meeting consisting of the governments of Angola and Namibia along with the UNHCR resulted in an agreement to restart the voluntary repatriation process. This voluntary repatriation process was still in the discussion stage as late as December 2015.

In keeping with these events, the government of Namibia opted not to move the Osire refugee camp in the early part of the new millennium. The majority of the refugees in the camp were repatriated to Angola and others returned voluntarily to other home countries, reducing the pressure for the relocation of the camp.

THE WORLD BANK IN LESOTHO

The World Bank is a multilateral development bank and international finance institution (IFI) based in Washington D.C., with more than 12,000 employees and consultants, and with operations in over 130 countries. It has more than seventy years of experience in development work, making it a leader in what might be termed the "financializing of development" (Rich 2013: 177). The World Bank, along with the International Monetary Fund, the International Development Association (IDA), and the International Finance Corporation (IFC), are part of the World Bank Group (WBG) and the United Nations family of agencies. Together, these organizations are called the Bretton Woods institutions, named after the place in New Hampshire where the meeting was held that recommended their establishment in 1944.

Development costs a great deal of money. In order to undertake development projects, most countries, including many of those in the developing world, must borrow funds. They do this by seeking assistance from multilateral development banks and from private banks (e.g. Bank of America, Barclays, Standard Bank, and Mitsubishi Bank). As the most significant agency involved in state-sponsored development, the World Bank provides technical assistance, development aid, and loans to developing countries and also monitors and evaluates development projects and programs. Development assistance provided by the International Bank for Reconstruction and Development (IBRD) (the World Bank) has had significant impacts on the wellbeing of both states and individuals since its founding in 1944. Much of the development work carried out by international finance institutions is viewed by some individuals and organizations as having had negative effects on sizable numbers of people, especially the poor and vulnerable (Caufield 1996; Darrow 2003, 2009; Rich 2013; Chavkin et al. 2015). The Bank has attempted, in response to criticism, to diversify its approaches, establish internal controls, and put in place social and environmental safeguards and performance standards. To this end, the Panel of Environment Experts in Lesotho was established by the World Bank and the Lesotho Highlands Development Authority in 1988, with a mandate to assess the social, environmental, and health impacts of the Lesotho Highlands Water Project.[5]

---

[5] For discussions of the Lesotho Highlands Water Project, see World Bank (2007), Human Sciences Research Council (2009), Devitt and Hitchcock (2010), Hitchcock (2012b, 2015), and Meissner (2015). A major concern of the evaluators of the LHWP was "quality of life" of the project-affected people; for a discussion of quality of life assessments, see White and Abeyaselera (2014).

Panels of Environmental Experts and Panels of Engineering Experts (POE), for example, were convened by the World Bank in the 1980s with the responsibility for providing independent reviews of the handling of environmental, social, and engineering issues associated with a project, to be submitted to the Bank and to the government ministries concerned. The World Bank also established the International Advisory Group (IAG) to provide guidance to the Bank on how it can improve its treatment of environmental and social issues. Yet, centralized power continues to characterize the Bank's structure and mode of operation. Even when an Inspection Panel or Independent Evaluation Group produces a negative evaluation of a project, this has no effect on the promotion of those responsible for the project in headquarters (Sarfaty 2012: 81).

This avoidance of responsibility for controversial decisions is amply borne out by several studies of the World Bank. Galit Sarfaty (2012) in an ethnographic investigation of World Bank headquarters, for example, finds an "interpretive gap" between the Bank's lawyers and economists, which goes much further than mere differences in professional training and disciplinary subculture. This was manifested in a greater emphasis on disbursement of funds than what people achieve on the ground. This is very similar to what David Mosse (among others) refers to as "the internal dynamics of development's 'regimes of truth', the production of professional identities, disciplines and the interrelation of policy ideas, institutions, and networks of knowledge workers who serve the development industry and who organise, and are organised by, its ideas" (Mosse 2008: 1). Mosse finds that agency staff, project workers, and consultants

> *do* have to engage in the messy, emotion-laden practical work of negotiating ... compromise, rule bending, and meeting targets and spending budgets, not to mention personal security, loneliness, family relations, and stress. And yet they have to make themselves bearers of context-free "traveling rationalities" and transferable skills – whether in the realms of health-sector reform, plant science, economic analysis, or "people's empowerment." (2008: 122)

While member shares have varied over the years, the United States has always been the only country to hold the power of veto. This structure of power has allowed the World Bank to operate as a major actor on the world stage, controlling the direction and shape of internationally financed development with far-reaching consequences. Decisions to withhold aid funding can potentially bring down democratically elected governments or prop up autocratic governments. In some ways, the World Bank is able to operate with relative impunity.

This is particularly true in the area where development programs result in the resettlement of local people, which are seen by World Bank staff as highly risky – so much so that many of them prefer to avoid working on them if at all possible. Some of them said that working on resettlement and indigenous peoples' projects were "career killers" because they took so long, were so complex, and were often judged, in World Bank terminology, unsatisfactory.

Such remoteness of World Bank headquarters from the contexts in which projects are implemented is amply borne out by local experience of the Lesotho Highlands Water Project. This project, the second largest water transfer project in Africa in terms of cost, had significant impacts on local people, including loss of grazing and arable land, and the resettlement of 71 households in Phase 1A and 325 households in Phase 1B, with a total of 573 people being affected directly, and another 20,000 people affected indirectly (e.g. through loss of natural resources, disruption of travel routes, and loss of livelihood sources). Aimed at supplying water to South Africa and electricity to Lesotho, the LHWP Phase 1, which began in 1986 and was completed in 2009, involved the construction of two large dams (Katse and Mohale) and other infrastructure such as roads, bridges, and power lines.

The World Bank provided a loan of US $45,000,000 to Lesotho (World Bank 2007). This amount represented approximately 3 percent of the total project cost. Other funders were the government of Lesotho, the Development Bank of Southern Africa (DBSA), the European Investment Bank (EIB), the African Development Bank, and various commercial banks and institutions. The purpose of LHWP Phase 1 was to transfer water from the headwaters of the Gariep River (called the Senqu in Lesotho) to the Vaal river catchment in South Africa and on to the commercial and industrial heartland in Gauteng. Besides water transfer, the LHWP was also aimed at providing hydroelectric power to Lesotho. Phases 1A and 1B of the project saw the development of various kinds of infrastructure, including roads, power lines, administrative and engineering facilities, dams, and tunnels.

The Lesotho Highlands Water Project provided for some compensation, resettlement, and development initiatives aimed at ensuring that project-affected people will be "enabled to maintain a standard of living not inferior to that obtaining at the time of first disturbance" (Government of Lesotho and Government of South Africa [1986] *Lesotho Highlands Water Project Treaty*, Article 7, paragraph 18). Compensation was done both in kind (in the form of grains and pulses) and in cash (Devitt and Hitchcock 2010). Houses, schools, and churches were replaced, and payments were made for losses of other assets, including brushwood, trees, thatching grass, and stones used for construction. In addition, communal compensation was paid in the form of cash to community co-operatives or local legal entities (LLEs) both upstream and downstream of the dams.

In the 1980s and 1990s the World Bank arguably had some of the most comprehensive sets of guidelines on how to go about doing resettlement and ensuring environmental and social protection as development projects are implemented (Scudder 2010; Hitchcock 2015). The problem with these guidelines was that they called for the *restoration* of livelihoods of people affected by projects, but they do not argue for *improvement* of the standards of living of people who have been affected by projects (World Bank 2001: 1–2).

The two governments (South Africa and Lesotho) also claimed that they wished only to restore living standards to what they were before first disturbance.

Government spokespersons pointed out that this approach was in line with World Bank thinking. The World Bank's lawyers, for their part, pointed to its policy statements on resettlement, saying that restoration of living standards was all that was required.

As the LHWP progressed, several further issues arose between the World Bank, the LHWP, non-government organizations, and project-affected people. One disagreement was over the issue of Free, Prior, and Informed Consent (FPIC). The management of the World Bank and its lawyers argued that Free, Prior, and Informed *Consultation* was necessary, but not *Consent*. People in the highlands of Lesotho who were affected by the project, on the other hand, said that they not only wanted to be consulted, they also wanted to have a say in issues such as whether or not the project should go forward, what kinds and levels of compensation should be provided to project-affected people, and what kinds of land they should receive in exchange for the land that they lost in the project area. None of these arguments held sway with the two governments, the Lesotho Highlands Water Commission, or the World Bank.

MONITORING IMPACTS

When I worked in Lesotho, there were no regional-level offices of the World Bank in Southern Africa. A regional World Bank office was established in South Africa after the end of apartheid in 1994. The project supervision that occurred in Lesotho was handled out of headquarters in Washington D.C. The people who came out to Lesotho had a variety of backgrounds: economists, hydrologists, political scientists, engineers, fisheries experts, sociologists, and anthropologists. I was part of a POE that was convened to monitor and make recommendations to the governments of Lesotho and South Africa and the World Bank on the Lesotho Highlands Water Project. The original LHWP POE consisted of two people: a hydrologist (a former Minister of Water Affairs in Argentina) and an anthropologist; later, in 1990, two other members were added: an ecologist and an archaeologist and resettlement expert (the role that I played). In the early 1990s, a public health expert was added to the team, a position that varied over time. In 1996, a second ecologist was added to the team. One of the two anthropologists retired from the Panel in 2002, leaving a team of two ecologists, a medical doctor, and an archaeologist/anthropologist.

The POE visited Lesotho two or three times per year for periods of one or two weeks at a time. This is a form of research referred to by the Bank as "rapid rural appraisal (RRA)," with the speed of information-gathering suited to the Bank's time constraints for loan disbursement (Goldman 2005: 161). The team met with personnel from the Lesotho Highlands Water Commission, the Lesotho Highlands Development Authority, and ministry representatives from the two governments, worked with the Chief Executive of the LHDA, carried out fieldwork, and did formal public reports to the LHDA and LHWC. As part of the fieldwork, they visited the project areas and examined the infrastructure (the dams, power lines, roads, clinics, schools, and other facilities). Discussions were held with project-affected people, host community members, traditional authorities, community-based institutions such as co-operatives, non-government organizations, and individual households. Records were kept of the people visited, and a monitoring system was put in place in which households and individuals affected by the project were visited multiple times over a period of two decades.

Some of the findings revealed that there were problems with the Lesotho Highlands Development Authority's approach to issues such as resettlement and compensation and to the formation and running of community institutions such as co-operatives and LLEs, and this led to debates between the Panel and the LHDA, the Lesotho Highlands Water Commission, and the two governments. Fortunately, the POE was an independent entity and their reports could not be censored as they became public documents, which frequently were referred to by non-government organizations and individuals critical of the LHWP and the World Bank.

In some cases, World Bank project supervisory missions were carried out at the same time as the POE visits. The Panel took World Bank personnel with them on some of their field visits, and the Bank and POE staff shared information. Sometimes the Panel and the Bank took issue with the other group's observations and reports. To take an example, there were major debates between the Panel and the World Bank teams over issues such as in-stream flow requirements (IFR), downstream impacts of the dams, and the effects of the LHWP on household wellbeing. The POE was dissatisfied with some of the social and economic impacts of the project, notably with respect to declining incomes and lowered agricultural productivity and land access in the resettlement areas, something that led to tensions with the LHDA and LHWC. Interestingly enough, the World Bank supervisory missions were often supportive of the findings of the POE and took their side in debates with the Highlands Water Project authorities.

There were several cases where there was broad agreement between the Panel and the Bank, resulting in both groups putting pressure on the Lesotho Highlands Development Authority and the Lesotho Highlands Water Commission – for example, in the need to provide timely compensation to project-affected persons and expanding post-resettlement development efforts. There were close working relationships between the anthropologist who came as part of the World Bank supervisory missions and the anthropologists on the POE, all of whom had extensive experience with resettlement not just in Lesotho but also in dozens of other African, Asian, and Latin American countries. In some cases, the World Bank anthropologist visited Lesotho on his own, something that was also done by members of the POE in order to obtain additional information and insights about the impacts of the project on the people and environments of Lesotho.

One of the unintended consequences of the LHWP was an earthquake that occurred in November 1995, which caused damage in seven villages around the

Katse Reservoir. The earthquake destroyed eleven homes and, according to local people, caused a crack in the earth at the village of Mapaleng. This earthquake may have been a consequence of reservoir-induced seismicity (RIS) caused by the weight of the water in the Katse Reservoir, which had begun to fill in October 1995. Some local people blamed the project for the earthquake and subsequent seismic activity, while others placed the blame on a large malevolent "river snake" that they said had been disturbed by the construction activity in the Katse area.

Another environmental impact of the LHWP was the drying up of springs in the catchment areas of the project. Such an event occurred, for example, at the village of Ha Mensel near Katse, close to the Katse Township and the administrative offices that were built to oversee the project. It was ironic, villagers said, that there was a large water tank built by the LHDA in the village to provide water to the engineers and dam workers and their families in Katse, but they themselves had less access to water now than they did before the project began. At least half a dozen communities around the Katse Reservoir saw their springs dry up as a result of road and other construction.

Among the most significant impacts of the LHWP, which followed from flows of workers into the area, was an increase in HIV/AIDS in the population in the highlands of Lesotho. Estimates of the HIV/AIDS prevalence rate in the project area in the late 1980s was 0.9 percent of the population. Recent figures suggest that the HIV/AIDS prevalence rate was at a level of 22 percent, which is approximately the rate of urban areas in Lesotho such as Maseru, the capital of Lesotho. A question that had to be addressed by the panel and other evaluators of the project such as the Human Sciences Research Council (2009) was whether the LHWP itself was responsible for the increase in HIV/AIDS, and, if so, what kinds of mitigation measures could be implemented in order to ensure that the project-affected population was at least as well off as they were prior to the inception of the project, in keeping with the treaty obligations between the two governments of Lesotho and South Africa. Another issue revolved around the ways in which the World Bank assessed the health costs of projects; had the Bank included the costs of dealing with HIV/AIDS in the calculations at the beginning of the Lesotho Highlands Water Project, as it should have, it is unlikely that the project would have been viable from an economic standpoint and therefore may not have been funded.

Yet another consequence of the project related to cultural and socioeconomic impacts. Some of the people who were resettled felt bereft. While they were able to get cash compensation and have their dead relatives moved to their new locations, they felt that their new ways of life were seriously lacking compared to what they had experienced prior to the project. According to some of the resettled people, there were fewer traditional ceremonies being conducted in the new locations, and people had to go long distances to take part in culturally important activities.

The implementation of the Lesotho Highlands Water Project also led to a struggle over biodiversity conservation versus development in the highlands of Lesotho. The Maloti Minnow (*Pseudobarbus quathlambae*), a critically endangered fish, was identified early on in the implementation of the LHWP as the single most important component of the natural heritage and environment program. The introduction of smallmouth yellowfish (*Labeobarbus aeneus*) and trout (brown trout, *Salmo trutta* and rainbow trout, *Onchorhynchus mykiss*) into the Mohale Dam Reservoir posed grave risks for the survival of the Maluti Minnow. What this meant was that for the second time in decades, a large dam project could lead to the extinction of a species. The last time this happened was on the Tellico Dam on the Little Tennessee River in 1973. The National Environmental Policy Act (NEPA) ended up slowing the construction of the dam, but it did not prevent its construction. Both Lesotho and the World Bank argued that since this fish was unimportant to the economies of project-affected people, "it did not matter what happened to it."

One potentially can make a connection between this attitude about the extinction of a species and the approach that the World Bank has often taken to dam construction. As one World Bank official told me, "[i]f indigenous people are in the way, then they should get out of the way so the dam can be built." She went on to say that no "tribal group" should be allowed to stop a major dam project, no matter how well-connected they are to interfering NGOs. In 1998 and 1999, South Africa and Lesotho Africa filed formal complaints about the LHWP with the World Bank Independent Inspection Panel, an institution set up in the Bank in 1993 in response to criticisms from the outside (as well as some from the inside) to increase accountability and to address international and local concerns about World Bank project impacts. The South Africa and Lesotho complaints had no result, as the Inspection Panel did not complete the necessary investigations and did not make the findings that they did have public.

After the close of the World Bank supervisory missions in the mid-2000s, the POE continued to monitor the LHWP. The World Bank evaluation of the LHWP was published in 2007, and members of the panel as well as personnel from LHDA, the Lesotho Highlands Water Commission, the two governments, and project-affected people were interviewed. The Lesotho Highlands Water Project Phase 1A Panel wound up its work in 2012, and a new panel was appointed in 2013 to monitor Phase 2 of the LHWP. Reports of the POE were made public, as required in the original agreements about the role of the LHWP, and World Bank personnel in the Lesotho office and in Washington followed the results of the POE's assessments, which took place as often as four times a year up to 2012. Subsequent information on changes in the wellbeing of wetland areas in the highlands of Lesotho was collected by a team working with support from the Millennium Challenge Corporation (Hitchcock and Nonyana Hoohlo and Associates 2013) and by the World Bank and a POE working on a separate water project in the Metolong area of the lowlands, where some of the people from the Mohale Basin (LHWP Phase 1B) had been resettled. World Bank personnel have told me that the lessons that were learned from the Metolong Project will hopefully be employed in Phase 2 of the Lesotho Highlands Water Project, but that Phase 1 of the project is over and "cannot be revisited."

The POE reports on the first Phase of the Lesotho Highlands Water Project were used both by the LHDA and the World Bank as well as by non-government organizations such as International Rivers, the Transformation Resource Center, and the Highlands Church Action Group in discussions in Lesotho, South Africa, and Washington D.C. There were debates within the Panel about the degree to which the findings should be disseminated, and for a while the POE reports were placed on the LHDA website. But this practice stopped in the early part of 2000, and the transparency of the LHWP suffered as a result.

BROKEN PROMISES

South African, Basotho, American, and European NGOs continued to raise objections to the lack of attention by the Lesotho Highlands Development Authority to timely and adequate payment of compensation, provision of alternative land for people who were dispossessed, failure to follow planned benefit distributions from the royalties that accrued to Lesotho for the sale of the water to South Africa, and the lack of compliance with social and environmental safeguards. While much of the project (including the engineering portions) was deemed "satisfactory," the LHWP was judged "moderately unsatisfactory" in terms of its compliance with the social and environmental components of the project (World Bank 2007: 8–13).

Communal compensation in the form of a Rural Development Program for losses of grazing and other natural resources was supposed to be provided to project-affected communities and their hosts by the LHDA as part of its treaty obligations. To participate in the Rural Development Program, people were required to form co-operatives, grazing associations, or other kinds of LLEs. Some groups of livestock owners formed Range Management Associations (RMAs) (see Lawry 1986 for a discussion of these institutions). While the individual compensation and minimum threshold payments were intended to ensure that affected families were at least no worse off after than before resettlement, the "communal compensation" was meant to bring "development" and restore standards of living both to the affected families and to their hosts (Slater and Mphale 2009; Devitt and Hitchcock 2010). As it turned out, there were some serious tensions between some of the resettlers and the "host communities," as occurred, for example, at Makhoakoeng in Maseru (Panel of Environmental Experts 2004). The source of these tensions revolved around a decision by the host population in Makhoakoeng not to allow the resettled people to bury a member of their group who had died after their arrival.

Eventually, after the close of Phase 1 of the Lesotho Highlands Water Project, the LHDA and the Lesotho Highlands Water Commission opted to stop the distribution of communal compensation to the co-operatives and other community organizations and to keep the money in the hands of the agencies, contrary to all of the treaty obligations between Lesotho and South Africa and contrary to World Bank policy. This decision, which was made in late 2014, is being contested by local communities and their lawyers, who are in the process of suing the LHDA. Currently, efforts are being made to move the case from the Commercial to the Constitutional Court in Lesotho.

In response to their displacement without adequate compensation, some of the people of the highlands met anthropologists and other World Bank personnel in Maseru. A few Basotho went to headquarters in Washington, most of them high government officials. Some of the Basotho met with non-government organizations critical of World Bank policies and practices, including the International Rivers Network and Fifty Years is Enough. With the exception of a few World Bank project personnel and anthropologists, most of the World Bank officials were reluctant to meet with highlands organizations such as Survivors of Large Dams (SOLD). When asked if this was the case, a few World Bank staff members said that headquarters personnel might potentially retaliate against them for "consorting with the opposition."

One group of people who raised serious questions about the project and the World Bank's approach was the Amatola, who live in the Maluti-Drakensberg area (Francis 2009; Hitchcock, field notes). Sometimes called "secret San" (see Prins 2009), the people of the Maluti-Drakensberg Mountains claimed to be indigenous to the region. They argued that the World Bank's indigenous peoples' policy, Operational Directive (OD) 4.20 (World Bank 2005), should have been triggered by the implementation of the Lesotho Highlands Water Project. When the World Bank anthropologist and the POE anthropologist asked World Bank management in Washington D.C. about this issue, the management staff replied that "there were no indigenous people in Lesotho" and that OD 4.20 did not apply. The position of the local World Bank office staff was that they "did not get involved in politics."

It is also sad to note that the water and sanitation programs promised for the people in the Katse Basin (Phase 1A), which began in the 1980s, are still not completed, which is in violation of all the promises made to the people of Katse by the Lesotho Highlands Development Authority. The second tranche of communal compensation due to the communities affected by the LHWP has not been paid, and now the LHDA is maintaining that they should not provide the compensation to the communities, but, rather, set up a separate fund in Lesotho which the LHDA can manage and then "tell the communities what the money will be used for." The lack of a participatory approach goes against everything that the World Bank and the LHDA have stood for (at least on paper), and it is not surprising that the project-affected people in Lesotho are angry and that non-government organizations are calling for the World Bank to follow the guidelines and safeguards that had been produced by the World Bank and other international finance and development institutions over the past two decades.

Although there was diversity of opinion within the World Bank about its resettlement and compensation programs, I discerned a trend among Bank employees toward support of the Banks projects. When asked about whether they were satisfied with the World Bank's involvement in the Lesotho Highlands Water Project, nearly all of the World Bank management staff in headquarters said the LHWP was a "marked success." Several of them said that it was successful "because it disbursed most of the funds allocated to the project." The local office personnel in the World Bank office in Maseru said that they did not get involved with local policy matters, except insofar as they were concerned about Lesotho's HIV/AIDS policy. The fact that the Lesotho Highlands Water Project contributed significantly to the rise of HIV/AIDS and the expansion in the number of AIDS orphans and child-headed households in Lesotho was not seen as a policy issue, nor was the fact that the LHDA took years to develop a health policy that addressed HIV/AIDS seen as problematic.

As was pointed out in the World Bank's own evaluation of the project, which was done by two World Bank personnel (World Bank 2007: 13–24), the project appraisal document of 1998 did not include specific provisions for listing safeguard policies triggered by the project, a major oversight. There was seriously weak performance in the social protection programs throughout the first phase of the LHWP, from its beginnings in 1987 to 2007. These were highlighted during World Bank supervisory missions by the anthropologist working on the LHWP, but he said he had difficulties getting World Bank management to take the social issues seriously, something he was deeply distressed about. The field supervision teams of the Bank did frequently take note of lack of compliance with social and environmental safeguards, but their reports and verbal observations had only moderate impacts on World Bank management, who are now busily preparing to fund part of Phase 2 of the Lesotho Highlands Water Project, without taking into consideration some of the findings of their own field staff regarding Phase 1.

It is ironic that one of the areas where significant progress had been made in the past was in the rules and procedures relating to involuntary relocation or resettlement resulting from the establishment of large-scale water infrastructure projects (Cernea 2000; Scudder 2005). A critical problem now is that the World Bank is reducing its safeguards when it comes to environmental, social, and resettlement issues, in line with some current thinking on being less regulatory and more market-oriented. The World Bank is placing even greater emphasis on fast funds disbursement than it had in the past, and is rewarding Bank staff who are supportive of this approach. Given the experiences of large dam projects such as those in Lesotho, this trend will have severe negative impacts on people and habitats in Africa and around the world, especially the poor and those who are heavily dependent on natural resources.

HEADQUARTERS AND THE FIELD

Both the UNHCR and the World Bank have played significant roles in dealing with displacement, a complex process that has caused enormous misery among tens of millions of people. The institutional cultures of both UNHCR and the World Bank have focused on placing the blame for displacement and development failures on local people and nation-states. Both global institutions have tended to let states set the agendas, saying that they should not be concerned with "state sovereignty." This can be described as the "fiction of the non-political" (see the Introduction to this volume, pp. 11–14) or "anti-politics" in global agencies (see also Ferguson 1994). By emphasizing the non-political qualities of their interventions, agencies are able to justify their approach to policy, and in particular to get around what they see as the obstacles posed by human rights. Is it really true that the agencies I discuss cannot do any more that what is mandated by states? Do agencies have more of a say in what they do than is apparent from their public positions? The answers to these questions begin with the existence of an imbalance of influence within the organizations between headquarters and the field.

The relationships between states' personnel, international agencies, NGOs, experts, civil servants, and affected groups are in the context of national politics much more than international politics. In these cases, UN staff have to engage in diplomatic and state-guided processes where national decisions have the last say. There is not the pressure of an international public opinion at the same level one might find in an open meeting in UN Headquarters. Here, UN offices are on national ground, and it is up to the ruling government to make the decision to either close the doors of the organization or leave them open. At the same time, states such as those in southern African are highly dependent on international donors and projects for present and future financial aid.

Despite this basic similarity between the two agencies, the World Bank's willingness to act against local and even state interests seems to go further than in the UNHCR. World Bank officials from headquarters are shown to prioritize the project at all costs, even in defiance of human rights. Putting this defiance of human rights together with the Bank's sidelining of state concerns gives us a picture of an agency with considerable global power that is single-minded in its pursuit of an agenda of prosperity on a grand scale.

At the same time, it is apparent that there are internal divisions of opinion within these institutions. It is fortunate for both the UNHCR and the World Bank – and for people around the world – that there are people inside of these organizations, some of whom are working at the field level, who have social justice and human rights as their ultimate goals.

The World Bank, arguably the most powerful and global institution in terms of its impacts on the world's poor, has moved in the direction of a "loan approval culture" (Rich 2013: 12–13, 34; Sarfaty 2012: ch. 3), pushing through loans to countries with little if any regard for the social, environmental, economic, and governance impacts involved. The results can be seen in the case of Lesotho and many other countries around the world where World Bank projects have been implemented (Rich 2013; Chavkin et al. 2015). There is a distinct lack of data on project-affected people relating to large-scale water projects, in spite of the "audit culture" that exists within the bank.

The differences between World Bank management and field staff, especially those who are social scientists, are significant, especially in terms of the degree to which many field staff are committed to a human rights-based approach and have concerns for the welfare of project-affected people and the areas where they live. Taking positions that were supportive of local people by field staff was seen in World Bank headquarters as being "irresponsible" and "anti-Bank," in the words of two World Bank headquarters staff. As one World Bank manager put it, "We are not supposed to be political, and supporting human rights is a political act."

From the field, a critical position was more often expressed. A field staff member, speaking against this managerial position, said, "Our job should be to help the people, not spend money that makes their situations worse."

The managerial levels of the World Bank tend to see the people who are displaced by large projects as obstacles to prosperity rather than the proper subjects of efforts toward it. They are to be kept in the same conditions – even conditions of poverty and misery – in which they were living before the project forced them to move from their homes, communities, and territories. The distance here between management and field worker seems somehow bigger, the differences in perspective between the two levels of the agency more stark, than in the UNHRC, producing a regime of visibility (or invisibility), a form of structural concealment of the agency's decision-making processes (see Abélès, Chapter 2, this volume).

The UNHCR, by contrast, sees itself as a protection agency, not a relief or development agency (Gilbert 2009: 188). At the same time, however, it is strictly limited by its mandate. The 1951 Convention Relating to the Status of Refugees does not apply to refugees who benefit from the protection or assistance of a United Nations agency other than the UNHCR. This can be illustrated by a particular case in which the concerns of the UNHCR and the World Bank directly overlapped. In 2014, there were thirty refugees and asylum seekers recognized by the UNHCR in Lesotho. Yet, the UNHCR office in Lesotho only works with formally recognized refugees, not internally displaced persons or stateless persons. UNHCR Lesotho has not taken an interest in the people who were resettled involuntarily as a result of the Lesotho Highlands Water Project. The internally displaced people are seen as being "outside of its realm of concern," according to one UNHCR employee in Maseru. The same position was taken by several UNHCR personnel in Switzerland.

For the UNHCR, the refugees (however narrowly defined) are the focal point of intervention. The agency sees itself as "protective." It is for the refugees that the agency does its work, first to find temporary relief of the condition of displacement, with camps offering shelter, food, health care, etc., and then to help refugees toward new homes, sometimes together with new nationalities.

Both of the cases I have discussed show that field officers and consultants are subject to agency directives, their perspectives overruled by dominant agendas, their research findings ignored. This even reaches the point at which staff are afraid to offer ideas that are informed by their work with displaced people for fear that they themselves will be displaced – overlooked for promotion, demoted, or even fired, just for conveying information or making views known to those in headquarters who are not likely to be receptive to them. The UNHCR, preparing for a possible relocation of the Osire refugee camp, revealed this "deafness" of the head office, and in the World Bank, the same kind of reticence is prevalent in the relationship between headquarters and field programs.

There is thus one basic quality shared by the UNHCR and the World Bank, which might be more widely generalizable: avoiding political agendas seems to the way that not only global institutions but also states are operating. Claiming to be operating in the interests of humanitarianism and global and local economic growth, the UN agencies and many of the world's states are placing less emphasis on human rights and livelihood concerns than they have previously. The global experience with refugees' and displaced persons' resettlement reveals that the majority of resettled people are worse off. There appears to be a lack of political will on the part of global institutions as well as state governments to try to reduce the social and environmental impacts of involuntary resettlement. One reason for this situation is the high financial costs of mitigation. As one individual who was affected by the Lesotho Highlands Water Project put it, "We are seen as poor people who have nothing to contribute to the economy but our labor, and as a result the government and the World Bank do not care what happens to us." Fortunately for some of the people in the highlands of Lesotho and for the refugees in Namibia facing resettlement, there were World Bank and UNHCR field staff members who took the concerns of local people to heart and did everything they could to promote their human rights and wellbeing.

ACKNOWLEDGMENTS

I wish to acknowledge the many contributions of the United Nations High Commissioner for Refugees, the World Bank, the governments of Namibia and Lesotho, and non-government organizations working in these countries. I also wish to thank my colleagues in the Panel of Environmental Experts of the Lesotho Highlands Water Project for their comments and suggestions on an earlier draft of this paper. Support for the work upon which this chapter is based was provided by the Office of Refugee Resettlement, the US Department of State, the UNHCR, and the Lesotho Highlands Development Authority. People in the UNHCR and World Bank headquarters, consultants, and field staff were willing to share their opinions with me, for which I am very grateful. I also wish to thank the refugees and project-affected people in Namibia and Lesotho for their patience and willingness to discuss these complex issues. Considerable effort was invested in the editing and reworking of this paper by Ronald Niezen and Maria Sapignoli, the editors of this volume, and I thank them for their hard work, insights, and recommendations.

REFERENCES

Betts, Alexander, Gil Loescher, and James Milner. 2012. *The United Nations High Commissioner for Refugees (UNHCR): The Politics and Practice of Refugee Protection*. Second Edition. London: Routledge.

Biesele, Megan and Robert K. Hitchcock. 2013. *The Ju/'hoan San of Nyae Nyae and Namibian Independence: Development, Democracy, and Indigenous Voices in Southern Africa*. New York: Berghahn Books.

Bornstein, Erica and Peter Redfield, eds. 2010. *Forces of Compassion: Humanitarianism Between Ethics and Politics*. Santa Fe: School for Advanced Research Press.

Caufield, Catherine. 1996. *Masters of Illusion: The World Bank and the Poverty of Nations*. New York: Henry Holt and Company.

Cernea, Michael. 2000. Risk, Safeguards, and Reconstruction: A Model for Population Displacement and Resettlement. In *Risks and Reconstruction: Experiences of Resettlers and Refugees*, Michael M. Cernea and Christopher McDowell, eds. Washington, D.C.: The World Bank, pp. 11–55.

Chavkin, Sasha, Ben Hallman, Michael Hudson, Cecelie Schlis-Gallego, and Shane Shifflett. 2015. *How the World Bank Breaks Its Promise to Protect the Poor*. 16 April, 2015, Washington, D.C.: Center for Public Integrity.

Crisp, Jeffrey. 2001. Mind the Gap! UNHCR, Humanitarian Assistance, and the Development Process. *International Migration Review* 35(1): 168–191.

Darrow, Mac. 2003. *Between Light and Shadow: The World Bank, the International Monetary Fund, and International Human Rights Law*. Oxford: Hart.

⎯⎯⎯ 2009. World Bank and International Monetary Fund. In *Encyclopedia of Human Rights*, Volume 5, David P. Forsythe, ed. Oxford and New York: Oxford University Press, pp. 183–190.

Devitt, Paul and Robert K. Hitchcock. 2010. Who Drives Resettlement? The Case of Lesotho's Mohale Dam. *African Study Monographs* 31(2): 57–106.

Feldman, Ilana and Miriam Ticktin, eds. 2010. *In the Name of Humanity: The Government of Threat and Care*. Durham and London: Duke University Press.

Ferguson, James. 1994. *The Anti-Politics Machine: "Development," Depoliticization, and Bureaucratic Power in Lesotho*. Minneapolis: University of Minnesota Press.

Francis, Michael. 2009. Silencing the Past: Historical and Archaeological Colonisation of the Southern San in KwaZulu-Natal, South Africa. *Anthropology Southern Africa* 32(3 & 4): 106–116.

Fresia, Marion. 2013. The Making of Global Consensus: Constructing Norms on Refugee Protection at UNHCR. In *The Gloss of Harmony: The Politics of Policy-making in Multilateral Organizations*, Birgit Müller, ed. London: Pluto Press, pp. 50–74.

Gilbert, Geoff. 1998. Rights, Legitimate Expectations, Needs, and Responsibilities: UNHCR and the New World Order. *International Journal of Refugee Law* 10(3): 349–388.

⎯⎯⎯ 2009. United Nations High Commissioner for Refugees. In *Encyclopedia of Human Rights*, Volume 5, David P. Forsythe, ed. Oxford and New York: Oxford University Press, pp. 183–190.

Goldman Michael. 2005. *Imperial Nature: The World Bank and Struggle for Social Justice in the Age of Globalization*. New Haven: Yale University Press.

Government of Lesotho and Government of South Africa. 1986. *Treaty on the Lesotho Highlands Water Project Between the Government of the Kingdom of Lesotho and the Government of the Republic of South Africa*. Maseru: Government of Lesotho and Pretoria and Cape Town: Government of the Republic of South Africa.

Hitchcock, Robert K. 2001. *Anthropological Study in the Potential Impact of Refugees in M'Kata, Namibia*. Windhoek: United Nations High Commissioner for Refugees.
    2012a. Refugees, Resettlement, and Land and Resource Conflicts: The Politics of Identity Among !Xun and Khwe San of Northeastern Namibia. *African Study Monographs* 33(2): 73–132.
    2012b. The Lesotho Highlands Water Project (LHWP): Water, Culture, and Environmental Change. In *Water, Cultural Diversity, and Global Environmental Change: Emerging Trends, Sustainable Futures?* Barbara Rose Johnston, Lisa Hiwasaki, Irene J. Klaver, Ameyali Ramos Castillo, and Veronica Strang, eds. Geneva: United Nations Cultural and Scientific Organization (UNESCO). New York: Springer, pp. 319–338.
    2015. The Lesotho Highlands Water Project: Dams, Development, and the World Bank. *Sociology and Anthropology* 3(10): 526–538.
Hitchcock, Robert K. and Nonyana Hoohlo and Associates. 2013. *Community-Based Livelihoods Enterprises in Wetlands Project Areas: Final Report* (Two Volumes). Maseru: Millennium Challenge Account-Lesotho and Nonyana Hoohlo and Associates.
Human Sciences Research Council. 2009. *Socio-economic, Health, and Nutrition Survey in the Lesotho Highlands Water Project Areas, Volume 1: Main Report*. Contract 1204, LHDA. Pretoria: Human Sciences Research Council and Maseru, Lesotho Highlands Development Authority.
Hyndman, Jennifer. 2000. *Managing Displacement: Refugees and the Politics of Humanitarianism*. Minneapolis: University of Minnesota Press.
Kane, Hal. 1995. *The Hour of Departure: Forces that Create Refugees and Migrants*. Worldwatch Paper 125. Washington, D.C.: Worldwatch Institute.
Lawry, Steve. 1986. *Livestock and Range Management in Sehlabathebe: A Study of Communal Resource Management*. Maseru, Lesotho: Ministry of Agriculture.
Lewis, David and David Mosse. Eds. 2006. *Development Brokers and Translators: The Ethnography of Aid and Agencies*. London: Kumarian Press.
Loescher, Gil. 2001a. *The UNHCR and World Politics: A Perilous Path*. Oxford and New York: Oxford University Press.
    2001b. The UNHCR and World Politics: State Interests vs Institutional Autonomy. *International Migration Review* 35(1): 33–56.
McNeill, Desmond and Asuncion Lera Stclair. 2009. *Global Poverty, Ethics, and Human Rights: The Role of Multilateral Institutions*. Washington, D.C.: Georgetown University Press.
Meissner, Richard. 2015. *Interest Groups, Water Politics, and Governance: The Case of the Lesotho Highlands Water Project*. New York: Springer.
Mosse, David. 2008. International Policy, Development Expertise, and Anthropology. *Focaal: European Journal of Anthropology*. 52: 119–126.
    2011a. Introduction: The Anthropology of Expertise and Professionals in International Development. In *Adventures in Aidland: The Anthropology of Professionals in International Development*, David Mosse, ed. Oxford and New York: Berghahn Books, pp. 1–31.
    2011b. Social Analysis as Corporate Production: Non-Economists/Anthropologists at Work at the World Bank in Washington, D.C. In *Adventures in Aidland: The Anthropology of Professionals in International Development*, David Mosse, ed. Oxford and New York: Berghahn Books, pp. 81–102.
Oliver-Smith, Anthony. 2009a. Introduction: Development-Forced Displacement and Resettlement: A Global Human Rights Crisis. In *Development and Dispossession:*

The Crisis of Forced Displacement and Resettlement, Anthony Oliver-Smith, ed. pp. 3–23. Santa Fe: School for Advanced Research.

———. 2009b. Evicted from Eden: Conservation and the Displacement of Indigenous and Traditional Peoples. In *Development and Dispossession: The Crisis of Forced Displacement and Resettlement,* Anthony Oliver-Smith, ed. Santa Fe: School for Advanced Research, pp. 141–162.

Pakleppa, Richard. 2001. *Report on Community Consultancy and Human Rights Education Undertaken in Tsumkwe District West Between 5 and 22 April, 2001.* Windhoek, Namibia: Working Group of Indigenous Minorities in Southern Africa.

Panel of Environmental Experts. 2004. Lesotho Highlands Water Project. Special Mission on Resettlement and Development. Report No. 36 to the Lesotho Highlands Development Authority, Maseru, Lesotho (R. Hitchcock, February, 2004).

Prins, Frans. 2009. Secret San of the Drakensberg and Their Rock Art Legacy. *Critical Arts* 23(2): 190–208.

Redfield, Peter. 2013. *Life in Crisis: The Ethical Journey of Doctors without Borders.* Berkeley: University of California Press.

Republic of Namibia. 1996. *Nature Conservation Amendment Act of 1996.* Windhoek: Government of the Republic of Namibia.

Rich, Bruce. 2013. *Foreclosing the Future: The World Bank and the Politics of Environmental Destruction.* Washington, Covelo, and London: Island Press.

Sarfaty, Galit A. (2012) *Values in Translation: Human Rights and the Culture of the World Bank.* Stanford: Stanford University Press.

Scudder, Thayer. 2005. *The Future of Large Dams: Dealing with Social, Environmental, Institutional and Political Costs.* London: Earthscan.

Slater, Rachel and Matseliso Mphale. 2009. *Compensation, Welfare, and Development: One-off Lump-Sum and Regular Transfers in the Lesotho Highlands Water Project.* London: Overseas Development Institute.

Taylor, Julie J. 2012. *Naming the Land: San Identity and Community Conservation in Namibia's West Caprivi.* Windhoek: Demasius Publications and Basel, Switzerland: Basler Afrika Bibliographien.

United Nations High Commissioner for Refugees (UNHCR) Liaison Office (LON). 2001. *Country Report for the Year 2000, UNHCR LON, Windhoek, Namibia, 26 February 2001.* Windhoek, Namibia: United Nations High Commissioner for Refugees (UNHCR) Liaison Office.

United Nations High Commissioner for Refugees. 2006. *The State of the World's Refugees: Human Displacement in the New Millennium.* New York: Oxford University Press.

United Nations High Commissioner for Refugees. 2012. *The State of the World's Refugees: In Search of Solidarity.* New York: Oxford University Press.

Weiss, Thomas G. and Larry Minear, eds. 1993. *Humanitarianism across Borders: Sustaining Civilians in Times of War.* Boulder and London: Lynne Rienner Publishers.

Welch, Cameron. 2013. "Land is Life, Conservancy is Life": The San and the N≠a Jaqna Conservancy, Tsumkwe District West, Namibia. PhD Dissertation, McGill University, Montreal, Canada.

White, Sarah C. with Asha Abeyasekera. 2014. *Well-being and Quality of Life Assessment: A Practical Guide.* Stirling: Stylus Publishing.

Wilson, Richard, and Richard Brown, eds. 2009. *Humanitarianism and Suffering: The Mobilization of Empathy.* Cambridge: Cambridge University Press.

World Bank. 1996. *World Bank Participation Sourcebook.* Environment Department Papers 019. Washington, D.C.: The World Bank.

2001. Involuntary Resettlement. In *The World Bank Operational Manual, Operational Policies* 4.12, World Bank, ed. Washington, D.C.: The World Bank.

2005. Indigenous Peoples. In *The World Bank Operational Manual, Operational Policies* 4.10, World Bank, ed. pp. 1–13. Washington, D.C.: The World Bank.

2007. *Implementation Completion and Results Report (IBRD-43390) on a Loan in the Amount of US$45 Million to the Lesotho Highlands Development Authority for Lesotho Highlands Water Project – Phase 1B*. Report No. ICR168. Washington, D.C.: World Bank.

World Bank Operations Evaluation Department. 2004. *An OED Review of Social Development in Bank Activities*. Washington, D.C.: The World Bank.

World Commission on Dams. 2000. *Dams and Development: A New Framework for Decision-making. The Report of the World Commission on Dams*. London: Earthscan Publications.

9

Global Village Courts: International Organizations and the Bureaucratization of Rural Justice Systems in the Global South

Tobias Berger

INTRODUCTION

The ethnography of international organizations is new in a dual sense. On the one hand, for anthropologists, it is part of a larger project of leaving traditional field sites in search of contexts in which to conduct their ethnographic explorations of the intricate logics of everyday life (cf. Müller 2013). On the other hand, scholars of international relations – for whom the investigation of international organizations has been a staple ingredient of academic inquiry for decades (e.g. Barnett and Finnemore 2004; Martin and Simmons 2013) – are only slowly warming to the import of ethnographic methods and anthropological arguments more broadly (Vrasti 2008; Lie 2013). This chapter pursues the ethnography of international organizations from a rather unlikely place – rural Bangladesh. It focuses on documents and investigates how global and local institutions become intertwined in development programming through the coproduction of bureaucratic paperwork.

Bureaucratic paperwork assumes a central role in current development initiatives of international donor agencies with rural non-state justice institutions. After a growing fatigue with orthodox rule of law reforms, international donors are currently accelerating projects with non-state institutions. Yet these projects are fraught with ambiguity. On the one hand, non-state justice institutions often enjoy high degrees of popularity, especially (though not exclusively) in the Global South. They are often seen as efficient, authentic, and legitimate. On the other hand, non-state justice institutions are also frequently criticized for the perpetuation of power imbalances, gendered hierarchies, and non-compliance with international human rights standards. International donor agencies are now confronted with the challenging task of disentangling both views and rescuing the seeming benefits of non-state justice institutions from their perceived shortcomings. This chapter investigates one of the most frequent responses to this ambivalence: the bureaucratization of non-state justice institutions.

Focussing on one specific project that aims at 'activating' village courts in rural Bangladesh, I show how the bureaucratization of rural non-state justice institutions plays multiple roles simultaneously. Justified in the name of enhanced transparency and accountability towards the people who use them, the bureaucratization of village courts also fulfils a further purpose. It renders non-state institutions legible to international donor agencies. Legibility is not only a central problem in statecraft (Scott 1998), it is also a problem within international organizations. In order to make sense of rural non-state justice systems – and their programme interventions in these systems – international organizations crucially depend on the documentation of village courts proceedings in writing. Only through these written records can village court proceedings – and therefore also the effects of projects on these proceedings – be fed into the tightly knit monitoring and evaluation apparatuses that have become integral components of all contemporary donor interventions.

Analyzing the monitoring and evaluation apparatuses in place for the project on the activation of village courts in Bangladesh, I show how it translates the messy complexities of rural justice delivery into quantifiable entities and moves numbers back and forth between different actors involved in this project. These numbers, in turn, are based on the forms filed in the village courts – and it is the official bureaucratic paperwork that constitutes the material basis for their claims to validity. In combination, the numbers and the paperwork on which they are (seemingly) based underpin international organizations' claims to epistemic authority (Zürn et al. 2012). In this way, the proliferation of written paperwork becomes constitutive of transnational bureaucracies as such. It is only by producing an endless trail of paperwork – starting in the actual village courts themselves – that international donor agencies can make authoritative claims to knowledge about rural non-state justice institutions in the Global South.

The empirical core of this chapter is based on seven months of ethnographic field research in Bangladesh. While most of it was spent in different village communities where the European Union (EU) and the United Nations Development Program (UNDP) – in cooperation with the Bangladeshi Ministry of Local Government, Rural Development and Cooperatives (MLGRDC) and four local NGOs – aim to activate the so-called village courts, I also spent some weeks in Dhaka, conducting interviews at the headquarters of international donor agencies in the country's capital. Conducting a multi-sited ethnography throughout my field research, I have followed the artefacts of development initiatives with rural non-state justice institutions as they travelled back and forth between Dhaka-based headquarters and rural village communities (Marcus 1995; Cook 2004). These artefacts, however, are only part of a larger shift of international donor agencies towards increased engagement with non-state justice institution, also beyond Bangladesh.

INTERNATIONAL ORGANIZATIONS AND THE BUREAUCRATIZATION OF NON-STATE JUSTICE

One of the key ways in which international organizations claim authority is via the production of knowledge about social, economic, and political phenomena of global relevance (Barnett and Finnemore 2004; Zürn et al. 2012). Access to justice is deemed to be globally relevant, and two international organizations are currently engaged in the production of knowledge about non-state justice institutions and their potential for promoting the liberal *trias* of democracy, the rule of law, and human rights (Ehm 2010). The first is the World Bank. It is an odd contender for the engagement of non-state justice institutions. As its name already indicates, the World Bank's core competence is loaning money. Founded as one of the Bretton Woods Institutions in the mid-1940s (when it was still called the International Bank for Reconstruction and Development), its initial mandate was to stabilize the global economy by addressing capital deficiencies and facilitating reconstruction and development loans, initially to post-World War II European countries and, subsequently, the countries of the Global South that had recently gained independence. After the Structural Adjustment Programmes in the 1980s and the subsequent turn to 'good governance' in the 1990s, the World Bank has recently reinvented itself as a key player in the burgeoning field of poverty reduction. This has encompassed not only a turn towards institutional reforms at various levels, including prolific decentralization schemes, but also an overall shift from an exclusive funding agency to a 'knowledge bank'. With its rapidly expanding portfolio, the World Bank has become the key institution for the production and procession of any kind of development-related data. It has thereby established itself as "the super think tank among the aid agencies that, based on its extensive analytical work, knows what is good for the recipient countries but also what other aid agencies should support" (Steiner-Khamsi 2012: 5). The World Bank has thus become a pacesetter for changes within international development discourses themselves. And in these discourses, non-state justice institutions have recently re-appeared (Tamanaha et al. 2012).

In 2002, the World Bank launched its 'Justice for the Poor Programme' (J4P). Having employed roughly fifty people since then, the project has been located with the Legal Vice Presidency, i.e. an administrative rather than operational part of the Bank. It has run only a handful of projects and, in the words of two of its key protagonists – Michael Woolcock and Deval Desai – pioneered new forms of what they call 'experimental justice reform' (Desai and Woolcock 2015). 'Experimental', because it increasingly breaks with established orthodoxies that reduce 'the law' to its state-backed manifestations and thereby also opens the conceptual space to think about non-state justice institutions as viable sites for legal reform. The most prominent example of a World Bank-funded project today is the "Strengthening Access to Justice Programme" in Indonesia. Based on extensive research that resulted in the publication of a key report on "Forging the Middle Ground – Engaging non-state justice institutions in Indonesia" (2008), the project aims "to strengthen best practice informal dispute resolution in West Sumatera and West Nusa Tenggara, based on principles set down in the

Constitution."[1] This project is significant, as the report on which it is based exemplifies a broader strategy of international donor agencies that try to seize the identified advantages of non-state institutions while circumventing their seeming shortcomings. In the words of the report, they seek "to marry the social accessibility, authority and legitimacy of informal processes with accountability to the community and the state" (The World Bank 2008: 68).

Similar considerations also informed the recent turn of various United Nations bodies – and the UNDP in particular – towards programming with non-state justice institutions in the Global South. As with the World Bank, programming is tightly intertwined with the production of knowledge about such non-state courts. After a number of exploratory studies, in 2013 the UNDP published the most comprehensive study of non-state justice institution presented by an international donor agency to date. The almost 400-page strong report on "Informal Justice Mechanisms – Charting a Course for Human Rights-based Engagement" starts with the "recognition that Informal Justice Systems are an empirical reality, albeit a complicated one" (UNDP et al. 2013: 7). They are a complicated reality precisely because they are so popular in the Global South. This popularity – according to the report – has a number of complex and multifaceted reasons. The two most prominent ones concern the efficiency and legitimacy of non-state justice institutions vis-à-vis their state-backed counterparts. As the report argues, for many people in the Global South, the state-backed courts are often geographically distant, generally inaccessible, and frequently marred by corruption and inefficiency. Non-state justice institutions not only offer faster, cheaper, and generally more accessible alternatives, they are also likely to be more in sync with local normative orders. This combination of efficient conflict resolutions and the resonance with local belief systems accounts for the popularity of non-state institutions. At the same time, these institutions are also frequently criticized by national as well as international human rights organizations for their patriarchal biases, the reproduction of local power relationships, and continuous marginalization of the concerns of women, children, and other vulnerable members of village communities. The key question for international donor agencies is thus how to evacuate the advantages of non-state justice institutions from these attested weaknesses.

The main response of both the World Bank and various United Nations organizations is to strengthen the accountability of non-state justice institutions. The UNDP study quoted above discusses accountability mechanisms under the broad headlines of "Transparency, Monitoring, and Oversight" (UNDP et al. 2013: 173). These mechanisms include possible rights of appeal against the decision of non-state justice institutions in the state-backed courts, the referral of cases from the non-state to the state courts, and the supervision of the former through the latter. All these

---

[1] http://web.worldbank.org/WBSITE/EXTERNAL/COUNTRIES/EASTASIAPACIFICEXT/0, contentMDK:23192809~pagePK:146736~piPK:146830~theSitePK:226301,00.html. Accessed February 4, 2016.

processes, however, require the bureaucratization of non-state justice institutions. In particular, this bureaucratization requires the increasing mediation of non-state justice processes through officially recognized paperwork. The recording of case outcomes is thus also one of the key recommendations of the UNDP report, which reasons that "the recording of case outcomes promotes legal certainty and transparency and can enhance oversight" (UNDP et al. 2013: 173). Only with officially recognized records in place, the report continues its line of argument, could decisions of non-state courts become appealable in the state-backed judiciary. And only on the basis of written records could state agencies as well as civil society organizations exercise meaningful control over processes of non-state justice delivery. Although conceding that the infiltration of paperwork might distort the nature of non-state justice institutions, the report concludes that the bureaucratization of these institutions is a central component of forging the kind of middle ground between the state and non-state courts that the World Bank also tries to seize.

Official paperwork is thus a centrepiece of international donors' recent engagement with non-state justice institutions. This is hardly surprising. Official documents play a central role in virtually all state-backed legal processes; there is no legal process that is even imaginable without some correlative paperwork (Nemeth 2011; Vismann 2000; 2008). Despite this centrality, written documents have received scant or – at best – rather one-dimensional treatment in the analysis of court proceedings (whether by state or non-state institutions) as well as by the exploration of national or transnational bureaucracies more generally.[2] Following a Weberian intuition, documents have been largely taken for granted and treated as neutral carriers of information. They have thus been predominantly seen as sources of information rather than as artefacts entangled in complex social processes. Scholars have, in the words of Ben Kafka, "discovered all sorts of interesting and important things by looking *through* paperwork, but seldom paused to look *at* it" (Kafka 2009: 341 emphasis in the original). To a lesser degree, this diagnosis also holds for anthropological scholarship in particular, as Matthew Hull has argued in his recent review of 'Documents and Bureaucracy' (Hull 2012a: 252). Yet notable exceptions do of course apply. As ethnographic artefacts, documents have been placed centre-stage in the seminal work of Annelise Riles (2006b), who explained the anthropological neglect of documents in her ethnographic exploration of the 1995 World Conference on Women in Beijing through the all-too-close proximity between the production of bureaucratic and academic knowledge. As Riles argues, anthropologists rely on a certain distance between analyst and object of analysis. Yet bureaucratic and academic practices of knowledge production both revolve around the reading and writing of documents as well as their circulation, so that "the problem of making documents a subject of ethnographic inquiry is a problem of studying knowledge practices that draw upon and overlap with the anthropologist's own" (Riles 2006a: 79).

[2] A notable exception is Latour (2010: 70–106).

Responding to this challenge, anthropologists, and especially anthropologists researching bureaucracies in South Asia, have recently turned to the close investigation documents as key bureaucratic artefacts (Hull 2012b; 2013; Gupta 2012; 2013; Mathur 2015). As Matthew Hull has argued, a key insight of this scholarship is that "documents are not simply instruments of bureaucratic organizations, but rather are constitutive of bureaucratic rules, ideologies, knowledge, practices, subjectivities, objects, outcomes, even the organizations themselves" (Hull 2012a: 251).

The bureaucratization of non-state justice institutions in the Global South through international donor agencies is a privileged site for the investigation of such processes in which bureaucratic writing becomes constitutive of international organizations themselves. Although the bureaucratization of rural justice institutions in the Global South is justified in the name of enhanced transparency and accountability of these institutions towards the people who approach them, the prolific distribution of bureaucratic paperwork that accompanies most international programming with non-state justice institutions also fulfils a second purpose. It renders rural institutions legible to international donor agencies. And it is only through the constant production of paperwork – for example, for monitoring and evaluation purposes – that international donor agencies can actually constitute themselves as transnational bureaucracies with correlative claims to authoritative knowledge about global programme interventions in the social, political, and economic life of diverse contexts in the Global South. Before turning to transnational knowledge claims, and their material basis in written documents, the next section introduces the village courts in Bangladesh.

THE VILLAGE COURTS IN BANGLADESH

The village courts in Bangladesh are a curious institution. They are located right at the intersection of state-backed and non-state legal systems and are designed to remedy the shortcomings of both. The state-backed courts are frequently criticized for their corruption and inefficiency; there are currently over two million cases pending in the lower courts alone, and resolving a land dispute through the state's judiciary might take well over a decade. Among many of my interlocutors in rural Bangladesh, the state courts had a reputation of being "a waste of time, money, and energy". In contrast to the state legal system, the shalish courts enjoy significantly higher degrees of popularity. The shalish courts are neither regulated nor recognized by the state. They therefore exist in all shapes and sizes; I have seen shalish with as few as 5 and as many as 150 people, negotiating absolutely everything from disputes arising from trespassing cattle to serious criminal offences, including murder cases. Based on committees comprised of influential people within rural communities, they resolve conflicts by reference to customary practices as much as to religious principles and Islamic law.

The shalish courts capture the overall ambiguity of international donor agencies towards non-state justice institutions outlined above. On the one hand, shalish courts have been repeatedly criticized by both national and international human rights organizations for their patriarchal bias, the perpetuation of unequal power relations, and their non-compliance with international human rights standards.[3] On the other hand, international donor agencies have displayed an increasing interest in shalish courts as an alternative avenue to enhance access to justice for poor and marginalized people in the rural parts of the country (Akmeemana et al. 2008: 1). Trying to forge a middle ground, international donor agencies have subsequently started to focus increasingly on the village courts as an alternative institution. Usually classified as "semi-formal", the village courts are recognized by the state yet resemble the shalish in terms of set-up. They therefore aim at maintaining a high degree of informality (like the shalish) while, at the same time, imposing formal procedural requirements.

The procedural requirements pertain to the composition of the village courts, their jurisdiction, and their relation to the state-backed judiciary. The 2006 Village Court Act circumscribes their jurisdiction to minor civil and criminal cases with a pecuniary limit of 25,000 Thaka.[4] Such cases include cattle trespassing, trifling assaults against people or property, unlawful assembly, rioting, mischief, provocation, wrongful restraint or confinement, intentional insult with intent to provoke breach of the peace, or criminal intimidation.[5] For such cases, the village courts have exclusive jurisdiction. Neither civil nor criminal courts ought to try cases falling within the competences of the village courts; and in the event that any such case is filed with the state-backed courts, these courts ought to forward to the case to the responsible village court. In the village courts, the respective civil and criminal laws of Bangladesh are suspended. Instead of applying the respective provisions from the Codes of Civil or Criminal Procedure, the village courts try cases by jury. The head of the jury is a local elected political – the Union Purishad Chairman.

A Union Purishad (UP) is the smallest administrative unit in Bangladesh; each of the roughly 4,500 Union Purishads in the country is presided over by an elected council with thirteen members, and the chairmen are the heads of these councils. They are usually closely connected to one of the dominant political parties in Bangladesh and, as locally highly influential figures, in control of dense formal and informal networks reaching into both the village communities that constitute a Union Purishad and into the upper echelons of Bangladesh's political system

---

[3] For much more nuanced accounts of the complexities in shalish processes, see Siddiqi (2011a; 2011b; 2011c) and Shehabuddin (2008).

[4] The Village Court (Amendment) Bill 2013 (also discussed below) increased the pecuniary limit of the village courts to 75,000 Thaka.

[5] The full list of cases triable by the village courts is specified in Schedules I and II of 2006 Village Court Act with reference to the Code of Civil Procedure (1908) and the Code of Criminal Procedure (1989).

(Lewis and Hossain 2008: 31–33). In addition to the UP chairman, each of the conflicting parties nominates two representatives to the village court's five-member jury. One of the two representatives for each party has to be a ward member, i.e. a member of the elected Union Council. The jury passes judgment by voting – and the composition of the vote is decisive for subsequent possibilities of appeal.

Only village court decisions that have been passed by a narrow 3:2 majority are appealable in the state's District or Magistrate Courts. All other decisions are legally binding and can be enforced with recourse to the state's enforcement agencies. Importantly, the village courts are only entitled to demand the return of property and/or compensation payments; they can neither imprison people (though they can refer cases involving crimes that might be punished with imprisonment to the responsible Magistrate Courts) nor impose any kind of physical punishment. Before the village court is constituted, the accused party can admit the claim(s) of the petitioner under a provision in Rule 33 of the 1976 Village Court Act. Cases solved though Rule 33 are legally binding. If no pre-trail compromise is found in accordance with Rule 33, the village courts are constituted by the UP chairman for nominal administrative fees of 2 and 4 Thaka for criminal and civil cases, respectively. Yet, despite these low court fees, the implicit reliance on local authorities, and the formal integration of the village courts into the state-backed judiciary through possible avenues of appeal as well as support through the state's enforcement agencies, the village courts exists primarily in the law books of Bangladesh. In the local practice of conflict resolution in the country's 87,000 villages, they are largely absent (Lewis and Hossain 2008: 20).

THE PROJECT 'ACTIVATING THE VILLAGE COURTS IN BANGLADESH'

Recently, various international donor agencies have started trying to change this. Between 2009 and 2015, the EU and UNDP – in concert with Bangladeshi state agencies as well as local non-state actors – have mobilized 10 million Euros for the project "Activating the Village Courts in Bangladesh". Whereas the EU is the main donor of the project and provides roughly 90 per cent of the project funding, the UNDP is its intellectual powerhouse. It links the EU with the Ministry of Local Governance, Rural Development and Cooperatives as well as with the four local NGOs that are in charge of implementing the project on grassroots levels. On grassroots levels, the local NGOs employ one fieldworker for the dissemination of information about the village courts and one court assistant whose one and only task is the administration of all the paperwork that village courts session necessitate. These court assistants are thus virtually tasked with writing the village courts into the complex landscapes of conflict resolution in rural Bangladesh, where – with additional staff at Sub-District, District, and Division levels – the four local NGOs employ in total more than 1,000 people, working on the activation of village courts in 350 Union Purishads. These 1,000 members of staff are both trained and supervised by UNDP's Dhaka-based project team.

For the project, UNDP set up its own project office. This office is an odd transnational space. Located in Dhaka's Diplomatic Quarter, it displays all the insignias of the international. Hidden behind a solid white wall, it is flagged with the blue banner of the United Nations. So are the four-wheel drives parked on both sides of the wall. Passing from the national streets of Dhaka into the international realm of the United Nations is only possible through a small gate, guarded by a private security guard, dressed in a military-like uniform. He diligently registers the movement of people in and out of the UN compound as they move back and forth between the national and the international.

Inside the building, this neat dividing line between the international and the national starts to blur. All members of staff employed by the project are Bangladeshi citizens. Yet most of them, at least those in leading positions, have a significant degree of international experience. Some of them have had long and distinguished careers within the state's judiciary before either being seconded to the project or joining the project's team directly as full members of staff. The professional biographies of UNDP's village court experts thus undermine established analytical categories that separate the global from the local or the state from the third sector (Lewis 2011). A key example is the project's senior legal advisor, with whom I had several long conversations in 2011 and 2012. After gaining his law degree from Dhaka University, he joined Bangladesh's state-backed judiciary in 1991 and has worked as a judge for almost two decades. In addition to his distinguished national judicial career, he has received ample legal training outside of Bangladesh. He earned a second MA degree in Human Rights and Intellectual Property Law from a Swedish University and received training in legislative drafting from renowned institutions in London and New Delhi. He has been on deputation from the judiciary to the national parliament in Bangladesh as well as to the Ministry of Law. Being seconded to the project on the activation of village courts, he has been in charge of the reform of the legislative framework of the 2006 Village Court Act (see above: "The Village Courts in Bangladesh"). As a high-ranking officer of the EU stressed when I talked to him a few weeks later, this legislative reform is given a very high degree of importance within the architecture of the project as a whole.

Almost two years after our conversation, the central piece of legislation was passed in parliament as the Village Court (Amendment) Bill 2013. The bill increases the pecuniary level of the village courts from 25.000 to 75.000 Thaka. It also makes the presence of at least one female ward member compulsory for all village court proceedings. This policy in particular displays the overall aim of supporting the empowerment of women through the village courts. The fine for filing a false village court case is increased to 5.000 Thaka, and contempt for village court is fined with up to 1.000 Thaka. The bill has been decisively prepared by the project. It has been drafted by the senior legal advisor following consultations with judicial officers,

NGO representatives, journalists, further members of civil society, and local politicians in different parts of the country (see also Murshed 2012).

All of these changes are fully in line with transnational aspirations of "forging the middle ground" between state and non-state legal systems. In order to translate this aspiration into practice, UNDP's Dhaka-based project team is organized in three further pillars: Monitoring and Evaluation, Communication, and Capacity Building units administer the activation of village courts from the Dhaka headquarters. These three units are in charge of translating rather fluid transnational ideas about the rule of law and access to justice through non-state institutions into tangible project activities, including training workshops as well as artefacts through which information about the village courts can be disseminated in the rural parts of the country.

DOCUMENTS AND OTHER ARTEFACTS TRAVELLING DOWNWARDS

How do these transnational ideas actually materialize in rural Bangladesh? The most immediate way in which these ideas travel is the communication and training materials provided by the project. Whilst talking to the head of the Communications Unit at UNDP in the beginning of 2012, he highlighted how the project pursued different communication strategies for different audiences. For international donors (and foreign researchers, such as myself), they had recently started publishing an English-language newsletter called "Smile." For the rural population whose access to justice ought to be enhanced through the actual project, the communications team had designed a multiplicity of so-called "knowledge products," including different training and other communication materials. Most of these materials contain a combination of pictures and texts, such as the stickers that are prolifically distributed in the rural areas of the country where the project is active. There are at least eight different motifs, including, for example, one which depicts a young man filing an application to the Union Purishad Chairman. He hands the chairman a piece of paper, which he holds with both hands. The paper is at the very centre of the sticker. Besides the chairman, who sits at a desk, another man (presumably the court assistant employed by one of the local NGOs) remains in the background, yet is always ready to help in case need arises. Underneath the depicted scene is a banner saying "My village is the way I like it. We have the Village Courts."

In addition to these kinds of stickers, other central artefacts through which the village courts are being activated as semi-formal institutions in rural Bangladesh are the capacity building materials, and in particular the flipcharts that the fieldworker and court assistants use to disseminate information about the village courts in their court yard meetings. The court yard meetings are the backbone of the project. In these meetings, the "target audience" – mainly women, poor, and marginalized people – come together to discuss day-to-day conflicts and learn about the avenues opened up by the village courts for adjudicating minor civil and criminal disputes. The flipcharts used in these meetings contain roughly twenty pages, giving information about the kinds of cases that can be tried in the village courts, the correct procedures to initiate a village court, the respective legal provisions on which the village courts are based, the necessary documents that facilitate village court trials, possible rights of appeal, and the actual constitution of the village court. On each and every page, there is the Bengali version of the name of the project – "Activating the Village Courts in Bangladesh" – as well as the logo of the Ministry of Local Governance, Rural Development and Cooperation. This logo is framed by the logos of UNDP/Bangladesh to the right and the EU to the left of the governmental emblem.

These three emblems are omnipresent throughout the entire project. They are printed onto virtually all artefacts through which the village courts are introduced – or "activated" – in rural Bangladesh. They are not only on the flipcharts and the stickers (described above), but also on the signboards of project offices at the district level as well as the billboards outside the Union Purishad offices in which the village courts take place. Within these offices, the EU and UNDP have installed functioning village courtrooms, which are equipped with magnificent wooden furniture. The so-called *Eljas* resemble formal courtrooms quite closely. They include a judge's bench, usually decorated with beautiful wooden panels or red cloths. At the bench, the five-member jury can follow the entire court proceedings. With the chairmen slightly elevated and placed in the middle, the two representatives for each conflicting party are located to his left and right sides. At a ninety degree angle from the judges' bench is the witness stand, where both the aggrieved and the responding party as well as potential witnesses give their testimonies. Opposite the witness stand is a table for the court assistant, who is in charge of keeping all written records of the village court session as well as the village court register in order, while the village court audience faces the judges' bench. Funded by the EU and distributed by the UNDP, the village courtrooms are the most tangible material manifestation of transnational ideas about the rule of law in rural Bangladesh.

The physical set-up of the village courts mirror that of the state-backed courts and endow their rural counterparts with an air of formality. So does the omnipresence of official paperwork at all stages of village court processes. The government prescribes no less than eleven different forms for the administration of village court proceedings; and the EU, UNDP, and four local NGOs are currently distributing these files into each and every one of the roughly 350 Union Purishads where project activities take place. The forms themselves bear the logos of neither international donors nor national government agencies. Yet each and every form is encased within a Cover Sheet. On the front page of the Cover Sheet is the logo of the Ministry of Local Government as well as a text box. Within the text box, the number of the form is given first (counting from 1 to 13), followed by the heading 'Case Register', and three subsequent dotted lines for the inscriptions of 'Union', 'Upuzilla' (Sub-district), and

'Zila' (District). On the backside of the sheet, the logos of the EU, the UNDP, and the Ministry are imprinted above the "Activating the Village Courts in Bangladesh" slogan.

On the inside, the first of these forms is designed for filing a formal application to the village court. This application contains information on (a) the name of the Union Purishad in which the application is made, (b) the name and place of residence of the petitioner, (c) the name and place of residence of the respondent, (d) the name of the Union in which the offence was committed, (e) the actual complaint and/or the valuation of the claim made against the respondent, and (f) the relief claimed by the petitioner. The application has to be signed by the petitioner and submitted with the fees of 2 or 4 Thaka for criminal or civil cases, respectively. If the application is accepted by the chairman, it is given a registration number and its particulars are registered in the specific Village Court Register of the Union Purishad. Then, further paperwork ensues. There are letters summoning the respondent as well as potential witnesses to the village courts, a Compromise Sheet to prevent the constitution of a Village Court under Rule 33 (see also "The Village Courts in Bangladesh", above), a form for the transfer of village court cases to the respective state-backed civil and criminal courts, a form to file a case of contempt of court and the corresponding fine that ensues, a form for the final village court decree, and a register for recording the appropriate implementation of village court verdicts. The entire village court process is thus mediated by a seemingly endless trail of bureaucratic paperwork – yet charting this trail is strongly supported by the project.

THICK DESCRIPTION: WORKSHOP – HOW DO THESE ARTEFACTS COME TO LIFE?

Although the village courts in many ways aim at drawing their authority from mimicking practices of the state-backed courts, the ways in which the village courts are introduced to the people living in rural Bangladesh starts from the institution they are most acquainted with – the shalish. Discussions about the shalish figured prominently in all kinds of project activities that I observed through multiple rounds of field research in Bangladesh between 2011 and 2014, including court yard meetings, workshops with local political authorities and religious leaders, and training sessions with villagers organized in so-called community-based organizations. I attended one of those training sessions in the northern part of Bangladesh in early 2012. About two dozen people had gathered in the classroom of the primary school. The only 6 women present sit on the left side of the room, on two benches in two rows. Next to them, some 17 men, ranging from between roughly 20 and 60 years of age, sat on benches and chairs on the remaining two sides of the room, facing the teacher's desk where the trainers were standing. The trainers were two men in their mid-thirties, both of whom were on the payroll of the local NGO in charge of implementing the project in this part of the country. One of them was in charge of coordinating all training activities of the NGO within the entire division. The slightly younger one, who delivered most of the training, was working primarily within this specific district.

The classroom is flagged with a polypropylene banner advertising the village court and their activation through the EU and UNDP. In blue letters, it states "Activating the Village Courts – A Cooperation between the Ministry of Local Governance, Rural Development and Cooperation, the European Union, and UNDP." Next to the banner, there are two posters, attached to the wall with sticky tape, depicting scenes from village court processes. The meeting begins. With my colleague and translator, I squeeze into the far-end corner of the room. All eyes rest on me as I am introduced as a researcher from Germany, interested in the ways in which people in rural Bangladesh solve their day-to-day conflicts in rural communities. The eyes only slowly wander off to the front, where the trainer starts his elaborations on rural justice systems. He begins with pointing to the banner, explaining that the village courts are owned by the Ministry of Local Governance, but that they are paid for by the EU. UNDP Bangladesh gives technical assistance – he says this in English – "technical assistance"; they provide the village court rooms, the training booklets, and all the documents for the village courts. The topic for this session is the village courts and how they are different from a shalish.

The session begins with an imaginary conflict between two fictional characters, Karim and Rahmin. The trainer vividly introduces the conflict, in which a quarrel between Rahmin and Karim has resulted in severe injuries that eventually turned into physical violence of the latter against the former. The audience is clearly taken by the narration, and their sympathies lie with Karim, as their repeated comments attest. The trainer then suggests that in order to solve the conflict, Karim could apply to local elites and ask for a shalish. Broad approval from the audience – this is the obvious thing to do. The trainer continues: deliberating behind closed doors, the local elites constituting the shalish board have decided that Rahmin owes an apology as well as 500 Thaka to Karim, to compensate him for his injuries as well as the costs he had incurred as he needed to purchase some medicine from the local village shop. Yet, in spite of this decision, the victim does not receive the money he is owed. What should be done? This question opens the floor. A vivid discussion develops between the trainer and the audience as well as among different members within the audience. One participant questions the plausibility of the hypothetical example presented by the trainer. If the shalish board was comprised of local influential figures, and if these figures had ruled against Rahmin, they would surely be able to enforce their verdict. Another participant disagrees; he quotes an example from a neighbouring village community, where a similar case had actually occurred. The majority of participants seem to be persuaded by this example, and the work on the fictional case continues. A third villager suggests that the shalish board should impose a deadline for the delivery of the 500 Thaka, and they should demand that the money be paid to them directly. "And what if the money is still not paid, not even to the Shalish board?" the trainer asks. "Then further discussions have to follow," a fourth man (so far only men have spoken) replies. The trainer agrees. Shalish discussion can only be based on the mutual understanding of both parties, and this understanding can only be reached in deliberative processes in which all involved parties continue the discussion until a decision is found that is acceptable to everybody. This is what they have debated in the previous meeting. Yet the trainer keeps pressing: what if – after all the discussions and the seeming agreement – the money is still not forthcoming?

Eventually, one of the participants argues that the real problem at the heart of the issue is that in shalish, all negotiations are verbal, nothing is written down, and no formal record documents the judgment. Most (but not all) of the participants nod affirmatively. This is a big problem. The trainer is delighted. Now, the introduction of the village court starts. He moves over to the flipchart, and starts explaining the key differences between a village court and a shalish. Unlike a shalish, a village court is recognized by the state. It is instituted through the 2006 Village Court Act, and its decisions can be enforced through the police. The majority of the training session is then dedicated to the exploration of village courts rules and procedures. The trainer discusses the jurisdiction of the village courts, the procedures leading to its constitutions, and the ways in which decisions are reached as well as how they are enforceable is discussed (as introduced in "The Village Courts in Bangladesh," above).

Throughout the session, documents play a predominant role. They become the key artefact that distinguishes the village courts from shalish. It is because of documents that the village courts qualify as an institution of the "strong law" – i.e. the state-backed laws. The trainer explains the different forms that are required for the administration of village court proceedings. He also highlights the support that is available for the court assistants. In every Union Purishad, one person is employed full time in order to help people in rural Bangladesh to file applications to the village courts and navigate the ensuing paper trail. In this way, the village courts are quite literally written into the landscape of rural conflict resolution – and the importance of documents is repeatedly stressed throughout the workshop, as well as throughout all other training activities that I attended in the course of my field research. In a way, then, the fieldworkers and court assistants who implement the project at grassroots levels introduce the village courts by bureaucratizing rural justice systems through the introduction of official documents.

The documents provided by the project are undoubtedly important – but not in the ways advocated by the trainer within this particular workshop. As I have argued elsewhere (Berger 2014), the documents do not necessarily record what happens in specific village court processes. They therefore do not produce the kind of accountability aspired to by international donor agencies. Yet they are highly important nonetheless. By distributing bureaucratic paperwork through the court assistants, the project equips poor and marginalized people with access to official paperwork that would otherwise be out of reach to them. Access to this paperwork, in turn, allows poor and marginalized people to approach local elites for support in processes of conflict resolution.

Take the case of Saheli as an example. One day she observes her neighbours taking some crops from her little plot of land. After unsuccessfully trying to resolve the issue with her neighbours directly, she approaches the local ward member for support – also unsuccessfully. Only when she files a formal complaint with the village courts and returns with the official paper do both the ward member and her neighbours agree to an informal settlement. They pay a lump sum for the crops and apologize to her. Although the sum does not amount to what is demanded in the village court application, she accepts the compromise. No village court is constituted and the case is filed under Rule 33 as a pre-trial settlement. The case of Saheli is exemplary of larger patterns of the effects of bureaucratizing rural justice institutions through the introduction of official paperwork that I observed in Bangladesh throughout the course of my field research. This bureaucratic paperwork thus becomes a form of symbolic capital that forges social relationships and potentially alters local dynamics of conflicts resolution, often quite independent of what is inscribed on the actual papers. Ironically, the distribution of paperwork thereby realizes one key aspiration of the project. It enhances access to local justice fora for poor and marginalized people, yet it does so without producing the kind of transparency that international donors expect from the bureaucratization of village courts through the distribution of official paperwork.

DOCUMENTS TRAVELLING UPWARDS

The documents distributed by UNDP via the local NGOs, however, also fulfil a further purpose. They quite literally render the village courts legible to international donor agencies. By documenting village court cases, the fieldworker and court assistants on the payroll of international organizations not only create a record of what did (and did not) happen for the people in rural Bangladesh. They also, perhaps more importantly, produce a record of project activities for international donors. And they do so by producing yet more paperwork.

Besides the eleven government-prescribed forms, the court assistants (who are on the payroll of the local NGOs) record all village court proceedings with a further thirteen non-government-prescribed forms, most of which are used by UNDP's Dhaka-based staff to monitor project activities. These forms record who filed a village court case, how long it took to resolve the case, how long it took to enforce the village court verdict, and how much money was recovered in terms of compensation payments. Additional forms also records project activities not directly related to village court trials but to training activities. Thus, the fieldworkers need to record how many court meetings they have held, how many community-based organizations (CBOs) have been formed and how regularly they met, and how many of the participants in all of these activities were women. These forms then start travelling upwards. They are sent to the Upuzilla and then the District and Divisional offices of the local NGOs, where the numbers are checked by specialized staff employed exclusively for project-monitoring and evaluation.

At the Divisional level, the case-related data from the individual Unions is aggregated. It is here that Monthly, Quarterly, and Annual Reports are prepared and passed on to UNDP's Monitoring and Evaluation experts in Dhaka. Again, these reports contain, above all, numbers. The most important numbers are the case-related ones, as representatives of one local NGO told me in late 2012 as we discussed the current monitoring and evaluation practices of the project. We were sitting in a spacious office of an unpretentious building, which is located in a narrow side-ally and not easily detectable. Only a small placard alerts the informed and searching eye to the presence of the NGO's headquarters within the one-storey building. There is no fence, no guard, and no four-wheel drive. There is also no flag. It took me some time and three phone calls to find the building. My hosts are half amused, half impressed as I arrive. I arrive on foot – and this is probably the most tangible way of articulating that, although being a citizen of the EU, I am not representative of the funding agencies that pay for the activation of village courts in the rural areas of the division.

For our first meeting, a District Coordinator and the Monitoring and Evaluation Expert of the NGO sit with me at the conference table in their office. We have a long discussion about the intricate complexities of rural conflict resolution, the history of the project in this particular Division, and their experiences with the trainings and workshops they have facilitated. I also ask about the reporting of project activities – and they highlight the importance given to monitoring and evaluation within the project. It is a lot of work. All the monitoring forms are provided by the UNDP, but they have kept changing throughout the implementation of the project. New requests for information have been added, for example about the actual amount of money recovered through village court sessions. If new information is required, they need to go back to the Districts, Upuzillas, and often even Union Purishad levels, make the court assistants go through the registers and any other documentation they have, and try to deliver the requested information. The regular reporting never stops. At least some members of staff are always engaged in producing either a monthly, quarterly, or annual report for the project managers in Dhaka. Most important are the numbers, they frequently stress. But recently, there have also been requests for brief case histories, so they started collecting anecdotes about village court proceedings and have passed them on to Dhaka headquarters as well. It is the first time, they tell me, that they had to pass such case histories on to Dhaka, but they have prepared them in the past, for the visits of the Head of the EU Delegation or the Country Director of UNDP Bangladesh. However, such visits are exceptional. Regular monitoring proceeds through the reports that are based on the documents they receive from the Districts, and – the most recent compilation of case studies aside – from the numbers that can be wrought out of these documents.

The current numbers requested by the project management in Dhaka fall into the following categories:

- Number of total reported cases
- Total number of cases resolved
- Total number of cases implemented (i.e. of village court decisions that have been enforced)
- Number of cases pending in the village courts
- Number of cases received from the higher courts
- Number of cases sent to the higher courts
- Total number of pending cases
- The number of representatives present on a village court panel
- Number of petitions to the village courts that have been dismissed for default

These categories themselves have been subject to frequent changes, as my interlocutors have stressed. Yet the insistence on numbers has remained constant throughout the entire project, and therefore also throughout the entire reporting period. Numbers are therefore crucial. They constitute a mathematical lingua franca through which very different actors in very different contexts are connected within the context of the project. As Theodore Porter has argued, what is special about this lingua franca is that "quantification is a technology of distance [and] since the rules for collecting and manipulating numbers are widely shared, they can easily be transported across oceans and continents" (Porter 1995: 9). Numbers travel lightly; they do not contain the contextual baggage of the places from whence they emerge. In some respects, numbers and documents are thus remarkably similar. They both seem independent of the people that have produced them (Porter 1995; Hull 2012a: 253); and, in combination, numbers based on documents make strong claims to the objective validity of the information they carry.

These claims to objective validity are crucial within the logic of international project interventions. With the advance of New Public Management Technologies within development discourse, performance indicators, rankings, and efficiency assessment tools of various other kinds have rapidly gained in importance (Desrosières 2015; also see Merry, Chapter 7, this volume). Consequently, the numbers relating to village court cases are complemented with numbers of specific training activities and other "deliverables" such court yard meetings, rallies, and street drama performances disseminating information about the village courts. For each of these activities, the staff members of the local NGO have to meet predefined targets, and the various reports submitted to the authorities in Dhaka always measure project activities against these targets.

There is thus a constant flow of information between the Dhaka offices of UNDP and the local NGOs implementing the project at grassroots levels. Yet this information remains fluid and elusive. Throughout the entire project phase, the so-called Objectively Verifiable Indicators that ought to track the progress of the project have been subject to constant contestation and redefinition, as several people involved in monitoring processes at different levels of the project confirmed in our conversations throughout 2011 and 2012. What emerged in these conversations was a rather different aspect of the importance of "Objectively Verifiable Indicators." These indicators were widely considered to be highly important; but not so much in order to control and track project outcomes, as for reasons to do with internal processes of legitimation within transnational bureaucracies.

In our conversations in their Dhaka offices, representatives of both the EU and the UNDP highlighted the constant pressure for the production of numbers. Above all, these numbers were required to give an account of project activities to superiors in headquarters in Brussels and New York. Ironically, all high-ranking international bureaucrats with whom I talked were well aware of the impossibility of fully trusting these numbers. As they told me, they had seen how quickly they change, or how many different numbers might circulate at any given point in time for the seemingly same phenomenon. Yet numbers were (almost) all they had.

Take the case of representatives of the EU. The building of their Delegation is literally only a stone's throw from the project offices of the UNDP. Yet the Delegation is even more secured. There are the familiar four-wheel drives, the high walls, and the blue flags (this time, of course, slightly darker and with yellow stars). But the wall is more solid. It is also higher and seems more imposing. There are heavy concrete road blocks surrounding the gate, and in order to enter the compound, one has to pass through a little house in which a security guard not only registers the movement of people but also x-rays their bags and equips them with a visitor pass (in case they do not belong to the Delegation). Yet this security is a double-edged sword, and entering the Delegation is almost as difficult as leaving it – at least metaphorically. In order to visit the projects that are funded by the Delegation, some of their representatives tell me, they have to apply for special permits. They are then escorted by an entourage of ministerial officials, press representatives, and United Nations experts to village sites where they can observe the functioning of village courts. All of this needs to be organized well in advance. And it is anticipated by thorough preparations within the respective village communities that are going to be visited. The boundaries of the international are thus carefully policed, from both sites. All that can permeate these boundaries is the endless trail of seemingly neutral paperwork – and the numbers it carries. This is the key reason why the very production of numbers within development projects seems almost more important than what these numbers actually ought to represent.

CONCLUSION

The fetishization of numbers is not limited to the two international agencies working on the activation of village courts in Bangladesh. It also applies to a diverse set of global organizations operating in rather different contexts. A telling example is given by Desai and Woolcock, the World Bank experts working in the Justice for the Poor initiative introduced at the outset of this chapter. With reference to traditional Rule of Law projects, which they characterize as "legal orthodoxy," they argue that virtually all development agencies tend to prioritize the production of tangible (i.e. measurable) results over genuine impact on the ground. As they argue, project initiatives follow primarily bureaucratic imperatives in global headquarters and capital cities. In accordance with these imperatives, projects will "reliably generate a seemingly impressive array of discrete deliverables that can be readily photographed, counted, tracked, aggregated, and compared" (Desai and Woolcock 2015: 163). This ceaseless production of discrete and measurable "deliverables" has been firmly institutionalized. Enumerable targets have become an intrinsic part of Memoranda of Understanding signed between governments in the Global South, international organizations, and non-state actors. They are also a constitutive element of Project Designs, Implementation Plans, Risk Assessments, and the various kinds of Monitoring Reports that accompany every project. In short, these innumerable deliverables are an intrinsic part of the rule of project law that shapes the interactions between transnational donor agencies, their state-based partners, and the variously defined groups of recipients (Benda-Beckmann et al. 2009: 4; Günter and Randeria 2001: 70).

As I have argued in this chapter, the imperatives of producing enumerable project results are also an integral part of the current bureaucratization of non-state justice institutions through international donor agencies. Justified in the name of enhanced accountability and transparency for the people who use them, the proliferation of official paperwork also renders rural non-state institutions legible to international donors. It is only on the basis of written paperwork that project outcomes can be tracked, enumerated, and fed-back to international headquarters through monitoring and evaluation apparatuses. These apparatuses, in turn, ground international organization's claims to authoritative knowledge about rural non-state justice systems in the Global South more generally. The village courts in Bangladesh are only a case in point. Once the village courts in Bangladesh have been cleared of the messy complexities of rural justice delivery and translated into neat numbers as well as correlative case stories, they can start travelling; and, as they travel, they become a reference point for further project interventions. Starting with the forms that are filled out by the local court assistants and passed on to sub-district, district, and divisional supervisors and then further on to the national and international headquarters of the EU and the UNDP, the village courts in Bangladesh become part of global templates for donor intervention in rural non-state justice systems, not only in Bangladesh but elsewhere too.

REFERENCES

Akmeemana, Saku, Naomi Hossain, Ferdous Jahan, and Erik Jensen. 2008. 'Survey: Citizens' Experiences of the Legal System in Bangladesh'. Available at microdata.worldbank.org /index.php/catalog/616/download/15824, accessed 14 February 2016.

Barnett, Michael N. and Martha Finnemore. 2004. *Rules for the World. International Organizations in Global Politics*. Ithaca: Cornell University Press.

Benda-Beckmann, Franz von, Keebet von Benda-Beckmann, and Julia Eckert. 2009. 'Rules of Law and Laws of Ruling: Governance and Law between Past and Future', in Franz von Benda-Beckmann, Keebet von Benda-Beckmann, and Julia Eckert (eds.), *Rules of Law and Laws of Ruling. On the Governance of Law*. Farnham: Ashgate.

Berger, Tobias. 2014. *Global Norms and Local Courts: Translating 'the Rule of Law' in Bangladesh*. Berlin: PhD Dissertation, Freie Universität Berlin.

Cook, Ian. 2004. 'Follow the Thing: Papaya', *Antipode*, 36(4): 642–664.

Desai, Deval, and Michael Woolcock. 2015. 'Experimental Justice Reform: Justice for the Poor – Lessons from the World Bank and Beyond', *Annual Review of Law and Social Science*, 11: 155–174.

Desrosières, Alain. 2015. 'Retroaction: How Indicators Feed Back onto Quantified Actors', in Richard Rottenburg, Sally E. Merry, Sung-Joon Park, and Johanna Mugler (eds.), *The World of Indicators. The Making of Governmental Knowledge through Quantification*. Cambridge: Cambridge University Press.

Ehm, Frithjof. 2010. *The Rule of Law. Concept, Guiding Principle, and Framework*. Trieste. European Commission for Democracy through Law.

Günter, Klaus, and Shalini Randeria. 2001. *Recht, Kultur und Gesellschaft im Prozeß der Globalisierung*. Bad Homburg: Werner Reimers Stiftung.

Gupta, Akhil. 2012. *Red Tape. Bureaucracy, Structural Violence, and Poverty in India*. Durham: Duke University Press.

2013. 'Messy Bureaucracies: Comment on Hull, Matthew. 2012. Government of Paper: The Materiality of Bureaucracy in Urban Pakistan. Berkeley: University of California Press', *HAU: Journal of Ethnographic Theory*, 3:435–440.

Hull, Matthew S. 2012a. 'Documents and Bureaucracy', *Annual Review of Anthropology*, 41(1): 251–267.

2012b. *Government of Paper. The Materiality of Bureaucracy in Urban Pakistan*. Berkeley: University of California Press.

2013. 'The Materiality of Indeterminacy. On Paper, at Least', *HAU: Journal of Ethnographic Theory*, 3(3): 441–447.

Kafka, Ben. 2009. 'Paperwork: The State of the Discipline', *Book History*, 12(1): 340–353.

Latour, Bruno. 2010. *The Making of Law. An Ethnography of the Conseil d'Etat*. Malden: Polity.

Lewis, David. 2011. 'Exchanges of Professionals between the Public and Non-Governmental Sectors: Life-work Histories from Bangladesh', *Modern Asian Studies*, 45(3): 735–757.

Lewis, David, and Abul Hossain. 2008. *Understanding the Local Power Structure in Rural Bangladesh*. Stockholm: Sida.

Lie, Jon H. S. 2013. 'Challenging Anthropology: Anthropological Reflections on the Ethnographic Turn in International Relations', *Millennium – Journal of International Studies*, 41(2): 201–220.

Marcus, George E. 1995. 'Ethnography in/of the World System: The Emergence of Multi-Sited Ethnography', *Annual Review of Anthropology*, 24(1): 95–117.

Martin, Lisa L., and Beth A. Simmons. 2013. 'International Organizations and Institutions', in Walter Carlsnaes, Thomas Risse, and Beth A. Simmons (eds.), *Handbook of International Relations*. London: Sage.

Mathur, Nayanika. 2015. *Paper Tiger. Law, Bureaucracy and the Developmental State in Himalayan India*. Cambridge: Cambridge University Press.

Müller, Birgit. 2013. 'Introduction: Lifting the Veil of Harmony: Anthropologists approach International Organizations', in Birgit Müller (ed.), *The Gloss of Harmony. The Politics of Policy Making in Multilateral Organisations*. London: Pluto Press.

Murshed, Mahboob. 2012. *Review Report on Village Courts Legal Framework*. Dhaka: UNDP.

Nemeth, Charles P. 2011. *Law and Evidence. A Primer for Criminal Justice, Criminology, Law, and Legal Studies*. Sudbury: Jones and Bartlett Publishers.

Porter, Theodore M. 1995. *Trust in Numbers. In Pursuit of Objectivity in Science and Public Life*. Princeton: Princeton University.

Riles, Annelise. 2006a. '[Deadlines] – Removing the Brackets on Politics in Bureaucratic and Anthropological Analysis', in Annelise Riles (ed.), *Documents. Artifacts of Modern Knowledge*. Ann Arbor: University of Michigan Press.

ed. 2006b. *Documents. Artifacts of Modern Knowledge*. Ann Arbor: University of Michigan Press.

Scott, James C. 1998. *Seeing Like the State. How Certain Schemes to Improve the Human Condition Have Failed*. New Haven: Yale University Press.

Shehabuddin, Elora. 2008. *Reshaping the Holy. Democracy, Development, and Muslim Women in Bangladesh*. New York: Columbia University Press.

Siddiqi, Dina M. 2011a. 'Crime and Punishment: Laws of Seduction, Consent, and Rape in Bangladesh', *Social Difference Online*, 1:December, 46–54.

2011b. 'Islam, Gender, and the Nation – The Social Life of Bangladeshi Fatwas', in Deana Heath and Chandana Mathur (eds.), *Communalism and Globalization in South Asia and Its Diaspora*. London, New York: Routledge, pp. 181–203.

2011c. 'Sexuality, Rights, and Personhood: Tensions in a Transnational World', *BMC International Health and Human Rights*, 11:3.

Steiner-Khamsi, Gita 2012. 'For All by All? The World Bank's Global Framework for Education', in Steven J. Klees, Joel Samoff, Nelly P. Stromquist, and Xavier Bonal (eds.), *The World Bank and Education. Critiques and Alternatives*. Rotterdam, Boston: Sense Publishers.

Tamanaha, Brian Z., Caroline M. Sage, and Woolcock, Michael J. V, eds. 2012. *Legal Pluralism and Development. Scholars and Practitioners in Dialogue*. New York: Cambridge University Press.

The World Bank. 2008. *Forging the Middle Ground – Engaging Non-State Justice Institutions in Indonesia*. Washington D.C.: The World Bank.

UNDP, UNICEF, and UN Women. 2013. 'Informal Justice Mechanisms: Charting a Course of Human Rights-based Engagement'. Retrieved from www.undp.org/content/dam/undp/library/Democratic%20Governance/Access%20to%20Justice%20and%20Rule%20of%20Law/Informal-Justice-Systems-Charting-a-Course-for-Human-Rights-Based-Engagement.pdf, accessed 14 February 2016.

Vismann, Cornelia. 2000. *Akten. Medientechnik und Recht*. Frankfurt am Main: Fischer.

2008. *Files: Law and Media Technology*. Stanford: Stanford University Press.

Vrasti, Wanda. 2008. 'The Strange Case of Ethnography and International Relations', *Millennium – Journal of International Studies*, 37(2): 279–301.

Zürn, Michael, Martin Binder, and Matthias Ecker-Ehrhardt 2012. 'International Authority and its Politicization', *International Theory*, 4(1): 69–106.

10

Contrasting Values of Forests and Ice in the Making of a Global Climate Agreement

Noor Johnson and David Rojas

INTRODUCTION

On Tuesday, December 8, 2009, in historic Nytorv square in central Copenhagen, sculptor Mark Coreth put the final touches on his ice bear sculpture in front of the World Wildlife Fund's (WWF) Arctic Tent, an unofficial side-event venue at the UN Framework Convention on Climate Change (UNFCCC). Carved from a ten ton block of ice encasing a 500 kg bronze cast of a bear skeleton, Ice Bear measured 1.8 meters – "as high as the disappearing arctic sea ice is thick," according to WWF's website. With temperatures above freezing, by mid-week, the bear was showing visible signs of shrinkage as the ice dripped into a puddle growing at its base. Mirroring feedback dynamics in the Arctic, as the sun's rays reached the dark bronze skeleton, it absorbed more heat, further accelerating the melting. By the end of the week, only a few scraps of ice remained attached to the center of the bear skeleton's coppery ribs.

The sculpture not only dramatized climate change but, in the various interpretations it elicited, it also exemplified the diverse values at play in climate change diplomacy. While for the WWF the bear was seen as an argument in favor of limiting human activities leading to environmental change in places such as the Arctic, others argued that the sculpture illustrated climate change risks as well as opportunities (van Mensvoort 2009). These opposing interpretations mirror the gap between environmentalists who use scientific arguments to advocate for limiting human impacts on the environment and increasingly dominant approaches that align environmental goals with continuing economic expansion.

WWF's performative use of sea ice metrics reflects a growing insistence on quantification and measurement in global environmental governance (Merry 2011; Dalby 2013). For example, the most important climate change diplomacy outcome to date, the 2015 UNFCCC "Paris Agreement," sets its goals in numeric terms. The UNFCCC decision adopting the Agreement states that "global greenhouse gas emissions should be consistent with holding the increase in the global average temperature to well below 2°C above preindustrial levels and pursuing efforts to limit the temperature increase to 1.5°C above preindustrial levels" (UNFCCC 2015). Scientists and environmental groups argue that, in order to stabilize temperatures below 2°C, atmospheric carbon dioxide concentrations should not rise above 450 parts of per million (ppm). Meanwhile, keeping atmospheric temperatures below 1.5°C would require limiting CO_2 concentrations to less than 350ppm.[1] Functioning as boundaries, these numbers could justify strict measures such as limiting deforestation in Amazonia or curbing oil extraction in new "energy frontiers" such as the Arctic (McGlade and Eakins 2015). Supporters of this strict policy approach draw on quantitative assessments and computer models of the Earth System (Edwards 2010) to draft global policy documents wherein numbers inform global objectives that cascade into regional, national, and local policy strategies. Policy success from this viewpoint would require bringing human actions within the planetary boundaries set by experts (Rockström et al. 2009).

The Paris Agreement, however, also reflects the UNFCCC's more recent economic approach that is supported by business interests and pro-market environmentalists who champion using monetary metrics to assess risks and opportunities in a climate change context. From their perspective, climate policies should minimize the economic costs of future environmental disruptions *and* limit the negative impacts that global environmental agreements could have on economic growth. In this approach, scientific metrics do not result in decisions to set firm limits on human activity, but are only a factor within "green economy" strategies guided by monetary metrics. Article 10 of the Paris Agreement, for instance, establishes that "accelerating, encouraging and enabling innovation is critical for an effective, long-term global response to climate change and promoting economic growth and sustainable development" (UNFCCC 2015; see also Fairhead et al. 2012).

As we discuss in this chapter, indigenous social movements at the UNFCCC offer a contrasting approach to policy proposals organized around both environmental and economic values. They stress that global issues such as atmospheric pollution are the legacy of long political histories whereby indigenous livelihoods are undermined by national and transnational political and economic projects (Doolittle 2010; Powless 2012). From this viewpoint, limiting atmospheric temperature increases to 1.5°C requires first guaranteeing the cultural and territorial rights of indigenous populations whose livelihoods are interwoven with non-human dynamics that compose the ecosystems of regions such as the Arctic and Amazonia. While still using quantitative (scientific and monetary) metrics, indigenous proposals are designed to create socio-environmental conditions that facilitate living in ways that can be *qualitatively* evaluated as "good" or "desirable." Differently put, their proposals advance socio-environmental values that will enable indigenous peoples to define, in their own terms, political and economic relations. Such ideas

---

[1] This means that, in order to have a good chance of avoiding runaway environmental crises, environmental policies should prevent a future situation in which, when randomly selecting 1 million particles from the atmosphere, more than 450 of such particles would be carbon dioxide.

found expression in the Paris Agreement, which states that "when taking action to address climate change, respect, promote and consider their respective obligations on human rights, the right to health, the rights of indigenous peoples, local communities, migrants, children" (UNFCCC 2015).

In this chapter, we explore the interplay between economic, ecological, and indigenous values at the UNFCCC, and in particular in the meetings leading to the recent Paris Agreement. Our analysis draws on Jane Guyer's concept of "scales of value" (Guyer 2004: 19). As Guyer defines it, scales of value are collective conventions that allow people to classify, compare, and pass judgment on entities and processes in the world. For example, Guyer documents the expansion of monetary transactions in West Africa, focusing on the ensuing combination of monetary and non-monetary metrics. She demonstrates that socio-economic transformations leading to the monetization of economic life take place through varied actions whereby persons and groups combine nominal qualifiers (*more* and *less*, *desirable* and *undesirable*) with ordinal qualifiers (numeric gradations in terms of a standardized quantity such as money) (Guyer 2004). Such analysis convincingly contradicts portrayals of capitalist dynamics as leading to a homogenous world in which all non-monetary values are destroyed (Roitman 2007). Rather, capitalist expansion is seen to produce heterogeneity, wherein various standards of commensuration are combined.

Drawing on anthropological literature on bureaucratic practice (Riles 2000; Hetherington 2011; Hoag 2011, 2014; Hull 2012), we examine different proposals that influenced the Paris Agreement by bringing into its landmark text various scales of value. Our starting point is to consider the UNFCCC as a global institution produced through a succession of formal and informal meetings. In these gatherings, politicians, scientists, business people, and, on some occasions, non-experts (including indigenous social movements) take part in a chain of document production whereby drafts, declarations, studies, reports, written claims, and formal agreements are composed. These practices, and the coalitions that form around them, effectively extend the work of climate diplomacy into unofficial meetings and events that, beyond the official meeting halls of the UNFCCC, result in alternative policy proposals.

Collaborative ethnography allowed us to examine the role played by indigenous actors in mobilizing and resisting various articulations of value in global climate forums (Brosius and Campbell 2010). Johnson studied the mobilization of Inuit knowledge about climate change, and participated in UN climate talks as a collaborator of the Inuit Circumpolar Council (ICC), an organization that represents Inuit in international and circumpolar governance arenas. For the three months leading up to the 15th Conference of Parties (COP 15) in Copenhagen, she volunteered with ICC Canada in their office in Ottawa, and then accompanied them to the meetings. Johnson also attended COP 18 in Doha on behalf of the ICC. Meanwhile, Rojas researched climate change science in the Amazonian rainforest and followed coalitions of scientists and NGOs as they engaged in UN political arenas in partnership with indigenous social movements – among them Coordinadora de las Organizaciones Indígenas de la Cuenca Amazónica (COICA), an organization representing indigenous peoples from the Amazon basin. After meeting up at the Doha climate talks in 2012, we began to collectively examine contrasting values at play in opposing policy proposals (Rojas and Johnson 2013). This chapter draws primarily on our research in this venue, but is also informed by our broader projects on knowledge production and climate change in the Arctic and Amazonia, which included long-term fieldwork in the aforementioned regions.

THE UNFCCC'S OFFICIAL SPACES

Since negotiations began in 1992, the products of climate change diplomacy have oscillated between general texts that offer only broad expressions of intent, and precise quantitative targets that have proven hard to enforce. For example, the text that established the UNFCCC states that the main objective of this body is the "stabilization of greenhouse gas concentrations in the atmosphere at a level that would prevent dangerous anthropogenic interference with the climate system" (UNFCCC 1992: Article 2). The convention leaves ample room for various interpretations of what "stabilization" and "preventing anthropogenic interference" may mean.[2] Article 2 goes on to suggest that stabilization of carbon concentrations "should be achieved within a time frame sufficient to allow ecosystems to adapt naturally to climate change, to ensure that food production is not threatened and to enable economic development to proceed in a sustainable manner" (UNFCCC 1992: Article 2). Neither statement offers specific metrics by which to gauge action or progress. In contrast, the UNFCCC's 2015 Paris Agreement establishes that signatory countries shall make "emission pledges" that will establish in precise numeric terms the limits below which they will strive to keep their annual CO_2 emissions until 2020 (UNFCCC 2015). Nevertheless, these pledges are voluntary, there are no mechanisms to guarantee that each country's objectives are consistent with global goals, and countries that fail to meet their own pledges will face no juridical sanctions.

The Paris Agreement thus revolves around precise quantitative targets that are, at the same time, vague expressions of intent. This is the outcome of painstaking political negotiations that produced in 2015 the most important climate change diplomacy agreement to date. At UNFCCC forums leading up to the 2015 Paris meeting, official delegates, abiding by diplomatic etiquette, wrote draft after draft of legalistic, dry, and often convoluted text. This process reflects what Florian Weisser has described as a chain of document production:

[2] Conventional environmentalists read these lines as an argument for strict measures to arrest carbon emissions even at the cost of limiting economic expansion. Meanwhile, those who see climate change through the looking glass of economics interpret the Convention to allow for various degrees of climate interference – which would be compatible with continuous economic growth.

Agendas structure the negotiations in the various bodies of the Convention; *reports* inform the parties on diverse matters such as the latest findings of climate science; *submissions* express states' and observer organizations' interests in the negotiation process; *draft texts* indicate a common ground on which to start negotiating; [official UNFCCC] *decisions* launch and determine worldwide implementation; *technical guidelines* specify and demonstrate what this might look like. (Weisser 2014: 46, emphasis added)

The technical language deployed in meetings and documents conveys the sense that climate change is governable, or at least manageable, if only all parties in the room can agree on the right words in the right order. This belief in the capacity of effecting profound worldly changes through bureaucratic writing reflects the first of two intersecting processes that Tania Li described as "the practice of government, in which a concept of improvement becomes technical as it is attached to calculated programs for its realization," and the "practice of politics; the expression, in word or deed, of a critical challenge" (2007: 12).

Those who engaged within the UNFCCC to translate perceived challenges into measurements that were ultimately included in the Paris Agreement included scientists, politicians, corporations, and social movements. As Bruno Latour described in reference to the negotiations around the earlier Kyoto Protocol agreement, efforts to link abstract will and quantitative targets undermined the roles traditionally assigned to the diverse actors involved. In these negotiations, Latour points out, "politicians and scientists, industrialists and militants found themselves on the benches of the same assembly" (Latour 2004: 26). In this chapter we add to this list indigenous actors. First, we present a brief overview of the roles played by the other members of Latour's assembly.

Politicians played the most visible role in drafting the texts that translated the idea of preventing "dangerous anthropogenic interference with the climate system" (UNFCC 1992: Article 2) into the Paris Agreement. They composed a heterogeneous group of "official" national delegations that, although having equal voice and vote, had extremely dissimilar capacities to influence a negotiation process that disproportionally favors rich nation-states. Less affluent states were often represented only by one or two individuals, and often relied on voluntary workers. Because many official diplomatic meetings were held simultaneously, these small delegations struggled to keep abreast of the agenda of negotiations and to identify the best venues to shape diplomatic outcomes. Meanwhile, economic powerhouses such as the United States brought to UNFCCC encounters large delegations comprised of dozens of experts equipped with reports and discussion drafts that they used to set the terms of the discussions.

Before the 2015 Paris meeting, climate change diplomats met twenty times at major UNFCCC summits. At these events, diplomats drew on previous agreements, reports, and new submissions in order to contribute to draft official documents that eventually led to the Paris text. Official negotiation can be seen as an exercise in producing a "clean" text, wherein a lack of brackets denotes consensus among the parties regarding matters of form and substance (Riles 2000). Most of this work takes place within closed-door meetings, in which only "official" delegates are admitted. Heated exchanges take place in these venues regarding minute details of wording that are of crucial importance. A small difference of terms could transform a simple statement of intentions into a legally binding agreement that imposes strict limits on the behavior of individual nation-states.

Although poor and rich delegations had different opportunities to influence the process that produced the "clean" Paris Agreement text, all official delegations were in a much better position than non-state delegations (NGOs, religious groups, trade organizations, corporations, and indigenous peoples' organizations such as the ICC and COICA) that were given "observer" credentials. Although these credentials allowed access to the official convention centers in which negotiations took place, as "observers" indigenous peoples could only sit in open-door plenary sessions; these are largely symbolic gatherings in which previously "cleansed" texts are brought for an official vote (although on some occasions, as the negotiations ran late, the plenary hall became a venue for drafting and un-bracketing).[3] Despite these significant constraints, the Paris Agreement does express concerns important to indigenous peoples. This is the outcome of the strategic use by indigenous groups of various institutional resources at the UNFCCC that allowed them to insert in the final text wording that supports climate policy strategies that further qualitative values.

UNOFFICIAL DIPLOMACY AT THE UNFCCC

Despite barriers to participation in the negotiations that resulted in the 2015 Agreement, observers were able to influence the drafting of the final text. They did so by drawing on tactics that included lobbying delegates and taking part in "side events" that focused on themes that ranged from pro-business environmental schemes to climate justice. At the UNFCCC, side events include both officially sanctioned sessions, similar to conference panels, that are held in the secured convention hall, as well as more informal events held in more accessible public spaces. While these side events are often perceived as peripheral to the "real" work of climate change diplomacy, we contend that they are fundamental to the functioning of the UNFCCC bureaucracy and were thus central to the drafting of the Paris text (Bernstein et al. 2010; Descheneau and Paterson 2011). Side events facilitate participation of a number of constituents whose expertise is crucial to the highly technical work required at the UNFCCC to combine economic policy, ecological projects,

---

[3] Observer delegations have to leave the room the moment a single party requests the meeting to be classified as "parties only." This request is made in the vast majority of meetings. Observers can nevertheless attend plenary meetings, but there they can only voice their opinions in a restricted time slot apportioned at the very end of the session.

and political decisions. NGOs, social movements, and scientists use side events to present their own documents, such as reports on cutting-edge scientific research, new policy ideas, human rights petitions, and demands for social equity. Such events are attended by official state delegates, who use these spaces to gather data, establish strategic alliances, and learn about or build support for policy strategies and positions.[4] Moreover, side events offer observers the opportunity to express views that may influence official discussions and are thus also spaces in which those attending UNFCCC summits may reclaim a sense of hope for climate change diplomacy, even as official negotiations fail to produce desired results (Bernstein et al. 2010; Descheneau and Paterson 2011).

Scientists who are not part of official delegations attend the UNFCCC to take part in research-oriented side events in which they present measurement techniques and visualization technologies that have the potential to be used in setting limits on greenhouse gas concentrations. By far the most important scientific side events are those organized by the Intergovernmental Panel on Climate Change, established in 1988 to "provide the world with a clear scientific view on the current state of knowledge in climate change and its potential environmental and socio-economic impacts" (IPCC 2015). IPCC side events combine science and policy arguments in image-laden presentations in which dry quantitative assessments of intensifying climate change are displayed together with images of recent events illuminating climate hazards such as the devastation wrought by Hurricane Katrina in New Orleans. In side events such as these, scientists strive to elicit a sense of urgency through presentations of hot-off-the-press scientific analyses, struggling to further the position that scientific knowledge plays in the agreements. Occasionally, scientific side events include activists, or vice-versa. For example, Stephen Schneider, an atmospheric scientist from Stanford University who conducted research on the Greenland ice sheet, joined the ICC at their side event on Arctic ice and snow at COP 15.

Scientists may also join corporate actors at side events in which pro-market policies are promoted. At Rio+ 20, for example, the International Union of Concerned Scientists joined a side event on deforestation and climate change that was co-hosted by billionaire Richard Branson, whose fortune comes from emission-intensive companies such as Virgin Airlines.[5] Branson's event was one of several that advocated for a "green economy" approach wherein "environmentally responsible corporations" would help achieve climate change diplomacy targets. This would be possible by making emissions reductions into a business opportunity that would incentivize entrepreneurs to innovate in reforming established economic operations and creating new fields of economic

---

[4] Of course, delegates juggle multiple demands and have very limited time, as was illustrated when I (Johnson) invited a Swiss diplomat to attend ICC's side event on Inuit knowledge in 2009. "I *wish* I could be there," she lamented. "I never have enough time to go to side events."

[5] For an examination of Branson's brand of environmentalism, see Prudham (2009).

activities. In a similar vein, proposals advanced by corporations such as Shell suggest that signatories to the Paris Agreement could meet their emission pledges, at least in part, through a for-profit and decentralized carbon trading system rather than by establishing binding juridical limits.

Pro-business events are sometimes the target of interventions by activists who see them as benefiting powerful economic interests in ways that distort environmental objectives in pursuit of economic goals. Branson's Rio+ 20 event, for example, was disrupted by activists who stood up to loudly argue "we will not stand aside as NGOs work hand in hand with the corporations that are polluting and killing the planet!" Although social movements such as the ICC and COICA may agree with the spirit of such claims, their interventions are more systematic and, rather than disrupting the flow of other side events, they focus on creating their own venues, side events in which they may advance struggles in a language unlike that of scientists, politicians, and corporations.

TERRITORIAL STRUGGLES AT THE UNFCCC

Many indigenous peoples' organizations, including the ICC and COICA, seek and are granted observer status within the UNFCCC. Once granted observer status, these groups can then choose to participate in a voluntary affinity group: the "Indigenous Caucus." The caucus meets daily to share organizing strategies and collaboratively lobby delegations for collective goals that often center on indigenous and human rights. Throughout the proceedings, caucus members exchange information by email and text message, allowing the relatively small delegations representing each indigenous population to divide up among relevant side events and meetings, thereby extending their reach.

Unlike scientists and business participants who take part in side events in which climate problems are framed in scientific and economic terms, indigenous actors use side events to introduce alternative political visions. Their efforts link general global objectives, specific targets, and local actions through narratives featuring non-quantitative values that frame climate problems in the language of justice, vulnerability, and human rights. Take, for example, an intervention by a leader of COICA at a side event on forests at the United Nations Conference on Sustainable Development held in Rio de Janeiro in 2012 (Rio+20). At the end of his formal presentation, the speaker put down his notes and, addressing the audience directly, advanced an argument that offered a singularly indigenous view on the stakes of environmental debates: "People say that, after our current wars, which are wars fought over petroleum, nations will clash over water. That is wrong," he argued, "the [current] war is about forests."

The speaker's comments alluded to struggles over the control of Amazonian territories over the past half-century in which indigenous lands have been targeted for exploitation by settlers, illegal loggers, gold miners, ranchers, and industrial farmers. In other instances, land struggles have involved state bureaucracies and large transnational companies that took control of vast areas for mining or infrastructure projects. In both cases, conflict sometimes led to deadly violence against indigenous leaders (Garfield 2014; Hecht and Cockburn 1990).

Amazonian peoples responded to aggressions against their members and lands through a mix of strategies that ranged from direct confrontation to peaceful protest and legal action. Joining other indigenous groups, they worked to transform global institutions such as the UN General Assembly, the International Labor Organization (ILO), the UN High Commission for Human Rights, and the Organization of American States into spaces wherein juridical and bureaucratic tools could be used to claim control over territories threatened by national governments and large private companies (Niezen 2003; Anaya 2004; Price 2011; Sawyer 2004; see also Sapignoli, Chapter 4, this volume). From this perspective, the "war" to which the COICA speaker referred also included bureaucratic struggles partly carried out in international institutions. The UNFCCC is one such institution in which indigenous groups have striven to advance an agenda based on ideas of rights that often collide with the economic, environmental, or geopolitical considerations of the institution's most powerful members.

From its inception, critics were concerned that the UNFCCC would adopt a "fortress conservation" approach whereby environmental degradation would be framed as a technical problem that Northern experts should solve, silencing the grounded knowledge of those experiencing climate change first hand and erasing the histories of territorial struggles born by indigenous communities. From this angle, COICA's description of UN environmental forums as the continuation of wars over territory by diplomatic means was part of a broader project by which, through direct participation in this venue, indigenous actors sought to minimize potential negative impacts on indigenous rights *and* to transform this arena into a platform to pursue indigenous claims.

Like COICA, the ICC, which represents Inuit from Alaska, Canada, Greenland, and Chukotka (Russia), in pan-Arctic and global policy arenas, has sent representatives to the UNFCCC for more than a decade in order to inject an Inuit perspective on climate change in the Arctic into the negotiations. The ICC is itself a political structure that was established in a way that mirrors global institutional norms, with elected regional representatives who attend a General Assembly meeting held every four years. At the General Assembly, chairmanship of the ICC is transferred from one country to another, a new chair is elected, and an action agenda for the next four years is adopted in the form of an official declaration. The wording of the declaration is subject to behind-the-scenes political negotiations among the delegates that, though rarely quite as contentious, bear a striking resemblance to the processes involved in drafting texts within the UNFCCC and other UN bodies. Between General Assembly meetings, an Executive Council comprised of the President and

Vice President from each of the four Inuit country delegations issues additional direction for the organization. The ICC's involvement in global climate negotiations was established by an Executive Council resolution in 2003 directing Sheila Watt-Cloutier, who was serving as ICC Chair, to "[b]ring Arctic/Inuit perspectives on climate change to the attention of decision-makers in North America, Western Europe, United Nations agencies, and to governments that participate in the Conferences of Parties to the UN Framework Convention on Climate Change with the aim of positioning Inuit to influence international discussions and decisions" (ICC 2003).

As anthropological studies of bureaucratic practices show, bureaucracies are "hope-generating machines" (Nuijten 2003: 16; Hoag 2011: 86, 2013), built through formalized rules and procedures that include modes of drafting and discussing documents (Hull 2012). Although imperfect, hierarchical, and resistant to change, the formalism of bureaucracies may also elicit the hope that, one day, such spaces may fulfill collective expectations (Hoag 2014). In other words, bureaucracies such as the UNFCCC conduct "future-work," offering publics procedures that allow them to imagine a future when the "machine" will work as expected and collective goals will be attained (Hoag 2014).

Indigenous social movements and other non-state actors participate in this politics of hope when they choose to engage within the UNFCCC venue, although they do so in strategic and pragmatic ways. A common goal is to influence the negotiating text through back-stage lobbying of delegates; another is to use the venue and the media and global audience it draws to introduce indigenous conceptions of climate justice intended to influence action outside the framework of a global climate agreement. In 2005, for example, Watt-Cloutier, working with several environmental law organizations, held a press conference at a side event in which she announced that the ICC was bringing a petition to the Inter-American Commission on Human Rights. The petition sought to hold the United States accountable for violating the Inuit "right to be cold" by failing to regulate its greenhouse gas emissions (Watt-Cloutier 2015). While the petition focused on a single country's actions and the ultimate venue for the petition was regional rather than international, the UNFCCC provided a strong staging ground for the announcement, which was covered by numerous media outlets, including the *New York Times* (Revkin 2004).

In addition to functioning as staging grounds for sharing alternative visions for climate action beyond the UNFCCC, at key historical moments in which diplomatic stalemates led observers to fear the collapse of the UNFCCC process, non-state delegations at side events have kept the UNFCCC machinery running and hope alive. One such moment involved Amazon-based scientists who, working closely with indigenous social movements, profoundly transformed the metrics used to frame deforestation as a climate problem.

COMBINING SCALES OF FOREST VALUE

At the 2012 UNFCCC meeting in Doha one of us (Rojas) had the opportunity to talk with a senior member of COICA about the relationship the organization maintained with scientists who advocated for novel strategies to address deforestation as a climate problem. At one point in the discussion, she underlined the tension between the diverging scales of value used by scientists and indigenous peoples to organize their relationships with forest territories:

> It is very hard for [the scientists with whom we work] to understand. They do understand, but is hard for them to accept how we defend and how we see [our territories]. For [the scientists] the carbon is what has value and is important. For us what is of value is the forest [*mato*] standing. Not because carbon is inside [trees], but because for us forests have another value, something like [pause] like more sacred? I don't know, is a relation, a whole relation of life itself.

Her statement conveys the sense that in discussions regarding climate change, perspectives that fashion singular scales of value converge and collide. On the one hand, Amerindian communities assess the forest in terms of the moral and social ("holistic") relations they establish between humans and non-humans – relations that some Westerners would feel tempted to describe as "sacred" (Viveiros de Castro 2011). On the other hand, scientists assess forests pragmatically, in terms of carbon stocks that forest populations could maintain by avoiding deforestation – a measurement that, as we will explain, can be used to value forests in terms of money. And yet, this statement of seemingly incommensurable values conveys a singular connection between these two approaches: they both assume that humans are part of Amazonian environments.

This recognition that humans are part of forested territories occurred only recently within the UNFCCC. When the Convention was signed at the Rio meeting in 1992, forests were framed in terms of a contradiction between conservation and economic growth (Corrêa do Lago 2009; Hecht 2011). Delegations from North American and European states argued that economic development in forested nations would lead to higher deforestation rates and higher atmospheric temperatures. In contrast, delegations from countries such as Brazil, Indonesia, and India were concerned that preserving forest cover would result in enduring poverty and dependency on wealthy nations (Gupta 1998; Lahsen 2009; Rojas 2015). Given the radical disconnect between the scales of value used by the delegations of northern and southern states, forests were initially excluded from the UNFCCC's chain of document production (Boyd 2010). Similarly excluded were indigenous movements such as COICA, given that indigenous populations were seen to benefit neither the plans of those who pursued the preservation of "pristine" forests nor the schemes of those who sought higher rates of economic growth (Rajão 2013; Claeys and Delgado 2015).

At the turn of the millennium, non-state parties organized side events to introduce scientific studies and policy proposals that combined socio-environmental, economic, and scientific metrics and thus created the necessary diplomatic conditions for forests to be discussed at the UNFCCC. This shift was a long time in the making. In the late 1990s and early 2000s, Amazonian environmentalists published a series of increasingly detailed scientific studies which showed that, in the forested regions in which rubber tappers and indigenous communities lived, deforestation was lower than in areas targeted by development projects (Schwartzman et al. 2000; Santilli et al. 2005). This supported the long-standing argument that legal recognition of indigenous and traditional territories and support for their socio-economic wellbeing would further their stewardship of forests and have positive global environmental impacts (Hecht and Cockburn 1990; Hecht 2011).

A group of scientists working in the region knew about these cases first-hand (Rojas 2016). Some of them were born in Amazonia, while others had worked in the region for decades and understood the role that indigenous and traditional communities could play in advancing global environmental goals. Drawing on their scientific expertise, Amazonian environmentalists formalized the claims of Amazonian social movements and traveled to UNFCCC meetings armed with studies showing that low-deforestation areas coincided with the territories of indigenous and communities. In the side events in which this research was shown, they systematically questioned the prevalent Western narratives of pristine wilderness removed from human use. They claimed that rather than keeping humans out of the forest, UNFCCC delegates should recognize the "service" provided by indigenous and traditional communities, who reduced carbon emissions and contributed to a more stable global environment by avoiding the deforestation that would have taken place in their absence (Nepstad et al. 2006).

Eventually, this economic framing of human/non-human relations would be known as REDD+ (an acronym for Reducing Emissions From Deforestation And Forest Degradation; the "+" is for improving carbon stocks). The approach used novel computer modeling techniques to integrate scientific and economic studies and provide an understanding of the ways in which future economic growth could contribute to global environmental goals (Soares-Filho et al. 2010). In order to align economic growth and forest conservation, scientists proposed rewarding landholders for keeping forests standing. Resources for these initiatives would be delivered through carbon trading schemes whereby, instead of reducing their own emissions, persons and institutions from rich parts of the globe would offset their environmental impacts by supporting forest conservation projects.

A preliminary REDD+ proposal was presented by Amazonian scientists and NGO officials at a UNFCCC side event in 2004, with immediate success. Of particular appeal for state delegations was that REDD+ integrated previously irreconcilable positions. Rather than advocating for the establishment of absolute limits on human activities in Amazonia, or for the abandonment of environmental objectives in order to pursue economic expansion, REDD+ proponents found a third way. New markets would render conservation an economic opportunity by reducing the amount of forest loss required per unit of economic growth. The interest in this proposal was such that two state delegations (Costa Rica and Papua New Guinea), working together with NGOs, drafted a document that was taken into the official negotiations, where it was gradually integrated as a new item in the formal negotiations.

While indigenous organizations such as COICA were skeptical about the use of market-based approaches to deal with unfolding climate crises, they strategically positioned themselves within these discussions in a variety of ways. Concerned about the potential of carbon market solutions to further empower large landholders to the detriment of indigenous forest communities, they negotiated with pro-REDD+ NGOs to provide training in climate change diplomacy issues for indigenous groups. Moreover, they secured financial support from NGOs that not only allowed them to attend UNFCCC meetings, but also helped indigenous leadership organize side events. Indigenous groups then used these side events to argue *against* REDD+ and advance policy alternatives such as an "indigenous REDD+" approach wherein scientific and economic metrics are subordinated to socio-environmental values.

In a proposal entitled "Indigenous Territories of Harmonious Life to cool the planet" (COICA 2013), COICA made support for carbon trading mechanisms contingent upon recognition of indigenous territorial rights, the expansion of the political autonomy of indigenous communities, a moratorium on macro-development projects in the Amazon basin, and more stringent limits on global carbon emissions (Long 2013). A key assumption in this proposal was that economic metrics are intrinsically flawed. "Industrial carbon does not have the same value as indigenous carbon," COICA argued (COICA 2013: 4), given that trees are not mere lumps of carbon but are linked to humans and non-humans in a multiplicity of ways. Moreover, the main objective for COICA was not efficiency (which can be measured in monetary terms), but attaining "Full Life," wherein indigenous peoples set the terms of their relations with states, markets, and non-governmental organizations.

To achieve these goals, COICA introduced documents such as the *Indigenous REDD+ Alternative: Life Plans of Peoples and Communities*. The Life Plans (Planes de Vida) to which the title alludes are essentially indigenous development planning proposals increasingly popular among Latin American indigenous communities. Similar in form to the documents used by national and international bureaucracies, these documents put in writing a vision of the community's future in terms of rights, environment, economics, and political relations within and beyond the group. Crucially, the plan offers an understanding of a "good life" (*vida plena*) or a desirable situation in terms of the relationship that humans establish with other humans and non-human companions in their territories. Once formalized in a document that is recognized by outsiders and guides decisions within the communities' leadership, the idea of the "good life" functions as a classificatory metric whereby some economic and environmental projects may be judged unacceptable. In short, the Life Plans have the potential to subordinate REDD+'s economic and scientific metrics to qualitative, socio-environmental values (van Dam 2011).

Despite COICA's attempts to reframe REDD+ in non-economic terms, several indigenous social movements and some COICA members express concerns with any relation between indigenous social movements and economic approaches to climate politics. Their opposition is expressed in documents such as the *Carta de Belém*, drafted in 2009, which contends that the underlying logic of seeking monetary recognition for forest preservation forecloses the opportunity of seeking profound reforms to environmentally destructive dynamics. As an alternative, the institutions supporting the *Carta* advocate for "a new model of production, distribution, and consumption based in agroecology, an economy of solidarity, and a diversified and decentralized economic matrix that guarantees food security and food sovereignty" (Grupo Carta de Belém 2009).

When the COICA leader expressed in Doha that it "is very hard [for scientists] to accept how we defend and see [our territories]," she was summarizing a multi-year process whereby indigenous communities creatively entered the UNFCCC's chain of document production. Although indigenous proposals are still marginal in climate politics, their strategic positioning in environmental discussions reflects bureaucratic dynamics at the UNFCCC that allowed them to shape some of the wording of the UNFCCC decisions that gave effect to the Paris Agreement. There we find that the UNFCCC "recognizes the importance of positive incentives for reducing emissions from deforestation and forest degradation ... *as well as alternative policy approaches ... while reaffirming the importance of non-carbon benefits associated with such approaches*" (UNFCCC 2015, emphasis added). These lines are partly the expression of COICA's continued struggle alongside key allies who work for a climate agreement based on qualitative values supportive of claims for justice and "good life" proposals (described in the document as non-carbon benefits). In spite of the UNFCCC's hermetic decision-making dynamics, COICA's experienced leadership succeeded in taking part in technical discussions at global forums by strategically holding side events in which they alluded to monetary and scientific values while also pushing for the inclusion of indigenous understandings in official documents. While the structural limitations COICA faced should not be underestimated nor its accomplishments overblown, is also useful to recognize their contributions to the Paris Agreement. The relative success of this movement is a reminder that more ambitious climate politics are possible.

INVALUABLE/UN-VALUABLE ICE AND SNOW

While scientists and environmental NGOs were successful in bringing forests into the UNFCCC's chain of documents, gradually moving forest carbon markets from the periphery of side events more directly into the policy negotiations, efforts to make the material qualities of ice and snow relevant in global climate talks have been less successful.

Dramatic satellite imagery of diminishing sea ice has offered an important metric for climate diplomacy (Dalby 2013), bolstering the legitimacy of climate science by proving models right. The biggest surprise in the Arctic has, in fact, been that models were largely too conservative, with the pace of change surpassing many predictions (Stroeve et al. 2007). In the UNFCCC, Arctic sea ice has figured as a harbinger of things to come, an apocalyptic vision of the future in the present. More broadly, ice and snow loss – particularly of the Greenland ice cap and the Antarctic ice sheet – figures in global climate discussions as an unknown dimension in predictions of future sea level rise.

Like forests, sea ice is valuable as a climate regulator. Through the albedo effect, the white Arctic surface reflects solar radiation and helps cool the ocean, while sea ice also plays a role in ocean and air circulation patterns (Serreze et al. 2007). Other "sea ice services" include shoreline protection from severe storms and currents, support for biodiversity, including polar bear and marine mammals, and as a platform for human activities such marine mammal hunting (Eicken et al. 2009). Sea ice also has a value-in-absence for the shipping industry, which will use the Northwest Passage and northern sea routes to shorten transits from Asia to North America, and for oil and gas companies interested in offshore development. As sea ice melts, these enterprises become more feasible, making it more difficult to place a specific value on sea ice, since its presence or absence has different value to different actors.

While melting Arctic ice has played a role in climate policy discourse, in practice the Arctic has been peripheral to the policies negotiated at the UN. Unlike forests, where a link between conservation and carbon storage can be leveraged through a series of calculations and studies into specific policy proposals, Arctic landscapes are difficult to act upon when it comes to mitigation policy.[6] Arctic tundra stores both carbon and methane, a climate forcer many times more powerful – though shorter lived in the atmosphere – than CO_2.[7] Tundra cannot be managed in the same way as forests, however, because the only thing that can halt melting permafrost is to limit global temperature rise. In other words, it has been difficult for NGOs, policy makers, and indigenous groups to bring Arctic territory into global climate discussions in tractable ways by rewarding Arctic populations for specific mitigation actions.

Because it could be challenging to get time to speak during the plenary sessions, the ICC used the alternative venue of the side event to share an Inuit perspective

---

[6] With the exception of sub-Arctic boreal forests; although largely excluded from REDD+ proposals, efforts to reduce carbon loss from boreal forests are underway.

[7] The IPCC calculated that methane is 35 times stronger than Co_2 over a one-hundred-year period (IPCC 2013).

with negotiators and observers. Within the side event forum, the ICC was able to redirect narratives about the Arctic that emphasized conservation or climate science themes from a more human perspective. At an ICC organized side event in 2009, for example, panelists spoke about different Inuit knowledge documentation projects they were involved with that examined environmental changes from the perspective of those who lived, traveled, and worked in the Arctic environment on a daily basis. Participants described the personal, in-depth knowledge that Inuit hunters accumulate of the physical characteristics of sea ice, but also, more importantly, the ways that sea ice is a social landscape that supports relationships among humans and between humans and non-humans. As one of the side event panelists later described, sea ice offers connections to "ideas of home, to physical, spiritual, and emotional nourishment from harvesting, sharing, and eating traditional food, to the gift of freedom, to travel, and to the practical and life-saving genius that goes into the tools and clothing used every day on the ice" (Gearheard et al. 2013: xxxv).

One of the panelists was a researcher from Clyde River, a small hamlet of around 1,000 residents on Baffin Island in Nunavut Territory where I (Noor) spent around five months during the course of my fieldwork. Connections between Clyde River and ICC's global engagements were generally sparse; one of the challenges that ICC has struggled to address over recent years is that although they are charged with representing Inuit, their work is poorly understood at the community level.[8] In this instance, ICC was familiar with the researcher's well-respected work in the community, and, since I knew her, I issued the invitation for her to participate in the panel.

In Clyde River, as in all coastal Inuit communities in Canada, residents hunt at seal breathing holes in winter months, and in spring often hunt at the floe edge where sea ice meets open water. Expert knowledge of ice conditions, gained from first-hand experience, is a necessary prerequisite for this kind of hunting. In springtime, as days become long, residents with dog teams prepare for the annual Nunavut Quest dogsled race, which celebrates the traditional role of dog teaming in travel. In 2010, the race route began in Pond Inlet, a community about 500 kilometers up the coast, and ended in Clyde River. The route crossed over sea ice a number of times, and those of us in Clyde awaiting news of the progress of the racers listened carefully for updates on the ice conditions; one night when they had set up camp on the sea ice, the teams had to scramble to move onto land when more experienced group members believed they detected signs that the ice may be breaking beneath them. Ice instability has caused fatal accidents in every community, as hunters try to navigate in conditions that are becoming less familiar.

One response to these kinds of changes, implemented in different parts of the Inuit Arctic, has been to bring together the qualitative observations of Inuit who

---

[8] This is a challenge that many global indigenous activists struggle with, as Sapignoli discusses in Chapter 4 of this volume.

travel on the ice and quantitative assessment of ice loss through satellite or field measurements to create locally scaled metrics in service to subsistence use (Huntington et al. 2009). In Clyde River, a community-based sea ice monitoring program installed ice measurement stations in locations where hunters regularly travel; a resident is paid to collect the data regularly, and the graphs are shared with residents to help them make informed decisions about when it is safe to travel. An expert group of hunters helps interpret the data, drawing as well on their own observations and knowledge of sea ice.

Like scientists who study sea ice loss using satellite data or conservationists from the WWF who mobilized metrics of sea ice loss through the ice bear sculpture, ICC's side event also drew on metrics to shape their arguments about the impact of climate change on Arctic ice. Unlike the former, however, in this context, the metrics were put in service to ICC's understanding of the Arctic as a human landscape. In addition to the examples provided by panelists, ICC distributed a document entitled *Call to Global Leaders: Act Now on Climate Change in the Arctic* (ICC 2009), which outlined their vision for successful climate diplomacy. The document combined scientific metrics, including limiting greenhouse gas emissions to stabilize global temperatures at 2°C, with proposals for social and economic equity, such as creating a global adaptation fund infrastructure that would facilitate assistance for Inuit and other indigenous groups. One of their points was to "recognize the impact of climate change on Inuit by designating *avoidance of climate change impacts on the Arctic* as one of the key benchmarks for effectiveness" of a successor climate agreement (ICC 2009, emphasis in original). This criterion reflected an attempt by ICC to reclaim authority over the Arctic from others, such as the WWF, who put forward alternative claims as spokespersons for the region. Gaining recognition of the Arctic in the text would potentially open other doors for Inuit to gain legibility within this political space. In its totality, the *Call to Global Leaders* can be seen as an effort by Inuit to participate in global climate politics on their own terms, and in a way that would support their claims to sovereignty and the right to be centrally involved in all governance decisions that might affect them or their traditional territories.

ICC spokespersons attempted to bring their proposal more directly to the table by approaching the lead negotiator for Canada with draft text that advocated for including "areas dependent on ice and snow" into language that singled out other vulnerable places, including small island states. The shift in language from "Arctic" to "ice and snow" reflected an effort to become more inclusive in ways that could lead to alliances with other regional spokespersons, since ice- and snow-dependent regions include not only the poles, but also high mountain regions such as the Himalayas and the Andes, as well as those dependent on mountain glacial and snowpack melt for water, such as the Ganges river basin in India and Bangladesh.[9]

[9] These interconnections and linkages were also highlighted at COP 15 in a report called "Melting Snow and Ice: A Call for Action" released at a separate side event hosted by Al Gore and Norway's Foreign Minister.

ICC's attempt to use documents to build alliances that might influence the official UNFCCC text met with limited success. Although the Canadian negotiator agreed to bring their proposed language to the negotiating table, since ICC was excluded from closed-door sessions, it was impossible to determine whether or not he actively advocated for the proposal; ICC only knew that at the end of the two weeks, their text was not incorporated into the final draft. Such occurrences are commonplace and reflect the hierarchical structure of the UNFCCC and the challenge of using bureaucratic tools to overcome it. While side events can facilitate policy proposals and discussions, structural barriers limit the success of observers in the official chain of document production.

Another challenge that ICC has faced in bringing an Arctic peoples' perspective to the UNFCCC is the tenacity of North/South discourses in this venue. Enshrined in the 1990 convention text is the notion of "common but differentiated responsibility," a vague concept that places a greater burden on European and North American nations to take the lead in emission reductions and transfer adaptation funding to developing states. Inuit spokespersons bring to their global engagements a postcolonial perspective that shares some similarities with those of developing states. They, too, have struggled to gain autonomy and authority over regional and local economies after years of policies administered by *qallunaat* (Euro-American) government officials that often went against local norms, customs, and even common sense. As with former colonies in the Global South, the legacies of these earlier policies are still visible in health, education, and income gaps within Inuit communities. In the context of climate change, these disparities lead to what Karen O'Brien and Robin Leichenko have termed "double exposure" (2000). In spite of these similarities, however, the UNFCCC draws on a state-centric, developmentalist discourse to determine who can qualify for adaptation assistance. The Global Adaptation Fund facilitates transfers from developed to developing states. Reflecting the geographic logic that Inuit follow, in which "South" denotes southern territories of North American and European nations, ICC has argued for global adaptation policy that would decentralize the transfer of adaptation support to the community level, and would make funding available to vulnerable communities within developed nations (ICC 2009), also with little success.

These vulnerability politics also created a public relations challenge for the ICC at COP 15 when the Canadian Broadcasting Corporation (CBC) ran a news story entitled "Exempt northerners from emissions cuts: Inuit leader" (CBC 2009a). The article cited ICC Chair Jimmy Stotts as stating that Inuit had needs "similar to developing nations when it comes to making their economies grow via such activities as mining and oil and gas exploration." According to the article, Stotts was requesting a "softening of the rules for northern peoples" when it came to emission reduction figures. The article concluded: "Stotts said he doesn't believe his call for an exemption undermines the Inuit Circumpolar Council's call for strong action to combat climate change" (CBC 2009a).

With rights to oil and gas revenues enshrined in Alaska Native Corporations and Canadian land claims processes, and with few jobs or other sources of development in the region, Inuit have conflicting views about non-renewable resource development. The Government of Greenland, a majority Inuit country, has pursued offshore oil and gas development based on the premise that the wealth it generates will secure Greenland's independence from Denmark (Nuttall 2012). Some citizens have raised concerns about threats to fishing and subsistence hunting, as well as the potential effects of seismic testing on marine mammals. Meanwhile, across Baffin Bay in Nunavut Territory, Inuit communities have sought to limit the Government of Canada's offshore seismic testing, raising concerns about consultation practices and the effects of increased shipping and spills on their lands and waters.

In the ensuing days, the article prompted discussion among Inuit leaders present at the COP about the balance between Inuit sovereignty and the right to govern natural resource development, on the one hand, and Inuit stewardship and the need for strong environmental protection and action on climate change on the other. A follow up article by the CBC suggested a "rift" was developing among Inuit who held differing and strong viewpoints on oil and gas development (CBC 2009b). These debates and discussions became a central theme of a second side event organized by the ICC, "Arctic Indigenous Peoples' Day," which featured political speeches by Inuit and other indigenous leaders from Alaska, Canada, Greenland, Sweden, and Russia. While their positions varied, what they had in common was an interest in ensuring that pathways into the future for Arctic communities offered the opportunity to improve wellbeing through economic and social development, as well as the ability to engage meaningfully with cultural traditions and life linked to ice. In this way, their position reflected elements of what COICA termed the "good life," which encompasses relations with humans and non-humans in traditional territories, yet does not rule out economic gain through landscape management or transformation.

The event's regional focus foreshadowed a retreat by the ICC from the UNFCCC venue in favor of pan-Arctic institutions such as the Arctic Council. Reflecting with one of us (Johnson) on COP 15 as a whole, one of ICC's leaders felt that a regional approach offered the best chance of supporting Inuit in the context of climate change. "COP15 is such a big thing and we are having dialogue with other parts of the world we don't even know anything about, other countries," he said. "I would hope that not only on climate change but other things – that the conversation could be kept within our area. There are a number of issues on climate change and other stuff too, that we should be talking closer to our national governments."

After the Copenhagen meetings in 2009, the ICC minimized participation in global climate forums, placing greater emphasis on dialogue with Arctic states and other Arctic indigenous groups on matters of regional concern, including oil and gas development. While the entire pan-Arctic ICC leadership was present at COP 15 in Copenhagen, only a single delegate participated in the following two COP gatherings. In 2012, when the meeting was held in the desert nation of Doha, Qatar, no one from ICC's staff had the time or inclination to participate, asking me (Johnson) to attend as an observer on their behalf.

This return to regionalism is, in many ways, consistent with the historic mission and vision of the organization, which was created in the late 1970s to build cohesion among Inuit living in different countries (Wilson 2007). But it also reflects the challenge of translating across scales of value, and the problems that can arise when the inherently messy deliberative process of the UNFCCC results in contradictions that are difficult to reconcile.

Within the UNFCCC, combining economic and ecological metrics is a daunting yet necessary challenge. The proposals that gain traction are those that link emission reductions with alternative mechanisms for monetary value creation. While COICA was somewhat successful at participating in REDD+ discussions to advance their own goals, the ICC had a much harder time gaining traction in this venue. We suggest that, fundamentally, this was due to the challenge of developing mitigation schemes in the Arctic linked to economic scales of value. Barring a huge increase in polar bear tourism or a donor willing to pay communities handsomely for conservation projects, the clearest pathways to monetary value in the Arctic are to develop non-renewable resources, yet these projects will inevitably contribute to rising global temperatures. The ICC's retreat from the UNFCCC therefore also reflects the challenge of balancing competing and sometimes contradictory values in a global, bureaucratic, state-centric venue.

CONCLUSION: HOPE AND EXHAUSTION IN GLOBAL CLIMATE POLITICS

The UNFCCC was launched in 1990 based on the hopeful premise that coordinated, international action could successfully limit greenhouse gas emissions and keep climate change in check. Twenty-five years later, the chain of meetings continues as carbon emissions reach record levels. In spite of persistent optimism on the part of committed parties, it seems unlikely that the UNFCCC will, on its own, achieve its initial goal of a single, global environmental framework capable of avoiding dangerous climate change. As we have tried to show in this chapter, however, assessments of success and failure at the UNFCCC must consider practices taking place far beyond the formal negotiating rooms. Through side events, scientists, social movements, and NGOs work across scales of value to develop innovative environmental approaches that sometimes enter into UNFCCC's chain of document production – thus changing the course of the negotiations. Perhaps more significantly, they create new coalitions capable of mobilizing resources and political will through more localized initiatives.

Hope in relation to an institution such as the UNFCCC is fleeting and unreliable, likely to give way to other emotions such as despair or, more commonly, fatigue. This was made apparent in a conversation that one of us (Rojas) had with COICA leaders at the end of the climate summit in Doha in 2012. As with other UNFCCC meetings, the gathering had required late nights and early mornings, and participants were physically and emotionally drained. Besides the poor food, lack of sleep, and much running around, the group discussed the sense of futility that came from trying to keep track of ever-shifting policy discussions held by thousands of persons in dozens of sessions and events held over two weeks. Moreover, COICA leaders discussed the growing sense of pessimism in the Doha meeting that a global agreement on climate change would not be forthcoming. The most they hoped for in Doha was an agreement to continue to hold more summits, draft more documents, and create more bureaucratic spaces.

In the midst of this conversation, however, a senior member of the Amazonian group also confided that he felt rather good about this meeting. Indigenous social movements, he explained, had been able to slow down discussions regarding the implementation of REDD+. From this perspective, the faint hopes that the UNFCCC process elicited among Amazonian indigenous leaders came, paradoxically, from the institution's *failure* to produce clear results or reach bureaucratic endpoints. A final agreement on REDD+ could render economic and scientific scales of value the only viable metrics in the negotiations, foreclosing alternative possible policy paths. For those such as COICA who struggled for the inclusion of socio-environmental values, inconclusive discussions regarding REDD+ were preferable to an agreement that ignored such values completely. The Paris Agreement was therefore a relative success insofar as it embraces REDD+ principles to reduce "emissions from deforestation and forest degradation" and yet leaves unsaid how such principles are to be implemented. The agreement in Paris only means that parties will continue to work on an agreement on the future implementation of REDD+ so that the mechanism may contribute to voluntary emission reduction pledges.

Observers such as COICA and the ICC contributed to a global climate agreement in which a singular kind of hope asserts itself – not necessarily hope for an ultimate global solution, but for keeping the UNFCCC's diplomatic machinery running. As long as the string of meetings continues and the chain of document production keeps on going, there is a chance for designing more meaningful policy approaches in the future. Keeping such hope alive often entails remembering how imperfect the UNFCCC current order of affairs is and how badly future diplomatic activity is needed. The text that adopts the Paris Agreement notes "with serious concern the urgent need to address the significant gap between . . . Parties' mitigation pledges . . . and aggregate emission pathways consistent with holding the increase in the global average temperature to well below 2°C" (UNFCCC 2015). These lines bring to mind that there are no mechanisms in the Paris Agreement that may be used to make the numbers add up by forcing more ambitious emission reduction pledges on the parties. The hope lies in social movements, private companies, and citizens who, energized by the Paris Agreement, would exert pressure on their governments to gradually increase the "ambition" of their emission targets.

In their prospective (forward looking) orientation, COICA's position brings to mind Hiro Miyazaki's interpretation of hope as a singular stance toward the future, wherein "there is no God's plan, no essential disposition of the world that will automatically unfold" (Miyazaki 2004: 15). Hope here is nourished not by the belief that the world will become what it should, or that a predetermined end will be reached, but by the sense of an open-ended horizon ahead that will bring change without resolution. The hope expressed by COICA delegates in climate politics is hope that the chain of document production at the UNFCCC will continue to be open to alternative scales of values. Perhaps in this way, the UNFCCC can gradually compose global strategies to advance situated actions capable of facilitating a "good life" for both humans and non-humans. The indigenous proposals that are advanced in pursuit of such objectives can be viewed neither as expressing unchanging core values incompatible with economic and scientific metrics, nor as reflecting co-optation by capitalist actors. Rather, indigenous proposals convey a profoundly creative stance wherein skilled interpretations of texts and combinations of documents allow them to broaden the range of values taken into consideration by global institutions. By keeping open institutional spaces in which powerful interests are challenged, indigenous social movements help to elicit much-needed hope in the UNFCCC's precarious functioning.

In contrast to COICA's commitment to continued engagement, however, the ICC gradually withdrew from participation in the UNFCCC venue. Although the venue helped draw some attention to Inuit perspectives on climate change, it became evident that there was little possibility for policy traction for the Arctic or for Inuit in this venue. For ICC staff, the bureaucratic hurdles to participation in the official negotiating spaces were a frustration that became impossible to ignore. One younger staff member for whom COP 15 was his first experience of a UN climate forum explained his disappointment:

> I thought we'd have *some* participation in the actual process. But for myself, I don't understand the process myself. So it's hard to know how you would be able to get your message in . . . I don't feel there was enough inclusion of indigenous peoples in the process. I guess I was expecting more participation than there was.

This suggests that there is no uniformity of hope in global institutions. The opportunities available to COICA to intervene in UNFCCC processes in order to champion non-economic and non-environmental values were not available to ICC delegates, who gradually lost their capacity to sustain their hope in global climate change diplomacy. From their perspective, the future of the negotiations was not open but – when it came to the possibility of injecting an indigenous Arctic perspective into policy outcomes – already decided. The terrain of hope is uneven for various indigenous actors who face dissimilar challenges that affect their capacity to bring non-quantitative values into a policy arena wherein policy goals are increasingly framed in monetary terms. As we have suggested in our discussion of conflicting values within this global institution, the stakes are much higher than merely offering ICC and COICA members a say in climate change diplomacy. Climate transformations are planetary processes that challenge persons and groups to link modes of action and care at global scales (Callison 2014). Given this necessity of mobilizing action at multiple scales, without an institutional framework that is truly open to a variety of perspectives and values, it is unlikely that the UNFCCC will achieve its stated goal of stabilizing greenhouse gases in the atmosphere before they create too much havoc on planetary systems. As such, the irregular persistence of hope at the UNFCCC can be seen as an indicator of the challenges and possibilities of a climate change diplomacy process that, while highly problematic, is still inconclusive.

REFERENCES

Anaya, J. 2004. *Indigenous Peoples in International Law.* Oxford: Oxford University Press.

Bernstein, S., Betsill, M., Hoffmann, M., and Paterson, M., 2010. "A Tale of Two Copenhagens: Carbon Markets and Climate Governance." *Millennium: Journal of International Studies.* 39 (1): 161–173.

Boyd, W. 2010. "Ways of Seeing in Environmental Law: How Deforestation Became an Object of Climate Governance." *Ecology Law Quarterly.* 37: 843–915.

Brosius, J.P., and Campbell, L.M., 2010. "Collaborative Event Ethnography: Conservation and Development Trade-Offs at the Fourth World Conservation Congress." *Conservation and Society.* 8 (4): 245.

Callison, C., 2014. *How Climate Change Comes to Matter: The Communal Life of Facts.* Durham: Duke University Press.

CBC NEWS, 2009a. "Exempt Northerners from Emission Cuts: Inuit Leader." December 10, 14–15. Retrieved from www.cbc.ca/news/canada/north/exempt-northerners-from-emission-cuts-inuit-leader-1.848239. Accessed August 27, 2016.

2009b. "Inuit Have Mixed Views on CO2 Cuts." December 13. Retrieved from www.cbc.ca/news/canada/inuit-have-mixed-views-on-co2-cuts-1.828264. Accessed August 27, 2016.

Claeys, P., and Delgado, D., 2015. "Peasant and Indigenous Transnational Social Movements Engaging with Climate Justice." Conference Paper No. 15, BRICS Initiatives for Critical Agrarian Studies. Retrieved from www.iss.nl/fileadmin/ASSETS/iss/Research_and_projects/Research_networks/MOSAIC/CMCP_15-_Claeys___Delgado.pdf. Accessed August 27, 2016.

COICA, 2013. Indigenous REDD+ Alternative. Indigenous Territories of Harmonious Life to cool the Planet, COICA's Directive Council. Retrieved from: http://theredddesk.org/sites/default/files/resources/pdf/coica_indigenous_redd.pdf. Accessed August 27, 2016.

Corrêa do Lago, A.A., 2009. "*Stockholm, Rio, Johannesburg: Brazil and the Three United Nations Conferences on the Environment.*" Fundação Alexandre de Gusmão, Brasília.

Dalby, Simon. 2013. "The Geopolitics of Climate Change." *Political Geography.* 37: 38–47.

Descheneau, P., and Paterson, M. 2011. "Between Desire and Routine: Assembling Environment and Finance in Carbon Markets." *Antipode*. 43 (3): 662–681.
Doolittle, A. 2010. "The Politics of Indigeneity: Indigenous Strategies for Inclusion in Climate Change Negotiations." *Conservation and Society*. 8(4): 286–291.
Edwards, P.N. 2010. *A Vast Machine: Computer Models, Climate Data, and the Politics of Global Warming*. Cambridge, Mass: MIT Press.
Eicken, H., Lovecraft, A., and Druckenmiller M. 2009. "Sea-Ice System Services: A Framework to Help Identify and Meet Information Needs Relevant for Arctic Observing Networks." *Arctic*. 62(2): 119.
Fairhead, J., Leach, M., and Scoones, I., 2012. "Green Grabbing: A New Appropriation of Nature?" *Journal of Peasant Studies*. 39 (2): 237–261.
Garfield, S. 2014. *In Search of the Amazon: Brazil, the United States, and the Nature of a Region*. Durham: Duke University Press.
Gearheard, Shari Fox, Holm, Lene Kielsen, Huntington, Henry, Leavitt, Joe Mello, and Mahoney, Andrew R.. 2013. *The Meaning of Ice: People and Sea Ice in Three Arctic Communities*. Dartmouth: International Polar Institute.
Grupo Carta de Belém, 2009. Carta de Belém. Retrieved from: http://terradedireitos.org.br/en/2009/10/15/carta-de-belem-os-efeitos-das-mudancas-climaticas-e-a-politica-de-redds/. Accessed August 27, 2016.
Gupta, A. 1998. *Postcolonial Developments: Agriculture in the Making of Modern India*. Durham: Duke University Press.
Guyer, J.I. 2004. *Marginal Gains: Monetary Transactions in Atlantic Africa*. University of Chicago: Chicago Press.
Hecht, S. 2011. "The New Amazon Geographies: Insurgent Citizenship, Amazon Nation, and the Politics of Environmentalisms." *Journal of Cultural Geography*. 28 (1): 203–223.
Hecht, S., and Cockburn, A., 1990. *The Fate of the Forest: Developers, Destroyers, and Defenders of the Amazon*. Chicago: University of Chicago Press.
Hetherington, K., 2011. *Guerrilla Auditors: The Politics of Transparency in Neoliberal Paraguay*. Durham: Duke University Press Books.
Hoag, C. 2011. "Assembling Partial Perspectives: Thoughts on the Anthropology of Bureaucracy." *PoLAR: Political and Legal Anthropology Review*. 34 (1): 81–94.
    2014. "Dereliction at the South African Department of Home Affairs: Time for the Anthropology of Bureaucracy." *Critique of Anthropology*. 34 (4): 410–428.
Hull, M.S. 2012. "Documents and Bureaucracy." *Annual Review of Anthropology*. 41: 251–267.
Huntington, H., Gearheard, S., Druckenmiller, M., and Mahoney, A. 2009. "Community Based Observation Programs and Indigenous and Local Sea Ice Knowledge." In *Field Techniques for Sea Ice Research*. H. Eicken, R. Gradinger, M. Salganek, K. Shirasawa, D. Perovich, and M. Leppäranta, eds. Fairbanks: University of Alaska Press, pp. 345–364.
ICC 2003. ICC Executive Council Resolution 2003–01. Re: Climate Change and Human Rights. Accessed online at: http://inuit.org/climate-change/icc-executive-council-resolution-2003-01/ on June 22, 2015 [no longer available at date of publication].
    2009. Call to Global Leaders: Act Now on Climate Change in the Arctic. Retrieved from www.inuit.org/fileadmin/user_upload/File/2009/PR-2009-11-13-call-to-action.pdf. Accessed June 21, 2015.
IPCC 2013. Working Group I, "Contribution to the IPCC Fifth Assessment Report, Climate Change 2013: The Physical Science Basis." Final Draft Underlying Scientific, Technical Assessment, September 26. 2013.
    "Organization." Retrieved from www.ipcc.ch/organization/organization.shtml. Accessed June 21, 2015.

Lahsen, M., 2009. "A Science–Policy Interface in the Global South: The Politics of Carbon Sinks and Science in Brazil." *Climatic Change*. 97: 339–372.

Latour, B. 2004. *Politics of Nature: How to Bring the Sciences into Democracy*. Cambridge: Harvard University Press.

Li, T. 2007. *The Will to Improve: Governmentality, Development, and the Practice of Politics*. Durham: Duke University Press.

Long, A. 2013. "REDD+ and Indigenous Peoples in Brazil." In *Climate Change and Indigenous Peoples: The Search for Legal Remedies*. R.S. Abate and E.A. Kronk, eds. Cheltenham: Edward Elgar Publishing.

Mcglade, C. and Ekins, P. 2014. "The Geographical Distribution of Fossil Fuels Unused When Limiting Global Warming to 2°C." *Nature*. 517(7533): 187–190.

Merry, S.E. 2011. "Measuring the World." *Current Anthropology*. 52(S3): S83–95.

Miyazaki, H. 2004. *The Method of Hope: Anthropology, Philosophy, and Fijian Knowledge*. Redwood City: Stanford University Press.

Nepstad, D., Schwartzman, S., Bamberger, B., Santilli, M., Ray, D., Schlesinger, P., Rolla, A. et al. 2006. "Inhibition of Amazon Deforestation and Fire by Parks and Indigenous Lands." *Conservation Biology*. 20(1): 65–73.

Niezen, R. 2003. *The Origins of Indigenism: Human Rights and the Politics of Identity*. Berkeley: University of California Press.

Nuijten, M. 2003. *Power, Community and the State: The Political Anthropology of Organization in Mexico*. London: Pluto Press.

Nuttall, M. 2012. "Imagining and Governing the Greenlandic Resource Frontier." *The Polar Journal*. 2(1): 113–124.

O'Brien, K. L., and Leichenko, R. M. 2000. "Double Exposure: Assessing the Impacts of Climate Change within the Context of Economic Globalization." *Global Environmental Change*. 10 (3): 221–232.

Powless, B. 2012. "An Indigenous Movement to Confront Climate Change." *Globalizations*. 9 (February): 411–424.

Price, R. 2011. *Rainforest Warriors: Human Rights on Trial*. Philadelphia: University of Pennsylvania Press.

Prudham, S. 2009. "Pimping Climate Change: Richard Branson, Global Warming, and the Performance of Green Capitalism." *Environment and Planning. A* 41 (7): 1594–1613.

Rajão, R. 2013. "Representations and Discourses: The Role of Local Accounts and Remote Sensing in the Formulation of Amazonia's Environmental Policy." *Environmental Science & Policy*. 30: 60–71.

Revkin, A. 2004. Eskimos Seek to Recast Global Warming as a Rights Issue. *The New York Times*. December 15.

Riles, A. 2000. *The Network Inside Out*. Ann Arbor: University of Michigan Press.

Rockström, Johan, Steffen, Will L., Noone, Kevin, Persson, Åsa, Chapin III, F. Stuart, Lambin, Eric, Lenton, Timothy M., et al., 2009. "Planetary Boundaries: Exploring the Safe Operating Space for Humanity." *Ecology and Society*. 14(2): 32, Retrieved from: http://pdxscholar.library.pdx.edu/iss_pub/64/. Accessed August 27, 2016.

Roitman, J., 2007. "The Efficacy of the Economy." *African Studies Review*. 50 (02): 155–161.

Rojas, D., 2016. "Climate Politics in the Anthropocene and Environmentalism Beyond Nature and Culture in Brazilian Amazonia." *PoLAR: Political and Legal Anthropology Review*. 39(1): 16–32.

Rojas, D. and Johnson, N., 2013. Landscapes of the Anthropocene in the UN Climate Negotiations, *Anthropology News*. October 2013.

Santilli, M., Moutinho, P., Schwartzman, S., Nepstad, D., Curran, L., and Nobre, C., 2005. "Tropical Deforestation and the Kyoto Protocol." *Climatic Change*. 71(3): 267–276.

Schwartzman, S., Moreira, A., and Nepstad, D., 2000. "Rethinking Tropical Forest Conservation: Perils in Parks." *Conservation Biology*. 14(5): 1351–1357.

Sawyer, S., 2004. *Crude Chronicles: Indigenous Politics, Multinational Oil, and Neoliberalism in Ecuador*. Durham: Duke University Press.

Serreze, M.C., Holland, M.M., and Stroeve, J. 2007. "Perspectives on the Arctic's Shrinking Sea Ice Cover." *Science*. 315 (5818): 1533–1536.

Soares-Filho, B., Moutinho, P., Nepstad, D., Anderson, A., Rodrigues, H., Garcia, R., Dietzsch, L., and Silvestrini, R., 2010. "Role of Brazilian Amazon Protected Areas in Climate Change Mitigation." *Proceedings of the National Academy of Sciences*. 107(24): 10821–10826.

Stroeve, J., Holland, M.M., Meier, W., Scambos, T., and Serreze, M. 2007. "Arctic Sea Ice Decline: Faster than Forecast." *Geophysical Research Letters*. 34(9): 1–5.

UNFCCC 1992. United Nations Framework Convention on Climate Change, United Nations, Retrieved from: https://unfccc.int/resource/docs/convkp/conveng.pdf. Accessed August 27, 2016.

  2015. *Paris Agreement*, United Nations, Retrieved from: https://unfccc.int/resource/docs/2015/cop21/eng/l09r01.pdf. Accessed August 27, 2016.

van Dam, C., 2011. "Indigenous Territories and REDD in Latin America: Opportunity or Threat?" *Forests*. 2 (1): 394–414.

van Mensvoort, K. 2009. Melting Polar Bear Reveals a Metal Skeleton, *NEXT NATURE*, blog at www.nextnature.net, entry for December 13, 2009. Accessed on February 25, 2010.

Viveiros de Castro, E. 2011. *The Inconstancy of the Indian Soul: The Encounter of Catholics and Cannibals in 16th-Century Brazil*. Chicago: Prickly Paradigm Press.

Watt-Cloutier, S. 2015. *The Right to Be Cold: One Woman's Story of Protecting her Culture, the Arctic and the Whole Planet*. Toronto: Allen Lane.

Weisser, F., 2014. Practices, Politics, Performativities: Documents in the International Negotiations on Climate Change. *Political Geography*. 40: 46–55.

Wilson, Gary N. 2007. "Inuit Diplomacy in the Circumpolar North." *Canadian Foreign Policy Journal*. 13(3): 65–80.

11

The Best of the Best: Positing, Measuring and Sensing Value in the UNESCO World Heritage Arena

Christoph Brumann

INTRODUCTION

The Convention Concerning the Protection of the World Cultural and Natural Heritage, adopted by the General Conference of the United Nations Educational, Scientific and Cultural Organization (UNESCO) in 1972, is widely seen as a very successful undertaking. Almost all states – that is, 191 – have ratified it by now, and despite the educational priorities of that UN special agency, World Heritage is the first thing that comes to mind for many people when they hear its name. World Heritage has been the single most influential force in making "heritage" the buzzword it is today and in spreading heritage discourses and practices across the globe, and it has also contributed to the formation of heritage studies as a new interdisciplinary field and the establishment of "World Heritage Studies" graduate programmes from Dublin over Cottbus to Tsukuba. A World Heritage title can be a huge boost for tourism, investments, aid, and local and national status. While the protective effect depends strongly on the susceptibility of the respective state to public pressure and on the nature of the domestic political debate, the World Heritage institutions – despite disposing of not more than "soft power," as outlined in the Introduction – have won major victories in battles against high-rises in historic town centres or highways through nature reserves. World Heritage has been significant enough to provoke war, such as when the World Heritage designation of the ancient Khmer temple Preah Vihear in 2008 – on territory disputed between Cambodia and Thailand – was followed by several bloody clashes between the two armies. So important has the UNESCO endeavour become that the World Heritage title may perversely thwart its own objective of protection: in 2012, the Islamist rebels then in control of northern Mali destroyed sufi tombs and mosque entrances in Timbuktu – as they claimed, precisely because this World Heritage site had been put on the sub-list of World Heritage in Danger a few days earlier. The provocative act produced the intended global headlines (Brumann 2016: 309–314). In accordance with this prominence, the annual World Heritage Committee sessions have grown from small gatherings of a few dozen conservationists to global events, with more than 2,000 participants attending the 2015 meeting in Bonn, Germany.

Central to the World Heritage operations is the World Heritage List which, by annual increments, has grown from an initial 12 inscriptions in 1978 to 1,031 items as of 2015, spread across 163 countries. As part of a new trend in international law that was also applied in roughly contemporary international treaties on Antarctica, the high seas, and outer space (Höhler 2014; Rehling and Löhr 2014; Wolfrum 2009), the Convention qualifies the World Heritage List entries as "common heritage of mankind," and it is the only one of these treaties where such global co-ownership and co-responsibility apply to sites on sovereign national territories. But according to the convention text,[1] such privileged treatment is restricted to "properties forming part of the cultural heritage and natural heritage ... consider[ed] as having *outstanding universal value*" (article 11.2, emphasis added). Academics know that disagreement about what is outstanding is a common occurrence, but when what is outstanding must be universal in addition, an anthropologist – adherent of a discipline that since Franz Boas's days has championed cultural relativism and been sceptical of conventional (or, for that matter, any kind of) rankings of culture – cannot help becoming curious. How do the World Heritage institutions define "OUV" – the standard abbreviation in World Heritage contexts – and how do they establish its presence in a given site? This chapter will offer an ethnographically grounded answer, comparing official norms and procedures with actual practices and giving special attention to what the unending stream of new additions to the erudite List is perceived as doing with the value of properties, the List as a whole, and the Convention.[2]

DEFINING OUV

"Value" was not part of initial World Heritage plans, and neither was a celebratory list. Instead, the (ultimately merged) initiatives of UNESCO for an international legal instrument for the protection of immovable cultural properties and of the International Union for Conservation of Nature (IUCN) and the US government

---

[1] See whc.unesco.org/en/conventiontext [all weblinks in chapter last accessed 9 September 2016].
[2] I base my analysis on what I have called, in a play on George Marcus (1995), 'multilateral ethnography' (Brumann 2012) – that is, a combination of participant observation, formal interviews, and documentary analysis similar to many other chapters in this volume. I attended all World Heritage Committee and General Assembly sessions in 2009–2012, a large part of the Committee session of 2015, and further statutory meetings and conferences, for all of which I was given 'observer' status by the secretariat, just like other academic researchers. Different from other chapters in this volume, I concentrated my participant observation on the formal meetings and their informal corona of hotel breakfasts and bar talk, lunches and dinners, receptions and special events, coffee breaks and shuttle-bus rides. I did not become part of any of the constituent organizations such as the Secretariat, the Advisory Bodies, or the state delegations, also due to not wishing to become too closely associated with any of them and their rivalries, but learned a lot about them from the formal interviews and an endless series of informal conversations.

for an UN-backed register of important natural sites had started out around the concept of a "World Heritage Trust" (Stott 2011: 283–285). With the widely publicized UNESCO safeguarding campaigns for the Nubian monuments of Abu Simbel (Hassan 2007) and its successors in Venice, Moenjodaro, and Borobudur as a point of reference, a mere register of sites in urgent need of international safeguarding efforts appeared sufficient to many (Titchen 1995: 147–151). Also, it did not require anthropological input for the consulted experts to predict difficulties when trying to decide which sites might have prime importance on a global scale (Titchen 1995: 101–102).

Despite these reservations, the drafting committee settled on keeping a list, and the UNESCO General Conference adopted a convention text[3] that mentions "outstanding universal value" no less than 13 times. The text does not define it, however, and (in article 11.2) passes on the task of establishing criteria for OUV to the World Heritage Committee, the intergovernmental decision-making body of the Convention. In its second session in 1978, this Committee adopted "Operational Guidelines"[4] that restricted OUV for "the most outstanding of these [*properties*] from an international viewpoint" (§ I.5 ii), a position which is upheld in the current 2013 version of the Guidelines[5] which stipulates that "Outstanding Universal Value means cultural and/or natural significance which is so exceptional as to transcend national boundaries and to be of common importance for present and future generations of all humanity" (§ 49; see also § 53). While "universal" may thus be operationalized to a certain extent, and while indeed a couple of candidates – such as parliament buildings – have been rejected as "too national," what is "outstanding" must be gleaned from the six criteria for cultural sites and four criteria for natural sites first formulated in the above-mentioned 1978 Guidelines, of which a World Heritage property must fulfil at least one (§§ I.B 7 and I.B 10). Slightly revised over the years, they currently read as follows:

The Committee considers a property as having Outstanding Universal Value ... if the property meets one or more of the following criteria. Nominated properties shall therefore:

(i) represent a masterpiece of human creative genius;
(ii) exhibit an important interchange of human values, over a span of time or within a cultural area of the world, on developments in architecture or technology, monumental arts, town-planning or landscape design;
(iii) bear a unique or at least exceptional testimony to a cultural tradition or to a civilization which is living or which has disappeared;
(iv) be an outstanding example of a type of building, architectural or technological ensemble or landscape which illustrates (a) significant stage(s) in human history;

[3] http://whc.unesco.org/en/conventiontext.
[4] whc.unesco.org/archive/opguide78.pdf.
[5] whc.unesco.org/archive/opguide13-en.pdf.

(v) be an outstanding example of a traditional human settlement, land-use, or sea-use which is representative of a culture (or cultures), or human interaction with the environment especially when it has become vulnerable under the impact of irreversible change;
(vi) be directly or tangibly associated with events or living traditions, with ideas, or with beliefs, with artistic and literary works of outstanding universal significance (the Committee considers that this criterion should preferably be used in conjunction with other criteria);
(vii) contain superlative natural phenomena or areas of exceptional natural beauty and aesthetic importance;
(viii) be outstanding examples representing major stages of earth's history, including the record of life, significant on-going geological processes in the development of landforms, or significant geomorphic or physiographic features;
(ix) be outstanding examples representing significant on-going ecological and biological processes in the evolution and development of terrestrial, fresh water, coastal and marine ecosystems and communities of plants and animals;
(x) contain the most important and significant natural habitats for in-situ conservation of biological diversity, including those containing threatened species of Outstanding Universal Value from the point of view of science or conservation. (World Heritage Operational Guidelines, 2013 version, § 77)

It will be immediately apparent that these are types or substantive aspects of heritage sites rather than "criteria" in the strict sense and that, rather than defining "outstanding," they themselves use that word or similar, equally undefined alternatives ("masterpiece", "important", "unique", "exceptional", "superlative", "significant", etc.).

Groping for guidance, one is next drawn to two compendiums prepared by the "Advisory Bodies" of the World Heritage Committee, the International Council of Monuments and Sites (ICOMOS), and the IUCN. For the cultural sites, former ICOMOS president Jukka Jokilehto (2006) reviews the past application of the criteria and the treatment of specific candidates, but something resembling an operational definition of OUV is nowhere in evidence. For the natural sites, a team around Tim Badman, Director of IUCN's World Heritage Programme, also takes stock of the past application of the criteria and the treatment of landmark candidates. Yet while the IUCN authors claim a more systematic approach of determining OUV than for the cultural sites and increasing strictness over time (Badman et al. 2008: 4, 6), again, a precise definition of the OUV threshold is missing. The official manual for World Heritage nominations confirms the centrality of OUV for the World Heritage endeavour and lists what appear to be common mistakes in demonstrating the OUV of a candidate site in a nomination file (UNESCO 2011: 56–58) but how to recognize OUV when one sees it is not explained. Also, attempts to set the OUV threshold at a more precise level for specific categories of heritage have not been engaged in, neither pre-emptively, before the first site of a new kind is nominated, nor in a post-hoc manner. This does not even happen in the thematic programmes that the secretariat of the convention, the World Heritage Center located in UNESCO headquarters in Paris, runs for specific, often neglected categories – such as astronomical heritage, earthen architecture, or modern heritage – by organizing expert studies and conferences.[6] During the World Heritage Committee sessions, I heard the complaint that OUV is far too rigidly conceived now, so the states of the Global South in particular struggle to comply with the many demands. But the above observations rather suggest the opposite, namely that OUV has never been properly spelt out.

FINDING OUV IN THE SITES: RARITY VALUE AND EXPECTATIONS OF GROWTH

Evidently, this lacuna has not prevented the World Heritage institutions from finding OUV more than a thousand times. For candidate sites, this is accomplished through an evaluation procedure that has been increasingly elaborated over the course of time. To have a site listed as World Heritage, a treaty state has to submit a nomination file to the World Heritage Center some 16 months ahead of the session in which it will be discussed. From a couple of typed sheets, these files have grown into huge tomes running into hundreds or even thousands of pages and supplemented by audiovisual documentation. The nomination file is then forwarded to either ICOMOS, an international membership NGO with national chapters whose headquarters are likewise in Paris, or IUCN, an "NGOGO" (Batisse and Bolla 2005: 20) with both government agencies and NGOs for nature conservation as members and headquarters in Gland near Geneva; mixed cultural and natural sites are considered by both ICOMOS and IUCN. These organizations whose role was already stipulated in the Convention (article 8.3) send the nomination file to up to several dozen experts and also dispatch one or two conservation experts to the site in order to examine its current condition and protection. Based on this input, internal ICOMOS and IUCN panels formulate a recommended decision which can be for 'inscription' of the property, outright and terminal rejection ("non-inscription"), or two forms of postponement for either minor revisions ("referral") or a major overhaul that requires a new expert mission to the site ("deferral"). Taking the decision, however, is reserved for the World Heritage Committee. Into this body, which meets every summer for an 11-day session, the 191 "States Parties" to the treaty elect 21 states from their own midst for staggered terms of 6 (now voluntarily 4) years. The states send delegations consisting of anything from a single person to several dozen. The Convention requires these be to "persons qualified in the field of the

---

[6] whc.unesco.org/en/activities.

cultural or natural heritage" (article 9.3), but in addition to experts, the state delegations also include the "Permanent Delegates" (i.e. ambassadors) to UNESCO, other diplomats, government personnel up to ministerial rank, representatives of listed and candidate sites, and other members according to what is each state's sovereign decision. State representatives are at the helm, and experts give advice but will influence final decision-making only as far as the respective Committee state allows. The Introduction to this volume calls attention to the details of the architecture of UN bodies and, indeed, the difference between the World Heritage Committee and, say, the Permanent Forum on Indigenous Issues where named independent experts occupy half the seats (see Sapignoli, Chapter 4 in this volume) is significant. Without nation-state dominance in the World Heritage arena, the "rebellion" described below and the general takeover by career diplomats (Brumann 2014) might not have happened.

On what, then, have the Advisory Bodies and the World Heritage Committee based their judgements of OUV? Since an intensional or connotative definition that characterizes OUV by its features has never been provided, this leaves an extensional or ostensive definition – that is, by reference to things that display the given quality, in this case the sites already on the World Heritage List. Obviously, the latter could not serve as a yardstick for the very first list inscriptions, but many of the early candidates were the famous and iconic sites that many people would expect to feature on such a list in any event, such as the Galapagos Islands, the Grand Canyon, the historic centre of Rome, Machu Picchu, and the Taj Mahal. Yet, soon enough, a solid body of World Heritage properties to relate to was assembled. A potential alternative method to ascertain OUV might have been the imposition of numerical limitations. There is only one Nobel Prize in Literature and one Academy Award for Best Picture each year, and the selectiveness this enforces is usually assumed to guarantee quality, whereas the opposite – mass accession – can raise doubts about the nature of a distinction.

Yet neither of these two logics – comparison with listed sites and inscription quotas – has ever been consistently applied in the World Heritage context. To begin with the latter, the drafters thought of around 100 sites as a target (Batisse and Bolla 2005: 74, 94). Very occasionally, a particular heritage category was declared as closed, such as when the Auschwitz concentration camp was listed in representation of all similar sites in 1979, or when the inscription of further reconstructions beyond the historic centre of Warsaw was ruled out in 1980. Yet, when in the first three years alone, Ethiopia obtained seven list inscriptions and Poland five,[7] it must have been obvious that there would eventually be a far larger number. After the annual total of new inscriptions peaked at 61 in 2000, and Italy alone had a record 10 candidates listed in the single year of 1997,[8] the World Heritage Committee imposed a nomination quota

---

[7] cf. whc.unesco.org/en/list.
[8] cf. whc.unesco.org/en/list/stat.

of 1 candidate per state and year, to a total of 30. But this was soon softened to (currently) 2 candidates per state and year, provided one of them is a natural site or a cultural landscape. This limitation is painful only to around a dozen very interested and resourceful countries since for most, even a single state-of-the-art nomination is a challenge. The overall cap has been raised as well, to 45 candidacies, a number that so far has never been exhausted. Crucially, however, limitations apply only to nominations, not inscriptions – if all candidates in a given year are found to have OUV, they must all go on the List. Attempts to impose a selective moratorium on the well-represented states have usually been fought with the argument that it is the Committee's sacred duty to put sites with proven OUV on the World Heritage List as soon as possible in order to ensure their protection, even if this means yet another inscription for the likes of Italy, Spain, or Germany and a continuation of European dominance on a list almost half-filled with the properties of that continent. For the natural and mixed sites, IUCN expects a ceiling of 250 to 300 sites, but this too is still some way ahead of the 229 sites in these categories (as of 2015), and ICOMOS has never said that the cultural World Heritage sites could be finite.

The World Heritage Committee could at any point restrict the nomination flow, but it is unlikely to do so. Committee states are held not to advocate their own national interests during the sessions, but there is no outright ban on World Heritage nominations by the 21 Committee members. Acknowledging what is an obvious conflict of interests, some of the latter voluntarily refrain from nominating during their tenure, but most states welcome the fact that a seat on the Committee helps them to advance their own nominations as it improves their lobbying position and ability to ensure support from their Committee peers. Often, there is little else that motivates states to serve on the Committee, and both nominations and inscriptions by Committee states have always been over-represented, up to a factor of two or three for inscriptions. Yet the very fact that Committee members come with anxiously anticipated nominations makes them soft and compromising on their peers' wishes, lest those other members might strike back and take revenge when their own candidates are up. For example, the admission of Palestine as a full state member of UNESCO in 2011 led to a severe budget crisis because of the pre-announced withdrawal of US funds. So, in the following Committee session, the proposal to halve the cap on nominations in order to ease the workload of the World Heritage institutions made sense to many. Yet Committee members Japan and Germany, which have their internal nomination schedules filled for years in advance, vehemently opposed the idea. And they had their way: while most other Committee states might not be affected one way or the other, they still did not want to estrange two influential Committee peers. The matter returned with renewed urgency in the 2015 session when the financial straits of the system – if anything, even more crippling than elsewhere in the UN universe, where they are chronic too (see Introduction) – had deepened. Now, a large majority of the states participating in an open working group meeting outside plenary session hours indicated their acceptance of a cap of

1 nomination per state and year up to a maximum of 25. Yet when the issue was taken up in the plenary session, a small number of vocal and influential Committee states, including India, Turkey, and Japan, staunchly resisted. Again, opposition was half-hearted, and the matter was eventually deferred to another working group, with the current, loose cap remaining in place.

The spectre of List inflation is regularly invoked in the World Heritage arena, and it is perhaps no accident that the most committed opponents to indiscriminate listing in the 2010–2012 sessions – Sweden, Switzerland, and Estonia – had already served themselves well in the past: with 14, 12, and 2 sites respectively, they had many more World Heritage properties per population than any of their 18 Committee peers or even the overall list leaders, and their 'Tentative Lists' of future candidates (see below) were almost empty. Yet with more than 1,000 properties, the marginal damage of an additional inscription to List exclusiveness has dwindled and is not nearly as much of a motivating force as the prospect of crowning a further candidate with World Heritage glory can be for the respective state. And despite negative press comments, obvious dents to the traction of the World Heritage title among the general public are not yet in evidence. This means that expecting restraint from the Committee is unrealistic.

To an insufficiently acknowledged degree, the entire World Heritage endeavour takes List growth for granted and depends on it. New inscriptions provide for scenes of jubilation in the hall, interrupting otherwise rather dry bureaucratic proceedings, with delegates cheering, hugging, waving national flags, and receiving the congratulations of their peers. New listings also make for happy global news, different from developments at already listed sites, which are often sobering and, even for what is perceived as the success stories of conservation, rather complex to tell. Without the promise of further inscriptions on the List, World Heritage might wane from public consciousness and quite a few states would lose interest, endangering the voluntary contributions on which the poorly funded system so much depends. The mechanism of the 'Tentative List' on which a state is to register its potential future candidates creates a pressure of its own: these nationally administered lists were introduced to give the Advisory Bodies a better grasp of what is in the offing and to enable synergies between the States Parties, and that is why they continue to be highlighted. Yet for the localities and communities committed to a site, having it registered on the Tentative List is generally taken as a promise of future nomination by one's government. As these national lists together contain more entries than the World Heritage List – 1,630, as of 2015 – there is ample material for further growth, and no treaty state has yet renounced its nomination right.

OUV BY COMPARISON

When numerical thresholds cannot determine value, comparison is left; and, indeed, in recent years, the "comparative analysis" as a compulsory part of each nomination file has been very much emphasized. Deficiencies in this regard are often a reason for negative evaluations, although rarely the decisive one. In the file, a candidate should be compared both with sites on the World Heritage List and with other potential candidates, and the analysis "shall explain the importance of the nominated property in its national and international context" (Operational Guidelines, 2013 version, § 132.3). One might expect the comparative exercise to rest on the simple logic that if a candidate site is shown to be as deserving as already listed sites whose OUV is thereby proven, it must itself have OUV. Yet while superiority to similar sites not on the List must indeed be demonstrated, a very precise aim of the comparative analysis with listed World Heritage sites is not given; instead, the comparative analysis is to demonstrate, in a rather vague formulation, "that there is room on the List for the nominated property" (UNESCO 2011: 68).

IUCN has a somewhat easier job here as there are more quantifiable indicators (such as numbers of plant and animal species or the number of endemic species), and it can rely on scientifically grounded, largely consensual classification systems for geological, climatic, and biological areas which allow identification of appropriate comparators and lacunae on the List that beg for coverage. Indeed, IUCN has repeatedly pointed out "gaps" on the List and sites with OUV potential which could help to fill them. Generally, comparison is applied in a more rigorous way in the evaluations, and in the sessions there is somewhat less readiness within the Committee to overturn IUCN recommendations. This is a different matter, however, for the cultural sites which make for almost four-fifths of both candidates and listings. Browsing through the states' nomination files and the evaluations by ICOMOS, one is often struck that the comparative analyses simply go over a number of similar sites and how the candidate site differs from them, but lack a clear conclusion: they do not say that the candidate site is as deserving as the already listed sites and more deserving than possible other candidates, nor do they raise the weaker claim that there is "room" for the site on the List. Sometimes in the evaluations, one also finds an outright rejection of the comparative logic, when it is said that the site is so unique that it cannot be compared at all. In marked contrast to how knowledge is conceived in the UN Statistical Commission (see Merry, Chapter 7 in this volume), and in defiance of the general "avalanche of indicators in global governance" (June and Wedel 2010), constructing numerical measures or indexes of OUV has never been attempted. Nor has anyone proposed to bring in indirect comparative measures, such as the number and national diversity of visitors or the presence of the site in print, on the internet, or in the specialized literature.

This leaves the assertion of OUV for individual sites – and, indeed, the "statement of OUV" to be formulated for each property has been foregrounded in recent years too, given that conservation is difficult to accomplish without an agreed baseline. Most of these statements, however, are extensive descriptions of the respective site's history and features rather than systematic argumentations for their OUV. Beyond the use of similar adjectives, as in the ten criteria such as "outstanding" or "unique," it is the sites that are presented, rather than their value.

REFORMING OUV

Partly, more stringent comparison may be absent because ideas of cultural heritage have changed considerably in the World Heritage arena, mainly by expansion rather than a complete overhaul of the established order. Responding to rising criticism, a package of reform measures devised during the 1990s aimed at conceptualizing cultural heritage in less Eurocentric ways. Adopted in 1994, the "Global Strategy for a Representative, Balanced and Credible World Heritage List"[9] urged getting away from palaces, cathedrals, and historic town centres to also include the vestiges of ordinary people and everyday life in their full diversity (Gfeller 2015). In the "Nara Document on Authenticity" of the same year,[10] previous notions were broadened to de-emphasize the material continuity that was privileging European-style stone monuments (Gfeller n.d.). The very popular new category of cultural landscapes – celebrating the physical or spiritual interaction between people and nature – was introduced in 1992 (Gfeller 2013; Mitchell et al. 2009; Rössler 2006). Modern and industrial heritage, sites of global movement and connectedness, and sites with a human-rights message have also become much more prominent. As a result of these measures, Belgian coal mines, wooden peasant churches in the Carpathians, sacred groves in Kenya, wetland gardens in Papua New Guinea, the Bikini nuclear test site, Indian mountain railways, and the landing place of indentured labourers in Mauritius are no less likely to make it onto the List now than Roman ruins, Gothic cathedrals, or Baroque palaces. Thematically, the World Heritage List has become considerably more diverse and, once again, a global institution has been more than a simple proponent of Westernization. Considerable amounts of the personal idealism described in the Introduction flew into these reforms, both from the civil servants of the World Heritage Center and the involved Advisory Body experts (Brumann 2014: 2181–2182, 2183).

Yet nothing deemed to have OUV before these reforms was principally discredited, and the very years of the reforms saw record numbers of European inscriptions of often rather conventional kinds, particularly in the late 1990s. Then, in the 2000s, which brought substantial procedural reform, nominations from the Global South often bumped into more elaborate nomination and evaluation requirements. I think that all this contributed to two consequences: it raised doubts about the existence of objective heritage standards when what counts as globally valuable cultural heritage could be expanded so much in such a short time; and, connected with this, it raised doubts about ICOMOS's true values when it denied Southern candidates OUV.

[9] http://whc.unesco.org/en/globalstrategy.
[10] whc.unesco.org/document/9379.

The organization and its functionaries continue to be perceived as European– or Western–dominated and as Eurocentric, and for many participants from the Global South, the gut feeling that World Heritage is essentially an affair of and for the Global North has never fully subsided.

ICOMOS does little to counter this view: in the critical 2009–2012 sessions, most of the "World Heritage Advisors" charged with drafting the evaluations and presenting and defending them – the "faces" of ICOMOS for session participants – were Europeans. Since they are not named and personally introduced, emphasizing the corporate rather than individual viewpoint they present, uninitiated participants probably also took the non-Europeans (such as a Mexican) for "Northerners." Nor did they learn that within ICOMOS, these Advisors – having published on such topics as African earthen architecture, the Umayyad Mosque of Damascus, or industrial heritage – were probably least suspect of Eurocentrism and a conventional architectural or art-historical point of view. IUCN diversified its speakers somewhat more, but it still happened that in the orientation meeting preceding the official session, all three Advisory Bodies – including the International Centre for the Study of the Preservation and Restoration of Cultural Property (ICCROM), which is not involved in evaluations – were represented by white British or Americans, without much thought about the impression this might make on a global audience.

The accumulated dissatisfaction finally led to an undeclared rebellion in the 2010 Committee session in Brasilia, led by political heavyweights from the Global South, such as the host nation Brazil, Mexico, Egypt, and China, also joined by the "other within" Europe, Russia. Starting with the debate over whether the state of conservation of the Galapagos Islands had sufficiently improved to justify removal from the List of World Heritage in Danger – as Ecuador demanded – Committee state representatives supported each other and the non-Committee states present as observers in over-ruling ICOMOS and IUCN recommendations and having national wishes fulfilled. To an unprecedented degree, decisions proposed for the problematic sites were softened, and the number of new inscriptions doubled from those recommended. Most of the "upgrades" in Brasilia benefitted the Global South, but the new mores have persisted through subsequent Committee sessions, with incoming Committee members such as India, Japan, Germany, and Turkey not resisting what, after all, serves their own interests of assuring World Heritage honours for the candidates they never fail to bring to the sessions.[11]

[11] For this development, Meskell (2013: 489–490) has emphasized the role of the BRICS alliance between Brazil, Russia, India, China, and South Africa, of which all except India were on the Committee in the 2010 and 2011 sessions, and Russia, India, and South Africa in the 2012 and 2013 sessions. Yet while these states certainly flexed their political muscle, South Africa was still relatively silent in 2010, China spoke up largely for its own properties, and non-BRICS states such as Mexico or Egypt in no way stood back behind Russia and Brazil in terms of assertively challenging the Advisory Bodies and supporting their peers. Claudi also sees the BRICS alliance in Committee politicking as "inconsistent and weak" only (2011: 67). In Meskell's account (2014), the new trend of national

CONSTRUCTING OUV IN THE WORLD HERITAGE COMMITTEE SESSIONS

But how do the state representatives within the Committee establish the presence of OUV when the Advisory Bodies fail to detect it? Largely in an ad hoc manner, and by using the superior power of the votes they have in a – most often open – decision in which ICOMOS and IUCN have none. There have indeed been inscriptions where it sufficed for one state to propose an over-ruling amendment of the recommended decision which, in the absence of any objections, was then adopted by the chairperson (him- or herself a representative of one of the Committee states). Normally, however, some degree of argumentative reasoning must be engaged in after ICOMOS or IUCN have finished their introductory presentation and the chairperson has opened the debate to the Committee states that then ask for the floor by raising their state-name plate. And here in the sessions since 2010, the instrumental nature of many interventions was transparent, down to unspecialized interpreters I talked to. The distribution of roles and arguments often appeared orchestrated, as became obvious when delegates struggled to read out slips of paper, suggesting that these were not their own notes but those that the concerned state delegation had drafted for them (see also Meskell 2015: 11). In their arguments, delegates either take promises as facts – when the Advisory Bodies are missing proper legal protection or management plans but the concerned state assures their imminent realization – or engage in very selective and forced readings of the evaluations: when the Advisory Bodies stress the need to demonstrate the presence of OUV more clearly, for example, this is turned into a confirmation of OUV, as ICOMOS is not convinced of its absence. Blanket assertions that the OUV of a given candidate is beyond doubt, without any supporting argument, are surprisingly common. In a rather popular move, delegates claim to have visited the property under debate, often very recently, and assert the absence of the alleged problems or the impressiveness of the site, no

---

self-serving at the cost of the Advisory Bodies appears to have arisen gradually over an entire decade. Attending both the 2009 session in Seville – where the Committee still went as far as delisting a site against a nation-state's wishes – and the 2010 session, however, I saw a clear rupture that, incidentally, is reflected in Meskell's own statistics (2014: 226–227, Figures 1 and 2). Pace Meskell, I also do not see "pacting" between nation-states (2014) and the transaction of "gifts" (2015) as the defining features of recent Committee sessions. Pacts make sense when two or more social actors join forces against an otherwise insurmountable opponent, but there was none such in the post-2009 sessions: for outvoting the three aforementioned European dissenters, a more or less spontaneously formed new orthodoxy of mutual support among the other Committee states was fully sufficient. It did not seem to me that elaborate games of building alliances had to be played when virtually every state that had done its advance lobbying – Committee member or not – received peer support. State parties did unite against the Advisory Bodies, but as these do not have a vote anyway, "pacting" is a big word for what looked more like crowd behaviour in a new situation where, to everyone's surprise, accustomed restraints have suddenly fallen away. Also, support is not much of a gift when it comes at no cost – given the aforementioned absence of an inscription cap, backing another state's World Heritage candidate cannot diminish the chances of one's own candidate; rather, it improves them by encouraging return support.

matter what the Advisory Bodies say. A case in point in 2012 was the German ambassador to UNESCO – a lawyer by training – who claimed that she was probably the only person in the room to have visited all of the three Russian kremlins under discussion (nominated together as a single, "serial" property) and urged us to believe her assertions of how exceptional they were.

Such self-declared and often unspecialized eye witnesses challenge an increasingly sophisticated and rationalized evaluation process in which dozens of specialists contribute to fact-finding about and comparative assessment of the sites. Not least because the charge of subjectivity is always in the air, however, the results of this process are presented in an invariably dry and textual way, doing little to fight the tendency of quite a few Committee delegates to give the pre-circulated reports little more than a cursory look. Because of the time pressure in the sessions, candidates are presented by the Advisory Bodies for not more than a couple of minutes, and with few visual cues.

The dissenting eye witness, by contrast, is a flesh-and-blood human being and maybe a cherished diplomatic colleague who makes fervent assertions, often imploring the Committee to believe him or her in such a sincere manner that one must fight down the urge simply to do so. The professional diplomats who most often speak for the delegations are not naïve, of course, but I still think that such testimony will help them to overcome any qualms about what their delegation's deals oblige them to say. Also, diplomatic etiquette discourages outright accusations of lying. Therefore, objections to obviously counterfactual claims will usually be made in measured language, and if the Advisory Bodies have supporting evidence, such as satellite images showing illicit construction activity, they will mention but usually not show it on the computer screens in the room. This means that OUV is constructed spontaneously, in a surprisingly improvised and often clumsy way that poorly hides the underlying interests. But since a majority of Committee members are committed to mutual support with almost every other state that has invested in a minimum of advance lobbying with them, these spontaneous constructions are turned into decisions, thus creating further World Heritage listings that themselves become precedents to which future candidates can refer.

CONSTRUCTING OUV IN THE EXPERT EVALUATIONS

Yet are the expert evaluations of OUV more objective and less interest-driven? ICOMOS officials, in their introductory statement to the discussion of nominations, never fail to emphasize the rigorous scientific standards applied in the evaluations. But ICOMOS is not a particularly scholarly organization to begin with, as became apparent in a rather humorous way when the president clarified that he was "just an ordinary person" after having been repeatedly referred to as "Dr. Araoz" by other delegates in the 2012 session. Responding to calls for more transparency, ICOMOS publicized the composition of its "World Heritage Panel" – the internal board to which the above-mentioned World Heritage Advisors submit their draft recommendations for final approval – for the first time before the 2015 session. Of the 19 Panel members listed in the report (ICOMOS 2014), not more than 6 (and not more than 1 of the 6 World Heritage Advisors) hold a doctoral degree. In terms of what the world over is regarded as the minimum requirement for competent scientific practice, there is thus little to boast about. Instead, what unites these individuals is their applied professional background: 13 of the 19 Panel members and 3 of the 6 Advisors are conservation architects or planners. A majority in the Panel also hold office on the ICOMOS international level: half of the 20 elected members of the current ICOMOS Board are included, among them the president, 4 of the 5 vice presidents, the secretary-general, and the treasurer,[12] and there is also a past ICOMOS vice president. Yet while these people thus enjoy the proven support of ICOMOS members, this may be based more on their leadership capacities than their scientific competence. All this is not to belittle the impressive practical experience, publication records (largely in applied fields), and teaching experience in universities (usually not the top-ranked ones) of many of these individuals, but it is still difficult to see this as a particularly scholarly and scientific assembly.

And while the six Advisors now hail from four continents, the composition of the Panel is also ill-equipped to counter charges of Eurocentrism. Eleven of the 19 members are Europeans or North Americans (a count that includes, in line with UNESCO practice, the one Israeli member), whereas there is only a single member each from sub-Saharan Africa and the Arab countries. The included representatives from five ICOMOS Scientific Committees and one "affinity organization" are all European (as are three of the six Advisors). In what appears to anticipate criticism, a concluding table to the report finds the proportional share of European and North American Panel members and that of the discussed European and North American candidate properties an identical 57 per cent. The very idea of making this comparison (and thereby implying that heritage sites are best judged by people from the same world region), however, is clearly at odds with the universalist mission of the World Heritage endeavour and OUV.

This situation can partly be explained by the specific organizational setup of ICOMOS. Its international office holders are elected at the triennial General Conferences, which usually have rather costly fees and often take place in a European or North American location. Support schemes exist for participants from the Global South, but numerically the latter are clearly outmatched by those from the North. In the elections, there is a cap of 20 votes per country, and voters hailing from countries with smaller numbers of attending participants may carry delegated votes. Yet at the 2008 General Conference in Quebec I attended, I talked to several such participants who were unsure about the respective procedures or who deplored hiccups in their implementation. Also, 81 of the 191 World Heritage treaty

---

[12] www.icomos.org/en/about-icomos/governance/general-information-about-the-executive-committee.

states do not have a national IMOCOS committee to begin with, meaning that their nationals cannot vote or stand for election. Both the blank spots and the less active national committees tend to lie outside Europe.

I do not want to imply conscious Eurocentrism, but it is obvious to me that the world view of such a body must be different than if it were dominated by non-Europeans, other background disciplines (for example, history or anthropology rather than architecture), and full-time scholars rather than practising conservationists. There is no reason to assume that the dominant professions have a lesser impact here than in the World Bank, for example. The resulting biases become rather apparent when, for example, in an ICOMOS attempt to take stock of the List and sort the properties on it, "Europe" is subdivided into no less than 12 categories combining regional and historic sub-divisions (such as "Eastern Medieval Europe", "Southern M. E." and "Western and Northern M. E."), whereas for "Asia" or "The Americas" no more than four, purely regional categories ("Indian subcontinent", "South-East Asia", "East Asia (Far East)", and "Central Asia" for Asia) are deemed sufficient (ICOMOS 2004: 16). I also see rather different depths of focus applied in some of the ICOMOS evaluations, meaning that the appreciation of what is better-known to much of its personnel is more nuanced and ready to acknowledge the details. For the 2013 session, for example, the Bergpark Wilhelmhöhe in Kassel, Germany, received an unconditional recommendation for inscription (ICOMOS 2013b: 161–168). The genre of the Baroque palace and park is, as everyone agrees, amply represented on the World Heritage List, but ICOMOS argued that the sophisticated waterworks make the site special and give it OUV. By contrast, the Japanese nomination of a series of sites in Kamakura was proposed for non-inscription and thereby declared as unambiguously devoid of OUV (ICOMOS 2013b: 116–125), despite its reputation as the "Number Three" of Japanese historic cities (after Kyoto and Nara) and its role in the rise of the shogun government and the samurai warriors. Loss of historic building substance was deplored in the evaluation, but nowhere in Japan have medieval cities and their wooden architecture survived intact, and while the remaining temples, shrines, and gardens of Kamakura may fall behind those of Kyoto or Nara, they can in most Japan specialists' eyes compete with those of World Heritage properties Nikkô or Hiraizumi, particularly as an ensemble. Yet while the eighteenth-century monumental sculpture of Hercules in the Wilhelmshöhe gardens – not much of a landmark in the history of European art – was specially praised in the justification for OUV, the thirteenth-century statue of Amida in the grounds of Kôtokuin temple – one of the most famous monumental sculptures of Buddhism – was not even mentioned. I think that such differences are difficult to explain other than in terms of the European lenses that much ICOMOS personnel are wearing.

As with applying truly universal standards, ICOMOS also has trouble remaining consistent over time. A series of five hill forts in Rajasthan nominated by India was recommended for non-inscription in 2012. According to the ICOMOS evaluation

(ICOMOS 2012: 121–134), the comparative analysis had neither demonstrated that these five were the best of their kind in that region nor that they were on a par with fortresses already inscribed on the World Heritage List. Serious problems of integrity (i.e. physical completeness) and authenticity were cited, and only a combined series of different types of Rajput forts (including water, forest, and desert forts) was deemed to stand a chance, if at all. In the general mood of ignoring the spoilsports, the Committee overrode the recommendation and decided for a referral, meaning that the revised nomination could come back to the 2013 session. Except for the addition of Jaisalmer Fort, the series was unchanged, and the new ICOMOS evaluation (ICOMOS 2013a: 22–35) voices the same concerns about the comparative analysis and the integrity and authenticity of the forts. Yet the conclusions are entirely different: integrity and authenticity are found to be sufficient now, with OUV being present for two of the three nominated criteria, and the recommendation is for inscription. Perhaps the verdict was formulated in anticipation of the inevitable: India was a (very vocal) Committee member, and a referral decision as passed by the Committee in the preceding year is usually taken to mean that the OUV of the candidate has been demonstrated so that in the new climate, a referral recommendation would have been overruled in any event. And indeed, the justification for the OUV criteria in the evaluation does not read as overly enthusiastic, suggesting what could have been internal divisions, with the Panel changing the Advisors' recommended decision but not bothering to revise the text. Yet still, ICOMOS has been steadfast in its opposition towards other re-nominated candidates, so the complete turnaround in this case – from outright rejection to unconditional support within a single year – finds no explanation.

All this is not to deny ICOMOS a universalist commitment, but, rather, to state the obvious: namely, that the represented nationalities and background disciplines – when conservation architects deliberate about sacred groves in Kenya or stone money sites on Yap – must constrain an organization's perspective. And when following the evaluations over the years, ICOMOS's judgements appear anything other than cast in stone, a fact that cannot escape the regular participants' attention.

SENSING AND BELIEVING IN OUV

But why does all this not lead participants in the World Heritage arena to the obvious conclusion – namely, that the emperor has no clothes and that conceptions of OUV and the set of sites deemed to display this elusive quality are products of sociohistorical processes driven by positioned interests and, to that extent, arbitrary? I think this is because most participants have not discarded the idea that OUV is intrinsic, whatever fallacies the evaluation and decision process might have. I am still struggling to find the reasons and have several hunches. For one thing, ICOMOS continues to be dominated by people with backgrounds in art history and architecture, disciplines that are perhaps more used to subjective but nonetheless authoritative judgements and to ideas of the intrinsic value of artistic masterpieces than other fields. This particularly applies to beauty, the silent guest at the World Heritage table: the ICOMOS and also the IUCN evaluations try to avoid aesthetic judgements since they are believed to be subjective, but, in my observation, it is often the aesthetic appeal of a site – brought in when the Advisory Bodies make their initial Powerpoint presentations – that gives their experts certainty and also encourages unspecialized delegates to make apodictic statements about the OUV of a site.

But a belief in intrinsic OUV also extends to the critics of the recent shift in Committee decision-making. When conversations and interviews turned to this point, such informants invariably began to enumerate examples such as Chichén Itzá, Yellowstone, the Mezquita of Cordoba, or the early List inscriptions in general to show that some sites indeed are outstanding beyond reasonable doubt, whatever else a questionable process might wash onto the List now. The intensional or ostentative definition is there again, but only for part of what is on the List, not its entirety. And should the Committee only return to focus on OUV, these critics often continue, all the current problems would simply fall away (rather than start, from having to work with a nebulous quality). In the assumption that these "wow sites" will simply blow away everyone who sees them, OUV transforms itself into something that, while not amenable to objectification, can nevertheless be sensed.

My favourite example of such thinking is a senior ICOMOS office-holder present at many recent meetings. He talked about the United Kingdom's revised nomination of "Darwin's Landscape Laboratory" – that is, the house in which the great naturalist passed his later life and the surrounding landscape in which he made many of his path-breaking observations. As in 2007, when the nomination had first been submitted (and then withdrawn before the session), ICOMOS recommended non-inscription since the house was massively restored and therefore inauthentic, and since the landscape, while deliberately chosen by Darwin for its specific natural features, bore no physical traces of his activities. In line with some (but not all) previous decisions, ICOMOS thus insisted that the World Heritage List is about the OUV of sites, not of famous people, and that the "Napoleon slept here" type of heritage is excluded. This was controversially debated in the 2010 session and, in the general spirit of catering to national wishes, the Committee deferred the nomination so that its future return remains a possibility. When the office-holder went for a family holiday to England, he thus decided to put the site on his itinerary. He was relieved – he told me – that upon visiting the house with the little museum, he *felt* that there was no OUV, something he texted immediately to other ICOMOS and IUCN officials involved in the process.

I have some affection for the fact that people as fully aware of all the shady sides of the World Heritage process as this informant still believe in the poetry of places (or lack thereof) that is accessible to direct, unmediated experience. And this is, after all, the promise that the World Heritage title also holds for tourists, who likewise hope to be overwhelmed when visiting something that is on the list of glory. If the myth of immediately perceptible site magic were gone, I think this would harm the World Heritage endeavour more than the current inconsistencies and suspicions of arbitrariness. After almost forty years of trying to grasp what its judgements are based on, the ultimate reliance on sensing OUV may appear regressive, but a value that is so intrinsic and complex as to defy objectification and measurement is perhaps the most outstanding of all.[13]

CONCLUSION

Particularly when applied to cultural heritage, the notion of an intrinsic "outstanding universal value" of heritage sites will strike most anthropologists as rather absurd. How could any such claim be more than a subjective reflection of positioned interests and of particular professional and disciplinary biases? But even when working from questionable premises, many would – in the age of indicators – probably still expect the UNESCO World Heritage institutions to describe and then find this elusive "OUV" in a more systematic, better theorized, and less improvised way than they actually do. For one thing, this is a lesson in power politics: when the interests of most of the crucial actors – the states currently serving on the World Heritage Committee – converge, this is a strong incentive to simply create the desired facts by consensual agreement, no matter if those deemed more knowledgeable about the subject matter disagree. The operations of agencies in the UN system are full of such political facts, often of a much more obviously constructed nature, and, often enough, the acceptance of such "facts" allows them to continue their work, producing certainty where there would be none otherwise (see the Introduction). And so it happens in the World Heritage arena where a vague

---

[13] The *degree* to which OUV must be present in a given World Heritage site is also barely theorized. Sometimes, OUV appears to be seen as a continuous quality rather than either fully present or fully absent, such as when the conservation reports of ICOMOS and IUCN speak of the OUV of a property as being "degraded" by such factors as lack of maintenance, new construction, etc. One ICOMOS official I interviewed was struck by how in the debate about deleting the Arabian Oryx Sanctuary in Oman from the World Heritage List in 2007 – oil prospecting had destroyed the nature reserve, and the remaining oryx antelopes had been taken to zoos – delegates were striving to find at least some traces of OUV left somewhere in the site. To her ears, this sounded as if, upon inscription, the sites were awarded a vessel with OUV liquid which they then either preserve or use up. But, in general, OUV appears to be imagined as evenly distributed throughout the property, even when it is a large site such as a cultural landscape or a so-called serial property consisting of two or more discrete components. This is at least the general ICOMOS and IUCN line in the many Committee debates where delegates try to excuse deficiencies of specific site components or partial damages: the new bridge built against Committee advice in the Dresden Elbe Valley led to the deletion of the entire cultural landscape of more than 20 kilometres in length from the List in 2009 – the last "strict" session – even when the bridge is visible from only part of it. This means that OUV is either fully there or not at all, and, contrary to most other values, there cannot be a little more or a little less of it.

definition of the threshold increases the argumentative leeway to push questionable candidates onto the List.

Yet without the widespread conviction that at least some World Heritage sites are great beyond question, transcending all cultural biases, and that such greatness can be experienced by everyone – even if not properly put into words or indicators – I think the system could not be sustained. To a certain degree, this may be true for all systems of cultural heritage designation, but when comparing the World Heritage system with what Natalie Heinich has described for the French national *Inventaire* (2009), I still think that the mythical element is significantly stronger on the world level. Maybe the UN system is more in need of myths, having so few tools of a more substantive nature to do its work, and maybe the world must be enchanted and hold the promise of greatness to remain bearable.

So is the UNESCO World Heritage Committee a palace of hope in the way outlined in the Introduction? It certainly has become much less likely to destroy the hopes of people who have invested years of work into a nomination. Conservation in some sites has indeed been boosted, and it has been claimed that the World Heritage arena performs many of its routine functions in an unobjectionable way (Terrill 2014). But the number of knowledgeable participants who would qualify the arena as a reason for hope rather than for concern or cynicism has certainly decreased. What the World Heritage system appears to accomplish through the List, however, is that the entire world becomes a palace of hope, with the World Heritage properties as its furniture. Some of the latter may be bad taste, fake, or clumsily repaired, but there are real gems among it whose value cannot escape even the most undiscerning eye. In the imagined world palace, these gems keep up the vague hope that beyond all that divides us, there are some things in whose appreciation and for whose care we can finally be united.

REFERENCES

Badman, Tim, et al. 2008 Outstanding Universal Value: Standards for Natural World Heritage. Gland, Switzerland: IUCN. https://portals.iucn.org/library/efiles/documents/2008-036.pdf.

Batisse, Michel, and Gérard Bolla 2005 *The Invention of 'World Heritage'*. Paris: Association of Former UNESCO Staff Members.

Brumann, Christoph 2012 Multilateral Ethnography: Entering the World Heritage Arena. Max Planck Institute for Social Anthropology Working Papers 136. http://www.eth.mpg.de/cms/en/publications/working_papers/wp0136.

——— 2014 'Shifting Tides of World-Making in the UNESCO World Heritage Convention: Cosmopolitanisms Colliding'. *Ethnic and Racial Studies* 37(12): 2176–2192.

——— 2016 'Imagining the Ground from Afar: Why the Sites Are So Remote in World Heritage Committee Sessions'. In *World Heritage on the Ground: Ethnographic Perspectives*. C. Brumann and D. Berliner, eds. Oxford: Berghahn, pp. 294–317.

Claudi, Ida Breckan 2011 The New Kids on the Block: Brics in the World Heritage Committee. MA thesis, University of Oslo.

Gfeller, Aurélie Elisa 2013 'Negotiating the Meaning of Global Heritage: "Cultural Landscapes" in the UNESCO World Heritage Convention, 1972–1992'. *Journal of Global History* 8(3): 483–503.

2015 'Anthropologizing and Indigenizing Heritage: The Origins of the UNESCO Global Strategy for a Representative'. *Balanced and Credible World Heritage List. Journal of Social Archaeology* 15(3): 366–386.

n.d. The Geography of Global Cultural Norms: The Authenticity of Cultural Heritage from Venice to Nara, 1964–1994. Unpublished ms.

Hassan, Fekri 2007 'The Aswan High Dam and the International Rescue Nubia Campaign'. *African Archaeological Review* 24(3): 73–94.

Heinich, Nathalie 2009 *La fabrique du patrimoine: De la cathédrale à la petite cuillère*. Paris: Maison des sciences de l'homme.

Höhler, Sabine 2014 'Exterritoriale Ressourcen: Die Diskussion um die Tiefsee, die Pole und das Weltall um 1970'. In *Global Commons im 20. Jahrhundert: Entwürfe für eine globale Welt*. I. Löhr and A. Rehling, eds. Berlin: de Gruyter, pp. 53–82.

ICOMOS 2004 *The World Heritage List: Filling the Gaps – An Action Plan for the Future*. Paris: ICOMOS. whc.unesco.org/document/102409.

2012 Evaluations of Nominations of Cultural and Mixed Properties to the World Heritage List: Icomos Report for the World Heritage Committee, 36th Ordinary Session, Saint Petersburg, June–July 2012. http://whc.unesco.org/document/116681.

2013a Addendum: Evaluations of Nominations of Cultural and Mixed Properties to the World Heritage List: Icomos Report for the World Heritage Committee, 37th Ordinary Session, Phnom Penh, June 2013. http://whc.unesco.org/document/123033.

2013b Evaluations of Nominations of Cultural and Mixed Properties to the World Heritage List: Icomos Report for the World Heritage Committee, 37th Ordinary Session, Phnom Penh, June 2013. http://whc.unesco.org/document/122862.

2014 Icomos News: Icomos World Heritage Panel 2014. http://www.icomos.org/images/DOCUMENTS/World_Heritage/ICOMOS_World_Heritage_Panel_2014.pdf.

Jokilehto, Jukka 2006 *What Is OUV? Defining the Outstanding Universal Value of Cultural World Heritage Properties*. Berlin: Bäßler Verlag.

June, Raymond, and Janine Wedel 2010 'The Avalanche of Indicators in Global Governance: Implications for the Anthropology of Policy'. *Anthropology News* 51(7): 25–26.

Marcus, George E. June, Raymond, and Janine Wedel 1995 'Ethnography in/of the World System: The Emergence of Multi-Sited Ethnography'. *Annual Review of Anthropology* 24: 95–117.

Meskell, Lynn 2013 'UNESCO's World Heritage Convention at 40: Challenging the Economic and Political Order of International Heritage Conservation'. *Current Anthropology* 54(4): 483–494.

2014 'States of Conservation: Protection'. *Politics, and Pacting within UNESCO's World Heritage Committee. Anthropological Quarterly* 87(1): 217–244.

2015 'Transacting UNESCO World Heritage: Gifts and Exchanges on a Global Stage'. *Social Anthropology* 23(1): 3–21.

Mitchell, Nora, Mechtild Rössler, and Pierre-Marie Tricaud, eds. 2009 *World Heritage Cultural Landscapes: A Handbook for Conservation and Management*. Paris: UNESCO.

Rehling, Andrea, and Isabella Löhr 2014 '"Governing the Commons": Die global commons und das Erbe der Menschheit im 20. Jahrhundert'. In *Global Commons im 20. Jahrhundert: Entwürfe für eine globale Welt*. I. Löhr and A. Rehling, eds. Berlin: de Gruyter, pp. 3–32.

Rössler, Mechtild 2006 'World Heritage Cultural Landscapes: A UNESCO Flagship Programme 1992–2006'. *Landscape Research* 31(4): 333–353.

Stott, Peter H. 2011 'The World Heritage Convention and the National Park Service, 1962–1972'. *The George White Forum* 28(3): 279–290.

Terrill, Greg 2014 'Politics before Lunch? A Morning's Work by the World Heritage Committee'. *Historic Environment* 26(2): 24–36.

Titchen, Sarah M. 1995 On the Construction of Outstanding Universal Value: UNESCO's World Heritage Convention (Convention Concerning the Protection of the World Cultural and Natural Heritage, 1972) and the Identification and Assessment of Cultural Places for Inclusion in the World Heritage List. PhD dissertation, Australian National University.

UNESCO 2011 Preparing World Heritage Nominations. Paris: UNESCO. http://whc.unesco.org/uploads/activities/documents/activity-643-1.pdf.

Wolfrum, Rüdiger 2009 Common Heritage of Mankind. In *Max Planck Encyclopedia of Public International Law*. R. Wolfrum, ed. www.mpepil.com.

12

Propaganda on Trial: Structural Fragility and the Epistemology of International Legal Institutions

Richard Ashby Wilson

INTRODUCTION

From the first stirrings of anthropology as a discipline in the nineteenth century, anthropologists have been concerned with knowledge systems for making sense of the material object and social worlds – in short, the epistemology of the population they are studying. At the heart of any system of knowledge are ideas of cause and effect, and twentieth-century social anthropology was characterized by a tendency to relativize theories of causation. Perhaps the epitome of this trend was Evans-Pritchard's *Witchcraft Among the Azande*, but the predisposition toward subjecting scientific ideas of causation to the relativizing gaze continued in recent anthropological studies of science and biomedicine (see Franklin 2003). Legal anthropology has always been attentive to the unique rules of evidence and procedure that make criminal and torts law a specialized system of knowledge whose ultimate aim is to determine causation. Without reliable tests for cause and effect, a court cannot perform its most basic functions – namely, to attribute responsibility, punish the wrongdoer, or provide remedy for the plaintiff.

More recently, anthropologists have detailed "how law knows" in a variety of legal settings, in part as a result of their own participation as expert witnesses. Appearing as an expert in dozens of British immigration court cases, Anthony Good (2007) provides rich material on the divergences between anthropological and legal understandings, in large part as the result of their distinctive ways of handling causation. Good reminds us that, "For lawyers ... an event's cause is inseparable from allocation of responsibility for it" (p. 30). These insights from legal anthropology have been recently transposed from the domestic to the international setting of criminal tribunals, many of them founded inside the United Nations system. The methods by which international criminal courts come to comprehend and adjudicate armed conflict have come under increased scrutiny from anthropologists such as Anders (2014), Clarke (2009), Eltringham (2013) and Wilson (2011). Wilson's book on historical debates in international criminal trials (2011) documented how prosecutors called historians as experts to build their case that there existed a longstanding animus toward opposing religious or national groups and prove genocidal *mens rea* (criminal intention). Defense attorneys turn to historical arguments about the origins and causes of a conflict to mount a *tu quoque* defense that conjures up a litany of previous atrocities. Instead of construing law and history as two incommensurable epistemological systems, Wilson argued that we might be better off understanding how the parties to the trial advance concrete legal strategies using expert witness testimony.

Similarly, Gerhard Anders (2014) analyzed the role of two anthropologists (Danny Hoffman and Dorte Thorsen) who appeared as expert witnesses at the Special Court for Sierra Leone. They were called by the defense to rebut the expert reports of the prosecution from a British military officer and Sierra Leonean civil rights activist. The anthropologists' testimony assisted the defense's claim that the prosecution experts were overly universalistic and simplistic in their claims about certain local cultural practices, namely the organization of *kamajor* hunting groups and forced marriages. The bench rejected the anthropologists' thick descriptions of everyday practices and their efforts to challenge both universalistic legal categories as well as what they saw as the anecdotal and sloppy nature of the prosecution experts' methodology. The judges were unconcerned by the fact that the military expert had only interviewed nine local sources during a fourteen-day stay in the country, or the fact that the civil rights activist had formulated his conclusions on the basis of his past experience rather than a systematic study. From this case at the Special Court for Sierra Leone, one could draw a set of conclusions about legal epistemology and about the narrow confines of what international criminal law considers "context," as well as how criminal courts value an expert's experiential knowledge, seemingly regardless of the methodological rigor of his or her study.

This chapter examines a precedent-setting "propaganda trial" at an international criminal tribunal established in 1993 under the auspices of the United Nations Security Council. Its central question is: how do international criminal prosecutors seek to demonstrate beyond a reasonable doubt that there exists a causal connection between a public speech and a set of subsequent crimes? In answering, we need to examine the prosecutors' case theory and the ways that they marshaled evidence for causation. Our case study is the trial of Serbian political leader Vojislav Šešelj at the International Criminal Tribunal for the Former Yugoslavia in The Hague (ICTY). Prosecutors, judges and defense counsel refer to the Šešelj case as the only clear-cut "propaganda trial" at the Tribunal, and they often equate it to the "Media Trial" (*Nahimana*) at the International Criminal Tribunal for Rwanda (ICTR).[1]

As we will see, proving that a leader's public utterances prompted his followers to murder and deport members of other national, religious, ethnic, or racial groups is an arduous undertaking, for reasons of both law and logistics. Even though there may

---

[1] While there might arguably be some ICTY antecedents such as Brđanin, Gvero, Krajisnik, Kordić and Čerkez, none had the prominence of the Šešelj case, nor the reliance on evidence of speeches to prove the charges against the defendant.

exist a surfeit of evidence of *mens rea* (criminal intention) against political leaders who mobilize their base through public expressions of discriminatory animus against the out-group, there is often very little in the way of evidence of *actus reus* (the wrongful act) and what prosecutors call "linkage evidence" that connects the accused to the actual crimes committed. Political leaders in conflict situations, including the most ostensibly irresponsible of demagogues, generally steer clear of issuing direct orders for, or participating in, physical acts of violence. Leaders such as Šešelj are seldom accused of materially perpetrating murder, torture, or other offenses beyond the use of their words to instigate and encourage their followers, who may only loosely be described as their "subordinates."

The "legal realist" approach adopted here highlights the strategies of legal actors and the structural conditions in which international tribunals operate, rather than formal legal doctrine. The material for this chapter is based on my review of the indictment, trial transcripts, exhibits and briefs submitted by the prosecution, as well as interviews with many of the main protagonists in the trial, including six members of the prosecution team, three judges and two prosecution expert witnesses. From these qualitative interviews, I developed a sense of a structured field of knowledge and action in which a variety of tactics are possible, rather than a monolithic and deterministic system of international criminal law doctrine. The strategies of prosecutors unfolded contingently throughout the trial, illustrating the balance between the volition of the agents and the structural constraints on their exercise of agency.

THE HISTORY AND STRUCTURE OF THE INTERNATIONAL CRIMINAL TRIBUNAL FOR THE FORMER YUGOSLAVIA

The ICTY and ICTR were established in the early 1990s in a unique conjuncture in international politics. As the Soviet Union disintegrated and its client regimes in eastern Europe were replaced by elected governments, many politicians and commentators lauded the triumph of liberal democracy and foretold a new era of peace and prosperity. Liberal exuberance receded rapidly with the Gulf War in 1991 and the onset of ethno-nationalist conflicts in Yugoslavia in 1991 and Rwanda in 1994. Even though the end of the Cold War did not augur an era of international peace, for a decade the United Nations Security Council was less characterized by stalemate and deadlock, allowing a consensus to coalesce around the creation of new international justice institutions.

Despite the many violations of international humanitarian law during the Cold War, it was not until after 1989 that the UN Security Council invoked Chapter VII of the UN Charter and established international courts to hold senior officials accountable for crimes committed within their sovereign territories. The ICTY and ICTR were both founded as temporary, ad hoc international tribunals to prosecute violations of international humanitarian law committed over a defined time period in one country or set of countries. Envisaged as short-lived courts that would prosecute a handful of symbolic cases, they have endured for more than two decades.

The ICTY was established by the UN Security Council in May 1993, two years after the Balkans conflagration began, after Croatia had fought a war of secession from the Socialist Federal Republic of Yugoslavia, and at the height of the armed conflict in Bosnia. The three European countries with greatest military capacity – Britain, France and Germany – were unwilling to intervene militarily to end the bloodshed. The tribunal was seen by many observers as a token effort on the part of the United States and Europe to assuage their guilt for standing by while innocent civilians were slaughtered in their tens of thousands on European soil. It was initially funded on a shoestring budget by the UN and received a financial lifeline from the US State Department, private foundations such as the Open Society Institute, and the European Union.

In the early years, the Tribunal proceeded at a sluggish pace, with few indictments, arrests, or trials. The first convictions were four years in coming, and these concerned low- or middle-ranking defendants; the ICTY and ICTR came under pressure from the UN Security Council to speed up the trials. However, once the indictments issued by the Tribunal (161 in total) started accumulating, the ICTY became more effective. A number of high-level perpetrators were arrested and convicted. General Radislav Krstić was found guilty of committing genocide at Srebrenica in 1995, a conviction that was reduced on appeal to aiding and abetting genocide. The trial of the most high-profile defendant, former Yugoslav President Slobodan Milošević, was an unmitigated disaster, dragging on for over four years and ending in his death in 2006, only weeks before his judgment and sentence was due to be delivered.[2] Subsequent trials of senior leaders from all sides in the conflict proved more procedurally effectual, and the budget from the United Nations Security Council swelled to more than US$350 million at its peak.[3] At the time of writing, only a handful of trials are still ongoing. They happen to be among the most important trials of all, as they include former Vice-President of Serbia, Vojislav Šešelj, Bosnian Serb President, Radovan Karadžić, and the Commander of the Bosnian Serb army (VRS), General Ratko Mladić. The latter two accused are charged with committing genocide in Bosnia. An overall assessment of the ICTY's accomplishments must wait until after this final round of trials is concluded.

The aim of this chapter is to understand how an international legal institution established under the auspices of the UN Security Council came to comprehend and adjudicate acts of violence committed in an armed conflict. Given that the ICTY was the first truly international court, it immediately faced the problem of

---

[2] See Boas (2007) on the Milošević trial.
[3] "Budget Committee Takes Up Proposed 2010–2011 Financing for International Criminal Tribunals for Rwanda, Former Yugoslavia." Sixty-fourth General Assembly, Fifth Committee, 19th Meeting, GA/AB/3936, December 10, 2009. www.un.org/press/en/2009/gaab3936.doc.htm. Accessed September 1, 2016.

what rules of procedure and evidence – and, indeed, body of law – it would use. Trials at the ICTY, like their Anglo-American common law counter-parts, are propelled by the adversarial process wherein the prosecution musters its best case against the accused on the basis of the available evidence, and the defense counsel contests every allegation it can. The legal process edged more toward a Continental civil law system as judges assumed more control over the scope and conduct of the trials. Its rules of procedure and evidence are not drawn entirely from either the Anglo-American system or the Continental system, and tribunal statements appropriately define the ICTY and ICTR as a "hybrid system."[4] Such hybridization, while understandable given the international nature of the ICTY, gives rise to uncertainty and unpredictability since it essentially creates a novel language of law that no one legal actors speaks fluently, at least at the outset. As a result, judges interpret their mandate and authority differently from one another, depending on their country of origin, and this can create turmoil and confusion in the courtroom.

The second structural feature of international courts that affects their investigative and adjudicative functions is that they are not constituted within the institutional framework of the nation-state. Therefore, they possess limited coercive capacity of their own, understood as an independent police force, prison system, and overarching ministry of criminal justice integrated into the legislative and executive branches. The courts have their own investigators, mostly former policemen who do not speak the local languages. The ICTY is sited outside of the countries where the crimes took place, and they must rely on the local nation-state for access to sites, witnesses, and documentary evidence. Positively, this means that the ICTY has not had to rely directly on the same institutional apparatus of the state that committed and/or condoned the mass violations to investigate and adjudicate the violations. Although international courts are administered by an international bureaucracy – and a highly politicized one, even – at least they are not subject to the bureaucracy of a nation-state with experience of administering criminal justice institutions.

United Nations tribunals are still, however, susceptible to political interference by nation-states, and they rely upon the benevolence of the UN Security Council to insist that recalcitrant states cooperate with investigations.[5] As ICTY Deputy Prosecutor David Tolbert admitted, "without state cooperation you can't conduct a proper trial; you can't conduct any trial at all." And states famously have not always cooperated. According to Carla Del Ponte (2008: 245), Croatian state civilian and military intelligence services tampered with evidence, intimidated witnesses, leaked to the press the names of protected prosecution witnesses, and helped indicted persons escape arrest, all the while assuring the international community that they were doing their utmost to assist the Tribunal. On occasion, the ICTY President

---

[4] ICTY Press Release. "Blaskic Case: Defense Objection to the Admission of Hearsay is Rejected." The Hague, January 23, 1998.
[5] On state interference, see Hazan (2004) and Peskin (2008), as well the memoir of ICTY prosecutor Carla Del Ponte (2008).

appealed directly to the UN Security Council and this resulted in greater state cooperation, but at other times the Security Council was slow to act or completely declined to act. There were also times when the Council acted but the local state actors successfully resisted international pressure. Croatia and Serbia in particular launched diplomatic counter-offensives to win over powerful allies on the UN Security Council, at which point the arrow of causation was reversed and the ICTY came under inordinate strain, with deleterious consequences for its independence and neutrality. A sea-change in state compliance with the ICTY came after 2003, when the European Union offered the carrot of accession to Croatia and Serbia, conditional on their cooperating with the Tribunal.

Both of these structural conditions – a hybrid legal model and a dependency on the United Nations and nation-states for key enforcement functions – have consequences for the type of knowledge about the armed conflict in the former Yugoslavia that has been produced at the ICTY. Epistemology is not, however, an epiphenomena of geo-politics and structural factors. Legal fact-finding is also embedded in internal legal procedures and the contingent and shifting assumptions, principles and strategies of the legal actors. Our analysis must hold both structure and agency in mind simultaneously to arrive at a comprehensive understanding of how international law knows what it claims to know.

INSTIGATING CRIMES AGAINST HUMANITY

Nobody cares about criminal law except theorists and habitual criminals.

Sir Henry Maine[6]

In 2007, the ICTY prosecutor indicted Vojislav Šešelj on nine counts of war crimes and crimes against humanity for acts committed between August 1991 and September 1993.[7] The indictment alleged that, acting individually or as part of a joint criminal enterprise with high-ranking Serb political and military leaders such as the late Serbia President Slobodan Milošević,[8] Vojislav Šešelj, "planned, ordered, instigated, committed or otherwise aided and abetted in the planning, preparation or execution" of crimes against humanity and war crimes that included persecutions, murder, sexual assaults, torture, deportation, and forcible transfer of Croats and Muslims.[9]

Compared with other cases at the Tribunal, the indictment was unusual in the degree to which the charges alleged indirect forms of participation that occurred at a distance from the actual crimes. The indictment largely conceived of the accused's

---

[6] Quoted in Dressler and Garvey (2012: 465).
[7] While the first indictment was issued in 2003, this discussion references the indictment used in the actual trial beginning in 2007, namely the Third Amended Indictment of December 2007.
[8] Third Amended Indictment of December 7, 2007, IT-03-67-T, (henceforth TAI), §8(a).
[9] TAI, Count 1, §15.

participation and criminal responsibility as vicarious – that is, as resulting from public speeches that prompted proxies to perpetrate the material crimes. "Instigating" and "aiding and abetting" in particular invoke vicarious forms of liability that allow the accused to be held responsible for crimes carried out by other perpetrators, often subordinates.[10] More than any other case, *Šešelj* foregrounds the form of criminal responsibility that most directly bears on the problem of causation in international speech crimes: instigating persecutions on political, racial or religious grounds (a crime against humanity).

The indictment defined "instigation" in the following way: "that the accused Vojislav Šešelj's speeches, communications, acts and/or omissions contributed to the perpetrators' decision to commit the crimes alleged."[11] More concretely, the indictment alleged that, "In public speeches Vojislav Šešelj called for the expulsion of Croat civilians from parts of the Vojvodina region in Serbia and thus instigated his followers and the local authorities to engage in a persecution campaign against the local Croat population."[12] Persecuting a civilian population and forcibly displacing civilians from a territory was a widespread and systematic practice used by all sides in the Balkans conflict of 1991–1995, a conflict that resurrected a disconcerting euphemism used in earlier conflicts: "ethnic cleansing."

One of the most notorious speeches the defendant gave in the Vojvodina region in northern Serbia was at an election rally in the small village of Hrtkovci on May 6, 1992. According to the prosecution, the speech allegedly triggered the ethnic cleansing of 700–800 Croats in the community of less than 2,000 persons. Indeed, it is fair to say that the speech at Hrtkovci is the heart of the prosecution case against Vojislav Šešelj, and Hrtkovci is mentioned 42 times in the indictment, more than any other "crime base" in the trial. Given the centrality of the May 6, 1992 Hrtkovci speech in the Šešelj trial, it is worth reproducing a passage from it here:

> In Hrtkovci ... there is no room for Croats ... [they] must clear out of Serbia ... Serbian refugees will move into their houses ... We have to give those Serbs a roof over their heads and feed the hungry mouths. We have no money to build new housing. We do not have the capacity to create new jobs for them. Very well, then, if we cannot do that, then we should give every Serbian family of refugees the address of one Croatian family. The police will give it to them, the police will do as the government decides, and soon we will be the government. Fine, then. Every Serbian family of refugees will come to a Croatian door and give the Croats they find there their address in Zagreb or other Croatian town. Oh, they will, they will. There will be enough buses, we will drive them to the border of Serbian territory and they can walk on from there, if they do not leave before of their own accord.[13]

---

[10] This statement also applies to the mode of liability of joint criminal enterprise, as the indictment makes clear: "Vojislav Šešelj is responsible for all the crimes the *actus reus* of which was carried out by a person used by him or any other participant in the joint criminal enterprise." TAI, §8(c).

[11] TAI, §5.

[12] TAI, §10(d).

[13] Prosecution's Closing Brief, IT-03-67-T, February 5, 2012 (hereafter Prosecution's Closing Brief), §496.

Šešelj's intentions are on full display here, as he transparently sanctions and encourages forced deportations. Šešelj declared that Croats "must clear out" and soon afterwards, in an atmosphere of extreme intimidation, they fled their homes. This speech was also given in a particularly violent context – the early phase of the deadliest armed conflict in Europe since the Second World War, a war that claimed approximately 130,000 lives.[14] The majority of the fatalities in this conflict were civilians who were murdered during forcible removals known as "ethnic cleansing." Given this context, and with such strong evidence of the defendant's intentionality to commit widespread and systematic crimes against a civilian population, it may seem that prosecutors had a straightforward task in convicting Šešelj of crimes against humanity and war crimes. This impression, however, is not widely held at the Tribunal. The Šešelj trial was generally viewed as one of the weakest cases against a political leader at the ICTY from an evidentiary point of view, and indeed, the prosecution case ultimately failed in the Trial Chamber. As noted previously, in most international trials, there is ample evidence of *actus reus*, and the primary responsibility of the prosecution is to prove that the defendant had knowledge of the intentions of the material perpetrators.

In the Šešelj trial, the challenge was the reverse: the prosecution possessed an abundance of evidence of discriminatory animus and *mens rea*. Šešelj openly used denigrating language toward Croats (against whom he often cast the ethnic slur "Ustaše" or "Ustashas")[15] and Muslims during the conflict, some of it openly encouraging *ex ante* or condoning *ex post facto* the persecution and deportation of non-Serb civilians, as in the paragraph from the Hrtkovci speech cited above. Throughout the trial, prosecutors turned the defendant's own words against him with great effect. During the prosecution's closing arguments, each assertion about the defendant's actions or intentions was accompanied by a ferocious and colorful proclamation from Šešelj that matched their claim.[16] The accused was even disposed to outbursts of ethno-nationalist hatred during the trial, for instance stating at one point in the proceedings, "As far as I am concerned, I really would like all Ustashas to be dead because Ustashas are such an evil, they are even worse than Hitler's Nazis."[17]

Moreover, the prosecution possessed ample material evidence of the *actus reus* of crimes against humanity and war crimes. During the period of the indictment

---

[14] The most widely accepted conservative estimate of deaths during the armed conflict come from demographers Tabeau and Bijak (2005: 207). Based upon voting registers and municipal and census records, they estimate 100,000 dead in Bosnia and Herzegovina alone (i.e., not including Croatia and Kosovo), with civilians making up the majority (54%) of the fatalities.

[15] Ustaše refers to members of the Croatian Revolutionary Movement, a fascist group that began in Croatia in the 1920s and established a pro-Nazi regime in Croatia during the Second World War. Since then, the term Ustaše has been used as an ethnic slur against Croats. Prosecutors cited the accused's use of this term in the Prosecution's Closing Brief at ¶51–53 and ¶162.

[16] See T.17143.

[17] T.16624, March 7, 2011.

(1991–1993), hundreds of non-Serbs had been murdered, ethnically cleansed, sexually assaulted, or tortured by self-styled ultra-nationalist followers of Šešelj. What the prosecutors struggled to find was what they called "linkage evidence": evidence that could connect the gushing firehose of Vojislav Šešelj's animus to the commission of concrete material crimes on the ground in Serbia. Did the defendant's obvious ill-will, malice and spite have verifiable consequences of a magnitude that would justify imposing criminal liability, or was it all just empty rhetoric, ethnically charged hot air of the kind that is commonplace in the Balkans, and indeed elsewhere (including the location of the trial, the Netherlands)?

Staff interviewed at international tribunals identified a generalized sense of doubt hanging over the category of speech crimes. I began nearly all of my interviews with the question, "Is this an unsettled area of law and is there is greater uncertainty in demonstrating speech crimes compared with war crimes and other crimes against humanity?" All the prosecutors and the majority of criminal defense attorneys and judges acknowledged that as a practical matter, there was less certainty in the law of speech crimes than say, murder as a war crime, and that the standard of proof for causation was less predictable. One prosecuting attorney maintained, as a general proposition, "It is very difficult to prove that this speech or broadcast led to these crimes."[18] Another prosecutor responded that the investigation and evidence gathering process is the same for all kinds of cases; however, as a practical matter it is more difficult to persuade the judges: "When we speak about speech crimes, we have to recognize that this is an unsettled and new area of law. We prosecutors are learning about what we need to prove the crimes and what elements of the OTP [Office of the Prosecutor] case the judges will accept."[19]

Prosecutors' observations were largely borne out in my interviews with judges. When asked, "Is a speech act like other acts when determining causality?" one international criminal tribunal judge replied: "It is similar to other acts, but the quest to establish a causal relationship might be a bit more abstract. I have concrete things to consider if a person drives their car erratically and causes a crash. It's all concrete – the speed of the car, its direction and so on. I don't have to fill in the gaps. Whether a speech act is causal or not is mainly an evidentiary problem ... the problem with speech is that its effects are difficult to measure, they're not usually visible. Whereas if I hit a table with a hammer [pounds the table], it leaves a mark."[20] There is also uncertainty regarding where prosecution must begin its case: with causation and *actus reus*, as is customarily the case, or with intention, as the judge cited a moment ago explained, when answering my question, "how do judges determine whether a speech instigated a crime?"

---

[18] Author interview, 2013.
[19] Author interview, 2013.
[20] Author interview, 2013.

If we start with the speech, then we get a different answer than if we start with the crime committed. If we start with the crime, then we look at the criminal act and work outwards to other factors, we need to commence with the intention to commit the crime and ask, did the speech add to this? Which is different from a monocausal approach that starts with the speech and asks was it the causal act, did this speech cause the crime to happen and without the speech would it not have happened? It is difficult to isolate the speech as the main or primary cause.[21]

Given the precedent-setting nature of the Šešelj trial, and the uncertainty surrounding the status of the evidence and the variety of judicial approaches to proving causation beyond a reasonable doubt, speech crimes cases emerge as among the most demanding cases facing prosecutors at international criminal tribunals. When the integrity of the legal process is undermined at every step by a filibustering defendant who enjoys uncommon tolerance from the presiding judge, the task only gets more arduous, as we will see.

CIRQUE DU ŠEŠELJ

Propaganda is based on the fact that the vast majority of people are naturally ready to believe indiscriminately in everything they read, hear, or see on television.

Vojislav Šešelj[22]

Vojislav Šešelj's long and winding path to the dock at the International Tribunal for the Former Yugoslavia in The Hague began in 1954 in Sarajevo, Bosnia-Hercegovina, then part of the Socialist Federal Republic of Yugoslavia. Without romanticizing the era, Sarajevo was at that time a multicultural city where Croats, Muslims and Serbs mixed relatively freely. They intermarried, worked together and mostly got along without a pronounced sense of political identity based upon religion or national group (Bringa 1995).

A talented doctoral student in political science, Šešelj became one of youngest faculty members at Sarajevo University in 1981. Although initially a communist, he developed close relations with Serb nationalists at the university. His promising academic career was derailed when he was convicted by a Sarajevo court in 1984 of "counter-revolutionary activities." Upon his release from nearly two years in jail, he moved to Belgrade and intensified his involvement in nationalist circles. Šešelj gravitated to the "Chetniks," a group of Serbian nationalists that in the Second World War waged a brutal campaign against Josip Broz, Tito's communist partisans, and at various points the Chetniks both resisted and collaborated with the occupying Germans. In 1990, having received the endorsement of the elder statesmen of Serbian nationalism, Šešelj founded his own proto-political party, the "Serbian

---

[21] Author interview, 2013.
[22] Exhibit P1337, referred to in the Prosecution's closing arguments on March 5, 2012 (T.17157).

Chetnik Movement" (SCP). In 1991, as the communist one-party system disintegrated in Yugoslavia, he founded a far-right nationalist party, the Serbian Radical Party (SRS)[23] and was elected a member of the Assembly of the Republic of Serbia. At that point, the SRS only had one Member of Parliament, Vojislav Šešelj, who was still a relatively marginal political figure. Šešelj vaulted to political prominence during the 1991–1995 armed conflict in Yugoslavia, as the state media under the control of President Slobodan Milošević tapped into the popular appeal of nationalism and elevated Šešelj's status and visibility. The SRS's radical ethno-nationalist platform both created and gave voice to a growing constituency of Serbs who were alarmed by the disintegration of Yugoslavia, a state that they had dominated for much of the twentieth century. In the general election of December 1992, Šešelj's party took 73 seats out of 250 and become the second largest parliamentary party.[24] Radical nationalists projected a vision of power and nationalist pride, promising to seize territory and protect the rights of Serb minorities, reviving the nineteenth-century idea of a state that included all Serbs, or a "Greater Serbia."[25] To achieve this state encompassing all Serbs, many Chetniks advocated war against Serbia's "historic enemies"[26] – namely, the Croat, Muslim and Albanian populations within the former Yugoslavia.

As the armed conflict intensified, Šešelj proved an effective mobilizer of volunteers for the Serbian war effort. Šešelj inspired 30,000 Chetnik volunteers called the "Šešeljevci," or "Šešelj's Men," who were attached to various military and paramilitary units.[27] "Šešelj's Men" were notorious across eastern Croatia and Bosnia, murdering, sexually assaulting, robbing and torturing Croat and Muslim civilians. Šešelj himself simultaneously condoned and disavowed the Šešeljevci and studiously kept his position of authority and military command responsibility ambiguous. Despite the fact that his followers revered him as the anointed "Vojvoda" – meaning "Duke" or supreme Chetnik military and political leader[28] – the prosecution acknowledged that this title did not denote any official rank in the Yugoslav National Army (JNA) or Bosnian Serb Army (VRS),[29] and that Šešelj himself did not exercise conventional command responsibility over the men who acted in his name.[30] At the same time, the

[23] The SRS incorporated the pre-existing SCP into its party structure.
[24] http://en.wikipedia.org/wiki/Serbian_general_election,_1992.
[25] "Greater Serbia" is an imagined territorial aspiration for a Serbian state that encompasses all territories inhabited by Serbs. It is conventionally traced back to articulations of Serb nationalism in the mid-nineteenth century in founding documents such as the Načertanije ("Program" or "Principles"), produced in 1844 by the Serb Minister for Internal Affairs, Ilija Garašanin.
[26] TAI, §4.
[27] T.17185, March 6, 2012.
[28] "Vojvoda" is a military title traditionally conferred by Momcilo Djujić, the Second World War Chetnik leader. Šešelj was named Vojvoda in 1989, and the discussion of the significance of this during the trial can be found at T.17122, March 5, 2012.
[29] See the testimony of prosecution expert witness Theunens, February 19, 2008, T. 3815.
[30] "Prosecutors Seek 28-Year Jail term for Šešelj." Rachel Irwin. Institute for War and Peace Reporting. March 9, 2012. http://iwpr.net/report-news/prosecutors-seek-28-year-jail-term-seselj. Accessed September 1, 2016.

prosecution team reiterated that "Šešelj exercised ideological and moral authority over the Šešeljevci sent to the front by his politico-military organization."[31]

By 2000, the Balkans wars had ended, with mixed results for the nationalist proponents of Greater Serbia. Šešelj seemed washed up. He was out of government and his party clung to a few seats in the Serb Assembly. He voluntarily surrendered in 2003 after being indicted that year by prosecutors at the ICTY. The actual trial did not begin until late 2007, after a prolonged period of obstructionism by Šešelj, who engaged in hunger strikes and filed frivolous motions to disqualify prosecutors and judges on grounds of bias and ethics violations.[32] Even after the official trial got formally underway, the defendant was convicted three times for contempt of court and sentenced to more than four years for revealing the identities of protected witnesses. After the formal legal proceedings ended, one of the judges in the trial, Danish Judge Frederik Harhoff, was disqualified and removed in August 2013 for demonstrating "an unacceptable appearance of bias in favour of conviction."[33] Termed a "series of unfolding disasters" by one legal analyst,[34] the trial dragged on for nine years, making it the longest running trial in war crimes history. The Tribunal released the defendant on compassionate and medical grounds in early 2015, and he returned to Belgrade to give literally incendiary press conferences in which he burned the US and Croatian flags.

The trial is a classic illustration of the pitfalls of self-representation by a high-level defendant, especially one as talented at the art of *defense de rupture* as Vojislav Šešelj.[35] The courtroom mayhem could have been anticipated, given that Šešelj had made his attitude toward the Tribunal abundantly clear when he turned himself in: "With their stupid charges against me they have come up against the greatest living Serb legal mind. I shall blast them to pieces."[36] The accused was unfailingly boorish, constantly playing to his supporters back in Serbia and seizing any opportunity to make a mockery of the courtroom. In his cross-examination of prosecution witnesses, Šešelj was abusive and bullying: he regularly questioned their intelligence,[37] called them liars,[38] and accused them of being agents or plants of the Croatian intelligence service.[39]

---

[31] Prosecution's Closing Brief, §593.
[32] These claims were investigated and dismissed by the Tribunal.
[33] ICTY Press release "Judge Harhoff disqualified from Šešelj case." The Hague, August 29, 2013. www.icty.org/sid/11357. Accessed September 1, 2016.
[34] Marko Milanović, quoted in, "In Releasing Seselj, ICTY Solves One Problem – But Creates Many Others." Daisy Sindelar. November 20, 2014.
[35] "Defense de rupture" is a term coined by the flamboyant French criminal defense attorney Jacques Vergès to refer to his style of upending courtroom conventions.
[36] "Vojislav Šešelj: Fallen Leader of Great Serbia." Manja Ristic. *Balkan Transitional Justice*. March 15, 2012. www.balkaninsight.com/en/article/vojislav-seselj-fallen-leader-of-the-great-serbia. Accessed September 1, 2016.
[37] T.2148, December 12, 2007.
[38] T.2164, December 13, 2007.
[39] "Besmirching the Witness," *Sense Tribunal*, October 15, 2008. www.sense-agency.com/icty/besmirching-the-witness.29.html?cat_id=1&news_id=10977. Accessed Sept. 1, 2016.

Šešelj was not just any ordinary and irascible self-representing defendant. His behavior regularly went well beyond the pale of acceptable courtroom conduct and into terrain that was truly toxic. He brow-beat the senior trial attorney Christina Dahl to the point where she appealed to the presiding judge for his protection, as the defendant was threatening her and she felt like a battered woman.[40] Šešelj took advantage of the platform of the Tribunal to engage in vicious outbursts against Croats, Muslims, and Albanians, and to countenance violence against Albanians as Kosovo gained independence from Serbia: "Now, we are going to have big flows of blood, rivers of blood on account of Albanians. If they take Kosovo away from us now, blood is going to flow in streams, for hundreds of centuries."[41]

With a defendant this disorderly, the situation needed a presiding judge in firm control of his or her courtroom. No observer has ever described Presiding Judge Jean-Claude Antonetti in such terms, and many have evaluated his performance harshly, with legal analyst Marko Milanović writing that, "The trial itself has truly devolved into a travesty, with the presiding judge in particular showing an incredible lack of ability to manage the self-representing Šešelj."[42] Indeed, Judge Antonetti sat silently during the outburst above. Throughout the trial, he appeared to be unable or unwilling to rein in the excesses of the defendant. He allowed Šešelj to disrupt the proceedings at will, and, in the eyes of a number of commentators, the defendant was allowed to essentially run his own trial (see Zahar 2008: 241; Sluiter 2007: 529).

Between the extraordinary length of the trial, the disruptions of the defendant, the removal of one judge for bias and the dereliction of duty on the part of the presiding judge, it is more than likely that the case would have been ruled a mistrial in many municipal jurisdictions. At the very least, the procedural irregularities in the trial ought to be cause for concern for anyone who aspires to fair procedure and due process in international law. Having said that, the case is still an instructive one, since thus far it is one of the best illustrations we have of how international prosecutors construct a case against a political leader for instigating his followers to persecute civilians. It underscores the special challenges of such an undertaking, and offers lessons of both a practical-legal and theoretical kind.

THE PROSECUTION CASE AGAINST VOJISLAV ŠEŠELJ

Some people need no encouragement to go out and commit crimes, some need only a little encouragement, but most people require a lot of encouragement, and propaganda does this.

ICTY Prosecuting Attorney[43]

---

[40] T.2143, December 12, 2007.
[41] T.2133, December 12, 2007. Kosovo gained independence from Serbia the following year (2008).
[42] Marko Milanovic. "ICTY Trial Chamber Suspends Seselj Trial." *EJIL: Talk! Blog of the European International Law Journal.* February 11, 2009. www.ejiltalk.org/icty-trial-chamber-suspends-seselj-trial/. Accessed September 1, 2016.
[43] Author interview, 2013.

The essence of the prosecution case against Vojislav Šešelj was that he "was a fanatic propagandist contributing to an illegal enterprise"[44] who instigated material perpetrators to commit crimes in four principal ways: by using denigrating propaganda in press and public speeches, by traveling to the frontlines to encourage Serb forces, by dispatching members of his political party to spread a message of revenge and ethnic cleansing, and by failing to act against soldiers and irregular fighters who called themselves Šešeljevci, or Šešelj's Men, as they persecuted non-Serbs in a widespread and systematic fashion.[45] How did the prosecution seek to prove beyond a reasonable doubt that Šešelj's speeches instigated others and thereby made a "substantial contribution" to the commission of crimes?[46]

This section focuses on the heart of the instigation case against the accused: his speech at Hrtkovci on May 6, 1992. In the investigations phase and as the trial got underway, the prosecution held damning evidence from insider witnesses – individuals close to Šešelj and his organization – that might have persuaded a trier of fact. In their statements to the prosecution, four insider witnesses, who were local Serb leaders and Šešeljevci, provided information about the relationship between the accused and the group undertaking criminal acts, including the structure and character of his ultra-nationalist organization. One prosecuting attorney described the character of their evidence thus:

> We had insiders who talked about how powerful he [Vojislav Šešelj] was and how they looked up to him like he was a god, and how his influence is evidenced by his popularity and the number of volunteers he was able to recruit, and the number of people who identified their group by using his name – the Šešeljevci.[47]

Why would insiders turn against their Vojvoda ("Duke")? According to one prosecution team member who took statements from former Šešeljevci, they gave statements because they were young men when they fought in the armed conflict and now they were middle-aged and often unemployed. Many of them were debilitated by war injuries and were left feeling used and abandoned by their leadership.[48] However, this cornerstone in the prosecution's case fell apart over the course of the trial. All of the insiders, to a man, later recanted their testimony and refused to testify in The Hague, or testified but recanted on the stand. Some made allegations of ethics violations against the prosecution during their testimony – allegations that were investigated by a Tribunal-appointed inquiry and found to be baseless. The prosecution counter-alleged that "The recantations were the product of an organized campaign to deter witnesses from testifying truthfully."[49]

[44] T.17136, March 5, 2012.
[45] Prosecution's Closing Brief, 2012, §589.
[46] The Prosecution's Closing Brief (at §590) reminds us that the causal threshold of instigation is "substantial contribution."
[47] Author interview, 2014.
[48] Author interview, 2013.
[49] T.17148, March 5, 2012.

One insider, Zoran Rankić, retracted his earlier signed statement and dramatically switched to testify for the defense. Rankić, former deputy head of Vojislav Šešelj's Serbian Radical Party War Staff, ceased to cooperate with the prosecution and became a defense witness in 2007, citing excessive pressure on him and his family from prosecutors. Under cross-examination, another picture emerged, and prosecutors alleged that when they met with Rankić in 2006 to finalize a second statement, he reported that a group from Belgrade had warned him "not to play with your life," an assertion Rankić denied on the stand. The witness did admit, however, that his family had received a bomb threat by telephone.[50] Prosecutors continued to refer to the insider testimony as plausible statements of fact even after their repudiation, but their credibility and probative value was severely downgraded.

After its insider witnesses defected, the prosecution in *Šešelj* was forced to turn to the second best source of testimony – victim or bystander testimony – and it called six fact witnesses for the Hrtkovci part of the indictment. Five were Croats who quit the village after Šešelj's election rally: Katica Paulić,[51] Franjo Baričević,[52] and three protected witnesses.[53] Their testimony was accompanied by the report of expert witness Ewa Tabeau, a demographer who documented the radical population changes in the towns and villages of Vojvodina where Šešelj had given his speeches. The victims' statements were powerful and compelling in their own right. Katica Paulić was present at the election rally on May 6, 1992, and she offered her interpretation of Šešelj's speech: "You can't survive here. Get out of here, save your skin and that of your family, any way you know how. The message was that we Croats and Hungarians had to get out of that village."[54] She fled the village when Serb refugees simply moved into her house and informed her that she must leave.[55]

The most gripping testimony came from Aleksa Ejić, a farmer who had been born and raised in Hrtkovci.[56] Ejić is an ethnic Serb who was active in Serbian nationalist politics, and in 1992 he was a member of the Serbian Renewal Party (SPO), which shared the intensely nationalist ideology of Šešelj's Serbian Radical Party. (Initially, the parties were allies, but over time became bitterly opposed.) Moreover, during the war, he had joined the paramilitary Serbian Guard and fought with Serb units in Bosnia and Hercegovina. In the Hrtkovci context, Ejić was neither a victim nor a perpetrator, but a prominent local political actor without an ethno-nationalist axe to grind against Serbs. Ejić described how Serbs had always been the minority in Hrtkovci, constituting only 10 percent of the population, with Croats and

---

[50] "Šešelj Trial Hears Why Witness Switched Sides." Julia Hawes. *Institute for War and Peace Reporting*, May 18, 2010.
https://iwpr.net/global-voices/seselj-trial-hears-why-witness-switched-sides. Accessed September 1, 2016.
[51] T.11909, November 19, 2008.
[52] T.10626, October 15, 2008, onwards.
[53] VS-061, VS-067 and VS-1134.
[54] T.11909–11910. Testimony included in the Prosecution's Closing Brief at §508.
[55] Prosecution's Closing Brief at §517.
[56] Beginning at T10328, October 7, 2008.

Hungarians representing an overwhelming majority. This changed in 1991 as Serb refugees, fleeing persecution in Croatia and Bosnia, began to cross the border. At first there were only a few hundred, who were spontaneously received and cared for by the whole community. The refugees were housed on a farm in accommodation usually reserved for seasonal laborers, but as their numbers swelled, they began to enter vacant houses whose owners were away working in other European countries. By 1992, there were over a thousand refugees and the process became less orderly; after Šešelj's speech at the election rally of May 6, they began to invade the homes of non-Serbs by force.[57]

Aleksa Ejić described the men who accompanied Šešelj that day. They wore the black uniforms of Chetniks in the Second World War and sported pistols and army daggers. He reported that every one hundred meters or so a man stood vigil with an automatic weapon. Their objective, for Ejić, was "to create fear."[58] At the rally, Šešelj gave his speech to an audience of about three hundred, the majority of whom were Serb refugees not originally from the village. According to Ejić, the displaced and relocated were Šešelj's main constituency, not the longstanding Serb villagers of Hrtkovci who had co-existed with their Croat and Hungarian neighbors for decades:

> I believe that actually this was a message to them to the effect of, "Judge things for yourself and you know what you should do. You've been expelled. You have nowhere to go, whereas Croats and Hungarians are living here. Carry out an exchange with them." That was my understanding of ... these words, and that is what I took away with me from the rally.[59]

In effect, Šešelj was granting Serb refugees, who were themselves the victims of recent persecution in Croatia, the authorization for a property grab, and they responded enthusiastically. Šešelj's speech was greeted with applause and calls and chants of "Ustasha Out!" and "This is Serbia!"[60] Aleksa Ejić recounted how after Šešelj spoke, a certain Mr. Zilić, who was a Serb refugee from Croatia, took the microphone and read out the names of prominent Croats in the village, saying they were not loyal to Serbia and had no place in Hrtkovci.[61] At this point, Vojislav Šešelj interrupted and challenged the witness: "The people that are mentioned here were the people that went to [Croatian President Franjo] Tudjman's army to fight against the Serbian people. That was the essence of this speech, not just mentioning all Croats residing in this village."[62] Presiding Judge Jean-Claude Antonetti not only allowed the question, but reworked it and posed it himself to the witness, asking if the named Croats left to fight in the Croatian National Guard. With the defendant

---

[57] T.10328, October 7, 2008.
[58] T.10335, October 7, 2008.
[59] T.10355, October 7, 2008.
[60] Ejić, T.10343. This was confirmed by witness Baričević at T.10621.
[61] T.10335, October 7, 2008.
[62] T.10348, October 7, 2008.

providing ammunition, the judge hijacked the cross-examination of the witness, while the Italian prosecutor, Mr. Calogero Ferrara, stood by abjectly.

On March 5, 2012, the prosecution team made their final closing arguments, representing their last chance to convince the bench. Led by Danish attorney Mathias Marcussen, the prosecution's arguments opened with Vojislav Šešelj's threat made on March 5, 1992 – exactly twenty years earlier to the day – that if Bosnia declared independence, there would be "rivers of blood on Bosnia and Herzegovina's soil."[63] A month or so later, Marcussen pointed out, the town of Zvornik was attacked by irregular Serb forces, including Šešeljevci. Non-Serb men were separated from the women and children, who were expelled from the town. Eighty-eight Croat and Muslim men were then executed by firing squads. Indeed, this was the template for the prosecution team's verbal closing arguments and the accompanying Prosecution's Closing Brief. The evidence for each "crime base," be it Hrtkovci, Vukovar or Zvornik, was organized according to the same narrative structure and arc. The prosecutors started with a speech by Šešelj, and then showed the awful events that subsequently transpired, asserting that these events were the direct consequences of the speech. Each Šešelj speech represented the proximate cause in a chain of causation that culminated in the target crime. To prove instigation, the prosecution adopted a robust, direct causal argument in which speech acts, then crimes, marched in lock step. The prosecution theory of the case could be summed up in four words: Šešelj speaks, atrocities ensue. More abstractly, it could be stated in only three words: chronology proves causation.

Given the slim evidentiary proof for direct instigation, legal causation was demonstrated through a chronological ordering of the facts, as is apparent in the prosecution's narration of the Hrtkovci situation by American prosecutor Lisa Biersay. She recounted how Šešelj's infamous "hate speech" was delivered on May 6, the Serbian national holiday of St. George's Day, the most popular and celebrated patron saint day in the Serb Orthodox calendar. The accused and his Chetnik entourage, wearing black Second World War uniforms, roared into the village, blaring Chetnik music. They posted men armed with automatic rifles on street-corners, the prosecution alleged, all with the objective of creating an intimidating atmosphere for Croat villagers.[64]

Biersay parsed the content and meaning of the speech, and then claimed that, "Immediately after his speech, many Croats began preparing to leave Hrtkovci, showing they felt denigrated and threatened, just as the accused intended."[65] Directly following Šešelj's May 6 speech, recounted Biersay, Croats were harassed and threatened. Hand grenades were thrown into Croat homes, dogs were killed and Croats received bomb threats over the telephone.[66] Evidence of the exodus of the

[63] T.17115.
[64] T.17299–17302, March 6, 2012.
[65] T.17304.
[66] T.17310, March 6, 2012.

Croat population was displayed in the register of the Catholic Church, which showed a spike in requests for birth and marriage certificates, as Croats gathered their identity documents in preparation for emigrating to Croatia. According to the Prosecution's Closing Brief, Hrtkovci's Croat population, initially about 40 percent of the village, declined by 76 percent in 1992.[67] The prosecution was not precise about the actual numbers that were displaced from the village, and could only estimate a range of between 700–800 persons.[68] By August 1992, Serbs were a majority in the village for the first time in recent history, and the leadership changed its name to Srbislavci, or "Glorifier of Serbs."[69]

That the prosecution sought to demonstrate a causal connection between the threatening speech and the atrocities through their temporal proximity is explicitly acknowledged in the Prosecution's Closing Brief:

> In fact, a strong causal inference is raised by the temporal connection between Šešelj's speech and the departure of a large number of Croats from Hrtkovci. This mass departure is evidenced by the dramatic increase in the number of requests for marriage and christening certificates from the Catholic Church in Hrtkovci in May 1992 ... In light of the inflammatory content of Šešelj's 6 May 1992 speech and how rapidly news of its content spread through Hrtkovci, the logical inference from these figures is that a number of Croats made the decision to leave Hrtkovci, and did in fact leave, as a result of Šešelj's speech (§521–522).

The relevance of temporal proximity for determining proximate cause was reinforced by my interviews with prosecutors on the Šešelj trial. Speaking with a prosecuting attorney, it became apparent that a chronological prism for understanding causality was already present in the early investigations phase: "I was in charge of the initial investigation in the Šešelj case and drew up the indictment and the opening statement of the prosecution. We emphasized where he said something and what happened next, like his speech in Vukovar or his speech in Hrtkovci. We believed there was a clear connection between these speeches and crimes."[70] When asked "What convinced you that the speech at Hrtkovci caused the crimes against Croats?" the prosecutor responded, "Šešelj comes into this area with a lot of tension and says 'Let's get rid of the Croats.' And the Croats hear this and start to leave the area and the Serbs in positions of power start a persecution campaign against Croats, it starts immediately afterwards." "Is the speech a proximate cause?" I asked. "It's a trigger for the audience to remove Croats, speeches can be triggers of violence," she replied.

How do judges evaluate the prosecution's chosen method of determining causation through chronology? When asked how a judge might determine a link between

---

[67] Prosecution's Closing Brief, §520.
[68] Ibid., at §523.
[69] Prosecution's Closing Brief, §515.
[70] Author interview, 2013.

a speech and criminal acts, one ICTY judge who had served on the case replied in a manner that illustrated the importance he gave to immediacy and temporal proximity: "Sometimes there is a clear link to an upcoming conflict or link, like the taking of Vukovar. If a leader says 'It is of vital importance to take Vukovar' and the next day Vukovar is taken, then there is a nexus." I then asked, "How do you know that the speech was the main trigger of violence and not another factor?"; he replied "You don't." He then proceeded to elaborate, asserting that temporal contiguity was not enough in itself:

> It's not easy to determine causality. The psychological implications in an audience are so rich and multifaceted, so putting up a checklist [and he provides a verbal list of factors including the context of the conflict at the time, the reaction of the audience, the content of the speech, the manner of delivery and the references to prior conflicts] makes a lot of sense, in order to consider all the aspects active at the time of the speech and arrive at conclusions holistically.[71]

In its summing up, the prosecution claimed that across all the crime bases in the indictment, Šešelj's Men, the Šešeljevci, had killed at least 905 Croats and Bosniaks, tortured and raped numerous civilians, deported tens of thousands of non-Serbs and destroyed religious monuments. Senior Trial Attorney Marcussen appealed to the judges to impose a sentence of 28 years, adding that since the accused paraded his lack of remorse as a badge of honor,[72] there were no mitigating factors.

THE STRUCTURAL FRAILTY OF INTERNATIONAL CRIMINAL TRIBUNALS

International criminal law, also known as "ICL" to its proponents, sounds commanding, authoritative, and even intimidating. Able to leap tall jurisdictional boundaries, ICL is widely touted as the scourge of war criminals, mass murderers and tyrannical despots everywhere. In practice, however, international criminal tribunals are quite a bit less formidable, since they lack both a consistent and established body of law (especially when compared with municipal criminal jurisdictions) and any coercive capacity. Even a medium-sized state such as Indonesia, Brazil or South Africa has vastly more institutional capability to enforce arrest warrants and to implement powers of search, seizure, and subpoena. Most states possess a more established and recognized set of laws and criminal justice institutions than international tribunals. The institutional frailties of international justice institutions have a clear effect on the daily functioning of the international courts and, concretely, on the ability of prosecutors to construct an evidence-based narrative of the crimes and

---

[71] Author interview, 2013.
[72] "I am being tried for atrocious war crimes that I allegedly committed through hate speech as I preached my nationalist ideology of which I am proud." Vojislav Šešelj, "Vojislav Šešelj: Fallen Leader of Great Serbia." Manja Ristic. *Balkan Transitional Justice*. March 15, 2012. www.balkaninsight.com/en/article/vojislav-seselj-fallen-leader-of-the-great-serbia. Accessed September 1, 2016.

present this narrative to a court with the expectation that the court will apply predictable criminal law principles.

Elements of the Šešelj trial highlight the sharp contrasts between international and domestic criminal trials, and they draw our attention to two issues in particular. First, they illustrate the overwhelming challenges of judging war crimes in international courts that are amalgamations of distinctive national legal traditions, with all the complications that abruptly conceived admixtures generate. Presiding Judge Jean-Claude Antonetti's deportment in the Šešelj trial was more than just a question of his personality, as it also illustrated the clash of legal cultures in the international context. Antonetti, a French judge from the inquisitorial tradition, simply could not countenance the common-law-inspired adversarial structure of the ICTY courtroom. The judge balked at the idea that the prosecutor serves as the motor of the trial and he continually elbowed the prosecutor aside like an investigating magistrate or inquisitorial *judge d'instruction*, seizing control of the prosecution's examination of its own witnesses. At other times, he assumed the role of defense counsel, and, in violation of standard procedure, advanced exculpatory arguments during the prosecution's examination-in-chief of fact witnesses.[73]

Judge Antonetti's imperious manner in the Šešelj trial is part of a larger process of increased judicial control over cases – what Langer (2005) describes as the rise of a "managerial judging model" at the ICTY. In 2000–2001, the UN Security Council exerted unrelenting pressure on the ICTY leadership to expedite ICTY trials. In response, then ICTY President French Judge Claude Jorda unveiled his "completion strategy" for the ICTY in 2002,[74] proposing a civil-law-style framework that permitted judges to actively manage their cases in unprecedented ways. New rules were introduced, such as Rules 73*bis* and 73*ter*, that allowed judges to decide which witnesses to call and to limit the scope of their testimony. Rule 90(F) and 90(G) granted judges control over the order and manner of witness cross-examination and the presentation of evidence to "avoid needless consumption of time." Judges ordered prosecutors to drop a specific number of indictments, or cut their cases by a set figure, such as 25 or 30 per cent.[75] When prosecutors protested the arbitrary cuts, judges ruled that any time spent addressing an objection would be subtracted from the time allotted to the party making the objection.[76]

---

[73] See T.10419, October 8, 2008.
[74] Report on the Judicial Status of the International Criminal Tribunal for the Former Yugoslavia and the Prospects for Referring Certain Cases to National Courts, U.N. Doc S/2002/678 (2002). Completion Strategy of the International Criminal Tribunal for Rwanda, U.N. Doc S/2003/946 (2003).
[75] In 2006, judges gave the prosecution two weeks to reduce the scope of the indictment against Momcilo Perisić, by "at least a third." In November 2006, the Trial Chamber slashed the time allotted to the prosecution in the Prlić case by more than a quarter to meet the timetable decreed by the Security Council.
[76] See *Prlić* Trial Chamber, "Decision on Adoption of New Measures to Bring the Trial to an End Within a Reasonable Time." November 13, 2006, §18–22.

For some, the managerial judging model represented a welcome streamlining of the international criminal law process. For others, particularly those trained in the Anglo-American tradition, it was a scandalous violation of due process that valued fast and furious trials over fair trials. What is clear is that the changes came too quickly for either the defense or prosecution to adjust to the mercurial legal environment. Many domestic criminal justice systems developed organically over time, gradually introducing conventions and procedural safeguards which reflect their legal history and culture. By contrast, international criminal law is a hurried, impromptu fusion of different legal systems, in which the law administered today may not be the law administered tomorrow. This raises serious questions about procedural fairness and the rights of defendants to be judged according to a set of rules and procedures that are known in advance of the trial, and respected and upheld during the legal proceedings.

As noted at the beginning of this chapter, another distinctive aspect of international criminal courts founded under the auspices of the United Nations Security Council is that they lack any infrastructure of enforcement and are forced to rely on national governments – often the same governments they are holding to criminal account. This means that international courts seem to be state-like criminal justice apparatuses, but without the rest of the accompanying coercive apparatus of the state, rendering them particularly vulnerable to political actors who wish to interfere with their work and undermine due process. Of course, political interference is a feature of criminal law everywhere, but the problem does seem both especially acute and especially ignored in the international setting.

To focus on one aspect of interference in international trials, the recanting of prosecution witnesses is a feature of all types of criminal trials, yet the phenomenon does seem more endemic at international tribunals. At the International Criminal Court (ICC), in the Ruto and Sang case relating to ethnic violence during the 2007 Kenyan elections, the Court ordered nine prosecution witnesses to testify after they stopped communicating with the prosecution or recanted their statements.[77] Compelling the recalcitrant witnesses to testify against their will via a video link from Nairobi was ultimately counterproductive. As one witness after another defected to the defense, prosecutors scrambled to petition the court to declare a succession of witnesses as hostile witnesses, a designation that permits the prosecution team to cross-examine and challenge the witness.[78] Prosecutors alleged that the witnesses recanted their earlier testimony only after the prosecution's witness list was disclosed to the defense and they were approached and bribed by persons aligned with the defendants.[79]

[77] "Witness Testifies about Fundraising Event He Said Did Not Take Place." Tom Maliti, *International Justice Monitor*, September 16, 2014.
[78] Witnesses 495, 516, 604 and 637. "Witness 516 is Declared a Hostile Prosecution Witness." Tom Maliti. *International Justice Monitor*, September 25, 2014.
[79] "Prosecutor Asks Witness Whether He Fears Implicating Ruto or Sang." Tom Maliti, *International Justice Monitor*, September 10, 2014.

Issues also arose involving ICC defense witnesses, and in January 2015, Meshak Yebei, a defense witness in the Ruto/Sang case who had been under the court's protection, was found murdered in Nandi County in Kenya. The press release from the OTP indicated that it held "information indicating that Mr. Yebei was deeply implicated in the scheme to corrupt Prosecution witnesses in the case against Mr. Ruto and Mr. Sang."[80] In April 2016, the Trial Chamber vacated the charges against Ruto and Sang citing a "disturbing level of interference with witnesses."[81]

With swirling allegations and counterallegations of bribery, intimidation and murder, trials at international criminal tribunals are possibly comparable to major organized crime cases in domestic settings.[82] Unlike national governments, however, international criminal tribunals have significantly less capacity and security presence on the ground to enforce special protective measures for witnesses. The international criminal law model therefore requires unimpeachable witnesses in order to connect speech acts to crimes and convict the accused of instigating crimes against humanity, but it does not count on the supporting institutional framework to shield those witnesses from intimidation and retribution. It is fair to say that, in this context, their reliance on often recalcitrant national states for search, seizure, and arrest, as well as the protection of witnesses, is the Achilles' heel of international justice institutions. Max Weber's (1919: 78) definition of the state as the "monopoly of the legitimate use of physical force within a given territory" is applicable here. International institutions have come, in some instances, to replace the justice functions of states, but because they lack the customary state monopoly on violence, the type of justice they administer is often greatly diminished.

SCIENCE AND DOUBT IN INTERNATIONAL COURTS

The particular challenges facing prosecutors in the Šešelj trial provide a window into the wider epistemological framework of international courts. In both domestic and international criminal law, the ideal evidence to prove instigation would be provided by material perpetrators declaring that, but for the speech of the accused, the crimes in question would not have occurred. When asked what would constitute the clearest evidence of causation, prosecutors invariably replied "the testimony of an insider," and they gave illustrative examples of ideal testimony such as "I heard his words and I would die for him and do anything he says,"[83] "he was an authority

---

[80] Statement of the Office of the Prosecutor regarding the reported abduction and murder of Mr. Meshak Yebei. January 9, 2015. https://thehaguetrials.co.ke/article/otp-denies-involvement-yebeis-murder. Accessed September 1, 2016.
[81] Decision on Defence Applications for Judgments of Acquittal, Ruto and Sang (ICC-01/09-01/11-2027-Red), Trial Chamber, April 5, 2016.
[82] And in particular "RICO" cases in the United States: Racketeer Influenced and Corrupt Organizations Act, enacted by section 901(a) of the Organized Crime Control Act of 1970.
[83] Author interview, 2013.

figure who commanded my behavior" and "I heard his words and I acted."[84] Insiders gave evidence very close to this ideal for other crime sites such as the Vukovar front. Šešelj confidantes such as Zoran Rankić and Goran Stoparić described how Šešelj was a "sort of god" who held great moral sway over his followers and successfully incited them through declarations such as "Not a single Ustaša should leave Vukovar alive" (Prosecution's Closing Brief, paras. 161–165).

Prosecutors lacked such "smoking gun" testimony from perpetrators in Hrtkovci and therefore they were unable to directly document the mobilization and organization that translated a shared criminal intent into collective action. Circumstantial evidence, while it still might be compelling for the court, is more susceptible to the defense rejoinder that the defendant's speeches were all symbolic performance, *sturm und drang*, with no actual consequences. For the Hrtkovci crime base, prosecutors called victims who told the court about an atmosphere of fear and intimidation that included hand grenades being thrown into people's homes and dogs being killed. Yet victims possessed no direct knowledge about the network that coordinated the offenses or the role of the accused in the planning and execution of atrocities. Lacking evidence that would show "cause-in-fact" (or what law thinks of as "true causation") using the *sine qua non* test of causation, the prosecution turned to anecdotal, secondary evidence that might satisfy "legal causation," which is more a matter of policy than fact. In their theory of proximate cause, prosecutors connected the speech acts of the accused to the crimes by their temporal contiguity to prohibited acts of persecution and deportation.

Lacking insiders, demonstrating the direct nexus required by the charge of instigation was a steep hill for the prosecution to climb. It is worth addressing some of the wider issues raised by the prosecution's efforts to establish the *actus reus* elements of instigating crimes against humanity. We could start with the question of whether chronology constitutes sufficient proof of causation. In philosophy, the once commonly accepted idea that chronology implies causation was discredited by the Scottish Enlightenment philosopher David Hume, whose position was re-articulated by Hart and Honoré (1985) as, "not all events which follow each other in invariable sequence are causally related." Applying Humean skepticism to our subject, it is possible that in Hrtkovci in May 1992 there were many factors that induced Croats to flee the village apart from the speech by Šešelj. These might include, inter alia, the outbreak of armed conflict between two conventional armies, television and radio propaganda from Belgrade, the influx of 1,000 Serb refugees into the village and the movements of local Serb nationalists who hosted Šešelj's visit. How do we know what Šešelj's exact contribution was to the exodus of Croats, as compared with these other factors?

Judge Antonetti, ever-alive to exculpatory evidence, asked pertinent questions during his dissenting opinion in the Rule 98 *bis* decision: "what words uttered [by

---

[84] Author interview, 2013.

Šešelj] led to brutal and inhumane living conditions? ... What are the reasons [for these conditions]? The words uttered by the accused or some other reason?"[85] Prosecutors never argued that the May 1992 speech constituted a "but for" cause of the forcible transfer of non-Serbs, or that their expulsion would not have happened without Šešelj's election rally and speech. There were 1,000 Serb refugees with nowhere to go, prowling around the homes of local Croats. Even before the rally, displaced persons were breaking into the empty homes of Croats working abroad. The thrust of the prosecution's case was that Šešelj's words *hastened* the displacement of non-Serbs, and this is one reason why temporality assumed such a central role in the prosecution case for causation. The prosecutor's reliance on temporal proximity could only hope to satisfy "legal causation," rather than what law terms "material causation" with its standard of *sine qua non*.

What is striking is how, in international criminal law, there are no well-defined and accepted tests for determining whether a connection between two acts or events is the result of correlation, causation, or mere coincidence in time. In the physical sciences, the chronological juxtaposition of two events is insufficient to establish a causal nexus unless accompanied by other tests. In social science, demonstrating causation would necessitate a large sample study that controlled for other factors. Social researchers normally refrain from strong claims for causation on the basis of one speech, or even three speeches. Instead, a well-designed quantitative study would require a sample of thirty to fifty speeches and reliable evidence of their aftereffects within a defined range and time period in order to determine whether there was a statistical relationship between words and crimes, and, if so, whether this relationship was of sufficient significance to warrant attributing causation rather than mere correlation.

Criminal law's epistemology, and in particular its propensity to generalize on the basis of very few examples (or even just one example), militates against a more systematic and rigorous approach to mass crimes across a large area. The structure of the prosecution case at international tribunals seldom identifies a general pattern in a region based upon a large sample.[86] Instead, it reviews a few incidents in great detail. In *Šešelj*, there were just three: Hrtkovci, Vukovar and Zvornik. To prove its case beyond a reasonable doubt in each crime base, the prosecution requires unimpeachable witnesses able to testify in the trial chamber, and, in the adversarial process, this is a laborious and time-consuming exercise, requiring several days of examination-in-chief and cross-examination for each and every witness. The standards of the adversarial process, while necessary for the standards of

---

[85] "Seselj Trial Cleared for Defence Phase." Institute for War and Peace Reporting. Rachel Irwin. May 6, 2011. http://iwpr.net/report-news/seselj-trial-cleared-defence-phase.
[86] There are a few exceptions, such as the compendious Amended Indictment "Bosnia and Herzegovina" of November 22, 2002 against former Yugoslav President Slobodan Milošević, which alleged killings, illegal detentions and forcible transfers of a civilian population in 17, 24 and 45 municipalities respectively.

a criminal court, result in a deleterious reduction of the sample size in mass crimes. International courts are asked to adjudicate mass crimes with tools that are woefully inadequate for understanding mass crimes.

In *Šešelj*, a main issue at stake in the testimony of fact witnesses was "what did the intended audience understand by the words of the accused?" At a rally with 300 participants and onlookers, how does the court determine with great certainty the intention of the speaker and the reception of such a large audience? In the crime bases of Zvornik and Hrtkovci, the two sites where Šešelj's speeches allegedly instigated persecution and deportation, prosecutors relied upon a remarkably small number of fact witnesses. For Zvornik, the prosecution called only 6 witnesses to give testimony on the deportation of hundreds of non-Serbs and the murder of 88 persons.[87] As we have just seen, at Hrtkovci the prosecution only counted 6 fact witnesses testifying regarding the forcible transfer of 700–800 non-Serbs.[88] This pattern is reproduced in similar international trials. In *Akayesu* at the ICTR, the prosecution convinced the court on the basis of 6 fact witnesses that the 100–200 persons in the meeting at Gishyeshye during the early hours of April 19, 1994, understood Akayesu's calls to eliminate "the accomplices of the RPF" to mean all Tutsis.[89]

The enormity of international criminal indictments, combined with the difficulties in obtaining evidence, mean that in each crime base international prosecutors are compelled to generalize on the basis of insufficient evidence. When I asked an ICTY prosecutor, "If you had 2–3 credible witnesses saying, 'I was in the crowd and the speech had this meaning for me', how would you then infer the meaning of the rest of the crowd of hundreds of people?"; he replied, "If I had 2–3 witnesses, that would be quite good – I would feel that I had a solid case."[90] If the criminal liability of the defendant hinges on the meaning and content of his or her words and the understanding of the audience, an international court could arrive at a conclusion on the basis of 6 (or even fewer) fact witnesses. In social research, this approach would be considered woefully anecdotal. Any research claiming to have determined the meaning of a speaker's words beyond a reasonable doubt on the basis of interviews with 2 to 3 members of a crowd of 300 would likely face a negative evaluation in the peer-review process, and yet international courts are convicting defendants on the basis of such small and unrepresentative samples.

Ironically, while international criminal tribunals are accustomed to deciding cases on a small and unrepresentative sample, the stakes are higher than in most social science studies, and so is the threshold of proof. The beyond reasonable doubt standard lies well above any claim of certainty found in the social sciences, and in the physical sciences too. If we recall that in law, reasonable doubt is a qualitative

---

[87] Prosecution's closing arguments, T.17248.
[88] Counted in the Prosecution's Closing Brief at §509.
[89] *Akayesu* TC §361. The judgment reviews the six fact witnesses at §§333–338.
[90] Author interview, 2013.

not quantitative standard, then it is worth observing that qualitative social scientists seldom claim that one social fact directly causes another. If they do, they generally only do so in a general, umbrella causation sense that recognizes multiple causation. Biomedical science in randomized clinical trials and quantitative social science can identify causation on the basis of certain criteria and tests, but their statistical methods and definitions of proof are quite unlike those of law, and they eschew the category of beyond reasonable doubt.

These comments point toward a deeper chasm between law's ways of knowing and other approaches to knowledge, as noted by the anthropologists cited at the beginning of this chapter, and socio-legal scholars such as Shklar (1986), Jasanoff (1995), and Monahan and Walker (2014). They also remind us that not all universalistic, rationalist knowledge systems are the same. Science is interested in the nomothetic: classes of events and generalizations based upon wider patterns that explain those patterns. Science pursues causation in order to explain categories or types of events which regularly and frequently occur, rather than particular events which are exceptional, rare or unusual. Some branches of science (e.g., epidemiology) can embrace composite notions of causation, rather than the criminal law's unilinear chain of cause and effect. When applied to human societies, science is generally concerned with populations rather than single individuals. Law, and criminal law in particular, makes a shrine to the idiographic, the particular event. The individual case, with all its particularities, may serve as the basis of a new legal precedent that transforms the entire body of law on a particular topic. Findings of causation need not be based upon a pattern of regularly observed events. Indeed, such findings may be built upon an unusual, even bizarre concurrence of factors that has never transpired before and may never transpire again.

Criminal law, while it has formulated its own standards of logical reasoning and evidence, does not always recognize scientific principles of reasoning or methods of evaluating evidence. It is therefore a form of non-scientific rationalism. It proceeds by a formal logic, but the rules of logic are internal to legal epistemology. The law uses evidence to make determinations, but its evidence would be insufficient in other branches of human knowledge. Returning to our case study, chronology does not prove causation, and half-a-dozen victim/bystander witnesses is not proof of a broadly held view (if any exists) by a listening audience. Arguing that this is so is mere prosecutorial rhetoric, which complicates matters when considering a case that hinges on the damaging implications of rhetoric.

EPILOGUE

In March 2016, the ICTY Trial Chamber majority, Judge Flavia Lattanzi dissenting, acquitted Vojislav Šešelj of all nine counts of war crimes and crimes against humanity. The majority judgment stated that the defendant's speeches constituted a clear call to deport Croats, but there was no causal connection to specific acts of violence, nor was there a widespread and systematic attack on the Croat population (§333). As we have seen, the prosecution case had its shortcomings, but the poorly written and defectively reasoned judgment included incomprehensible statements such as "the buses which were chartered in this context were not forced transfer operations of population, but rather acts of humanitarian assistance to non- combatants who fled areas where they no longer felt safe" (§193). In this way, an international tribunal judgment coined a new concept: "humanitarian deportation." Judge Lattanzi dissented from the judgment in the starkest terms seen thus far at the ICTY: "with this Judgement we have been thrown back centuries into the past, to a period in human history when we used to say – and it was the Romans who used to say this to justify their bloody conquests and the assassinations of their political enemies during civil wars: *Silent enim leges inter arma*" (§150). The prosecution has appealed the decision.

REFERENCES

Anders, Gerhard (2014) "Contesting Expertise: Anthropologists at the Special Court for Sierra Leone." *Journal of the Royal Anthropological Institute.* 20(3): 426–444.

Boas, Gideon (2007) *The Milosevic Trial: Lessons for the Conduct of Complex International Criminal Proceedings.* Cambridge: Cambridge University Press.

Bringa, Tone (1995) *Being Muslim the Bosnian Way: Identity and Community in a Central Bosnian Village.* Princeton: Princeton University Press.

Clarke, Kamari (2009) *Fictions of Justice: The International Criminal Court and the Challenge of Legal Pluralism in Sub-Saharan Africa.* New York: Cambridge University Press.

Del Ponte, Carla (2008) *Madam Prosecutor: Confrontations with Humanity's Worst Criminals and the Culture of Impunity: A Memoir.* With Chuck Sudetic. New York: Other Press.

Dressler, Joshua and Stephen P. Garvey (2012) *Criminal Law.* Sixth Edition. St. Paul: West.

Eltringham, Nigel (2013) "'Illuminating the Broader Context': Anthropological and Historical Knowledge at the International Criminal Tribunal for Rwanda." *Journal of the Royal Anthropological Institute.* 19: 338–355.

Franklin (2003) "Re-thinking Nature-Culture: Anthropology and the New Genetics." *Anthropological Theory.* 3(1): 65–85.

Good, Anthony (2007) *Anthropology and Expertise in the Asylum Courts.* London: Routledge.

Hazan, Pierre (2004) *Justice in a Time of War: The True Story Behind the International Criminal Tribunal for the Former Yugoslavia.* Translated by James Thomas Snyder. College Station: Texas A&M Press.

Hart, H.L.A. and Tony Honoré (1985) *Causation in the Law.* Second Edition. Oxford: Clarendon Press.

Jasanoff, Sheila (1995) *Science at the Bar.* Cambridge: Harvard University Press.

Langer, Máximo (2005) "The Rise of Managerial Judging in International Criminal Law." *American Journal of Comparative Law.* 53(4): 835–909.

Monahan, John and Laurens Walker (2014) *Social Science in Law.* Eighth Edition. St. Paul: Foundation Press.

Peskin, Victor (2008) *International Justice in Rwanda and the Balkans: Virtual Trials and the Struggle for State Cooperation.* Cambridge: Cambridge University Press.

Shklar, Judith (1986) *Legalism: Law, Morals, and Political Trials*. Cambridge: Harvard University Press.
Sluiter, Göran. (2007) "Compromising the Authority of International Criminal Justice – How Vojislav Šešelj Runs His Trial." *Journal of International Criminal Justice*. 5(2): 529–536.
Tabeau, Ewa and Jakub Bijak (2005) "War-related Deaths in the 1992–1995 Armed Conflicts in Bosnia and Herzegovina: A Critique of Previous Estimates and Recent Results." *European Journal of Population*. 21: 187–215.
Weber, Max (1919/1996) "Politics as a Vocation." In Bryan Turner (ed.) *For Weber: Essays on the Sociology of Fate*. Second Edition. London: Sage, pp. 77–129.
Wilson, Richard Ashby (2011) *Writing History in International Criminal Trials*. Cambridge: Cambridge University Press.
Zahar, Alexander (2008) "Legal Aid, Self-Representation and the Crisis at The Hague Tribunal." *Criminal Law Forum*. 19: 241–263.

13

The Anthropology *by* Organizations: Legal Knowledge and the UN's Ethnological Imagination

Ronald Niezen

WHAT IS THE ANTHROPOLOGY *BY* ORGANIZATIONS?

We are used to thinking of global institutions in terms of how they respond to security crises, human rights abuses, and development opportunities in an uncertain world, but it is less often noted that they are also among the world's most significant producers of knowledge. This knowledge includes understandings of human life and its variety – something that we might recognize as "anthropology," or what I have referred to as "the law's legal anthropology" (Niezen 2012). They prioritize improving conditions in the world through the powers of bureaucracy and law, and often do so by first identifying and categorizing those who are in need of recognition and rights, or their particular qualities or practices that can be conducive to peace and prosperity. These ideas constitute, through the great variety of interconnected UN agencies and global NGOs, a kind of composite vision of human life, a form of instrumental, rights-oriented, managerial, but, oddly, at the same time, publicly engaged and participatory anthropology. The combination of ideas about the human with ideas having to do with rights, dignity, security, and development is powerfully compelling, influencing not just officials and activists, but also public consumers of ideas about rights and their human subjects. As I intend to show here, the involvement of these institutions in anthropological knowledge probably reaches a wider audience than (while drawing from and influencing) the concepts of academic anthropology.

Part of the intellectual history of anthropology *by* global organizations is fairly well understood, at least in the context of debates about relativism and rights-oriented universalism. The focal point here is the response from professional anthropologists to the ideas emerging out of the formulation of the Universal Declaration of Human Rights. In 1947, the American Anthropological Association (AAA) submitted its Statement on Human Rights to the United Nations, responding to a call from UNESCO for member states to draft statements on human rights to aid in the development of the Universal Declaration (Engle 2001; Goodale 2009). Under the influence of the Boasian anthropologist Melville Herskovitz, the Statement offered a counterpoint to the predominant universalistic positions in human rights discourse for tolerance of difference, or cultural relativism, famously arguing that "the individual realizes his personality through his culture, hence respect for individual differences entails a respect for cultural differences" (AAA 1947: 539). The Statement penned by Herskovitz, however, is only one part of the story, having to do mainly with the history and professional identity of anthropology; it had its counterpoint in a concept of humanity with a long history and still being articulated within the UN, with UNESCO struggling for predominance in formulating a universal, rights-oriented conception of human nature that stressed both the biological and moral universality of humanity. This was a conception of humanity that drew inspiration mainly from Enlightenment thought and the American and French Revolutions – all of which Herskovitz found woefully inadequate in terms of the minimal place given to the individual as a member of a social group with a cultural heritage (AAA 1947). As it happened, the intervention of the American Anthropological Association was given little attention outside academic circles and the Statement, despite having some impact on debates in the discipline of anthropology, "played almost no role at all in the drafting of the Universal Declaration of Human Rights" (Goodale 2009: 24).

Whatever their differences with respect to the relationship between culture and rights, anthropologists and UN experts in this formative period were at least agreed on the racial unity of "mankind." Proving this unity once and for all was the explicit aim of an early UN-sponsored foray into anthropological knowledge: the 1950 UNESCO report, "The Race Question," and its follow-up 1951 "Statement by Experts on Problems of Race," sponsored by what was then known as the United Nations Economic and Security Council and published in the flagship journal *American Anthropologist*. In this international effort, the central goal was clear: to combat the hate-inspiring ideas about race promoted by Nazism and to do so with recourse to science. Since the legitimacy of this project and the persuasiveness of its ideas depended on the solidity of its foundations, UNESCO spared no effort in assembling leading scholars – the committee included the anthropologists Ashley Montagu and Claude Lévi-Strauss and sociologist Morris Ginsberg – whose efforts were supported by input from wider academic communities. This collaboration was couched quite literally in terms of a life and death struggle, in which, "like war, the problem of race which directly affects millions of human lives and causes countless conflicts has its roots 'in the minds of men'" (1950: 1). UNESCO's ambition began with establishing a definitive scientific consensus on the fundamental unity of "mankind," then subjecting these ideas to a campaign of global dissemination. Although its efforts of scholarly collaboration were based on science, UNESCO expressed its main objective in terms of diplomacy: "to ... help to lessen the hatreds that separate human groups from one another" (1950: 1–2).

My main goal in this chapter is to show that the early relationship between professional anthropology and the development of human rights is a small part of a much wider phenomenon: the continued involvement of rights-oriented global organizations in cultivating and promoting a distinct form of anthropological knowledge. "The Race Question" may be the most ambitious foray by a UN agency into this knowledge, but, since then, many other initiatives have taken place to clarify, redefine, or reposition one or another aspect of human life, sometimes with strategic or instrumental goals expressed clearly, at other times more implicitly; sometimes with input from professional anthropologists, at other times working at a greater remove from academic concerns or standards. The concepts of "women," "children," "indigenous peoples," "refugees," "migrants," "persons with disabilities," and "lesbian, gay, bisexual and transgender (LGBT) persons" have all, with varying degrees of compulsion and state recognition, been written into international law, with corresponding efforts along the way to define or at least better understand their essence. Besides sketching out some of the main features of this "other anthropology," the concepts I will later focus on are those of "local community" and "indigenous peoples."

Unlike the Race Question initiative, these ideas are not always consistent with or concerned about professional consensus. The concept of "civilization," for example, long excoriated from professional anthropology, was reformulated in a 2005 UN peacemaking initiative as a counterpoint to discourse about the "clash of civilizations" in the context of concerns over global terrorism, given the title the Alliance of Civilizations (UNAOC), and positioned at the forefront of efforts to redefine attachments to and relations between the world's major civilizations (UNAOC 2015). The Alliance of Civilizations has in short order developed "youth-led" initiatives oriented toward the promotion of "intercultural and interfaith dialogue" (Alliance of Civilizations 2016). It also sponsored a Media Fund "aimed to finance mainstream film productions that promote cross-cultural understanding and combat religious stereotypes," striving to engage major Hollywood production, distribution, and talent management companies (Berkeley Center for Religion, Peace and World Affairs 2015).

Similarly, UNESCO has made use of the concept of "culture" in its World Heritage initiatives, connecting it closely to notions of "heritage," apparently without regard for the fact that anthropologists are divided about its utility (Brumann and Berliner 2016). Professional criticism of the concept of cultural heritage, Christoph Brumann points out, has not discouraged those who approach it as a form of belief, seeing in it possibilities for all sorts of desirable ends such as education, economic development, nation building, reconciliation between civilizations, or world peace (2014: 174). For its prominent role in promoting and acting on this belief, Brumann goes so far as to characterize UNESCO as a "Vatican" of the "global church of heritage" (2014: 183).

The UN's forays into anthropological inquiry have been cumulative, garnering relatively little attention as sources of knowledge, but, as these examples make clear, ultimately constituting a distinct institutional realm of understanding about the categories of human difference. They share some of this understanding and power of persuasion with the more prominent global NGOs engaged in ambitious programs of rights-defense and development (although the examples that I draw from in this chapter are focused on UN agencies). In the UN's legal/bureaucratic approaches to knowledge of the human that I consider here, the connections between social life and interpretive categories, including the fundamental priorities that guide conceptual interpretation and observation, produce a distinct vision of human life, an "anthropology" that originates in demands for peacemaking and prosperity and that produces conceptions about the beneficiaries of rights-oriented concern.[1]

It is curious that anthropologists have taken relatively little interest in this world-reforming rival to their discipline. This is an egregious oversight. The ambitions of the UN's anthropological ideas alone should offer enough justification to consider them more carefully (Eriksen 2001: 129). This is a conduit to knowledge that has not been sufficiently acknowledged or understood by those concerned with the consequences of legal process or the constitution of the social. Institutional experts are mostly seen as responsible for policies and their implementation, not as thinkers who in some ways could have equal or greater intellectual authority than academics (which overlooks their sometimes direct connections with academe), not as people who formulate key ideas and models with public influence, who bring their intuitions, personal experience, and professional backgrounds into the *conceptual* exchanges that take place in bureaucratic/legal processes – and beyond, to public understandings of human existence.

The central challenge in approaching this topic is getting as close to the sources of institutional knowledge as possible, the meetings, interventions, and conversations that constitute a process of knowledge-in-formation. To offer a glimpse of this process I will draw on some twenty years' experience of attending meetings of indigenous peoples sponsored by the UN, including those of the Working Group on Indigenous Populations in the 1990s, the World Health Organization's International Consultation on the Health of Indigenous Peoples in 1999, and the Permanent Forum on Indigenous Issues since its establishment in 2002, including three of its most recent annual sessions from 2012–2015. I also draw from the Internet, the UN's main vehicle of knowledge dissemination and transparency. I follow the ways that various UN agencies present online their current knowledge of specific categories of people and how they are acting on their behalf to a global public. In no part of this experience was I a UN "insider," but I hope nevertheless to describe some of the knowledge-oriented initiatives that I encountered along the way, which serve to illustrate the wider phenomenon of the anthropological thinking that emerges from the concerns of global governance.

---

[1] Here I am elaborating on an argument that I first made in a contribution to Mark Goodale's 2013 edited volume *Human Rights at the Crossroads* (Niezen 2013). I point to a similar phenomenon in a discussion of the Canadian Supreme Court's conceptions of culture (Niezen 2003b).

LEGAL KNOWLEDGE

The UN's legal/institutional conceptions of human life follow their own logics and produce ideas that are fundamentally different from those that emerge independently from scholarly disciplines, even when there is some connection between them. It is from four initial starting points that many of the distinct qualities of the anthropology of (or, to be clear, produced *by* or *from*) global institutions follow. First, consistent with the example I mentioned earlier of UNESCO's war against racism, there is a strong emphasis on the *strategic or applied purposes* behind anthropological concepts. This strategic orientation to knowledge can be found at the very pinnacle of the UN's occupational hierarchy. The Permanent Representative of Austria to the then Secretary-General of the United Nations, Kofi Annan, expressed the guiding principle behind some of the UN's most recent forays into anthropological knowledge in a paper known as the Salzburg Reflections: "As the reality of a more interdependent world is pushing us ever closer together, we will have to improve our management of diversity" (United Nations 2001). This indicates that, much as large corporations and government agencies attempt to "manage diversity" in the workplace, the UN promotes an applied understanding of difference and the practice of tolerance on a global scale (Niezen 2010: ch. 5). And to accomplish this it begins by cultivating a basic knowledge of those who represent human difference and whose differences must be more widely tolerated. What these Reflections tell us is that the ideas being put to use in global governance are just that: ideas that are being put to use – they are *meant* to have practical effects, to produce change for the better in conditions of human life. These strategic priorities are usually defined, first, by reports of a condition of crisis, the challenge of making known and ameliorating conditions of human suffering, the misery, despair, and premature end to life that results from hunger, poverty, disease, and bloodshed. This strategic purpose is of course not inconsistent with the policy approaches of, say, economics, political science, or interdisciplinary development studies, but in international institutions it is the starting point of all inquiry. The tendency toward application of ideas in global institutions is characterized by ambitious goals for change in conditions of crisis that do not have the luxury of being guided by time-consuming scholarly reflection, indecision, or ethics of non-interference.

Second, the categories of human belonging elaborated by international institutions are often *endowed with rights*. Legal knowledge of the social frequently involves elaboration of rights at the same time as categories of rights-holders are conceived. It is, in this sense, legislative rather than analytical, in that it begins with legal designs, from which follow possibilities for implementation and elaboration. This means that the rights inherent in a concept attract (or fail to attract) the participation necessary to confirm the validity of that concept. The effectiveness of their rights, rather than correspondence with some measure of reality, is the ultimate criterion of a concept's truth-value. This influence of rights on conceptual legitimacy and appeal has a tendency to produce a kind of reverse epistemology, in which the elaboration of a concept precedes the accumulation of evidence from the reality that it purports to describe. People with important collective claims tend to inhabit, perform, and thereby give reality to the concepts associated with the rights they are using to further their claims. Rights have the potential to take ideas of human belonging far beyond the original strategic goals of institutional knowledge. When they are (or become) associated with furtherance of rights in ways that correspond with the goals of lobby groups and their efforts, the anthropological ideas articulated by UN institutions are often able to attract globally influential efforts toward cultivation of belonging, loyalty, performance, and public persuasion.[2]

Third, following from the emphasis on rights, the categories elaborated by global institutions are informed by the legal demands for *clarity and certainty*. "By definition," Antonio Cassese (2012: xviii) writes, "law must be as unambiguous as possible, so as to constitute a stable and safe set of standards of behaviour for all legal subjects." The idea of a particular set of rights that apply to those facing distinct disadvantages calls for a clear understanding of who is and who is not a beneficiary of those rights. Where certainty does not exist through the assemblage of facts, law is able to produce it through its powers of construction, simply by writing in legal language the "fictions" that produce the desired reality. Some legal fictions tend toward the bizarre, at least by the standards of common sense thinking, an example being Chief Justice Goddard's 1951 ruling in a US court (*Garner v. Burr*, KB, 1951), which considers a poultry shed to be a vehicle within the meaning of the Road Traffic Act of 1930 (Constable 2014: 19), but other instances of fictional certainty might just as readily pass unnoticed. A hunting society without specific notions of property, for example, can be assigned a "territory" for the purposes of a treaty, which then becomes a point of reference for other rights and benefits, including subsistence rights. The need for certainty also invokes efforts toward definition and quantification, such as elaborating divisions of powers, mapping territories, and implementing censuses to count with precision those who do and do not benefit from judicial decisions or, more broadly and less practicably, developing indicators to measure human rights violations, effectiveness of protections, and, of course, numbers of victims. Mary Douglas, in *How Institutions Think*, adds some historical perspective to this point with the observation that the great growth in collecting statistics and ordering them into labeled categories in the nineteenth century resulted in new kinds of people coming forward to accept the labels and live

---

[2] The effects of law on ideas of the social can be understood through a dichotomy that is frequently cited in the context of the linguistic turn in science at the beginning of the twentieth century, which centers on the difference between descriptive language as a representation of the world – with the correspondence between language and the brute facts of reality as the touchstone of truth – and "speech acts" which can be performed, in which the (often legal) imperatives of language bring states of being into existence, as in the classic formula of a marriage ceremony: "I now pronounce you man and wife" (Austin 1962; Van Schooten 2007: 4–5). This dualism provides a point of departure to discuss something similar that can be found in the field sometimes known as socio-legal studies.

accordingly (1986: ch. 8; cited in Wright 1994: 22). The kind of rank-ordered, simplified data that Merry (in Chapter 7 and 2011 and 2013) discusses as central to institutional life are brought to bear on legal categories of belonging to achieve the kind of "factual" clarity required of legal process. Under these circumstances, the subjects of rights can be endowed with reality through their organized memberships, and distinct "cultures" can be invested with qualities that are definable, collectible, and measurable.

Finally, regimes of human membership with implications for rights are not only investigated – in one way or another, they are also *negotiated*. This can have important implications for conceptual coherence, because the elaboration of concepts sometimes involves parties with opposed interests and worldviews, whose most cherished ideas simply *have* to be expressed in a collectively drafted document. The contradictory conceptions of culture embodied in a UNESCO report, for example, can result not only from conceptual confusion, but also, as Brumann notes, from "accommodating each and every whim present on the drafting committee, in a consensus-oriented environment with . . . diverse professional backgrounds" (2014: 183). As parties to these negotiations, states and NGOs have become significant actors in the formulation of concepts of belonging in international institutions. As we will see, these "third party" interests are especially influential in the UN's knowledge system, acting as primary points of reference for the elaboration of ideas about human qualities, practices, or manifestations of difference, above all those with the potential for international recognition and legal protection.

LOCAL COMMUNITIES: EXOGENOUS IDENTITY

In one sense, this anthropology by global institutions is nothing new; legal conceptions of belonging were central to the colonization of the non-European world, with colonial administrators and missionaries exercising and imposing forms of legal discipline and identity on those who were the subjects of their reform efforts (see Comaroff and Comaroff 1997: ch. 8). It also sad but true that ethnologists were not always good listeners, particularly under European colonization when the concepts of "tribe" and "chiefdom" and the particular ethnic names and distinctions that went together with them were among those categories applied (for example, in the course of treaty negotiations) and "discovered" by anthropologists, sometimes in collaboration with colonial administrators (see Amselle 2010). Even with a starting point in human experience, there is not necessarily a close connection between institutional conceptions of belonging and the lives of those on which they are based.[3]

---

[3] One source of scholarly support for the idea of social conceptualization as something that can exert influence on the identities of those who are conceptualized comes from the 1990s literature on the formation of ethnic groups. Here we find the important (and seemingly forgotten) idea that naming is not only a particularly revealing aspect of inter-group relations, it is itself productive of the entities that

To habitual critics of the UN, it would probably come as no surprise to learn that its ethnology is often marked by a similar exogenous, authority-at-a-distance approach to interpreting the world.[4] To see just how detached from human actors this anthropology by global institutions can be, let us consider the sort of ideas that begin at the furthest remove from lived reality, with concepts sometimes based on little more than vague intuitions, which eventually become sources of reference for rights and identities. Clearly, not every concept that is articulated by experts attracts a following of claimants and supporting activists, particularly if it does not elaborate new possibilities for rights. This failure of a concept to "take" in terms of activist engagement is one of the best ways to illustrate the separation of justice-oriented ideas from the intended beneficiaries of justice initiatives. A concept that does not produce a justice movement reveals its conceptual foundations in expert knowledge all the more clearly. Its exogenous origins are not obscured by the reality-enhancement of participatory action.

The distance between a concept and its intended subjects or beneficiaries can be seen in vague outline in an expert opinion on the concept of "local communities," produced by the Secretariat of the Permanent Forum on Indigenous Issues for an "Expert Workshop on the Disaggregation of Data." The data that required disaggregation in this case arose in response to an item in the preamble and article 8(j) of the 1992 Convention on Biological Diversity, which invoked the dual concept "indigenous and local communities" – "recognizing the close and traditional dependence of many indigenous and local communities embodying traditional lifestyles on biological resources" (United Nations 1992: 1) – without further definition or explanation. Whatever "local communities" turned out to be, the Convention on Biodiversity gave them a more salient reality that then called for elaboration. Following from little more than the document in which the concept occurred, these communities clearly possessed attachments to some form or other of traditional heritage and intimate knowledge of the environment in which they lived; and with heritage endangered nearly everywhere, and with intimate knowledge of biological resources inherent in its faint outline – knowledge that could hold the key to some wider form of human improvement – the concept cried out for elaboration and elucidation. Without questioning the utility of the concept, but chasing after the

---

are the foundation of human belonging, inseparable from processes of ethnogenesis. "In situations of domination," Poutignat and Streiff-Fenart argue, "the imposition of a label by the dominant group has a truly performative power: the fact of naming has the power to make exist ... despite what the individuals so named might think of their membership in such a collectivity" (1995: 157). The argument here is broadly similar to other findings that emerge from the ethnography of international institutions: expert involvement in elaborating conceptions of human belonging has a broad reach, with particularly important consequences for those who see themselves described and categorized in knowledge with institutional origins.

[4] This claim is consistent with a recent body of ethnography that considers human rights and development advocacy in practice and finds "top down" exercises that ignore local challenges to prosperity and overlooks the concepts that express collective aspirations and ideas of justice (compare, for example, Bornstein [2005] and Englund[2006]).

assumption that local communities were an essential, at-risk category of human life, distinct from indigenous peoples, the Secretariat set about defining and describing them in more detail, encouraged by the puzzle inherent in the subtitle of its three-page report, "who are local communities"? (United Nations 2004). The answer to this question involved the well-intentioned elaboration of a distinct status in international law for those peoples who do not have primordial claims of attachment to territory, but who nevertheless have a longstanding and intimate knowledge of their environment, in this case with a regional focus on Latin America.

As with many seemingly innocuous uses of terminology with implications for rights-recognition, the dual mention of "indigenous peoples and local communities" in the Convention on Biological Diversity (CBD) was (and continues to be) a focal point of contention, described, for example, in a press release by the International Indigenous Forum on Biodiversity (IIFB) as the source of "an impasse" following from the persistent and, from their perspective, unwanted linkage of the terminology "Indigenous Peoples and local communities." This connection, the IIFB contended, was an outcome of state efforts (particularly on the part of Canada and Indonesia) to control and limit references to indigenous peoples as distinct rights-holders, "attempting to build a wall against any mention of Indigenous Peoples in a political or human rights context and any subsequent decisions or secondary texts of the CBD" (IIFB 2014). In other words, the compound term "indigenous and local communities" found in the Convention on Biodiversity and the texts and decisions that followed from it were seen as oppressive mechanisms used to dilute the rights of indigenous peoples by connecting them with an ill-defined and unrepresented category of people with only limited rights – "local communities." In this alternative explanation of the origins of "local communities," the development of the category of belonging again follows from the strategic intentions of experts, but in this case influenced by the less-than-positive motives of several state diplomats seeking to set limits to the collective rights of indigenous peoples.

Since the production of the "disaggregating" report, the concept of local communities has persisted in its use in several agencies, though in an almost spectral way, with very little in the way of participatory presence, not to mention anything that might be referred to as activism. There has long been a generic use of the term "local communities" in UN reports, particularly those of development-oriented agencies such as the International Fund for Agricultural Development (IFAD) and the United Nations Development Programme (UNDP), where it has been used to emphasize grassroots participation in their initiatives.[5] But a recent trend is toward the use of "local communities" to describe those who possess intimate knowledge of a place, a territory, or the environment. For example, this is the explicit starting point of a "toolkit" for local communities provided online by the United

---

[5] See, for example, a 2012 IFAD report, "Addressing poverty through mobilization of community resources." www.ifad.org/operations/projects/regions/pf/seeds/1.htm. Accessed April 14, 2015.

Nations Environment Programme World Conservation Monitoring Centre (UNEP-WCMC). Here, the definition of community reveals the emphasis on intimate knowledge: "a well-defined people or community possesses a close and profound relation with an equally well-defined site (territory, area or habitat) and/or species" (UNEP 2013).

Consistent with this starting point in local environmental intimacy, UNESCO's Venice headquarters sponsored a meeting in Montenegro in 2012 on the theme, "World Heritage and Sustainable Development: The Role of Local Communities," which was billed in publicity online as a "celebration" offering an opportunity to reinforce joint efforts toward the "development of effective policies and practices for the better management of cultural and natural heritage and all UNESCO designated sites, with a special focus on participatory approaches and community engagement." In practice, however, the "joint efforts" and community engagement involved state-sponsored "experts" from each invited country (Albania, Bosnia and Herzegovina, Bulgaria, Croatia, Greece, Macedonia, Montenegro, Romania, Serbia, Slovenia, and Turkey) "to present and discuss, in a comparative way, meaningful cases of heritage management and community engagement in selected UNESCO designated sites" (UNESCO 2012). That is to say, the communities in question, whose roles in sustainable development were being celebrated, were not represented in the meeting other than through the secondary accounts of states.

This marginality is consistent with local communities' potential to be "heritage victims" in UNESCO initiatives, those whose customary rights and practices are limited by the conservation requirements of heritage sites, without adequate action on their rights to consultation or needs for compensation (Meskell, cited in Brumann and Berliner 2016). Even where there are benefits to local communities to be had from world heritage status, they tend to be "spread to an increased number of recipients in the considerably expanded networks forming around World Heritage sites" (Brumann and Berliner 2016).

In another somewhat ghostly manifestation of "local communities," the World Intellectual Property Organization (WIPO) held a workshop in Geneva in December 2014, titled a "Practical Workshop for Indigenous Peoples and Local Communities on IP and Traditional Knowledge," with participants drawn from the seven "geo-cultural" regions recognized by the Permanent Forum on Indigenous Issues (about which, more later), and with indigenous rights and traditional knowledge (TK) taking the forefront in the agenda (WIPO 2014). Here, the front-and-center category was that of "indigenous peoples," both in the title of the workshop and the agenda, with "communities" having a strictly secondary role.

We can speculate that, aside from the structural exclusions of expert-centered meetings, this relative absence of grassroots engagement by representatives of "local communities" has occurred for two basic reasons. One is the non-specificity of the term: even though it is invoked and described formally in global governance initiatives, the concept "local community" is already part of the vernacular, with cognates in many languages. Alan Macfarlane (1977) has provided us with a succinct survey of the use of the term "community," reaching back as far as the mid-nineteenth century, which he describes as "one of the most powerful myths in industrial society, shaping not only policy and government, with the movement towards 'community centres', 'community welfare', 'community care', but also affecting thought and research. Expecting to find 'communities', the prophecy fulfilled itself and communities were found" (1977: 632). This means that in each of its current iterations, the concept of local communities has wider, deep-historical meanings, which tend to obscure the identification and recognition of particular claimants.

Second, in terms of the challenge of gaining momentum among rights claimants, the concept of local community in international law is not connected to a rights regime that offers any significant advantages to those who are the subjects of definition. The rights and recognition that did inhere in the concept did not appeal to existing coalitions of lobby groups. The rights and benefits that follow from UNESCO's connection of local communities with world heritage sites, as we have just seen, are not even sufficiently robust to prevent the occasional *violation* of human rights, the *loss* of autonomy and prosperity through heritage initiatives. As a term that applies to those with subsistence-based knowledge, "local communities" was likely in competition with a variety of already-established grassroots social movements, including the *"movemiento sem tierra"* in Brazil (internationalized in Spanish as *"sin tierra,"* or "landless") and the international Via Campesina, based in Jakarta, all of which possess their own opportunities and energy. Hence, the concept of "local communities" failed to acquire participatory energy, even though UNESCO and WIPO have kept it alive, at least conceptually.

The example of local communities, with the elaboration of the concept resulting from a contest with indigenous rights claimants and a "disaggregating" inquiry following from the wording of the Convention on Biological Diversity highlights a basic logic inherent in the social and cultural conceptualizations of experts: the identification of a category, community, or set of practices determined to be in flux and at risk of particular kinds of harm can provide the incentive for a redefinition of that category or community, determining its membership, identifying those who are to be the beneficiaries of the of the law and of development programs and those who are not, disaggregating the concept from others that might introduce ambiguity.

This example also shows that the odds that any given category of the oppressed will serve the strategic and identity-oriented purposes of rights claimants is an open question at the time that it is first exposed to view in an institutional context. Of course, the failure of a concept to garner a following is even more difficult to observe than the original formulation of it, for the simple reason that it tends to simply disappear, without public outcry, with no explicit reason or explanation. There is no secret graveyard of dead categories of belonging where one might try to assemble a sufficient mass of remains to determine the common reasons for their demise. These ideas are solitary, and tend to disappear quietly and discretely within the accumulating humus of the world's digital data.

INDIGENOUS PEOPLES: PARTICIPATION AND NATURALIZATION

One of the perplexing things about the concepts developed in global institutions is that they can be oxymoronic: exclusive and state-centric in their origins, but also participatory in their implementation and elaboration. That is to say, given the technical origins of some of the key concepts of belonging produced by global institutions, one of the most significant – and incongruous – qualities of these conceptualizations is that they have the potential to draw a crowd.

Nowhere is the transition from closed-door ideas to participatory engagement better illustrated than in the global indigenous movement, the early developments of which took the form of a fairly restricted conceptual elaboration, in which the category of the vulnerable was initially defined by experts at a remove from most of the relevant actors, only subsequently becoming elaborated within the global indigenous movement. Once the concept of indigenous peoples was taken hold of as a source of justice and identity, it eventually involved thousands of representatives of indigenous peoples and organizations, who, through their speeches and press releases, but also through their performances, through the music, movement, color and costume that they brought into UN buildings, made the concept "indigenous peoples" publicly familiar on a global scale (see Niezen 2003; Sapignoli, Chapter 4 in this volume). In this instance there are two overlapping and interpenetrating sides to the UN's anthropology – one legal/conceptual and the other performative – producing a tension between the remote, cautious, constrained abstraction of its guiding concepts and the public spectacle of claiming and elaborating rights and identities through these concepts.

The origins of this tension can be seen in the early phase in which the concept of "indigenous peoples" was elaborated in international law by the International Labour Organization (ILO). The main impetus behind the ILO initiatives of the 1950s on behalf of "indigenous, tribal, and semi-tribal peoples" came from an increasing awareness of the exploitation of those living on the margins of states in Central and South America, who were especially defenseless against gold mining, timber harvesting, and plantations. (The exploitation from mining had already been described in the early-nineteenth century by Alexander von Humboldt [2009: 271–274] in the diaries of his famous voyages to the Americas, in terms that correspond with our understanding of death camps.) The specifics of the formative discussions in which the concept of indigenous peoples was taken up at the ILO headquarters in Geneva in the 1950s are difficult to know with any kind of certainty. One of the few insights I have into this process is a proud confession from a high-level expert to the effect that he co-authored the first draft of a significant UN human rights instrument over the space of one night in a New York hotel room, while he and his colleague consumed a bottle of whisky – an account that confirms the now common observation that there is a certain level of informality behind formal processes. In the mid-1950s, the term "indigenous" had long been used in reference to the original inhabitants of colonial territories, without any positive implications for rights and in ways that were socially and politically condescending. ILO experts probably also drew on the concept of *indigenismo* that had been part of state-sponsored development programs in Latin America (particularly Mexico) in the 1940s, a concept around which elites engaged in the literature, art, and politics that were "designed for indigenous people, but not produced by them" (Lucero 2013: 194). We can be sure that sometime in the early 1950s the meetings and research efforts took place that produced the report titled simply *Indigenous Peoples: Living and Working Conditions of Aboriginal Populations in Independent Countries* (ILO 1953). The "features common to all such people," outlined in the first page of the report, include:

> considerable economic backwardness by comparison with the remainder of the population, the mythical concepts underlying their social organisation and economic activities, inequality of opportunity and the survival of anachronistic economic and land tenure systems that prevent indigenous peoples from fully developing their production and consumption and contribute to perpetuating their inferior social status. (International Labour Office 1953: iiv)

The forward-looking use of the term "indigenous peoples" in the title of this report, with its implications for self-determination in international law, does not correspond with its colonialist values and assimilationist policy orientation. With its socio-evolutionist overtones, this report in turn provided much of the impetus behind the 1957 ILO Convention (No. 107), Concerning the Protection and Integration of Indigenous and Other Tribal and Semi-Tribal Populations in Independent Countries (to which eighteen states are still signatory). The description of the beneficiaries of this Convention in Article 1 – as those "whose social and economic conditions are at a less advanced stage than the stage reached by the other sections of the national community" – reveals the classic colonial paradigms of "progress" versus "backwardness" as explanations of human difference and the conditions of misery of those on the margins of states, which call for legal intervention and remediation.[6]

---

[6] The complete text of the ILO definitions in article 1 of Convention (No. 107) reveals the use of the term "tribal" as a synonym for "backward," and hence in need of integration into the state:

(a) members of tribal or semi-tribal populations in independent countries whose social and economic conditions are at a less advanced stage than the stage reached by the other sections of the national community, and whose status is regulated wholly or partially by their own customs or traditions or by special laws or regulations;
(b) members of tribal or semi-tribal populations in independent countries which are regarded as indigenous on account of their descent from the populations which inhabited the country, or a geographical region to which the country belongs, at the time of conquest or colonisation and

A further preliminary definition of the indigenous inhabitants of states was made by Chilean diplomat Hernàn Santa Cruz (a former delegate in the drafting committee of the Universal Declaration), in a report, begun in 1966 and completed in 1970, on economic, social, and cultural discrimination toward minorities. Santa Cruz stressed the difficulties of arriving at a definition of the indigenous or aboriginal inhabitants of a given territory, observing that, "in many instances the first confrontation between 'inhabitants' and 'invaders' [sic] took place centuries ago. With the passing of time life in common broke down the physical and ethnic distinctions between the two groups and brought about varying degrees of biological and cultural hybridism" (1970: para. 346). As an outcome of such complexity, Santa Cruz describes "indigenous people" simply as those who are "disadvantaged in relation to the rest of the population: in some countries they are the victims of *de facto* discrimination and continue to suffer from prejudice" (1970: para. 1094). The key question of the distinct rights that might be associated with the concept "indigenous people" was not addressed in this report, and in fact, like the ILO efforts on behalf of indigenous peoples of the 1950s, it concluded with a recommendation that states adopt a policy of assimilation as the best way to achieve an end to discrimination faced by the marginalized indigenous populations.

Whatever its shortcomings, the Santa Cruz report did, however, create an opening for a new study, and with it a more precise definition of indigenous peoples. In a typical UN arrangement in which authorial attribution follows the occupational hierarchy, the resulting report was given the name of the Ecuadorian diplomat José Martínez Cobo, who had political responsibility for it, while his Guatemalan colleague Augusto Willemsen Diaz contributed its key definition of indigenous peoples, along with the conclusion and recommendations. Willemsen Diaz thus arrived at the widely cited working definition, which first appeared in the draft Marínez Cobo report of 1972:

> Indigenous communities, peoples and nations are those which, having a historical continuity with pre-invasion and pre-colonial societies that developed on their territories, consider themselves distinct from other sectors of the societies now prevailing in those territories, or part of them. They form at present non-dominant sectors of society and are determined to preserve, develop and transmit to future generations their ancestral territories and their ethnic identity, as the basis with their own cultural pattern, social institutions and legal systems. (Martínez Cobo 1982: para. 34)

which, irrespective of their legal status, live more in conformity with the social, economic and cultural institutions of that time than with the institutions of the nation to which they belong.

2. For the purposes of this Convention, the term *semi-tribal* includes groups and persons who, although they are in the process of losing their tribal characteristics, are not yet integrated into the national community.

ILO Indigenous and Tribal Populations Convention, 1957 (No. 107). www.ilo.org/dyn/normlex/en/f?p=NORMLEXPUB:12100:0::NO::P12100_ILO_CODE:C107. Accessed 12 April 2015.

There are two ways that this definition introduces an unusual element of flexibility to a UN-sponsored concept. First, according to Henry Minde (a Norwegian legal historian who conducted several interviews with him), Willemsen Diaz emphasized that this definition should be understood as preliminary, a point of departure to be subject to feedback, criticism, and revision. It thus opened the door to negotiation and self-representation, to indigenous peoples themselves taking part in refinement of the definition and the rights claims associated with the concept. What is more, key elements of the working definition, such as the self-identification implied by the term "considering themselves distinct," were influenced by the work of anthropologists, most notably Fredrik Barth, whose seminal 1969 edited volume *Ethnic Groups and Boundaries* emphasized the interface, interaction, and negotiation at the root of ethnic identity. In the final version of the report, the views of several indigenous organizations are also taken into account, including the World Council of Indigenous Peoples and the Consejo Indio de Sud America, inspiring the observation that "indigenous populations themselves have claimed the right to define themselves as an exclusive right on their part" (Martínez Cobo 1982: para. 8). Nevertheless, in keeping with the rejection of ambiguity in legal thought, ever since it first appeared this "working definition" has been used as a reference point for understanding just who indigenous peoples are, a kind of "official definition in UN matters" (Minde 2008: 80).

One of the most important contributions of the Martínez Cobo report, embodied in its flexible definition of indigenous peoples, was its path-breaking emphasis on indigenous peoples with distinct rights, not to be subsumed into discussions of minority peoples and their rights. Taking the implications of this distinction to their logical conclusion, the report found that self-determination "must be recognised as the basic precondition for the enjoyment by indigenous peoples of their fundamental rights and the determination of their own future." And since the key UN bodies, including ECOSOC, did not disassociate themselves from this aspect of the report, it appeared to create an opening for indigenous representatives and their allies to expect greater acceptance of their right to self-determination in the UN system (Minde 2008: 77).

It did not take long for this call for self-determination to be taken up as indigenous organizations and representatives made connections with national and international NGOs and themselves acquired expertise, recognition, and leverage in the UN system. Shortly after the initial drafting of the Martínez Cobo report, high-profile meetings of indigenous peoples took place, nationally, regionally, then fully internationally, resulting in the participation of indigenous peoples' organizations in meetings at the UN headquarters starting in the late 1970s (see Engle 2010: ch. 2). Prominent among them was the 1977 International NGO Conference on Discrimination against Indigenous Peoples in the Americas, held at the Palais des Nations in Geneva, sponsored in part by the Women's International League for Peace and Freedom. The 1977 NGO Conference was a meeting that gave a burst of life and energy to the ILO's previously abstract concept of indigenous peoples, bringing together representatives from throughout the Americas, who, through their very presence, offered tangible displays of human variety, and through their words offered more profound similarities in their experiences of marginalization and dispossession. Those from Latin American dictatorships who managed to obtain the visas needed to travel added poignancy to the exchange, with stories of state-sanctioned violence, political imprisonment, and assassinations. (Today the 1977 NGO Conference is seen nostalgically by indigenous representatives, who consider the roughly thirty surviving original participants as "elders" of the indigenous peoples in the UN. In the 2014 Session of the Permanent Forum on Indigenous Issues there was an agenda item of the plenary session dedicated to these pioneers of the global indigenous movement.)

These meetings at the UN headquarters in Geneva were followed in 1982 by the creation of a more permanent entity: the Working Group on Indigenous Populations (WGIP), a subsidiary body overseen by the Sub-Commission on the Promotion and Protection of Human Rights. From its inception and until it was disbanded in 2006, the Working Group adopted an open-door policy to the participation of indigenous peoples' organizations, bringing into the high-vaulted, art deco meeting rooms, corridors, and cafeterias of the UN headquarters in Geneva (see the cover photo of this book) the presence of often colorfully-dressed delegates attending the annual two-week Session, who shared both common experiences of dispossession and certainty about their status as "indigenous peoples" – with rights of self-determination. From its inception, the Working Group was oriented toward elaborating new human rights standards for indigenous peoples, a challenge that was directly taken up in 1985 with the beginning of the drafting process of the Declaration on the Rights of Indigenous Peoples (completed as a draft in 1993 and ratified as a Declaration in 2007). With the impulse of emerging rights standards behind it, the Working Group's annual Session grew exponentially, from approximately 100 delegates at the first meeting in 1982 to nearly 800 twelve years later when the draft Declaration was completed. More than any other meeting or entity in the UN system, the Working Group was responsible for the emergence of a global indigenous movement, both because of its wide geographical representation of indigenous peoples, and, perhaps above all, because of their sense of common cause, of struggling together for rights and recognition in the face of resistance from states. In the words of Mick Dodson, who attended Working Group meetings in his capacity as Aboriginal and Torres Straits Social Justice Commissioner, "We had gathered there united by our shared frustration with the dominant systems in our own countries and their consistent failure to deliver justice. We were all looking for, and demanding, justice from a higher authority" (1998: 18–19).

The involvement of indigenous representatives in the elaboration and expression of their rights and identities was particularly clear to me in a February 2000 meeting in Geneva on the structure and mandate of the soon-to-be created Permanent

Forum on Indigenous Issues. Indigenous delegates to this meeting, which consisted mainly of experienced participants with membership in NGOs with ECOSOC status, were active in the elaboration of the "socio-cultural regional groupings" from which the eight indigenous experts were to be elected to the Forum, an exercise of legal-geographical imagination in which the world was eventually divided into seven categories: Africa, Asia, Central and South America and the Caribbean, the Arctic, Eastern Europe, North America, and the Pacific. The states, by contrast, limited themselves to five regions: Africa, Asia, Eastern Europe, Latin America and the Caribbean, and "Western Europe and other countries." As these regional groupings illustrate, indigenous delegates did not want to be "Latinized" by a dominant language and culture through the term "Latin America"; and they saw themselves as having distinct regional ways of life that fell into the additional categories of "Arctic" and "the Pacific," which did not correspond with the state-centric way of dividing the world. Indigenous experts with long experience in UN meetings were active in the formulation of an anthropological/geographical design of "socio-cultural" regions – themselves the outcome of the legal imperatives of an equitable distribution of global representation of indigenous peoples in the Permanent Forum.

There is more to the conception of indigenous peoples in the contemporary UN system than the term itself or the socio-cultural regions into which they can be divided. There are also key ideas that follow from their common essence as those on the margins of states, often with durable attachments to a primordial past. The outcome of institutional collaboration between indigenous representatives and UN experts is a constellation of ideas that do not always fit well together, but that resonate with popular expectations of what collective difference and suffering should be: Indigenous peoples are those who represent human diversity in the face of the leveling forces of modernity, including those who possess the collective virtues of unbroken heritage, living connections to humanity's primordial origins; they are sources of deep experiential knowledge that can be used for humanity's benefit, providing models for living in harmony with the natural world, and quite possibly for overcoming the worst consequences of environmental abuse. The management by indigenous peoples of their resources, for example, was characterized by a delegate from Morocco to the 2014 meeting of the Permanent Forum on Indigenous Issues as having "a remarkable harmonization with nature," while the UN itself recognizes the "positive role of the traditional knowledge of indigenous peoples in the areas of biodiversity and climate change" (Handaine 2014). If these peoples indeed represent cultural virtue and new hope for a perfect (or at least perfectible) world, then their rights claims must be the focus of our concern, the injustices from which they suffer addressed, their territory mapped and defended, their culture described and saved from outside influence, and their distinct status recognized.

At the same time, they have inherited legacies of dispossession and often face very real conditions of collective suffering; hence, they are able to effectively represent themselves as the victims of political neglect, removal, forced assimilation into dominant societies, even the targets of mass killing and genocide. The challenges facing indigenous peoples cover the entire range of serious human rights abuses, as in a 2014 account of the state-sanctioned violence occurring in the Chittagong Hills in Bangladesh, which the Asia Indigenous Peoples Caucus described as "mostly related to abduction, arbitrary arrest and detention, harassment and intimidation, extrajudicial killing, indiscriminate firing and bombing, use of persons as human shields, destruction and divestment of property, torture, and for women, rape and sexual harassment," while the most common violations of collective rights were "land grabbing [and] forced displacement, [relating] to economic land concessions for plantations, mines, dams, and other energy and resource extraction projects" (Chakma 2014). The stories that indigenous delegates bring to UN meetings – of past and present victimization at the hands of states – may be restricted to passionate five-minute interventions and later couched in the dispassionate language of reporting, but they consistently meet the UN's criteria of crisis, of conditions of victimization, at least to the extent that the wheels keep turning, the meetings keep being held, information continues to be gathered, and reports written and made available to the interested parties. The UN's anthropology is given shape, substance, and momentum through participatory engagement with the basic principles of collective virtue and victimhood.

In short, the identification of indigenous, tribal, and semi-tribal peoples as objects of international law and intervention first took place in meetings of technocrats and with the pens of international jurists; only some years later was the term "indigenous peoples" taken up and transformed by representatives and organizations that made use of it and situated themselves and their constituents within it. (It is noteworthy that, as categories of beneficiaries of rights in ILO Convention 107, "tribal" and "semi-tribal" peoples fell by the wayside, mainly because they did not carry the legally significant connotations of descent from populations which inhabited the country at the time of conquest or colonization, with rights deriving from original occupation of a territory.) Under these latter circumstances, the reality of the concept of indigenous peoples was permanently transformed: from the original ILO conception of people "hindered" by their ways of life from "sharing fully in the progress of the national community" and in need of assimilation as equal citizens of states, it became, through the intercession of a few far-seeing international jurists, together with the voices of self-identifying indigenous spokespeople, irrevocably associated with forced removal, dispossession, and oppression at the hands of states and industries.[7]

---

[7] The basic process by which concepts with legal potential become naturalized through activism can be understood with reference to Keck and Sikkink's (1998: 12) account of the "boomerang pattern of influence," also known as the "boomerang effect".

DISAMBIGUATION

So far, I have described the conceptual categories elaborated by international institutions as top-down, with ideas and opportunities associated with forms of collective belonging elaborated in board rooms – and at the same time as participatory, with global coalitions of rights claimants shaping the discourse that applies to them and lobbying for greater rights and recognition in the international system. It would be misleading to choose one or the other as a defining quality of UN conceptions of belonging when the structure of international institutions is such that in some circumstances small groups of experts can have wide latitude in elaborating (or reconceiving) concepts that include notions of social membership; while at the same time a concept of belonging can be linked to activist networks, particularly when that concept is elaborated in association with rights, venues for gathering, and focal points for public influence.

Another part of the answer to the top-down/participatory conundrum is that the space for and influence of participation have changed over time. The international movement of indigenous peoples illustrates the transformation that took place from the post–World War II institutions that zealously guarded the prerogatives of states, ultimately yielding to the exponentially growing influence of NGOs, including their development as significant actors in the designated public processes of international institutions. In these circumstances people are not just defined by legal process; they are able, perhaps even called upon, to define themselves. The new space for self-representation through legal concepts means that rights can produce a participatory kind of anthropology, which encourages representation from rights claimants themselves. It is through participation in the pursuit of justice and prosperity that concepts of human belonging elaborated in global institutions become populated, and in the process reconsidered, reformulated, reasserted, publicized, and naturalized.

One of the unique things about the ethnological imaginations of international institutions is that their concepts of belonging are not inert or restricted to academic analysis. The relation between people and the things they name – or the institutions that name *them* – is never static (Douglas 1986: 101). As categories become infused with rights, they have the potential to attract active responses from those who fit within them as claimants. They serve as focal points for strategic engagement, including public lobbying. This produces a distinct process for determining the legitimacy or illegitimacy of a concept. Successful rights-based categories are validated by those who have strong incentives to match their self-representation with their place in the law. They depend, further, on the ability of these rights claimants to make effective use of the category, to be impactful and persuasive in representing their claims and identities both to those experts, officials, and advocates assembled in the meeting room at the UN headquarters and to more distant, abstract public audiences reading newspapers or browsing the Internet.

At what point – and in what ways – do the rights-holders and peacemakers who are the subjects of rights or conceptual diplomacy make their presence felt? How do they enter the scene, engage in the debates, and possibly reform the foundations of their participation in the initiatives originally conceived for their benefit, in which their essence is given shape and substance?

There are clearly certain parameters within which grassroots participation is given expression and autonomy in international institutions, parameters that have to do with rights and peacemaking. Effective rights regimes are populated with the living representatives of victim communities or of diversity-in-jeopardy, to the point that the public spectacle of claims-making confirms the anthropological assumptions at their origins. To be a member of a youth population representing one's civilization or a member of a delegation representing an indigenous people, it is as simple as meeting some basic criteria (such as age, birth origin, and NGO affiliation respectively) and completing an online registration form. Through being populated and naturalized by claimants, legal conceptions of belonging can acquire the reality and the truth-value that most of us associate with trustworthy knowledge. The fit between a concept and the social reality it purports to name comes about above all through the effectiveness (or limits) of the rights built into the concept, rights that then attract (or repel) participation, performance, debate, and renegotiation of the concept. Compared to the struggle involved in ethnographic descriptions by anthropologists or the meticulous data collection in other human sciences, this pathway to legitimacy is almost like cheating. All you have to do is describe a social world within an emerging regime of law with enough promise of practical (or, better, political) benefit and the world itself gives it truth-value.

In its extreme form of knowledge-oriented managerialism, the UN's anthropology can begin with the formulation of an interpretive concept, which then acquires currency, not by any kind of observation, testing, or scholarly peer review, but by the strategic adaptations of participating human actors. Institutional knowledge of the forms and variety of human belonging can constitute a kind of exogenous ontology, in which experts describe the categories and qualities of human life according to the exigencies of rights, peacemaking, and prosperity, and in which reality conforms and adapts to these concepts. In some circumstances, as illustrated by the concept of "local communities," this approach to typology not only identifies the beneficiaries of global initiatives, it begins by "disaggregating" and elaborating the categories that bring them into being for instrumental purposes.

Such detachment of human rights conceptions of social belonging from the lives of human actors comes not from a defiance of the logic of social construction, but simply from the structural removal of conceptualization from the context in which it naturally occurs. The experts involved in the management of diversity sometimes conduct their work in the abstract, describing categories of the virtuous-oppressed in the absence of the active participation of those described and categorized. This removal, in turn, is an outcome of the strategic and instrumental imperatives of legal thought. Institutions arise and are maintained, Searle (1995: 40) argues, through "continued human cooperation in the specific forms of recognition, acceptance, and acknowledgment" of the institutional forms of human society. But Searle's emphasis on cooperation within a language community as a foundation for the creation and maintenance of institutional facts overlooks the extent to which new conceptual and institutional realities can be developed at a remove from those people whom the new language of belonging is intended to describe, and possibly to liberate. That is to say, institutions of global governance are able to take knowledge out of context, find what is essential in it for the purposes of diplomacy or development, translate it into the languages of bureaucratic fact finding or law, and return it to its source of origin in new form, connected to visions of rights and diplomatic opportunities. Through this process of institutional translation, the way that people collectively identify themselves is sometimes secondary to the rights-orientation and other strategic objectives of conceptual construction. It is almost as though, in Ptolemy's universe, the sun could be conferred recognition and rights for revolving around the earth in an effort to make unnecessary the heleocentrism of Copernicus.

Critical scholars of human rights as social practice have become aware of a tendency for the interventions of experts to overlook or intervene inappropriately in local practice; but the power of concepts of belonging in human rights has the same global reach as the rights themselves, and the potential for mistranslation and misuse of conceptual/legal power has a corresponding wide reach. As with any significant source of public influence, it is the locus of both opportunity and error. The recent history of the indigenous peoples' movement shows the great potential for legal concepts to produce conditions of empowerment, but even here, the scope of what we might call "beneficiary-oriented participation" – making peoples' own social constructions part of the avenues for legal recognition and redress – is restricted by the conceptual foundations of legal categories formulated by experts who are attentive to state interests and the popular resonance that might (or might not) be achieved through activism.

The question arises, then, of whether the study of legal social construction can ever be disambiguated from its strategic or practical application. Annelise Riles addresses this issue with the argument that in the context of global legal activism (the "Network," in her terms), "the performance of culture ultimately fails to produce a position 'outside' legal instrumentalism"; in other words, the form and content of culture "are already (negatively) dictated by the form of the legal instrument itself" (2006: 62). The legal instrumentalism of global activism is thus a kind of trap or cage that takes hold of every form of cultural knowledge for its own purposes and doesn't let go.

Does this mean that it is impossible to disambiguate a critically oriented, comprehensive anthropology of law from the anthropology produced by global institutions or from the contested and processual self-knowledge and representation of claimants, or even from the anthropology of "engaged," "activist," or "vernacularizing" anthropologists? Under the influence of the ideas produced and naturalized in global institutions, have legal fictions (or some permutation thereof) now inevitably and inexorably become a foundation for our understanding of human life?

Perhaps the appeal of the legal/strategic anthropology originating in non-academic institutions is too powerful for there to be any option other than an "if you can't beat them, join them" kind of acquiescence, or willful acceptance of the instrumentally oriented concepts of collective virtue and victimhood as the ultimate source of our knowledge of the world. After all, these are concepts that sometimes take hold and become focal points of narrative and dialogue on suffering, sources of dignity for the marginalized, that through public exposure hold powerful, oftentimes abusive actors to account. But, as I have tried to show here, the mere fact that these questions can be posed means that the potential remains for the strategically oriented anthropology of global institutions to be disambiguated from an approach that, at a remove from strategic choices, includes the process of institutional conceptual construction in its subject matter, as one of the emerging ways that human belonging can be understood in its variety, complexity, flux, and reflux. It is important to consider both the managerial origins and performative effects of concepts, as they appeal to, or are rejected by, those who are seeking conditions of redress and prosperity through processes of public justice.

REFERENCES

Alliance of Civilizations. 2016. Youth Solidarity Fund. www.unaoc.org/what-we-do/grants-and-competitions/youth-solidarity-fund/. Accessed September 5, 2015.

American Anthropological Association. 1947. "Statement on Human Rights." *American Anthropologist*. 49(4): 539–543.

Amselle, Jean-Loup. 2010. *Vers un multiculturalisme français: l'empire de la coutume*. Paris: Éditions Flammarion.

Austin, J. L. 1962. *How to Do Things with Words*. Cambridge, MA: Harvard University Press.

Berkeley Center for Religion, Peace and World Affairs. 2015. Alliance of Civilizations Media Fund. http://berkleycenter.georgetown.edu/programs/alliance-of-civilizations-media-fund. Accessed July 12, 2015.

Bornstein, Erica. 2005. *The Spirit of Development: Protestant NGOs, Morality, and Economics in Zimbabwe*. Stanford: Stanford University Press.

Brumann, Christoph. 2014. "Heritage Agnosticism: A Third Path for the Study of Cultural Heritage." *Social Anthropology/Anthropologie Sociale*. 22(2): 173–188.

Brumann, Christoph and David Berliner (eds.). 2016. "Introduction: UNESCO World Heritage – Grounded?" In *World Heritage on the Ground: Ethnographic Perspectives*, Christoph Brumann and David Berliner, eds. New York and Oxford: Berghahn.

Cassese, Antonio. 2012. "Introduction." In *Realizing Utopia: The Future of International Law*, Antonio Cassese, ed. Oxford: Oxford University Press, pp. xvii–xxii.

Chakma, Mangal Kumar. 2014. "Agenda Item 4: Human Rights." Asia Indigenous Peoples Caucus, Statement to the 13th meeting of the Permanent Forum on Indigenous Issues, New York, 12–23 May.

Comaroff, John and Jean Comaroff. 1997. *Of Revelation and Revolution: The Dialectics of Modernity on a South African Frontier*. Chicago: University of Chicago Press.

Constable, Marianne. 2014. *Our Word Is Our Bond: How Legal Speech Acts*. Stanford: Stanford University Press.

Dodson, Mick. 1998. "Linking International Standards with Contemporary Concerns of Aboriginal and Torres Strait Islander Peoples." In *Indigenous Peoples, the United Nations and Human Rights*, Sarah Pritchard, ed. London: Zed / Federation.

Douglas, Mary. 1986. *How Institutions Think*. Syracuse: Syracuse University Press.

Engle, Karen. 2001. "From Skepticism to Embrace: Human Rights and the American Anthropological Association from 1947–1999." *Human Rights Quarterly*. 23: 536–559.

  2010. *The Elusive Promise of Indigenous Development: Rights, Culture, Strategy*. Durham and London: Duke University Press.

Englund, Harri. 2006. *Prisoners of Freedom: Human Rights and the African Poor*. Berkeley and Los Angeles: University of California Press.

Eriksen, T. H. 2001. "Between Universalism and Relativism: A Critique of the UNESCO Concept of Culture." In *Culture and Rights: Aanthropological Perspectives*. J. K. Cowan, M.-B. Dembour, and R. Wilson (eds.), Cambridge: Cambridge University Press, pp. 127–148.

Goodale, Mark. 2009. *Surrendering to Utopia: An Anthropology of Human Rights*. Stanford: Stanford University Press.

  (ed.). 2013. *Human Rights at the Crossroads*. Oxford: Oxford University Press.

Handaine, Mohammed. 2014. "Déclaration de la délégation amazighe, instance permanente, New York." Delegation amazighe, Afrique du Nord. Statement to the 13th meeting of the Permanent Forum on Indigenous Issues, New York, May 12–23.

IFAD 2012. "Addressing Poverty through Mobilization of Community Resources." www.ifad.org/operations/projects/regions/pf/seeds/1.htm. Accessed April 14, 2015.

International Indigenous Forum on Biodiversity. 2014. Statement to the Press. Pyeongchang, Republic of Korea, October 13. www.forestpeoples.org/sites/fpp/files/news/2014/10/IIFB%20Press%20Statement.pdf. Accessed April 10, 2015.

International Labour Office. 1953. *Indigenous Peoples: Living and Working Conditions of Aboriginal Populations in Independent Countries*. Studies and Reports, No. 35. Geneva: International Labour Office.

Keck, Margaret and Kathryn Sikkink. 1998. *Activists Beyond Borders: Advocacy Networks in International Politics*. Ithaca and London: Cornell University Press.

Lucero, José Antonio. 2013. "Encountering Indigeneity: The International Funding of Indigeneity in Peru." In *Who Is an Indian?: Race, Place and the Politics of Indigeneity in the Americas*, Maximilian Forte, ed. Toronto: University of Toronto Press, pp. 194–217.

Macfarlane, Alan. 1977. History, Anthropology and the Study of Communities. *Social History*. 2(5): 631–652.

Martínez Cobo, José. 1982. *Study of the Problem of Discrimination Against Indigenous Populations*, Chapter 5, Definition of Indigenous Populations. UN Doc no. E/CN.4/Sub.2/1982/2/Add.6. www.un.org/esa/socdev/unpfii/documents/MCS_v_en.pdf. Accessed September 18, 2015.

Merry, Sally Engle. 2011. "Measuring the World: Indicators, Human Rights, and Global Governance." *Current Anthropology*. 52 (3): 583–595.

2013. "Human Rights Monitoring and the Question of Indicators." In *Human Rights at the Crossroads*, Mark Goodale, ed. Oxford: Oxford University Press, pp. 140–150.

Metraux, A. (communicator). 1951. "United Nations Economic and Security Council, Statement by Experts on Problems of Race." *American Anthropologist*. 53(1): 142–145.

Minde, Henry. 2008. "The Destination and the Journey: Indigenous Peoples and the United Nations from the 1960s through 1985." In *Indigenous Peoples: Self-Determination, Knowledge, Identity*, Henry Minde, ed. Delft: Eburon Publishers, pp. 49–86.

Niezen, Ronald. 2003a. *The Origins of Indigenism: Human Rights and the Politics of Identity*. Berkeley and Los Angeles: University of California Press.

2003b. "Culture and the Judiciary: The Meaning of the Culture Concept as a Source of Aboriginal Rights in Canada." *Canadian Journal of Law and Society*. 18(2): 1–26.

2010. *Public Justice and the Anthropology of Law*. Cambridge: Cambridge University Press.

2013. "The Law's Legal Anthropology." In *Human Rights at the Crossroads*, Mark Goodale, ed. Oxford: Oxford University Press, pp. 185–197.

Poutignat, Philippe and Jocelyne Streiff-Fenart. 1995. *Théories d'ethnicité*. Paris: Presses Universitaires de France.

Riles, Annelise. 2006. "Anthropology, Human Rights, and Legal Knowledge: Culture in the Iron Cage." *American Anthropologist*. 108(1): 52–65.

Santa Cruz, Hernàn. 1970. *Study on Racial Discrimination in the Political, Economic, Social and Cultural Spheres*. United Nations Publication, Sales No. E.71 XIV.

Searle, John, 1995. *The Construction of Social Reality*. New York: The Free Press.

UNAOC 2015. UNAOC United Nations Alliance of Civilizations: Who We Are. www.unaoc.org/who-we-are/. Accessed 8 July 2015.

UNEP 2013. A toolkit to support conservation by indigenous peoples and local communities: Building capacity and sharing knowledge for Indigenous Peoples' and Community Conserved Territories and Areas (ICCAs). www.unep.org/dewa/portals/67/pdf/ICCA_toolkit.pdf. Accessed April 14, 2015.

UNESCO. 1950. The Race Question. http://unesdoc.unesco.org/images/0012/001282/128291eo.pdf. Accessed July 7, 2015.

2012. World Heritage and Sustainable Development: The Role of Local Communities. www.unesco.org/new/en/venice/resources-services/multimedia/photo-stories/world-heritage-and-sustainable-development-the-role-of-local-communities/. Accessed March 29, 2015.

United Nations. 1992. Convention on Biological Diversity. www.cbd.int/doc/legal/cbd-en.pdf. Accessed March 29, 2015.

2001. Letter dated 27 September 2001 from the Permanent Representative of Austria to the United Nations addressed to the Secretary-General. U.N. doc no. A/59/419.

2004. The Concept of Local Communities. Background paper prepared by the Secretariat of the Permanent Forum on Indigenous Issues for the Expert Workshop on the Disaggregation of Data. UN doc no. PFII/2004/WS.1/3/Add.1.

Van Schooten, Hanneke. 2007. "Law as Fact, Law as Fiction: A Tripartite Model of Legal Communication." In *Interpretation, Law and the Construction of Meaning* A Wagner et al. eds. New York: Springer, pp. 3–20.

Von Humboldt, Alexander 2009 [1799–1804]. *Amerikanische Reise: Rekonstruiert und Kommentiert von Hanno Beck*. Wiesbaden: Edition Erdmann.

World Intellectual Property Organization (WIPO). 2014. Practical Workshop for Indigenous Peoples and Local Communities on IP and Traditional Knowledge. Geneva, December 3–5, 2014. www.wipo.int/tk/en/indigenous/workshop.html. Accessed March 29, 2015.

Wright, Susan. 1994. "Culture in anthropology and organizational studies." In *Anthropology of Organizations*, Susan Wright, ed. London and New York: Routledge, pp. 1–32.

Index

!Kung, 176–178
"studying up", 4, *See* Nader, Laura
15th Council of Parties (COP 15), 221, 225, 235n.9, 235–238, 240
18th Council of Parties (COP 18), 221, 229

access, 57
  fieldwork, 65, 99, 106, 118, 224
  of NGOs to global organizations, 17
  to organizations, 6, *See* global institutions; methods of ethnography
  to the WTO, 36
  to Universal Periodic Review (UPR), 111–113, 115, 118
access to justice, 200, 204, 207
accountability, 14, 20, 24
  audits and, 11, 14–15, 123
  bureaucratization and, 199, 201, 203
  documentation and, 211
  human rights and, 93
  mechanisms of, 201
  paperwork and, 216
  statistics and, 11, 15, 161
  Universal Perdiodic Review (UPR) and, 108–114
  World Bank and, 187
acronyms, in the UN, 78
activism, 20, 23, 302, 314
  anthropology and, 315
  belonging and, 312
  bureaucracy and, 103
  business and, 226
  challenges to, 85
  climate change and, 25
  expertise and, 267, 301
  human rights and, 130, 142, 144, 267, 294
  in Amazon, 230
  NGOs, 1, 16–17, 111, 120
  San activists, 79
  United Nations and, 26, 85, 87
  United Nations Permanent Forum on Indigenous Issues, 23, 79, 99
  United Nations Security Council and, 153
  United Nations treaties and, 142
  Universal Periodic Review and, 110, 113, 119, 120
activists, 3, 11, 19, 23, 26, 79, 80, 83–85, 96, 98, 110, 113, 114, 119, 120, 130, 142, 144, 153, 225, 226, 234n.8, 267, 294, 301, 302, 312, 315
  civil servants and, 86–87, 103, 130
  human rights and, 119, 142, 144, 301
  in science, 225
  indigenous, 79, 80, 83, 85, 86, 96, 98, 103
actus reus, 268, 273, 274, 288
albedo effect, 233
Albania, 278, 303
Amazon, 220, 222, 226–231, *See* Reducing Emissions From Deforestation And Forest Degradation (REDD+)
  climate change and, 222
  climate change metrics and, 220, 228
  environment of, 229
  evironmentalists of, 230
  indigenous peoples in, 222, 227
  social movements in, 230
American Anthropological Association, 295
American Anthropological Association, Statement on Human Rights, 294
Anders, Gerhard, 266, 267
Angola, 168, 176, 177, 179–181
Annan, Kofi, 10n.7, 67, 298
Antarctica, 233, 246
anthropology
  as science, 123
  by organizations, 294, 301, 315
  colonialism and, 4, 300
  culture, 246, *See* World Heritage List
  engaged, 294, 315

European biases in, 259
expansion of field sites, 5
globalisation and, 33
history, 18, 31, 33, 34, 294–295
human rights and, 148
international relations and, 72
knowledge production and, 27, 34, 122
methods of, 4
of bureaucracy, 221, 228
of global governance, 3, 27
of humanitarianism, 173
of organizations, 4, 18, 33, 34, 62, 294, 300
of the state, 5
proximity and ethnographers, 7
subjects of, 4, 5
Arctic, 219, 220, 222, 225, 227, 228, 233, 234, 235, 237, 238, 240, 310
economics and, 238
indigenous peoples of, 236, 237, 240
language and, 235
states of, 237
Arctic Council, 237
Argentina, 37, 42, 153, 154, 184
artefacts
activated, 208
of development, 199
audit
accountability and, 14–15, 123
as ritual, 23, 106, 109, 110, 114, 120, 149, See Universal Periodic Review (UPR)
as soft power, 109
assessment of assets, 165
knowledge production and, 123
mechanisms of, 14
power relations and, 109
state practices, 14
statistics and, 161
Universal Periodic Review and, 14, 109
audit culture, 14, 23, 24, 109, 192
Australia, 41, 50, 51, 95, 147, 164, 167
authority
academic training and, 261

Badman, Tim, 248
Balkans conflict, 269, 272, 277
Bangladesh, 25, 159, 198, 199, 203, 204, 205, 206, 207, 208, 209, 210, 211, 212, 215, 216, 235, 311
in NGO publicity, 208
judicial system of, 204, 205, 206
UNDO Bangladesh, 213
Bauer, Raymond, 158, See indicators
Belgium, 112, 118, 119
belonging, 300, 313
activist networks and, 312

categories of, 300, 304, 313
cultivation of, 299
global institutions and, 305, 312
human rights and, 298, 314
in international institutions, 300
indigenous peoples and, 302
Benin, 43, 46
biodiversity
conservation and, 186, 233
black box, 120
Bolivia
Chaco region, 85n.8
indigenous government and, 95
Bosnia, 269, 273n.14, 275, 276, 281, 282, 303
Botswana, 79, 91, 94
boundaries
in climate change, 220
within the United Nations, 78
Branson, Richard, 225
Brazil, 41–44, 50–52, 154, 161, 162, 164, 229, 235, 252, 254, 255, 255n.11, 284, 304
Cancun Conference, 42
social movements in, 304
BRICS, 255n.11
bureaucracy, 2, 221, See ethnography; activism
anthropology of, 5, 6, 228
changes through, 223
cooperation in, 34
documents and, 228
hope and, 228
international courts and, 270
of climate change, 224
of United Nations, 96, 99
organizations and, 294
paperwork, 199
transnational, 215
United Nations human rights regimes and, 130, 142
bureaucratization, 198, 203
Burkina Faso, 43

Cambodia, 128, 245
Cameroon, 37, 159
Canada, 37, 52, 95, 167, 221, 227, 234, 235, 237, 302
Canadian Broadcasting Corporation (CBC), 236, 237
CAP reform, 42
capacity building, 207
carbon markets, 98, 220, 222, 226, 229–233, 233n.6
causation, 26, 291
legal anthropology, 266
responsibility and, 266
speech crimes and, 274
censuses, national, 159
center-periphery dynamic, 130, 131, 142, 149

Central African Republic, 96
centralization, 182
Chad, 43
China, 32, 37, 42, 44, 48, 50–52, 59, 61, 64, 135, 142, 255, 255n.11
civil-law, 270
civil society, 3, 16, 23–24, 26, 33, 40, 79–81, 86, 89, 99, 107, 110–111, 113–114, 119–120, 143, 153, 179, 202, 207
classification systems, 253
climate change, 25, 26, 83, 90, 219–241, 310
  diplomacy, 222
  governable, 223
climate change regulator
  sea ice, 233
Clyde River, 234, 235
Cold War, 68, 268
Coldplay, 44
common law, 270
community-based organization, 212
Compaoré, Blaise, 43, See IDEAS Centre
consensus, 22, 44–45, 50
  performance criteria, 123
  United Nations Security Council and, 55, 60–61, 67, 75
  World Trade Organization (WTO) and, 32–33, 41, 50
control
  indigenous people over territories, 227
  of Amazonian territories, 226
  state, 202
  through indicators, 215
Convention Against Torture (CAT), 117
Convention Concerning the Protection of the World Cultural and Natural Heritage, 245–247, 249
Convention on Biological Diversity (CBD), 301, 302, 304
Convention on the Elimination of All Forms of Discrimination Against Women (CEDAW), 132
Coordinadora de las Organizaciones Indígenas de la Cuenca Amazónica (COICA), 222, 224, 226, 227, 229, 231, 232, 237–241
Costa Rica, 231
cotton, 38, 40, 43, 45–48
  global market, 44
  subsidies, 45
  World Trade Organization (WTO) and, 44, 46
Cotton 4, 45, 46, 47, 48
Cotton Initiative, 45, 46
cotton sector, 43
  and International Monetary Fund (IMF), 43
  as part of GDP, 43

Country Common Assessment, 88
crime
  against humanity, 273
  speech, 26, 267, 272–275, 279–284, 287–297
  war crimes, 273
cultural heritage, 296
cultural landscapes, 254
culture
  anthropological developments, 34
  as analytical perspective, 72
  Canada's Supreme Court, 297n.1
  classifications of, 300
  cultural relativism, 295
  for political struggle, 100
  groups shaped by statistics, 300
  in UNESCO, 300
  in United Nations Security Council (UNSC), 56
  incompleteness, 53
  indigenous, 100, 310
  legal, 285
  legal instrumentalism, 314
  of expertise, 9
  of global institutions, 8, 53
  of power, 4
  of United Nations Security Council, 62, 64, 73
  of United Nations work, 80
  organizations, 72n.14
  rankings of, 246
  relationships between, 34
  rights and, 295
  United Nations Educational, Scientific and Cultural Organization (UNESCO) concept of, 296

decentralization, 232
Declaration on the Rights of Indigenous Peoples (DRIP), 89, 91, 96, 309
Deeb, Hadi Nicholas, 7, 38
Del Ponte, Carla, 270
Delors, Jacques, 36
demographics. *See* indicators
  as political, 161
Denmark, 82, 95, 237
Department of Economic and Social Affairs (DESA), 80
Desai, Deval, 200, 216
developing countries
  imports and, 50
  non-governmental organizations (NGOs) and, 44
  subsidies and, 42
  Universal Periodic Review of, 113
  WTO and, 33

Index

development
  and United Nations Educational, Scientific and Cultural Organization (UNESCO), 303
  anthropologists and, 5
  approaches to, 2
  as a discipline, 298
  economic, 41
  financialization of, 181
  global governance and, 314
  indigenismo and, 306
  management staff, 179
  NGOs and, 297, 302
  study of, 11
  United Nations and, 302
  World Bank and, 181
development discourse, 200, 214
diplomacy, 86, 90, 100, 116
  as ethic, 13
  climate change, 224, 241
  experts and, 13
  language of, 11
  politics of, 12
  United Nations High Commissioner for Refugees, 175
disenchantment, 81
displacement, 5, 16, 173, 191, 192, 289, 311
dissensus, 48
distinction, and quality, 250
diversity
  management and, 298
document production, chain of, 222
documents, 1, 3, 9, 14, 23–26, 42, 57, 58, 80, 86, 88, 91, 101, 106n.1, 108–117, 120, 124, 131n.1, 134, 136–140, 155, 185, 190, 198, 199, 202, 203, 208–214, 220–225, 228–240, 249, 270, 300, 301
  as bureaucratic artefacts, 203
  ethnographic artefact, 202
  legibility and, 24
Doha Development Agenda, 41, 42
  development and, 48
  trade, inequality in, 41
Doha Round, 22, 32, 32n.1, 40, 41, 49, 50, 53, *See* World Trade Organization
domination, 301n.3
  through WTO rankings, 48
drought, 186
Dunckel, Arthur, 43, *See* IDEAS Centre

Earth System, 220
economic measures
  changes in categories of, 160
  problems with, 158
Egypt, 46, 255, 255n.11
enchantment, 26, 263

epistemology, 26, 266, 267, 271, 289, 291
Estonia, 252
ethnic cleansing, 272
ethnography
  "from below", 5
  as approach, 7
  collaboration, 8, 21, 37, 78, 122–123
  empathy, 7
  ethics and practice of, 122
  immersion, 7
  knowledge production, 122
  methods, 6–8, 34, 37, 80, 131, *See* anthropology of organizations
  modernity and, 4
  multilateral, 246n.2
  multi-positioned, 22, 80
  multi-sited, 80, 132, 199
  observation and, 7
  para-ethnography, 34, 58, 122
  transnational, 114
Eurocentrism, 254, 255
European Commission, 36
  Commissioner for Trade, 42
European Investment Bank, 183
European Union (EU), 199, 205, 206, 208, 209, 210, 213, 215, 216
  Delegation of, 213, 215
  funded projects of, 208
  in NGO publicity, 208
  International Criminal Tribunal for the Former Yugoslavia (ICTY) and, 269, 271
  subsidies and, 43
  tariffs and, 42
  trade, 42
Evangelical Lutheran Church in Namibia, 179
Evans-Pritchard, E. E., 266
evidence, 11, 15, 18, 257, 266–268, 270, 273–275, 279, 282–290
expertise. *See* activism
  activism and, 144, 301
  anthropologists and, 172
  consultants and, 179
  in international criminal trials, 266
  in statistics, conflicts in, 155
  in UN Security Council, 56
  knowledge, 18
  knowledge and, 267
  non governmental organizations and, 83
  Panels of Engineering Experts, 182
  Panels of Environmental Experts, 182
  Permanent Forum on Indigenous Issues, 22–23
  politics of neutrality, 13
  statistical. *See* United Nations Statistical Commission (UNSC)

expertise (cont.)
    United Nations Permanent form on Indigenous Issues and, 81
    United Nations Security Council (UNSC) and, 22, 56, 62
    World Trade Organization (WTO), 40
experts
    relation to global organizations, 10–11
    UNDP Monitoring and Evaluation, 213

Farm Bill, 2002, 41, 43
fear, 131, 288
    as motivation for not reading statement, 93
    of administrative reprisal in UNHCR, 193
    of government retaliation, 176, 178
Field Operations and Technical Cooperation Division, 115, 116
fieldwork. *See* ethnography
Finland, 95, 137–148, 161
food security, 232
food sovereignty, 232
formality and informality, 6
Forward Studies Unit, 36
fragility, 15–16, 18–19, 27, 132, 155, 266
France, 37, 45, 59, 60, 63, 157–159, 167, 269
Free, Prior, and Informed Consent (FPIC), 96, 99, 184
Fundamental Principles of Official Statistics, 154

G-20, 42, 45
Galanter, Marc, 55, 62, 67, 71, 72, 73
General Agreement on Tariffs and Trade (GATT), 39, 45, *See* Imboden, Nicholas
    World Trade Organization (WTO) and, 31
Geneva, 5, 24, 31, 32, 33, 38, 49, 51, 79, 87, 91, 106, 118, 121, 127, 130, 131, 133, 134, 135, 137, 139, 141, 143, 144, 147, 148, 174, 175, 249, 303, 305, 308, 309
    cost of, 141
Germany, 45, 159, 167, 210, 246, 251, 255, 259, 269
global north, 41, 223, 255
    data systems and, 158
global organizations, 1–27, 216, 294
    anthropologists and, 5
    definition of, 2, 10
    difficulty with conducting ethnography in, 35
    ethnographic methods of, 37
    ethnography of, 10, 31
    public opinion of, 16
global south, 41, 255
globalisation, 33, 40
globality, 2
Good, Anthony, 266

governance
    global, 2, 155
    global governance, 1–3, 5–6, 12, 15, 24, 27, 97, 155–156, 253, 297–298, 303
    multilateralism, 35
Greece, 112, 118–120, 154, 303
Greek National Commission for Human Rights, 120
green economy, 220, 225
Greenland, 225, 227, 233, 237
guidelines, 23, 69, 85, 88, 96, 114, 116, 143, 145–146, 154, 160–161, 175, 183, 189, 223, 247–248
Guyer, Jane, 221

heritage
    as discourse, 245
    modern, 254
    types of, 249
Herskovitz, Melville, 294
hierarchy
    ethnography and, 8, *See* ethnographic methods
    in UN and knowledge, 298
    in UN authorship, 307
    of audits within academic writing, 123
    UN, 89
historians
    as experts, 266
    in international court, 266
HIV/AIDS, 186, 190
Hoffman, Danny, 267, *See* Special Court for Sierra Leone
Holmes, Douglas, 7, 34, 122
hope, 9, 18–21, 95, 96, 103, 122, 225, 228, 238–241, 263, 310
    "palaces of hope", 19
    climate change and, 240
    global organizations and, 18
    indigenous groups and, 240, 241
Hrtkovci, 272
Hull, Matthew, 203
Human Development Index (HDI), 153, 159, 162–169
    controversy in, 162
    creation of, 159
    data within, 168
    definition of, 163
    measurements in, 163
    response to critique of, 168
Human Development Report Office, 163, 164, 167, 168, 169
    autonomy of, 168
    critiques of, 165–168
    indicators, 168
    mandate of, 164
    responses to criticism, 168

Index

human rights, 2, 5, 10, 14, 16–19, 23, 24, 27, 79, 82, 84, 87, 88, 93–96, 100–102, 106–124, 127–149, 172, 191–193, 200, 204, 223, 226, 254, 294, 295, 299, 302, 304, 309, 311, 313, 314
  discourse of, 131
  international development and, 16
  measures of, 158
  monitoring bodies, 16, 23, 24, 107, 112, 118, 122–124, 130–132, 138, 140–144, 147, 148
  relativism, 130
  violations, 19
Human Rights Committee, 17, 23, 127, 128, 131–149
Human Rights Council and Special Procedures Division, 115
Human Rights Treaties Division, 115
human, conceptions in anthropology, 294
humanity, and human rights, 295
hybrid legal system, 270

IDEAS Centre, 43
Imboden, Nicholas, 43, 45, *See* IDEAS Centre
IMF. *See* International Monetary Fund (IMF)
India, 42, 44, 45, 50–52, 154, 161, 162, 164, 229, 235, 252, 254, 255, 255n.11, 259, 260
indicator culture, 24
indicators, 159
  data collection, 129, 158
  development and, 214
  economic measurement, 160
  forest, 229
  global data systems, 158
  global governance and, 253
  government interest in, 159
  history of, 158
  ice, 231
  movement, 159
  Objectively Verifiable Indicators, 215
  purpose of, 162
  World Heritage, 26
  World Heritage Sites and, 253
indigenous peoples
  activism, 80, 83, 85, 87, 94, 96, 98, 103
  belonging and, 302
  climate change and, 310
  experts, 23, 80, 82–90, 310
  self-determination and, 306, 308
Indigenous Peoples of Africa Coordinating Committee (IPACC), 83
Indigenous Peoples' Organizations (IPOs), 79, 81, 224, 226, 308, 309
Indonesia, 140, 200, 229, 284, 302
informal justice institutions, 201
informality, 61
  United Nations Security Council and, 63

injustice
  indigenous delegates and, 90
  indigenous stories of, 81
  made legible, 92
  NGOs and, 17, *See* optics
  passion and, 90
  Permanent Forum and, 90
  United Nations management of discourse and, 86
instigation
  as a legal concept, 272
institutional ethnography. *See* ethnography
  history of, 4–6
  methodology of, 6–8
in-stream flow requirements, 185
intentionality
  as legal concept, 273
Inter-American Commission on Human Rights, 228
Intergovernmental Panel on Climate Change (IPCC), 225
internally displaced persons, 176n.3, 192
International Advisory Group, 182
International Atomic Energy Agency (IAEA), 111.1
International Bank for Reconstruction and Development, 181
  World Bank and, 200
International Centre for International Centre for the Study of the Preservation and Restoration of Cultural Property (ICCROM), 255
International Council of Monuments and Sites, 248
International Covenant on Civil and Political Rights (ICCPR), 23, 127, 131–133
international courts
  coercion and, 270
  local communities and, 270
  procedural irregularities of, 278
International Criminal Law (ICL)
  as fusion of legal systems, 286
  causation and, 289
  doctrine of, 268
  evidence in, 287
  expertise, 267
  image of, 284
  streamlining of, 286
  witnesses and, 287
International Criminal Tribunal for the Former Yugoslavia (ICTY), 26, 267, 269–271, 274
  United Nations Security Council (UNSC) and, 271
International Development Association, 181
International Finance Corporation, 181
international finance institution, 181

International Fund for Agricultural Development
    (IFAD), 2, 80, 96, 302
International Indigenous Forum on
    Biodiversity, 302
international justice insititutions
  force and, 287
  knowledge production and, 291
International Labour Organization (ILO), 22, 80,
    87, 91, 93, 96, 227, 305–307, 309, 311
  indigenous peoples and, 305–307, 309, 311
  International Labour Organization Convention
    (No. 169), 91, 93, 96
  International Labour Organization Convention
    (No. 107), 306, 306n.6, 307, 311
  training courses, 87
International Monetary Fund (IMF), 12, 15, 31, 33,
    43, 181
International Rivers Network, 189
International Union for the Conservation of
    Nature (IUCN), 246, 248
International Union of Concerned Scientists, 225
Inuit, 228, 234, 235, 240
Inuit Circumpolar Council (ICC), 221, 233, 234,
    235, 236, *See* Arctic
  constructions of the Artctic, 235
  discourse, 236
  documents, 236
  events of, 234, 235
  exclusion of, 236
  mandate of, 234
  narratives about the Arctic, 234
  negotiations, 236
Iran, 168
Iraq's Weapons Declaration, 63, 65–66, 70, 73

Japan, 41, 42, 50–52, 161, 162, 251, 252, 255, 259
Jokilehto, Jukka, 248
Jorda, Claude, 285
Ju/'hoan, 178
jurisdiction, 204

Kelly, Tobias, 17, 117
Kenya, 44
  in World Heritage List, 254
  International Criminal Court (ICC) and, 286
  Maa Forest, 96, *See also* United Nations
    Environment Programme
  *The Prosecutor v. William Samoei Ruto and
    Joshua Arap Sang*, 286, 287
  World Heritage List and, 260
knowledge, 297
  of experts, 267
knowledge production
  authority and, 199

  by global organizations, 18
  in academia, 202
  in bureaucracy, 202
  knowledge products, 207

Laboratoire d'Anthropologie Sociale, 37
Lamy, Pascal, 36, 38, 42, 49, 50, 51
Latour, Bruno, 120, 223
League of Nations, 59, 115, 127, 131
legal anthropology.*See also* anthropology
  evidence and, 266
  outside academia, 315
legal instrumentalism, 314
legal realism, 268
legibility
  international development, 203
  legal systems, 199
  of courts, 212
legitimacy
  climate science and, 233
Lesotho Highlands Water Project, 174, 175, 181, 183,
    184, 186, 188
  assets, 183
Li, Tania, 223
liability
  war crimes and, 272
linkage evidence, 268
local legal entities, 183, 185, 188

Macedonia, 118, 303
magic, 262
Malloch-Brown, Mark, 8–9
Mali, 43, 245
Manchester School, 4
Marcus, George, 7, 34, 38, 122, 246n.2
Martínez Cobo report, 307–308
measurable facts
  Universal Periodic Review (UPR), 117
media, 16, 17, 27, 33, 44, 50, 67, 92, 177,
    178n.4, 228
  Social media, 87, 92, 145
  World Trade Organization (WTO) and, 53
mediation
  between state and non-state legal systems, 207
  between states, 17
  of non-state justice institutions, 202
  of place, 261
  paperwork, 209
mens rea, 267, 268, 273
Merry, Sally Engle, 11, 12, 14, 24, 26, 87, 102, 131, 144,
    253, 300
Meskell, Lynn, 255n.11
Mexico, 46, 67, 255, 255n.11, 306
Milanović, Marko, 278

Millennium Development Goals, 20, 88, 160, 162, 165
Milošević, Slobodan, 269, 271, See International Criminal Tribunal for the Former Yugoslavia (ICTY)
Ministerial Conference of Cancun, 44
  failure of, 44–45
Miyazaki, Hiro, 240
modernity
  ethnography and, 4, 5
  financial accounting, 14
  indigenous peoples and, 310
  statistics and, 169
Morales, Evo, 95
Morocco, 165, 166, 310
multilateralism, 40, 48
myth, 263

N≠a Jaqna Conservancy, 177
Nader, Laura, 4
Namibia, 91, 94, 173–181, 193
  refugees in, 176
Namibia Red Cross Society, 179
National Household Survey Capability Program, 160
negotiation
  as collaboration, 92
  as gambling, 51
  as public drama, 52, 53
  documentation of, 211
  favoring global north, 223
  formality and, 100
  legitimacy and, 116
  quantitative targets and, 223
  spatiality of, 51
  structuring of, 223
  World Trade Organization (WTO) and, 48–51
neoliberalism, 1, 25, 31, 109
New York, 5, 19, 22, 56, 57, 58, 60n.6, 62, 71, 73, 78, 79, 80, 85, 86, 89, 91, 95n.13, 99, 100, 101, 131, 133, 145, 152, 161, 215, 305
New Zealand, 95
non-governmental organizations (NGOs)
  accreditation of, 81, 89, 313
  activism and, 1, 3, 16, 17, 23, 80, 110, 297, 311n.7
  engagement with state governments, 119
  global climate change and, 98, 222, 225, 226, 230–233, 238
  influence of, 312
  participation of, 1, 12, 15, 19, 24, 25, 40, 78, 128, 133, 135, 294
  Permanent Forum on Indigenous Issues and, 15, 78, 79–81, 83–85, 87–89, 94, 96, 99, 101
  states, tension with, 137

United Nations High Commissioner for Refugees (UNHCR) and, 172, 175, 176, 178
United Nations Human Rights Committee (UNHRC) and, 23, 128–130, 131n.1, 133–149
Universal Periodic Review (UPR) and, 24, 107, 110, 113–116, 119–121, 124
non-state justice institutions, 201
Village courts and, 25, 199, 207–210, 213
World Bank and, 187, 188, 191
World Trade Organization (WTO) and, 38, 40, 43–45, 49, 53, 60n.5
Norway, 56, 58, 60, 63–67, 67n.10, 70–74, 139, 235n.9
Norwegian permanent delegation to the UN, 60
Norwegian Permanent Mission to the UN, 58
numerical measures. See indicators
  of outstanding universal value, 253
Nyqvist, Annette, 57

Office of the Prosecutor, 274, 287
Oman, 168, 262n.13
Operational Directive, 189
optics
  hope and, 20
  NGOs, 44–45, See media
  of the UN, 20
Organization for the Prohibition of Chemical Weapons (OPCW), 2n.1
Organization of American States, 227
Osire Refugee Camp, 174–181, 193
outstanding universal value (OUV), 26, 246–248, 262, 262n.13
  as intrinsic, 262
  comparative analysis, 252, 253
  definition of, 26
  how to determine, 256
  spontaneously constructed, 257
Oxfam, 38, 44, 45

Pakistan, 164
Palestine, 251
Panel of Environmental Experts, 174, 188
paperwork, 198–199, 202–205, 208–212, 215–216
  courts, 208–209
  development initiatives, 198
  non-state legal processes and, 202
Papua New Guinea, 231, 254
para-ethnography, 7, 34, 58, 122, See ethnography
Paris Agreement, 219–221, 223–224, 232, 239–240
  influence of observers on, 224
participant observation. See ethnography
Permanent Forum on Indigenous Issues, 8, 22, 27, 78, 79, 81, 82, 297, 309, 310
  creation of, 82

Permanent Forum on Indigenous Issues (cont.)
  expertise and, 301
  kaleidoscopic form, 79, 101
  May revolt, 98
  makeup of, 250
  mandate of, 82, 310
  statement-making, 90
plasticity
  in UNSC, 64
poetry of places, 261
politics of shame, 17
polymorphous engagement, 58
Population Division, 160
Porter, Theodore, 214
Preparatory Commission for the Comprehensive Nuclear Test-Ban Treaty Organization (CTBTO), 2n.1
publicity. *See* optics media
publics, 3, 16, 26, 92, 106, 228
  global governance and, 3
  UNFCCC, 228
purchasing power parity, 152, 162, 163

quantification. *See* indicators
  of justice, 199

Rancière, Jacques, 48
Range Management Associations, 188
rationality, 4, 26, 56
rationalization, process of, 4
Reducing Emissions From Deforestation And Forest Degradation (REDD+), 25, 96, 98, 230, 231, 232, 238, 239
  indigenous peoples and, 231
refugee camp, 174–181, 193
  economic benefits of, 177
repeat players
  of UNSC, 55–57, 62, 67, 69, 71–74
reservoir-induced seismicity, 186
resettlement, 173, 177
Riles, Annelise, 202, 314
Rio+20, 225
rule of law, 157, 198, 200, 207, 208, 216
Rules of Procedure
  UNSC, 63
Russia, 61, 68, 68n.11, 83n.7, 128, 227, 237, 255, 255n.11, 257
Russian Association on Indigenous Peoples of the North (RAIPON), 83

Salzburg Reflections, 298
scales of value, 221
Schneider, Stephen, 225
Searle, John, 314

Secretariat of the Permanent Forum on Indigenous Issues (SPFII), 80, 83, 85, 86–90, 92, 93–96, 97–99, 102
Secretariat of the World Trade Organization(WTO), 33, 36, 38, 40, 49, 50
secularism, 131
self-determination, 308
  indigenous peoples and, 306, 308, 309
Serbia, 269, 271, 272, 274–278, 276n.25, 278n.41, 280–282, 303
Serbian Chetnik Movement, 276
Serbian Radical Party, 276, 280
Šešelj, Vojislav, 26, 267, 271, 272, 275–277, *See* International Criminal Tribunal for the Former Yugoslavia (ICTY)
  during Balkan Wars, 277
  trial of, 275–277, 278
Šešeljevci, 279, *See* Šešelj, Vojislav
shadow reports, 136
shalish, 209
  description of, 203–204, *See* non-state justice institutions
Shell Oil Company, 226
Sierra Leone, 267
Singapore, 45, 46
slowness
  negotiation and, 20, 53
social survey, 157
Soderberg, Nancy, 100
soft power, 109, 245
South Africa, 91
  Human Development Index (HDI), 165, 166
  San, 79, 91, 93–95, 174–181
  World Heritage Committee and, 255n.11
South Korea, 37, 41, 46
sovereignty
  indigenous groups and, 235
  Inuit, 237
  of states, 191
  United Nations and, 19
Spain, 251
spatial arrangement
  Palais des Nations, 121
  rural courts, 208
  United Nations Committee on Human Rights, 135
  United Nations Human Rights Committee, 127
  United Nations Security Council (UNSC), 61
  Universal Periodic Review (UPR), 121
  WTO, 49
Special Court for Sierra Leone, 267
Special Rapporteur, 10, 81n.1, 84, 91, 93, 97
Special Safeguard Mechanism, 50, 51, 52
speech acts, 282, 287, 288
  explanation of, 299n.2

speech crimes, 26, 267, 272–275, 279–284, 287–292
  ethnic cleansing and, 272
  evidence for, 273, 275
  instigation and, 272, 274
  intentionality and, 273
  liability, 274
  propaganda and, 279
State under Review, 107, 108, 111, 112, 113, 116, 117, 118
Statistical Commission, *See* United Nations Statistical Commission(UNSC)
statistics. *See* indicators
  global governance and, 156–157
  governance and, 155–157
  implications for sovereignty, 169
  knowledge creation and, 24
  rendering populations countable, 157
  rendering visibility and, 157
  states and, 24
  tensions between wealthier and poorer nations, 169
Strathern, Marilyn, 109, 123
Structural Adjustment Programmes, 200
subjectivities
  of institutions, 35
Survivors of Large Dams (SOLD), 189
Syria, 1, 57n.1, 66, 67
systematization
  of cultural heritage designation, 263
  of cultural value, 262

technical assistance, 14, 33, 46, 46n.3, 165, 176, 181, 210
temporality, 53
The Prosecutor v. William Samoei Ruto and Joshua Arap Sang, 286–287
The Race Question, 295, 296
thick description, 267
Thorsen, Dorte, 267, *See* Special Court for Sierra Leone
Timor-Leste, 117
Tolbert, David, 270
torture, 16, 117, 268, 271, 274, 284, 311
  depoliticization, 117
traditional authority, 177, 178, *See* !Kung; N≠a Jaqna Conservancy
traditional knowledge, 90, 99, 303, 310
training intitiatives, 22, 23, 80, 87–88, 96–99, 103, 121, 158, 160, 168, 176, 206–214, 231
  on indigenous issues, 22, 23, 80, 88–89, 96, 99, 103
transnational. *See* bureaucracy
  bureaucracies, 199, 202, 203
  consensus building, 131
  human rights, 131
  ideas, 207
  office space, 206
  organizations, 34
  politics, 106
  publics, 106
  workers, 121
transnationalism, 34
treaty body proceedings, 137
Turkey, 168, 252, 255, 303

Uganda, 117
Ukraine, 140
uncertainty, legal, 274
Union Purishad, 204
  documents of, 229
United Kingdom, 16, 59, 60, 159, 167, 173, 261
United Nations Alliance of Civilizations, 296
United Nations Charter
  Chapter VII, 268
United Nations Children's Fund (UNICEF), 87, 121
United Nations Committee Against Torture, 117
United Nations Conference on Sustainable Development, 226
United Nations Country Teams, 25, 86, 88, 96, 172, 179
United Nations Declaration on the Rights of Indigenous Peoples (UNDRIP), 82, 91, 96, 309
United Nations Development Programme (UNDP), 24, 199, 201, 205, 302
United Nations Economic and Social Council (ECOSOC), 81–83, 89, 98, 111, 113, 308, 310
  non-governmental organizations (NGOs) and, 81, 111, 113, 310
  Permanent Forum on Indigenous Issues and, 82, 83
United Nations Educational, Scientific and Cultural Organization (UNESCO), 26, 27, 99, 165, 166, 168, 245–251, 257, 258, 262, 263, 295, 296, 298, 300, 303, 304
  anthropology and, 295
  culture and, 296
  diplomacy and, 295
United Nations Framework Convention on Climate Change (UNFCCC), 219–223, 236, 237–241, *See* 15th Council of Parties, 18th Council of Parties; Coordinadora de las Organizaciones Indígenas de la Cuenca Amazónica
  forests and, 229–230
  Indigenous Caucus, 226
  indigenous groups and, 227
  signing of, 229

United Nations Fund for Population Activities (UNFPA), 161
United Nations General Assembly, 19, 59, 60, 68, 154, 227, 246n.2
United Nations High Commission for Human Rights, 227
United Nations High Commissioner for Refugees (UNHCR), 11, 25, 31, 174–180, 190–193
United Nations Human Rights Committee, 127, *See* spatial organization
  history of, 133–134
  meeting process, 127–128
  NGOs, 128, 135
United Nations Interregional Crime and Justice Research Institute (UNICRI), 9
United Nations Permanent Forum for Indigenous Issues (UNPFII), 8, 11, 17, 22, 23, 27, 78–103, 143, 250, 297, 301, 303, 309, 310
  expertise, 81
United Nations Security Council (UNSC), 55–75
  "one-shotters", 73, 75
  description of, 59–60
  E10, 61
  expertise and, 22
  formality and, 100
  influence of, 15
  informality of, 22
  internal dynamics of, 62
  international criminal courts and, 286
  International Criminal Tribunal for the Former Yugoslavia (ICTY) and, 267, 268, 269, 271, 285
  international justice institutions and, 268, 270
  NGO access and, 17
  P2, 61
  P3, 60, 61
  P5, 60, 61
  penholder, 60, 61
  politics of, 74
  power disparities and, 12
  processes of, 22, 63
  repeat players, 55, 57, 73
  Rules of Procedure of, 59, 64
  Statement by Experts on Problems of Race, 1951, 295
  states and, 154
  United Nations Charter Chapter VII, 268
  working culture of, 56, 67
United Nations Statistical Commission (UNSC), 9, 24, 152–156, 160–169, *See* indicators
  cost to states of, 159
  Human Development Index and, 153, 159, 163–169
United Nations Statistical Division (UNSD), 153
  history of, 160

United Nations Treaty Bodies, 132–133
United Nations Universal Periodic Review (UPR), *See* Universal Periodic Review (UPR)
United States
  in Security Council, 60, 64, 66
  subsidies and, 43
  tariffs and, 42
  United Nations Statistical Commission (UNSC) and, 161, 164, 167
United States Agency for International Development (USAID), 158, 161
Universal Declaration of Human Rights (UDHR), 129, 131n.1, 294, 295, 307
Universal Periodic Review (UPR), 8, 12, 14, 17, 106, 119, 124, 132, 144
  Belgium, 112, 119
  definition, 107
  developing countries, 113
  ethnographer in, 118
  fieldwork in, 119
  Finland, 139, 140–148
  Greece, 112, 119
  human rights in, 23
  NGOs and, 17, 137
  states and, 137
universalism, 129, 131, 148, 267
  human rights, 127
  ICOMOS and, 260
  myth of universalism, 129
  relativism and, 130
  Universal Declaration of Human Rights (UDHR), 129
universality
  as dynamic, 129
  as plurality, 132
  audits and, 110
  biological, 295
  cultivated, 143
  embodied, 139
  human rights and, 129, 130, 132, 142
  moral, 295
  of global institutions, 2
USSR, 59
utopia, 19, 19n.10, 20, 131, 147

validity, 214
Van Maanen, John, 62

Ward, Michael, 160
Watt-Cloutier, Sheila, 228
Weber, Max, 202, 287
Weisser, Florian, 222
Westernization, 254
Wilson, Richard Ashby, 266

Woolcock, Michael, 200, 216
Working Group of Indigenous Minorities in Southern Africa (WIMSA), 178
Working Group on Indigenous Populations (WGIP), 27, 82n.5, 85, 86n.10, 91, 297, 309
World Bank, 9, 11, 15, 20, 25, 31, 33–34, 45–46, 96, 98–99, 117, 153, 164, 166, 172–178, 181–193, 200–202, 216, 259
   as justice institution, 199–200
   competing interests and, 191
   cotton and, 45
   data production and, 200
   definition of, 181
   developing countries and, 181
   humanitarianism and, 25
   in Lesotho, 174, 185, 187, 189
   indigenous people and, 187, 189
   Justice for the Poor Programme, 200
   mandate of, 172
   refugee assistance, 174
   resettlement, 190
   Strengthening Access to Justice Programme, 200
World Bank Group, 1, 181
World Food Program, 176
World Heritage
   as influencing force, 245
   indicators, 26
   list, 250, 251
   Operational Guidelines, 2013, 248
   outstanding universal value (OUV), 246
   title, 245
   value and, 246
World Heritage Advisors, 255
World Heritage Committee, 247, 248, 249, 262, *See* UNESCO

   2010 Brasilia Committee Session, 255
   sessions, 245
World Heritage Convention
   outstanding universal value and, 26
World Heritage List, 26, 246, 263
   definition, 246
   description of, 246
   diversity of sites in, 254
   genres in, 259, 260
   growth of, 252
   outstanding universal value (OUV) and, 26, 262n.13
   Tentative List, 252
   The Global Strategy for a Representative, Balanced and Credible World Heritage List, 1994, 254
World Heritage site
   designation of, 26
   Guidelines, 1978, 247
   nominations, 248, 250–251
   process, 249–250
World Heritage Studies, 245
World Heritage Trust, 247
World Intellectual Property Organization, 303, 304
World Trade Organization (WTO), 7n.6, 13, 15, 21–22, 31–53, 121
   cotton and, 48
   Dispute Settlement Body, 39
   Doha Round, 22, 32, 40–42
   ethnography of, 31, 38
   expertise, 40
   incompleteness, 53
   metaphor and, 51
World Wildlife Fund (WWF), 219, 235

Books in the Series

China and Islam: The Prophet, the Party, and Law
Matthew S. Erie

Diversity in Practice: Race, Gender, and Class in Legal and Professional Careers
Edited by Spencer Headworth and Robert Nelson

Diseases of the Will
Mariana Valverde

The Politics of Truth and Reconciliation in South Africa: Legitimizing the Post-Apartheid State
Richard A. Wilson

Modernism and the Grounds of Law
Peter Fitzpatrick

Unemployment and Government: Genealogies of the Social
William Walters

Autonomy and Ethnicity: Negotiating Competing Claims in Multi-Ethnic States
Yash Ghai

Constituting Democracy: Law, Globalism and South Africa's Political Reconstruction
Heinz Klug

The Ritual of Rights in Japan: Law, Society, and Health Policy
Eric A. Feldman

The Invention of the Passport: Surveillance, Citizenship and the State
John Torpey

Governing Morals: A Social History of Moral Regulation
Alan Hunt

The Colonies of Law: Colonialism, Zionism and Law in Early Mandate Palestine
Ronen Shamir

Law and Nature
David Delaney

Social Citizenship and Workfare in the United States and Western Europe: The Paradox of Inclusion
Joel F. Handler

Law, Anthropology and the Constitution of the Social: Making Persons and Things
Edited by Alain Pottage and Martha Mundy

Judicial Review and Bureaucratic Impact: International and Interdisciplinary Perspectives
Edited by Marc Hertogh and Simon Halliday

Immigrants at the Margins: Law, Race, and Exclusion in Southern Europe
Kitty Calavita

Lawyers and Regulation: The Politics of the Administrative Process
Patrick Schmidt

Law and Globalization from Below: Toward a Cosmopolitan Legality
Edited by Boaventura de Sousa Santos and Cesar A. Rodriguez-Garavito

Public Accountability: Designs, Dilemmas and Experiences
Edited by Michael W. Dowdle

Law, Violence and Sovereignty Among West Bank Palestinians
Tobias Kelly

Legal Reform and Administrative Detention Powers in China
Sarah Biddulph

The Practice of Human Rights: Tracking Law Between the Global and the Local
Edited by Mark Goodale and Sally Engle Merry

Judges Beyond Politics in Democracy and Dictatorship: Lessons from Chile
Lisa Hilbink

Paths to International Justice: Social and Legal Perspectives
Edited by Marie-Bénédicte Dembour and Tobias Kelly

Law and Society in Vietnam: The Transition from Socialism in Comparative Perspective
Mark Sidel

Constitutionalizing Economic Globalization: Investment Rules and Democracy's Promise
David Schneiderman

The New World Trade Organization Knowledge Agreements: 2nd Edition
Christopher Arup

Justice and Reconciliation in Post-Apartheid South Africa
Edited by François du Bois and Antje du Bois-Pedain

Militarization and Violence Against Women in Conflict Zones in the Middle East: A Palestinian Case-Study
Nadera Shalhoub-Kevorkian

Child Pornography and Sexual Grooming: Legal and Societal Responses
Suzanne Ost

Darfur and the Crime of Genocide
John Hagan and Wenona Rymond-Richmond

Fictions of Justice: The International Criminal Court and the Challenge of Legal Pluralism in Sub-Saharan Africa
Kamari Maxine Clarke

Conducting Law and Society Research: Reflections on Methods and Practices
Simon Halliday and Patrick Schmidt

Planted Flags: Trees, Land, and Law in Israel/Palestine
Irus Braverman

Culture under Cross-Examination: International Justice and the Special Court for Sierra Leone
Tim Kelsall

Cultures of Legality: Judicialization and Political Activism in Latin America
Javier Couso, Alexandra Huneeus, and Rachel Sieder

Courting Democracy in Bosnia and Herzegovina: The Hague Tribunal's Impact in a Postwar State
Lara J. Nettelfield

The Gacaca Courts and Post-Genocide Justice and Reconciliation in Rwanda: Justice Without Lawyers
Phil Clark

Law, Society, and History: Themes in the Legal Sociology and Legal History of Lawrence M. Friedman
Robert W. Gordon and Morton J. Horwitz

After Abu Ghraib: Exploring Human Rights in America and the Middle East
Shadi Mokhtari

Adjudication in Religious Family Laws: Cultural Accommodation, Legal Pluralism, and Gender Equality in India
Gopika Solanki

Water on Tap: Rights and Regulation in the Transnational Governance of Urban Water Services
Bronwen Morgan

Elements of Moral Cognition: Rawls' Linguistic Analogy and the Cognitive Science of Moral and Legal Judgment
John Mikhail

A Sociology of Constitutions: Constitutions and State Legitimacy in Historical-Sociological Perspective
Chris Thornhill

Mitigation and Aggravation at Sentencing
Edited by Julian Roberts

Institutional Inequality and the Mobilization of the Family and Medical Leave Act: Rights on Leave
Catherine R. Albiston

Authoritarian Rule of Law: Legislation, Discourse and Legitimacy in Singapore
Jothie Rajah

Law and Development and the Global Discourses of Legal Transfers
Edited by John Gillespie and Pip Nicholson

Law against the State: Ethnographic Forays into Law's Transformations
Edited by Julia Eckert, Brian Donahoe, Christian Strümpell, and Zerrin Özlem Biner

Transnational Legal Process and State Change
Edited by Gregory C. Shaffer

Legal Mobilization Under Authoritarianism: The Case of Post-Colonial Hong Kong
Edited by Waikeung Tam

Complementarity in the Line of Fire: The Catalysing Effect of the International Criminal Court in Uganda and Sudan
Sarah M. H. Nouwen

Political and Legal Transformations of an Indonesian Polity: The Nagari from Colonisation to Decentralisation
Franz von Benda-Beckmann and Keebet von Benda-Beckmann

Pakistan's Experience with Formal Law: An Alien Justice
Osama Siddique

Human Rights under State-Enforced Religious Family Laws in Israel, Egypt, and India
Yüksel Sezgin

Why Prison?
Edited by David Scott

Law's Fragile State: Colonial, Authoritarian, and Humanitarian Legacies in Sudan
Mark Fathi Massoud

Rights for Others: The Slow Home-Coming of Human Rights in the Netherlands
Barbara Oomen

European States and their Muslim Citizens: The Impact of Institutions on Perceptions and Boundaries
Edited by John R. Bowen, Christophe Bertossi, Jan Willem Duyvendak, and Mona Lena Krook

Environmental Litigation in China
Rachel E. Stern

Indigeneity and Legal Pluralism in India: Claims, Histories, Meanings
Pooja Parmar

Paper Tiger: Law, Bureaucracy and the Developmental State in Himalayan India
Nayanika Mathur

Contractual Knowledge: One Hundred Years of Legal Experimentation in Global Markets
Edited by Grégoire Mallard and Jérôme Sgard

Religion, Law and Society
Russell Sandberg

The Experiences of Face Veil Wearers in Europe and the Law
Edited by Eva Brems

The Contentious History of the International Bill of Human Rights
Christopher N. J. Roberts

Transnational Legal Orders
Edited by Terence C. Halliday and Gregory Shaffer

Lost in China?, Law, Culture and Society in Post-1997 Hong Kong
Carol A. G. Jones

Security Theology, Surveillance and the Politics of Fear
Nadera Shalhoub-Kevorkian

Opposing the Rule of Law: How Myanmar's Courts Make Law and Order
Nick Cheesman

The Ironies of Colonial Governance: Law, Custom and Justice in Colonial India
James Jaffe

The Clinic and the Court: Law, Medicine and Anthropology
Edited by Tobias Kelly, Ian Harper, and Akshay Khanna

A World of Indicators: The Making of Government Knowledge Through Quantification
Edited by Richard Rottenburg, Sally E. Merry, Sung-Joon Park and Johanna Mugler

Contesting Immigration Policy in Court: Legal Activism and Its Radiating Effects in the United States and France
Leila Kawar

The Quiet Power of Indicators: Measuring Governance, Corruption, and Rule of Law
Edited by Sally Engle Merry, Kevin Davis, and Benedict Kingsbury

Investing in Authoritarian Rule: Punishment and Patronage in Rwanda's Gacaca Courts for Genocide Crimes
Anuradha Chakravarty

Iraq and the Crimes of Aggressive War: The Legal Cynicism of Criminal Militarism
John Hagan, Joshua Kaiser, and Anna Hanson

Culture in the Domains of Law
Edited by René Provost

A Sociology of Transnational Constitutions: Social Foundations of the Post-National Legal Structure
Chris Thornhill

Shifting Legal Visions: Judicial Change and Human Rights Trials in Latin America
Ezequiel A. González Ocantos

The Demographic Transformations of Citizenship
Heli Askola

Criminal Defense in China: The Politics of Lawyers at Work
Sida Liu and Terence C. Halliday

Contesting Economic and Social Rights in Ireland: Constitution, State and Society, 1848–2016
Thomas Murray

Buried in the Heart: Women, Complex Victimhood and the War in Northern Uganda
Erin Baines

Palaces of Hope: The Anthropology of Global Organizations
Edited by Ronald Niezen and Maria Sapignoli

Printed in Great Britain
by Amazon

57267789R00195